Phillip K. Trocki

D1709564

Modern Curriculum Press

EXECUTIVE EDITOR Wendy Whitnah

PROJECT EDITOR Diane Dzamtovski

EDITORIAL DEVELOPMENT
DESIGN AND PRODUCTION The Hampton-Brown Company

ILLUSTRATORS Anthony Accardo, Joe Boddy, Harry Briggs, Roberta Collier-Morales, Mark Farina, Sandra Forrest, Carlos Freire, Ron Grauer, Meryl Henderson, Jane McCreary, Masami Miyamoto, Rik Olson, Doug Roy, John Sandford, Rosalind Solomon.

PHOTO CREDITS 5, Michael S. Yamashita/Westlight; 9, Catherine Ursillo/Photo Researchers; 13, Lawrence Migdale; 17, Henry Georgi/Comstock; 21, Janeart Ltd/Image Bank; 29, Steinhart Aquarium/Photo Researchers; 30, H.L. Parent/Photo Researchers; 31, E.R. Degginger/Earth Scenes; 33, Craig Aurness/Westlight; 35, Spencer Grant/Photo Researchers; 37, Michael Fredericks, Jr./Earth Scenes; 41, Mary Evans Picture Library/Photo Researchers; 44, Robert Landau/Westlight; 45, Masud Quraishy/Photo Researchers; 46, Leonard Lee Rue III/Photo Researchers; 53, Don Klumpp/Image Bank; 57, Don King/Image Bank; 61, Garry Gay/Image Bank; 69, Uniphoto/Pictor; 70, G. and V. Chapman/Image Bank; 72, Joel Glenn/ Image Bank; 77, Keith Gunnar/Photo Researchers; 78, Frans Lanting/Photo Researchers; 81, Spencer Grant/Photo Researchers; 85, Harry Angels N.A.S./Photo Researchers; 87, George R. Cassidy/Animals Animals; 93, Wilf Schurig/Animals Animals; 101, Lawrence Migdale; 105, Bob Daemmrich/Uniphoto; 106, Carson Baldwin, Jr./Earth Scenes; 109, Bob Daemmrich/Uniphoto; 113, Henry Georgi/Comstock; 116, Tom and Pat Lesson/Photo Researchers; 117, Lawrence Migdale; 133, Ron Blakeley/Uniphoto; 141, Jen and Des Bartlett/Photo Researchers; 143, Charles Mahaux/Image Bank.

COVER DESIGN The Hampton-Brown Company
COVER PHOTO G & J Images/Image Bank

Typefaces for the cursive type in this book were provided by Zaner-Bloser, Inc., Columbus, Ohio, copyright, 1993.

Modern Curriculum Press

An imprint of Pearson Learning
299 Jefferson Road, P.O. Box 480
Parsippany, NJ 07054–0480

ISBN: 0-8136-2843-1
Printed in the United States of America

9 10 11 12 13 14   06 05 04 03 02

1-800-321-3106
www.pearsonlearning.com

Table of Contents

Spelling Workout—Our Philosophy

Integration of Spelling with Reading and Writing

In each core lesson for *Spelling Workout,* students read spelling words in context in a variety of expository selections and genre, including poetry, riddles, and stories. The reading selections provide opportunities for reading across the curriculum, focusing on the subject areas of science, social studies, health, language arts, music, and art.

After students read the selection and practice writing their spelling words, they use List Words to help them write about a related topic in a variety of forms and innovations such as poems, letters, descriptive writings, newspaper articles, advertisements, jokes, and posters. A proofreading exercise is also provided for each lesson to help students apply the writing process to their own writings and reinforce the use of spelling words in context.

The study of spelling should not be limited to a specific time in the school day. Use opportunities throughout the day to reinforce and maintain spelling skills by integrating spelling with other curriculum areas. Point out spelling words in books, texts, and the student's own writing. Encourage students to write, as they practice spelling through writing. Provide opportunities for writing with a purpose.

Phonics-Based Instructional Design

Spelling Workout takes a solid phonic and structural analysis approach to encoding. The close tie between spelling and phonics allows each to reinforce the other. *Spelling Workout* correlates closely to *MCP Phonics, MCP Discovery Phonics I* and *II,* and other phonics material published by Modern Curriculum Press, although these programs are complete within themselves and can be used independently. In addition, lessons are correlated to the phonics strategies in Silver Burdett Ginn *New Dimensions in the World of Reading* Teacher's Editions.

Research-Based Teaching Strategies

Spelling Workout utilizes a test-study-test method of teaching spelling. The student first takes a pretest of words that have not yet been introduced. Under the direction of the teacher, the student then self-corrects the test, rewriting correctly any word that has been missed. This approach not only provides an opportunity to determine how many words a student can already spell but also allows students to analyze spelling mistakes. In the process students also discover patterns that make it easier to spell List Words. Students study the words as they work through practice exercises, and then reassess their spelling by taking a final test.

High-Utility List Words

The words used in *Spelling Workout* have been chosen for their frequency in students' written and oral vocabularies, their relationships to subject areas, and for structural as well as phonetic generalizations. Each List Word has been cross-referenced with one or more of the following:

Carroll, Davies, and Richman. *The American Heritage Word Frequency Book*

Dale and O'Rourke. *The Living Word Vocabulary*

Dolch. *220 Basic Sight Words*

Fry, Polk, and Fountoukidis. "Spelling Demons—197 Words Frequently Misspelled by Elementary Students"

Green and Loomer. *The New Iowa Spelling Scale*

Harris and Jacobson. *Basic Elementary Reading Vocabularies*

Hanna. *Phoneme Grapheme Correspondences as Cues to Spelling Improvement*

Hillerich. *A Written Vocabulary of Elementary Children*

Kucera and Francis. *Computational Analysis of Present-Day American English*

Rinsland. *A Basic Vocabulary of Elementary Children*

Sakiey and Fry. *3000 Instant Words*

Thomas. "3000 Words Most Frequently Written"

Thomas. "200 Words Most Frequently Misspelled"

A Format That Results in Success

Spelling Workout treats spelling as a developmental process. Students progress in stages, much as they learn to speak and read. In *Spelling Workout,* they move gradually from simple sound/letter relationships to strategies involving more complex word-structure patterns. The use of a sports format motivates and maintains student interest.

Sample Core Lesson

- *A **Warm Up** reading selection in each lesson uses spelling words in context.*

- ***On Your Mark** guides students to take the pretest and self-assess their spelling.*

- *The "Coach" explains spelling patterns in **Pep Talk**, providing a lesson focus.*

- *The **List Words** box contains high-frequency spelling words.*

- ***Game Plan** gives students an opportunity to practice new words.*

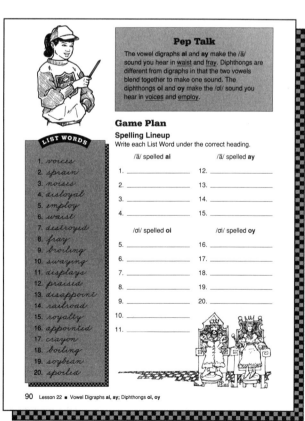

Name _____

Vowel Digraphs ai, ay; Diphthongs oi, oy

LESSON 22

Warm Up

How can a town be turned into a museum?

End of the Trail

The front door of Butch Cassidy's cabin stands open. A stagecoach is parked outside the General Store. No horses are restlessly pawing the gray dust. No **voices** can be heard from the well-traveled trail. In fact, the only **noises** that can be heard are the whispering breezes and chirping insects.

You may think this is a ghost town, but it's really a museum called Old Trail Town. It stands outside Cody, Wyoming. The town, which stands on five acres, was established by Bob and Terry Edgar. Among the **displays** are old cabins and treasures from the long-ago days of the Wild West.

Years ago, Bob noticed many old cabins standing empty on the range. "Some were falling in. Others were being **destroyed** by grazing cattle," he said. He decided to save them as a part of American history.

After working hard and sacrificing time and money, the Edgars' dream came to life. They should be **praised** for preserving a long-ago way of life. People are interested in seeing how cowhands and pioneers really lived. As Bob says, "The main thing is to enjoy the place and remember it."

Say each boldfaced word in the selection. How are the words with the /ā/ sound spelled? How are the words with the /oi/ sound spelled?

On Your Mark

Take your Warm Up Test. Then check your spelling with the List Words on the next page.

89

Pep Talk

The vowel digraphs **ai** and **ay** make the /ā/ sound you hear in waist and fray. Diphthongs are different from digraphs in that the two vowels blend together to make one sound. The diphthongs **oi** and **oy** make the /oi/ sound you hear in voices and employ.

Game Plan

Spelling Lineup

Write each List Word under the correct heading.

LIST WORDS

1. voices
2. sprain
3. noises
4. disloyal
5. employ
6. waist
7. destroyed
8. fray
9. broiling
10. swaying
11. displays
12. praised
13. disappoint
14. railroad
15. royalty
16. appointed
17. crayon
18. boiling
19. soybean
20. spoiled

/ā/ spelled **ai**	/ā/ spelled **ay**
1. _____	12. _____
2. _____	13. _____
3. _____	14. _____
4. _____	15. _____

/oi/ spelled **oi**	/oi/ spelled **oy**
5. _____	16. _____
6. _____	17. _____
7. _____	18. _____
8. _____	19. _____
9. _____	20. _____
10. _____	
11. _____	

90 Lesson 22 ■ Vowel Digraphs **ai, ay;** Diphthongs **oi, oy**

Rhyming

Write the List Word that rhymes with each word given.

1. train _____	5. toiled _____
2. grazed _____	6. playing _____
3. day _____	7. paste _____
4. annoy _____	8. replays _____

Classification

Write the List Word that belongs in each group.

1. pen, pencil, _____
2. baking, boiling, _____
3. bang, crash, _____
4. soprano, alto, _____
5. dissatisfy, fail, _____
6. rice, potato, _____
7. queens, kings, _____
8. untrue, unfaithful, _____
9. moving, rocking, _____
10. chosen, assigned, _____

Lesson 22 ▪ Vowel Digraphs **ai, ay;** Diphthongs **oi, oy** 91

- *A variety of activities that emphasize word meaning provide many opportunities to practice List Words.*

- *Students use dictionary skills.*

- *Word puzzles and games help to motivate students.*

Flex Your Spelling Muscles

Writing

Cowhands worked hard at herding cattle, and riding and mending fence. Yet, they had fun, too. Write a paragraph telling what you think it was like to be an Old West cowhand. Use as many List Words as you can.

Proofreading

The paragraph below has twelve mistakes. Fix the mistakes with the proofreading marks. Then write the misspelled List Words on the lines.

Proofreading Marks
◯ spelling mistake
⊙ add period
ℛ take out something

The pioneers who came west in covered wagons are to be praysed Even with an appoynted leader, they had to use all all their skills just to survive. Long days were spent riding in in the swaiying wagons in boyling hot or icy cold weather. Accidents could and did happen! A wagon wheel could be destroied by by the rough terrain or someone could have a sprained ankle with with no one to treat it When the ralroad came, traveling west became easier, but still an adventure.

1. _____
2. _____
3. _____
4. _____
5. _____
6. _____

Now proofread your paragraph about cowhands. Fix any mistakes.

Go for the Goal

Take your Final Test. Then fill in your Scoreboard. Send your mistakes to the Word Locker.

SCOREBOARD	
number correct	number wrong

★ ★ ★ ★ ★ ★ ★ **All-Star Words** ★ ★ ★ ★ ★ ★ ★

entertain   delay   embroider   loyal   raisin

Write a sentence for each word, but leave a blank in place of the All-Star Word. Then write a wrong All-Star Word in each blank. Trade papers with a partner. Try to write the correct All-Star Words in the sentences.

92   Lesson 22 ▪ Vowel Digraphs **ai, ay;** Diphthongs **oi, oy**

- *Flex Your Spelling Muscles encourages students to practice and apply the List Words in different contexts.*

- *Writing activities provide opportunities for students to write their spelling words in a variety of writing forms and genres.*

- *Proofreading practice builds proofreading proficiency and encourages students to check their own writing.*

- *Go for the Goal encourages self-assessment of students' final test by encouraging students to record their scores in the Scoreboard. Students keep track of words they are having difficulty with by writing them in a Word Locker provided in the Teacher's Edition as a reproducible sheet.*

- *All-Star Words offer more challenging words with similar spelling patterns. Students are given opportunities to practice the words with a partner.*

Sample Review Lesson

- The **Instant Replay** lesson allows students to review what they've learned.

- **Time Out,** signaled by the "Coach," briefly reviews the spelling patterns used in the previous five lessons.

- **Check Your Word Locker** suggests that students evaluate words they are having trouble with by reviewing the words they've written in their Word Locker. A partner activity provides practice for those words in a variety of learning modalities — kinesthetic, visual, and auditory.

- A variety of activities provide practice and review of selected List Words from the previous lessons.

- **Go for the Goal** encourages self-assessment of students' **Final Replay Test** by encouraging students to record their scores in the Scoreboard.

- **Clean Out Your Word Locker** provides further practice for students' troublesome words by suggesting that students write the words in a **Spelling Notebook,** a student-created word book that students can refer to whenever they need to check their spelling, or when they need a resource for writing.

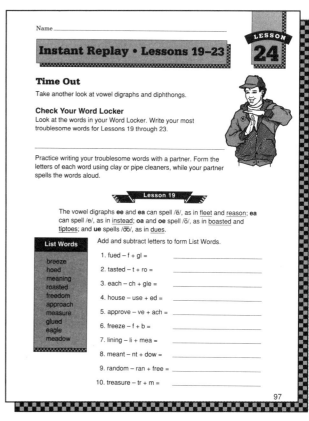

Name _____

Instant Replay • Lessons 19–23

LESSON 24

Time Out
Take another look at vowel digraphs and diphthongs.

Check Your Word Locker
Look at the words in your Word Locker. Write your most troublesome words for Lessons 19 through 23.

_____

Practice writing your troublesome words with a partner. Form the letters of each word using clay or pipe cleaners, while your partner spells the words aloud.

Lesson 19

The vowel digraphs **ee** and **ea** can spell /ē/, as in <u>fleet</u> and <u>reason</u>; **ea** can spell /e/, as in <u>instead</u>; **oa** and **oe** spell /ō/, as in <u>boasted</u> and <u>tiptoes</u>; and **ue** spells /ōō/, as in <u>dues</u>.

List Words	Add and subtract letters to form List Words.
breeze	1. fued – f + gl = _____
hoed	2. tasted – t + ro = _____
meaning	3. each – ch + gle = _____
roasted	4. house – use + ed = _____
freedom	5. approve – ve + ach = _____
approach	6. freeze – f + b = _____
measure	7. lining – li + mea = _____
glued	8. meant – nt + dow = _____
eagle	9. random – ran + free = _____
meadow	10. treasure – tr + m = _____

97

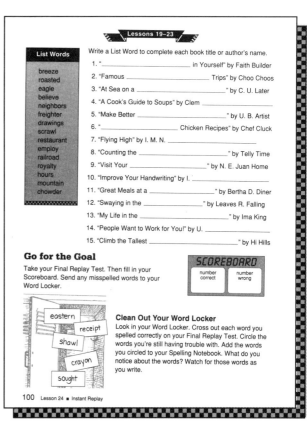

Lessons 19–23

Write a List Word to complete each book title or author's name.

List Words
breeze
roasted
eagle
believe
neighbors
freighter
drawings
scrawl
restaurant
employ
railroad
royalty
hours
mountain
chowder

1. "_____ in Yourself" by Faith Builder
2. "Famous _____ Trips" by Choo Choos
3. "At Sea on a _____" by C. U. Later
4. "A Cook's Guide to Soups" by Clem _____
5. "Make Better _____" by U. B. Artist
6. "_____ Chicken Recipes" by Chef Cluck
7. "Flying High" by I. M. N. _____
8. "Counting the _____" by Telly Time
9. "Visit Your _____" by N. E. Juan Home
10. "Improve Your Handwriting" by I. _____
11. "Great Meals at a _____" by Bertha D. Diner
12. "Swaying in the _____" by Leaves R. Falling
13. "My Life in the _____" by Ima King
14. "People Want to Work for You!" by U. _____
15. "Climb the Tallest _____" by Hi Hills

Go for the Goal
Take your Final Replay Test. Then fill in your Scoreboard. Send any misspelled words to your Word Locker.

SCOREBOARD

number correct	number wrong

eastern
receipt
shawl
crayon
sought

Clean Out Your Word Locker
Look in your Word Locker. Cross out each word you spelled correctly on your Final Replay Test. Circle the words you're still having trouble with. Add the words you circled to your Spelling Notebook. What do you notice about the words? Watch for those words as you write.

100   Lesson 24 ■ Instant Replay

10

Spelling Workout in the Classroom

Classroom Management

Spelling Workout is designed as a flexible instructional program. The following plans are two ways the program can be taught.

The 5–day Plan
Day 1 – Warm Up and Warm Up Test
Day 2 and 3 – Game Plan
Day 4 – Flex Your Spelling Muscles
Day 5 – Final Test

The 3–day Plan
Day 1 – Warm Up and Warm Up Test/Game Plan
Day 2 – Game Plan/Flex Your Spelling Muscles
Day 3 – Final Test

Testing

Testing is accomplished in several ways. A pretest is administered after reading the Warm Up selection and a final test at the end of each lesson. Dictation sentences for each pretest and final test are provided.

Research suggests that students benefit from correcting their own pretests. After the pretest has been administered, have students self-correct their tests by checking the words against the List Words. You may also want to guide students by reading each letter of the word, asking students to point to each letter and circle any incorrect letters. Then have students rewrite each word correctly.

Tests for Instant Replay lessons are provided in the Teacher's Edition as reproducibles following each lesson. These tests provide not only an evaluation tool for teachers, but also added practice in taking standardized tests for students.

Individualizing Instruction

All-Star Words are included in every core lesson as a challenge for better spellers and to provide extension and enrichment for all students.

Review pages called Instant Replay lessons reinforce correct spelling of difficult words from previous lessons.

A reproducible sheet called Word Locker allows each student to analyze spelling errors and practice writing troublesome words independently.

A reproducible individual Student Record Chart provided in the Teacher's Edition allows students to record their test scores.

Ideas for meeting the needs of ESL students are provided.

Dictionary

In the back of each student book is a comprehensive dictionary with definitions of all List Words and All-Star Words. Students will have this resource at their fingertips for any assignment.

The Teacher's Edition —Everything You Need!

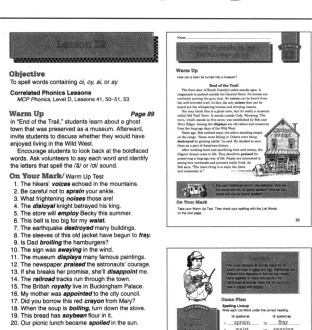

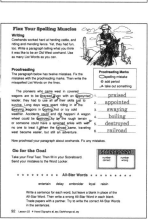

- *The goals of each core lesson are clearly stated.*

- *Spelling lessons are correlated to* MCP Phonics, MCP Discovery Phonics I *and* II, *and Silver Burdett Ginn* New Dimensions in the World of Reading. *Page references refer to Teacher's Edition pages.*

- *Ideas for introducing and setting a purpose for reading are given for each reading selection.*

- *A* **Warm Up Test,** *or pretest, is administered before the start of each lesson. Dictation sentences are provided.*

- *Concise teaching notes give guidance for working through the lesson.*

- *Ideas for meeting the needs of* **ESL** *students are given.*

- ***Spelling Strategy*** *activities provide additional support for reinforcing and analyzing spelling patterns.*

- *Suggestions for ways students can publish their writing complete the writing process.*

- *A* **Writer's Corner** *extends the content of each reading selection by suggesting ways in which students can explore real-world writing.*

- *A* **Final Test** *is administered at the end of the lesson. Dictation sentences are provided.*

Name _____

Instant Replay Test
Side A

Read each set of words. Fill in the circle next to the word that is spelled wrong.

1. ⓐ displays ⓒ launch
   ⓑ disloyal ⓓ shreak
2. ⓐ without ⓒ sprein
   ⓑ eagle ⓓ spoiled
3. ⓐ aproach ⓒ sauce
   ⓑ railroad ⓓ fault
4. ⓐ dawn ⓒ mountin
   ⓑ meadow ⓓ glued
5. ⓐ roasted ⓒ gnaw
   ⓑ soybean ⓓ distroyed
6. ⓐ brief ⓒ freedom
   ⓑ gawnt ⓓ swallowed
7. ⓐ drawings ⓒ howed
   ⓑ boiling ⓓ audience
8. ⓐ disapoint ⓒ meaning
   ⓑ believe ⓓ eastern
9. ⓐ chiefly ⓒ disloyal
   ⓑ hours ⓓ boquet
10. ⓐ frieghter ⓒ displays
    ⓑ sleigh ⓓ clues

78

- *Instant Replay lessons review spelling objectives, give guidance for further practice of List Words, and provide dictation sentences for a **Final Replay Test**. Reproducible two-page standardized tests to help prepare students for test-taking are supplied for assessment purposes after each Instant Replay lesson.*

1
TAKE IT HOME

Your child has learned to spell many new words and would like to share them with you and your family. Here are some great activities that will help your child review the words in Lessons 1–5 as your family has fun, too!

What Did You Say?
Have a sheet of paper and a pencil handy in several rooms of your home. That way, your child can listen for and record spelling words that are spoken in family conversations. Encourage your child to keep note of the number of times each word is used.

later
until
idea
dentist
musical
dream
banner
gifts

32 Take It Home Master ■ Lessons 1–5

Spelling Enrichment

Bulletin-Board Suggestion

Eggs-pert Spellers Display a picture of a large hen sitting near a nest. Make large eggs out of white construction paper. Encourage students to write words on the eggs that are similar in structure to the words in the week's spelling list. Post the eggs on the nest.

You may also want to display a chart showing the number of eggs each student has posted to the bulletin board during the year. It might then be fun to keep a basket in the classroom that contains plastic eggs with little surprises in them. The surprise might be a note telling them they can skip an assignment or have extra minutes of free time, or it could be a small trinket. Students could then pick an egg from the basket after they have posted a predetermined number of eggs on the bulletin board.

Group Practice

Fill-In Write spelling words on the board. Omit some of the letters and replace them with dashes. Have the first student in Row One come to the board to fill in any of the missing letters in any of the words. Then have the first student in Row Two continue the procedure. Continue having students in each row take turns coming up to the board to fill in letters until all the words are completed. Any student who is able to correctly fill in a word earns a point for his or her row. The row with the most points at the end of the game wins.

Erase Write List Words on the board. Then ask the class to put their heads down while you call on a student to come to the board and erase one of the words. This student then calls on a class member to identify the erased word. The identified word is then restored and the student who correctly identified the erasure can be the person who erases next.

Crossword Relay First draw a large grid on the board. Then, divide the class into several teams. Teams compete against each other to form separate crossword puzzles on the board. Individuals on each team take turns racing against members of the other teams to join List Words until all possibilities have been exhausted. A List Word may appear on each crossword puzzle only once. The winning team is the team whose crossword puzzle contains the greatest number of correctly spelled List Words or the team who finishes first.

Scramble Prepare letter cards sufficient to spell all the List Words. Distribute letter cards to all students. Some students may be given more than one letter card. The teacher then calls out a List Word. Students holding the letters contained in the word race to the front of the class to form the word by standing in the appropriate sequence with their letter cards.

Proofreading Relay Write two columns of misspelled List Words on the board. Although the errors can differ, be sure that each list has the same number of errors. Divide the class into two teams and assign each team to a different column. Teams then compete against each other to correct their assigned lists by team members taking turns erasing and replacing an appropriate letter. Each member may correct only one letter per turn. The team that corrects its entire word list first wins.

Detective Call on a student to be a detective. The detective must choose a spelling word from the list and think of a structural clue, definition, or synonym that will help classmates identify it. The detective then states the clue using the format, "I spy a word that . . . ." Students are called on to guess and spell the mystery word. Whoever answers correctly gets to take a turn being the detective.

Spelling Tic-Tac-Toe Draw a tic-tac-toe square on the board. Divide the class into X and O teams. Take turns dictating spelling words to members of each team. If the word is spelled correctly, allow the team member to place an X or O on the square. The first team to place three X's or O's in a row wins.

Words of Fortune Have students put their heads down while you write a spelling word on the board in large letters. Then cover each letter with a sheet of sturdy paper. The paper can be fastened to the board with magnets. Call on a student to guess any letter of the alphabet they think may be hidden. If that particular letter is hidden, then reveal the letter in every place where it appears in the word by removing the paper.

The student continues to guess letters until an incorrect guess is made or the word is revealed. In the event that an incorrect guess is made, a different student continues the game. Continue the game until every List Word has been hidden and then revealed.

161

- *Reproducible **Take It Home Masters** that also follow each Instant Replay lesson strengthen the school-home connection by providing ideas for parents and students for additional practice at home.*

- *Suggested games and group activities make spelling more fun.*

Meeting the Needs of Your ESL Students

Spelling Strategies for Your ESL Students

You may want to try some of these suggestions to help you promote successful language learning for ESL students.

- Prompt use of spelling words by showing pictures or objects that relate to the topic of each selection. Invite students to discuss the picture or object.
- Demonstrate actions or act out words. Encourage students to do the same.
- Read each selection aloud before asking students to read it independently.
- Define words in context and allow students to offer their own meanings of words.
- Make the meanings of words concrete by naming objects or pictures, role-playing, or pantomiming.

Spelling is the relationship between sounds and letters. Learning to spell words in English is an interesting challenge for English First Language speakers as well as English as a Second Language speakers. You may want to adapt some of the following activities to accommodate the needs of your students—both native and non-English speakers.

Rhymes and Songs

Use rhymes, songs, poems, or chants to introduce new letter sounds and spelling words. Repeat the rhyme or song several times during the day or week, having students listen to you first, then repeat back to you line by line. To enhance learning for visual learners in your classroom and provide opportunities for pointing out letter combinations and their sounds, you may want to write the rhyme, song, poem, or chant on the board. As you examine the words, students can easily see similarities and differences among them. Encourage volunteers to select and recite a rhyme or sing a song for the class. Students may enjoy some of the selections in *Miss Mary Mack and Other Children's Street Rhymes* by Joanna Cole and Stephanie Calmenson or *And the Green Grass Grew All Around* by Alvin Schwartz.

Student Dictation

To take advantage of individual students' known vocabulary, suggest that students build their own sentences incorporating the List Words. For example:

Mary ran.
Mary ran away.
Mary ran away quickly.

Sentence building can expand students' knowledge of how to spell words and of how to notice language patterns, learn descriptive words, and so on.

Words in Context

Using words in context sentences will aid students' mastery of new vocabulary.

- Say several sentences using the List Words in context and have students repeat after you. Encourage more proficient students to make up sentences using List Words that you suggest.
- Write cloze sentences on the board and have students help you complete them with the List Words.

Point out the spelling patterns in the words, using colored chalk to underline or circle the elements.

Oral Drills

Use oral drills to help students make associations among sounds and the letters that represent them. You might use oral drills at listening stations to reinforce the language, allowing ESL students to listen to the drills at their own pace.

Spelling Aloud Say each List Word and have students repeat the word. Next, write it on the board as you name each letter, then say the word again as you track the letters and sound by sweeping your hand under the word. Call attention to spelling changes for words to which endings or suffixes were added. For words with more than one syllable, emphasize each syllable as you write, encouraging students to clap out the syllables. Ask volunteers to repeat the procedure.

Variant Spellings For a group of words that contain the same vowel sound, but variant spellings, write an example on the board, say the word, and then present other words in that word family *(cake: rake, bake, lake)*. Point out the sound and the letter(s) that stand for the sound. Then add words to the list that have the same vowel sound *(play, say, day)*. Say pairs of words *(cake, play)* as you point to them, and identify the vowel sound and the different letters that represent the sound *(long a: a_e, ay)*. Ask volunteers to select a different pair of words and repeat the procedure.

Vary this activity by drawing a chart on the board that shows the variant spellings for a sound. Invite students to add words under the correct spelling pattern. Provide a list of words for students to choose from to help those ESL students with limited vocabularies.

Categorizing To help students discriminate among consonant sounds and spellings, have them help you categorize words with single consonant sounds and consonant blends or digraphs. For example, ask students to close their eyes so that they may focus solely on the sounds in the words, and then pronounce *smart, smile, spend,* and *special.* Next, pronounce the words as you write them on the board. After spelling each word, create two columns—one for *sm,* one for *sp.* Have volunteers pronounce each word, decide which column it fits under, and write the word in the correct column. Encourage students to add to the columns any other words they know that have those consonant blends.

To focus on initial, medial, or final consonant sounds, point out the position of the consonant blends or digraphs in the List Words. Have students find and list the words under columns labeled *Beginning, Middle, End.*

Tape Recording Encourage students to work with a partner or their group to practice their spelling words. If a tape recorder is available, students can practice at their own pace by taking turns recording the words, playing back the tape, and writing each word they hear. Students can then help each other check their spelling against their *Spelling Workout* books. Observe as needed to be sure students are spelling the words correctly.

Comparing/Contrasting To help students focus on word parts, write List Words with prefixes or suffixes on the board and have volunteers circle, underline, or draw a line between the prefix or suffix and its root word. Review the meaning of each root word, then invite students to work with their group to write two sentences: one using just the root word; the other using the root word with its prefix or suffix. For example: *My favorite mystery was* due *at the library Monday afternoon. By Tuesday afternoon the book was* overdue! Or, *You can* depend *on Jen to arrive for softball practice on time. She is* dependable. Have students contrast the two sentences, encouraging them to tell how the prefix or suffix changed the meaning of the root word.

Questions/Answers Write List Words on the board and ask pairs of students to brainstorm questions or answers about the words, such as "Which word names more than one? How do you know?" (foxes, *an* es *was added at the end)* or, "Which word tells that something belongs to the children? How do you know?" *(children's is spelled with an* 's)

Games

You may want to invite students to participate in these activities.

Picture Clues Students can work with a partner to draw pictures or cut pictures out of magazines that represent the List Words, then trade papers and label each other's pictures. Encourage students to check each other's spelling against their *Spelling Workout* books.

Or, you can present magazine cutouts or items that picture the List Words. As you display each picture or item, say the word clearly and then write it on the board as you spell it aloud. Non-English speakers may wish to know the translation of the word in their native language so that they can mentally connect the new word with a familiar one. Students may also find similarities in the spellings of the words.

Letter Cards Have students create letter cards for vowels, vowel digraphs, consonants, consonant blends and digraphs, and so on. Then say a List Word and have students show the card that has the letters representing the sound for the vowels or consonants in that word as they repeat and spell the word after you. Students can use their cards independently as they work with their group.

Charades/Pantomime Students can use gestures and actions to act out the List Words. To receive credit for a correctly guessed word, players must spell the word correctly. Such activities can be played in pairs so that beginning English speakers will not feel pressured. If necessary, translate the words into students' native languages so that they understand the meanings of the words before attempting to act them out.

Change or No Change Have students make flash cards for root words and endings. One student holds up a root word; another holds up an ending. The class says "Change" or "No Change" to describe what happens when the root word and ending are combined. Encourage students to spell the word with its ending added.

Scope and Sequence for MCP Spelling Workout

Skills	Level A	Level B	Level C	Level D	Level E	Level F	Level G	Level H
Consonants	1–12	1–2	1–2	1	1	1, 7, 9	RC	RC
Short Vowels	14–18	3–5	4	2	RC	RC	RC	RC
Long Vowels	20–23	7–11	5, 7	3	RC	RC	RC	RC
Consonant Blends/Clusters	26–28	13–14	8–9 29	5, 7	RC	RC	RC	RC
y as a Vowel	29–30	15–16	10–11	RC	RC	RC	RC	RC
Consonant Digraphs—**th, ch, sh, wh, ck**	32–33	28–29 32	27–28 31	9	RC	RC	RC	RC
Vowel Digraphs		25–26 33	21–22 25	19–22	7–10	11 13–16 19	25	RC
R–Controlled Vowels		19–20	13–14	8	RC	RC	RC	RC
Diphthongs	24	27	26	22–23	11	16–17	RC	RC
Silent Consonants			23	10	4	4–5	RC	RC
Hard and Soft **c** and **g**		32	3	4	2	2	RC	RC
Plurals			19–20	25–27 29	33–34	33	RC	RC
Prefixes		34	32–33	31–32	13–17	20–23 25	7–8	7–11 19–20
Suffixes	34–35	21–23	15–17	13–17	25–29 31–32	26–29 31–32	9 13–14 16, 26	5, 25–27
Contractions		17	34	28	23	RC	RC	RC
Possessives				28–29	23	RC	RC	RC
Compound Words				33	19	RC	RC	RC
Synonyms/Antonyms				34	RC	RC	RC	RC
Homonyms		35	35	35	RC	RC	RC	RC
Spellings of /f/ **f, ff, ph, gh**				11	3	3	RC	RC
Syllables					20–23	RC	RC	RC
Commonly Misspelled Words					35	34	17, 35	17, 29 35
Abbreviations						35	RC	RC
Latin Roots							11, 15 31	13–16

Skills	Level A	Level B	Level C	Level D	Level E	Level F	Level G	Level H
Words with French or Spanish Derivations							10, 29	RC
Words of Latin/French/ Greek Origin								21–23 28
Latin Prefixes							33	RC
List Words Related to Specific Curriculum Areas							19–23 28, 32	31–34
Vocabulary Development	●	●	●	●	●	●	●	●
Dictionary	●	●	●	●	●	●	●	●
Writing	●	●	●	●	●	●	●	●
Proofreading	●	●	●	●	●	●	●	●
Literature Selections	●	●	●	●	●	●	●	●
All-Star Words	●	●	●	●	●	●	●	●
Review Tests in Standardized Format	●	●	●	●	●	●	●	●

Spelling Through Writing

Skills	Level A	Level B	Level C	Level D	Level E	Level F	Level G	Level H
Poetry	●	●	●	●	●	●	●	●
Narrative Writings	●	●	●	●	●	●	●	●
Descriptive Writings	●	●	●	●	●	●	●	●
Expository Writings	●	●	●	●	●	●	●	●
Persuasive Writings			●	●	●	●		
Notes/Letters	●	●	●		●	●	●	
Riddles/Jokes	●		●					
Recipes	●	●	●			●	●	
Newspaper Articles		●	●	●	●	●		●
Conversations/Dialogues				●	●	●		●
Menus						●	●	
Questionnaires		●			●	●	●	●
Logs/Journals			●	●	●	●	●	
Advertisements		●	●	●	●	●	●	●
Reports					●	●	●	●
Literary Devices							●	●
Scripts							●	●
Speeches						●		●

Numbers in chart indicate lesson numbers
RC = reinforced in other contexts
● = found throughout

Lesson 1

Objective
To spell words with single and double consonants

Correlated Phonics Lessons
MCP Phonics, Level D, Lessons 1–2

Warm Up   **Page 5**
In this selection, students read to find out about a dangerous stunt that an adventurous woman performed nearly a century ago. Invite students to discuss what Anna Taylor did and what they thought about it.

Encourage students to look back at the boldfaced words. Ask volunteers to say each word and identify the consonant sounds.

On Your Mark/Warm Up Test
1. Each Olympic team carried its country's *banner.*
2. The number after ninety-nine is one *hundred.*
3. Babe Ruth achieved *fame* as a baseball player.
4. Did the school bus arrive *later* than usual?
5. The number between six and eight is *seven.*
6. Pam used a *hammer* and nails to fix the chair.
7. Do two sixes make *twelve?*
8. The farmer stored the apples in a wooden *barrel.*
9. There are twenty nickels in one *dollar.*
10. The first two *letters* of the alphabet are *A* and *B.*
11. When the movie started, everyone became *silent.*
12. Some *wild* animals are very colorful.
13. Ken studied his spelling words *until* dinner time.
14. In the springtime, the river currents are *swift.*
15. Please put the *bottles* on the shelf.
16. Aunt Maria brought us a *pineapple* from Hawaii.
17. That *film* was fantastic!
18. Four quarts make a *gallon.*
19. We were late because of the *traffic* jam.
20. Are there *eleven* people on a soccer team?

Pep Talk/Game Plan   **Pages 6–7**
Introduce the spelling rule and have students read the List Words aloud. Encourage students to look back at their Warm Up Tests and apply the spelling rule to any misspelled words.

As students work through the **Spelling Lineup,** **Definitions,** and **Vocabulary** exercises, remind them to look back at their List Words or in their dictionaries if they need help.

 See **Student Dictation,** page 14

Name _____

Consonant Sounds   LESSON 1

Warm Up
What stunt was performed by a woman nearly a century ago?

Free Fall
Every year, thousands of people travel to Niagara Falls. This 160-foot waterfall is between New York and Canada. Most people just watch the falls. On October 24, 1901, one person did more than just look. She was the first person to go over the falls in a wooden **barrel!**

Her name was Anna Taylor. This, her first real adventure, could have been her last. She was sure that if she survived the fall she would find **fame** and fortune.

Hundreds of people stood along the banks of the Niagara River. They cheered as the barrel was dropped into the river. The barrel floated with the **swift** current toward the falls. Then it tumbled down the **twelve**-story-high falls. For a while, there was no sign of Anna Taylor. The crowd was **silent.** Finally the oak barrel bobbed up.

The barrel was brought ashore. As Anna stepped out, the crowd cheered wildly. It wasn't **until later** that people found out that she couldn't swim!

 Look back at the boldfaced words. Say each word. What consonant sounds do you hear in each word?

On Your Mark
Take your Warm Up Test. Then check your spelling with the List Words on the next page.

5

Pep Talk
The vowels are **a, e, i, o, u,** and sometimes **y** and **w.** All the rest of the letters are **consonants.** In most words, you can hear the sounds of several consonants. Listen for the **w, l,** and **d** sounds in <u>wild</u>. Sometimes a consonant in a word is doubled, but you hear it only once. Listen for the one sound the double consonants stand for in <u>banner</u> and <u>dollar</u>.

LIST WORDS
1. banner
2. hundred
3. fame
4. later
5. seven
6. hammer
7. twelve
8. barrel
9. dollar
10. letters
11. silent
12. wild
13. until
14. swift
15. bottles
16. pineapple
17. film
18. gallon
19. traffic
20. eleven

Game Plan
Spelling Lineup
Write consonants to complete each List Word. Then circle any words with double consonants.

1. fa **m** e
2. twe **l v** e
3. (b̲o̲ **t t** l̲e̲s̲)
4. wi **l d**
5. (l̲e̲ **t t** e̲r̲s̲)
6. e **l e v** en
7. swi **f t**
8. la **t** er
9. (g̲a̲ **l l** o̲n̲)
10. (t̲r̲a̲ **f f** i̲c̲)
11. se **v** en
12. hun **d r** ed
13. fi **l** m
14. **s** i **l** ent
15. (d̲o̲ **l l** a̲r̲)
16. un **t i** l
17. (b̲a̲ **n n** e̲r̲)
18. (h̲a̲ **m m** e̲r̲)
19. (b̲a̲ **r r** e̲l̲)
20. (p̲i̲ n̲e̲a̲ **p p** l̲e̲)

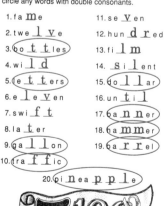

6 Lesson 1 ■ Consonant Sounds

18

Definitions
Read each definition clue. Write List Words in the spaces.
Then use the numbered letters to solve the riddle.

1. cars t r a f f i c
  ‾ ‾ ‾11‾ ‾4‾ ‾ ‾

5. not tame w i l d
  ‾ ‾ ‾8‾ ‾

2. 12 – 1 = e l e v e n
  ‾ ‾ ‾ ‾9‾ ‾ ‾

6. fast s w i f t
  ‾ ‾3‾ ‾ ‾5‾ ‾

3. a flag b a n n e r
  ‾ ‾ ‾ ‾ ‾7‾ ‾

7. popularity f a m e
  ‾1‾ ‾ ‾ ‾

4. quiet s i l e n t
  ‾2‾ ‾ ‾10‾ ‾6‾ ‾

Riddle: What runs and falls but never walks?

Answer: a s w i f t r i v e r
  ‾1‾ ‾2‾ ‾3‾ ‾4‾ ‾5‾ ‾6‾ ‾7‾ ‾8‾ ‾9‾ ‾10‾ ‾11‾

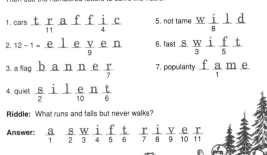

Vocabulary
Write List Words under the correct headings. The first one has been done for you.

numbers
1. hundred
2. seven
3. twelve
4. eleven

fruit
5. pineapple

money
6. dollar

tool
7. hammer

measurement
8. gallon

containers
9. bottles
10. barrel

time words
11. until
12. later

Lesson 1 ■ Consonant Sounds 7

Flex Your Spelling Muscles

Writing
Imagine that you were among the crowd who watched Anna Taylor float down Niagara River and go over Niagara Falls. Write a brief news report telling what you saw, heard, and felt. Don't forget to include what happened when it was all over. Use as many List Words as you can.

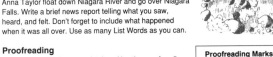

Proofreading
This travel article has ten mistakes. Use the proofreading marks to fix each mistake. Write the misspelled List Words correctly on the lines.

Proofreading Marks
◯ spelling mistake
≡ capital letter

Niagara Falls Is Worth the Trip
  When traveling to niagara Falls during the summer, be ready for some delays. The (traffik) can be heavy. When you finally get to the falls, spend some time watching the (wyild) (swiff) water. Don't worry. it's unlikely that a (barral) will come crashing down. (Latar) after you leave, your ears will still hear the roar of the water. take plenty of (filmm) and send (leterz) and postcards home to friends. There are many scenic places you'll want to share.

1. traffic
2. wild
3. swift
4. barrel
5. later
6. film
7. letters

Now proofread your news report. Fix any mistakes.

Go for the Goal
Take your Final Test. Then fill in your Scoreboard. Send your mistakes to the Word Locker.

SCOREBOARD	
number correct	number wrong

★ ★ ★ ★ ★ ★ ★ ★ **All-Star Words** ★ ★ ★ ★ ★ ★ ★ ★

vessel   slipper   splendid   enemy   instant

Work with a partner to write one paragraph using all the All-Star Words. Trade papers with other students to see how they used the words. How are the paragraphs alike or different?

 **Spelling Strategy**   To help students figure out whether to double the consonant in the middle of a two-syllable word, point out that double consonants usually follow short-vowel sounds. Ask students to say *traffic/trader* and *hammer/tamer* and to tell you whether
- the *a* in each word is long or short
- a single consonant or double consonants follow *a*.

Flex Your Spelling Muscles   *Page 8*
As students complete the **Writing** activity, encourage them to brainstorm ideas, write a first draft, revise, and proofread their work. The **Proofreading** exercise will help them prepare to proofread their news reports. To publish their writing, students may want to
- read their reports as radio broadcasts
- illustrate their reports.

✍ **Writer's Corner**

> Invite students to bring in news clippings about bungee-jumping, skydiving, or other wild stunts. Ask students to write paragraphs telling whether or not they think these activities are safe.

Go for the Goal/Final Test
1. We did not get home **until** after dark.
2. Pablo gave the soccer ball a **swift** kick.
3. Can we return these **bottles** for money?
4. Mom put **pineapple** rings on the ham.
5. We made a **banner** to welcome home the band.
6. Can you count backward from one **hundred?**
7. The young singer dreamed of **fame** and fortune.
8. I will clean my room **later,** after Cody leaves.
9. Antonio has to put **film** in his camera.
10. Paul carried the **gallon** of paint up the ladder.
11. **Traffic** is heavy around 5:00 in the evening.
12. Karla will be **eleven** on her next birthday.
13. Beautiful flowers grow **wild** on the hillside.
14. If you are **silent,** you will hear crickets chirp.
15. There are twenty-six **letters** in the alphabet.
16. Luwanda tried to save one **dollar** every week.
17. The clown came out wearing a **barrel.**
18. There are **twelve** eggs in a dozen.
19. Stop banging that **hammer!**
20. Miss Yee's class is in room **seven.**

Remind students to complete the Scoreboard and write any misspelled words in their Word Locker.

★★ **All-Star Words**   You may want to point out that the All-Star Words follow the spelling rule. Before students write, suggest that they brainstorm topics that relate to all the words.

Lesson 2

Objective

To spell one- and two-syllable words with short-vowel sounds

Correlated Phonics Lessons

MCP Phonics, Level D, Lessons 3–4

Warm Up   *Page 9*

In "Dig It," students read about a type of sculpture that only lasts until the tide comes in. After reading, students may enjoy telling what kind of sand sculpture they would like to make.

Encourage students to look back at the boldfaced words. Ask volunteers to say each word and identify the vowel sound or sounds.

On Your Mark/Warm Up Test

1. Amy's **hands** moved swiftly across the keyboard.
2. The **dentist** showed Pete how to brush his teeth.
3. Kim **lifted** the heavy sack by herself.
4. There is a small **crack** in the old teacup.
5. The **bumps** in the road make drivers go slowly.
6. Keshia will **practice** the song before she sings it.
7. If the ice isn't frozen **solid,** don't walk on it!
8. The dancers will **clasp** hands and form a circle.
9. He rubbed two **sticks** together to start a fire.
10. Last night I **spent** two hours on my homework.
11. Daniel **locked** the chest and put the key away.
12. The teacher decided to **adopt** the students' plan.
13. Dad was chosen to **judge** the dog show.
14. Can your team win the tug-of-war **contest?**
15. They had to **stand** in line for twenty minutes.
16. I would like **shrimp** and clams for dinner.
17. How much does a **stamp** for a postcard cost?
18. Luis can **trust** John to keep a secret.
19. I waxed the **fender,** the hood, and the door.
20. Maiko's **pencil** has her name printed on it.

Pep Talk/Game Plan   *Pages 10–11*

Introduce the spelling rule and have students read the List Words aloud. Encourage students to look back at their Warm Up Tests and apply the spelling rule to any misspelled words.

As students work through the **Spelling Lineup, Alphabetical Order,** and **Hidden Words** exercises, remind them to look back at their List Words or in their dictionaries if they need help. For the **Spelling Lineup,** point out that in two-syllable words, one syllable is stronger than the other (the *stressed* syllable).

 See **Letter Cards,** page 15

Short-Vowel Sounds

Warm Up

What type of sculpture disappears with the tide?

Dig It

It all starts when the tide goes out. The artists come to the beach with their pails and shovels. They lift and sift and make **bumps** in the sand, but they aren't making just sand castles. This is the annual sand castle **contest** in Carmel, California, which happens every October. In this contest, artists make not only castles, but also animals, fish, and anything else they can think of.

Artists mold and carve the wet sand for hours. They use pails, shovels, **sticks,** and other small tools, but mostly their **hands.** They build as far as the water's edge. The results are sometimes wacky, but always creative and fun to look at. The **judges** must have a hard time choosing a winner.

When the contest is over, the sculptors don't have to put the sand back. Before long the tide will come in and take care of things.

Look back at the boldfaced words. Say each word. Listen for the vowel sounds. What vowel sound do you hear in each word?

On Your Mark

Take your Warm Up Test. Then check your spelling with the List Words on the next page.

Pep Talk

The letters **a, e, i, o,** and **u** are vowels. You hear short-vowel sounds in these words:
/a/ in <u>stand</u>
/i/ in <u>sticks</u>
/e/ in <u>spent</u>
/ä/ in <u>locked</u>
/u/ in <u>judge</u>
Listen for the short-vowel sounds in each List Word.

LIST WORDS

1. hands
2. dentist
3. lifted
4. crack
5. bumps
6. practice
7. solid
8. clasp
9. sticks
10. spent
11. locked
12. adopt
13. judge
14. contest
15. stand
16. shrimp
17. stamp
18. trust
19. fender
20. pencil

Game Plan

Spelling Lineup

Write each List Word under the correct short-vowel sound. If a word has two short-vowel sounds, use the stressed one.

/a/	/u/
1. hands	10. bumps
2. crack	11. judge
3. practice	12. trust
4. clasp	
5. stand	/e/
6. stamp	13. dentist
	14. spent
/i/	15. fender
7. lifted	16. pencil
8. sticks	
9. shrimp	/ä/
	17. solid
	18. locked
	19. adopt
	20. contest

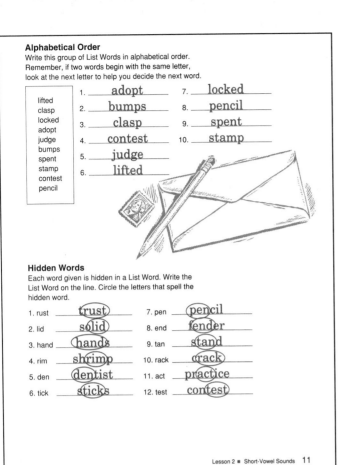

Alphabetical Order
Write this group of List Words in alphabetical order. Remember, if two words begin with the same letter, look at the next letter to help you decide the next word.

lifted	1. adopt
clasp	2. bumps
locked	3. clasp
adopt	4. contest
judge	5. judge
bumps	6. lifted
spent	7. locked
stamp	8. pencil
contest	9. spent
pencil	10. stamp

Hidden Words
Each word given is hidden in a List Word. Write the List Word on the line. Circle the letters that spell the hidden word.

1. rust	trust	7. pen	pencil
2. lid	solid	8. end	fender
3. hand	hands	9. tan	stand
4. rim	shrimp	10. rack	crack
5. den	dentist	11. act	practice
6. tick	sticks	12. test	contest

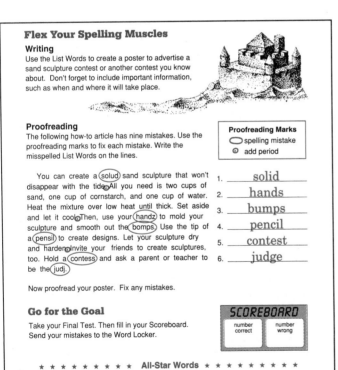

Flex Your Spelling Muscles

Writing
Use the List Words to create a poster to advertise a sand sculpture contest or another contest you know about. Don't forget to include important information, such as when and where it will take place.

Proofreading
The following how-to article has nine mistakes. Use the proofreading marks to fix each mistake. Write the misspelled List Words on the lines.

> **Proofreading Marks**
> ◯ spelling mistake
> ⦿ add period

You can create a solud sand sculpture that won't disappear with the tide. All you need is two cups of sand, one cup of cornstarch, and one cup of water. Heat the mixture over low heat until thick. Set aside and let it cool. Then, use your handz to mold your sculpture and smooth out the bomps. Use the tip of a pensil to create designs. Let your sculpture dry and harden. Invite your friends to create sculptures, too. Hold a contess and ask a parent or teacher to be the judj.

1.	solid
2.	hands
3.	bumps
4.	pencil
5.	contest
6.	judge

Now proofread your poster. Fix any mistakes.

Go for the Goal
Take your Final Test. Then fill in your Scoreboard. Send your mistakes to the Word Locker.

> **SCOREBOARD**
> | number correct | number wrong |

★ ★ ★ ★ ★ ★ ★ ★ **All-Star Words** ★ ★ ★ ★ ★ ★ ★ ★

timid   mascot   extend   public   fond

Make a list of the All-Star Words. Then, write a word or phrase that means the same or almost the same as each word. Check your definitions against your dictionary. Read each meaning aloud to a partner. Ask your partner to name the All-Star Word it goes with.

◎ **Spelling Strategy** Say each List Word aloud and invite the class to repeat it after you. Tell students that as they say each word, they should think about how to spell it by listening to the sounds the letters stand for in each syllable. You may also want to point out that the vowel in the middle of a one-syllable word usually has a short sound.

Flex Your Spelling Muscles   *Page 12*

As students complete the **Writing** activity, encourage them to brainstorm ideas, write a first draft, revise, and proofread their work. The **Proofreading** exercise will help them prepare to proofread their posters. To publish their writing, students may want to
• display the posters in the classroom or in a hall
• use the posters to publicize real contests.

✍ **Writer's Corner**

> Students might enjoy reading *Sand Castles Step-by-Step* by Wierenga/McDonald, which can be ordered from Meadowbrook Press (800-338-2232). Suggest that they use the book as a model to create activity books for younger children. You may want to photocopy students' books for other teachers.

Go for the Goal/Final Test

1. Let's use those **sticks** to make the kite frame.
2. Did you wash your **hands** before dinner?
3. I like a **pencil** with a good eraser.
4. Our school is having a poetry **contest.**
5. The earthquake caused the wall to **crack.**
6. I **locked** myself out of the house!
7. Please don't sit on the **fender** of the car.
8. You forgot to put a **stamp** on your letter.
9. Scott **lifted** that heavy box.
10. We **spent** two days in El Paso, Texas.
11. That was carved from a **solid** block of ice.
12. Did the **dentist** say that Julie needed braces?
13. Of course I **trust** you with my wallet!
14. Now **stand** by the door and I'll take your picture.
15. It was difficult to **judge** the swimming contest.
16. I like cold **shrimp** dipped in chili sauce.
17. The **clasp** on my purse is hard to turn.
18. It takes hours of **practice** to dive well.
19. My parents said I could **adopt** a kitten!
20. The road has lots of **bumps** in it.

Remind students to complete the Scoreboard and write any misspelled words in their Word Locker.

★★ **All-Star Words** You may want to point out that the All-Star Words follow the spelling rule and review the meaning of the word *synonym.*

Lesson 3

Objective
To spell one-, two-, and three-syllable words with long-vowel sounds

Correlated Phonics Lessons
MCP Phonics, Level D, Lessons 5–6

Warm Up   *Page 13*
Students can read to discover what to do to have a good but safe time on a playground. Afterward, invite the class to suggest additional playground rules.

Encourage students to look back at the boldfaced words. Ask volunteers to name the long-vowel sound or sounds in each word.

On Your Mark/Warm Up Test
1. I'll wear *these* boots on our hike tomorrow.
2. I can't *deny* that I missed the meeting.
3. It is important to follow bicycle safety *rules.*
4. Please see that they cross the street *safely.*
5. I can't *locate* my missing book.
6. It's a *crime* to dump garbage in the river!
7. I heated my soup on the *stove.*
8. Mother used a *scale* to weigh the vegetables.
9. Will I wear this *costume* in the play?
10. The train will *arrive* at four o'clock.
11. Jill *opened* the box of cereal.
12. The play is a *musical* called *Oklahoma.*
13. Please divide the apple into four *equal* pieces.
14. Connie has a terrific *idea* for a new game.
15. Put a *tight* cover on the container.
16. Cows like to eat *clover* out in the field.
17. Is a mouse a *rodent?*
18. The *tuba* is a heavy instrument to carry.
19. Put some ice *cubes* in the pitcher of lemonade.
20. The soldier saluted the flag with *pride.*

Pep Talk/Game Plan   *Pages 14–15*
Introduce the spelling rule and have students read the List Words aloud. Encourage students to look back at their Warm Up Tests and apply the spelling rule to any misspelled words.

As students work through the **Spelling Lineup, Classification,** and **Word Building** exercises, remind them to look back at their List Words or in their dictionaries if they need help. For the **Word Building** exercise, you may want to write on the board *debate – deb + loc =* and model how to arrive at *locate.*

 See **Tape Recording,** page 15

Name _____

Long-Vowel Sounds

Warm Up
What playground rules should you follow?

Playground Rules
A playground is a place to have fun. Getting hurt could spoil your fun, so here are some simple **rules** for playing **safely:**

- Ride the slide one person at a time. A pile-up could be dangerous. Always slide feet first and your head will thank you.
- Ride the seesaw with a person of **equal** weight. Never get off without first alerting your partner.
- Keep a **tight** grip when you ride the swings. Use both hands and always remain seated.
- Play games with others. Never be the only one on a playground. Wait for your friends.

If you follow **these** rules, you'll have a good time and stay safe.

 Say each boldfaced word. What do you notice about the vowel sounds?

On Your Mark
Take your Warm Up Test. Then check your spelling with the List Words on the next page.

13

Pep Talk
Long vowels sound like their names.
/ā/ as in <u>scale</u>
/ē/ as in <u>these</u>
/ī/ as in <u>arrive</u>
/ō/ as in <u>stove</u>
/yoo/ as in <u>cubes</u>
/oo/ as in <u>rules</u>
The long vowel sound of u is /yoo/ or /oo/. Listen for the long-vowel sounds in each List Word.

LIST WORDS
1. these
2. deny
3. rules
4. safely
5. locate
6. crime
7. stove
8. scale
9. costume
10. arrive
11. opened
12. musical
13. equal
14. idea
15. tight
16. clover
17. rodent
18. tuba
19. cubes
20. pride

Game Plan
Spelling Lineup
Write each List Word. Circle the letters that spell long-vowel sounds. Words of two or more syllables may contain more than one long-vowel sound.

1. these
2. deny
3. rules
4. safely
5. locate
6. crime
7. stove
8. scale
9. costume
10. arrive
11. opened
12. musical
13. equal
14. idea
15. tight
16. clover
17. rodent
18. tuba
19. cubes
20. pride

14   Lesson 3 ■ Long-Vowel Sounds

Classification

Write the List Word that belongs in each group.

1. sink, refrigerator, __stove__
2. piano, flute, __tuba__
3. find, place, __locate__
4. this, those, __these__
5. play, show, __musical__
6. mask, makeup, __costume__
7. laws, orders, __rules__
8. squares, boxes, __cubes__
9. thought, plan, __idea__
10. rat, mouse, __rodent__

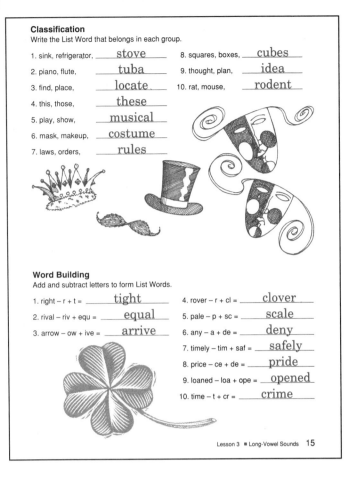

Word Building

Add and subtract letters to form List Words.

1. right – r + t = __tight__
2. rival – riv + equ = __equal__
3. arrow – ow + ive = __arrive__
4. rover – r + cl = __clover__
5. pale – p + sc = __scale__
6. any – a + de = __deny__
7. timely – tim + saf = __safely__
8. price – ce + de = __pride__
9. loaned – loa + ope = __opened__
10. time – t + cr = __crime__

Flex Your Spelling Muscles

Writing

Most sports and games have rules so that everyone can play safely. Choose a sport or game you know about. Then use the List Words to write some rules that go with it.

Proofreading

The following story has nine mistakes. Use the proofreading marks to fix each mistake. Then write the misspelled List Words on the lines.

Proofreading Marks	
◯	spelling mistake
∧	add something

The strangest thing happened yesterday. When Bo and I arrived at the school playground together the gate was shut tyght.
"Do you know why the gate is closed⌃" I asked Bo.
"No, it never has been before. Do you think someone didn't know the rooles⌃" he asked.
"Maybe. Let's try to get in," I said.
When we got the gate opened, we couldn't believe what we saw. By the swings sat a big cardboard stoove. On the slide was a tubah.
"What is all this⌃" I asked.
"I don't know!" said Bo.
Just then a clown wearing a silly catsume came walking through the gate. Bo and I had forgotten! It was the day of our school carnival!

1. __tight__   3. __opened__   5. __tuba__
2. __rules__   4. __stove__   6. __costume__

Now proofread your game rules. Fix any mistakes.

Go for the Goal

Take your Final Test. Then fill in your Scoreboard. Send your mistakes to the Word Locker.

SCOREBOARD
number correct	number wrong

★ ★ ★ ★ ★ ★ ★ **All-Star Words** ★ ★ ★ ★ ★ ★ ★

remove   spice   rude   cone   tomato

With your partner, write a silly recipe using the All-Star Words. Swap recipes with other students to see how they used the words.

◎ **Spelling Strategy** Write these words on the board: *crime, late, cube, pride.* Then list: *rim, stop, cub, bad.* With a partner, students can say the words in each list and compare the spellings. Help students conclude that one-syllable words with a long vowel followed by a single consonant usually end in *e.* Ask them to name other words that follow this rule.

Flex Your Spelling Muscles   *Page 16*

As students complete the **Writing** activity, encourage them to brainstorm ideas, write a first draft, revise, and proofread their work. The **Proofreading** exercise will help them prepare to proofread their rules. Before they begin the exercise, remind students that the proofreading mark ∧ is used to add something. It could be a space, a comma, a question mark, or an exclamation mark. To publish their writing, students may want to play rap music and sing their rules.

✍ **Writer's Corner**

The class may want to write to a local law enforcement agency to request a guest speaker on traffic or bicycle safety. Before the speaker arrives, students can write a list of questions to ask.

Go for the Goal/Final Test

1. Nick hopes for a role in the school *musical.*
2. Jeff's mother made him a snake *costume.*
3. Roger *opened* the envelope.
4. Will Rosa's train *arrive* at six o'clock?
5. I found a four-leaf *clover* in the yard.
6. A square has four *equal* sides.
7. Your dog's collar is too *tight!*
8. Ellen has a good *idea.*
9. Drive *safely!*
10. Each of us tries hard to follow the *rules.*
11. Could I borrow *these* books for a while?
12. Cindy may *deny* that she forgot your birthday.
13. The butcher weighed the steak on the *scale.*
14. Robbing a bank is a *crime.*
15. We have a new *stove* in our kitchen.
16. We tried hard to *locate* the missing cat.
17. I take *pride* in my work.
18. Is a squirrel a *rodent?*
19. My friend Robert plays the *tuba.*
20. Mother chopped the meat into *cubes.*

Remind students to complete the Scoreboard and write any misspelled words in their Word Locker.

★★ **All-Star Words** You may want to point out that the All-Star Words follow the spelling rule and inspire students by showing them some real recipes.

Lesson 4

Objective
To spell words with the hard and soft *c* and *g* sounds

Correlated Phonics Lessons
MCP Phonics, Level D, Lessons 7–8

Warm Up   *Page 17*
In "Cool as Ice," students read to find out what kind of sculpture never gets into a museum. Ask students whether they have ever seen an ice sculpture and why they would or would not like to try sculpting ice.

Call on volunteers to say each boldfaced word and identify the sounds made by *c* and *g*.

On Your Mark/Warm Up Test
1. We stood at the *edge* of the steep cliff.
2. White is a *common* color for houses.
3. The moon is in the shape of a *circle.*
4. A *cactus* plant grows well in a hot, dry region.
5. On their birthdays, Daryl and Pam exchange *gifts.*
6. A *gentle* breeze swayed the leaves of the tree.
7. Everyone laughed when the clown came on *stage.*
8. Did you hear a *strange* sound on the roof?
9. The cat slept in a chair in the *corner* of the room.
10. The audience applauded the *graceful* dancers.
11. The sun is the *center* of our solar system.
12. Tom put the *baggage* on the rack above the seats.
13. Put words with the hard *c* in one *category.*
14. It's time to feed our pet *gerbil.*
15. Don't step in the wet *cement!*
16. Does this store offer discount *prices?*
17. The *force* of the wind blew the roof off the barn.
18. This bunch of *celery* looks fresh.
19. Please *decide* if you plan to come for a bike ride.
20. It is important to conserve *energy* resources.

Pep Talk/Game Plan   *Pages 18–19*
Introduce the spelling rule and have students read the List Words aloud. Encourage students to look back at their Warm Up Tests and apply the spelling rule to any misspelled words.

As students work through the **Spelling Lineup, Classification,** and **Dictionary** exercises, remind them to look back at their List Words or in their dictionaries if they need help. You may also want to point out that some words, such as *circle* and *baggage,* contain both hard and soft *c* or *g.*

 See **Rhymes and Songs,** page 14

24

Hard and Soft <u>c</u> and <u>g</u>

Warm Up
What kind of sculpture never gets into a museum?

Cool as Ice

If you saw someone wearing ski pants, heavy kneepads, a warm jacket, a baseball cap, rubber boots, and warm gloves, who would you think the person was? A skier? A baseball player in the Arctic? Possibly, but that person could also be an ice sculptor. An ice sculptor carves works of art out of giant ice cubes. Not a very **common** job, is it?

Simple blocks of ice can become any creation—an animal, a mermaid, or maybe a horse-drawn chariot. A frozen cart could carry two icy riders. It can take a sculptor hours and hours of cutting, shipping, and smoothing to complete one carving.

Unlike most works of art, ice sculptures are not meant to last. Once they're displayed, they melt. The sculptures are often used as party decorations. These **graceful** figures are usually placed in the **center** of the food table, in a **corner,** or on a **stage** by themselves. Talking about the sculptures puts guests at ease. They can easily "break the ice" by talking about the frozen art.

 Say each boldfaced word. Listen for the sounds that **c** and **g** make. What do you notice about the sounds for **c** and **g**?

On Your Mark
Take your Warm Up Test. Then check your spelling with the List Words on the next page.

17

Pep Talk
The letter **c** can make a hard sound as in <u>common</u> and <u>cactus</u> and a soft sound as in <u>force</u> and <u>celery</u>. Listen for the hard and soft sound of **c** in <u>circle</u>.

The letter **g** can make a hard sound as in <u>gifts</u> and <u>graceful</u> and a soft sound as in <u>edge</u> and <u>stage</u>. Listen for the hard and soft sound of **g** in <u>baggage</u>.

LIST WORDS

1. edge
2. common
3. circle
4. cactus
5. gifts
6. gentle
7. stage
8. strange
9. corner
10. graceful
11. center
12. baggage
13. category
14. gerbil
15. cement
16. prices
17. force
18. celery
19. decide
20. energy

Game Plan
Spelling Lineup
Write each List Word under the correct heading. Four words will be written more than once.

hard **c** as in <u>carton</u>	hard **g** as in <u>grade</u>
1. common	14. gifts
2. circle	15. graceful
3. cactus	16. baggage
4. corner	17. category
5. category	

soft **c** as in <u>cent</u>	soft **g** as in <u>germ</u>
6. circle	18. edge
7. graceful	19. gentle
8. center	20. stage
9. cement	21. strange
10. prices	22. baggage
11. force	23. gerbil
12. celery	24. energy
13. decide	

18   Lesson 4 ■ Hard and Soft **c** and **g**

Classification
Write the List Word that belongs in each group.

1. ordinary, usual, __common__
2. square, triangle, __circle__
3. lettuce, cucumber, __celery__
4. middle, core, __center__
5. luggage, suitcases, __baggage__
6. group, set, __category__
7. actors, play, __stage__
8. tame, kind, __gentle__
9. desert, sand, __cactus__
10. mouse, hamster, __gerbil__
11. birthday, party, __gifts__
12. electrical, solar, __energy__
13. sidewalk, concrete, __cement__
14. cost, money, __prices__

Dictionary
Write the List Word that comes between each pair of guide words in the dictionary.

In a dictionary, **guide words** at the top of a page show the first and last entries on that page. **category/center**

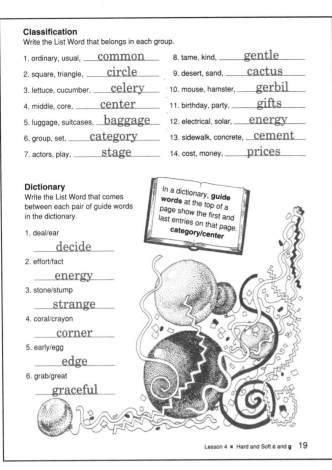

1. deal/ear
__decide__
2. effort/fact
__energy__
3. stone/stump
__strange__
4. coral/crayon
__corner__
5. early/egg
__edge__
6. grab/great
__graceful__

Lesson 4 ■ Hard and Soft **c** and **g**   19

Flex Your Spelling Muscles
Writing
Ice is only one material that sculptors use. Think of a sculpture you have seen in a picture, a store, or a museum. Write a paragraph telling what you liked or did not like about it. Use as many List Words as you can.

Proofreading
Mary's art review has ten mistakes. Use the proofreading marks to fix the mistakes. Write the misspelled List Words correctly on the lines.

Proofreading Marks
◯ spelling mistake
∧ add something

Sculpture Display Wows Crowds!
Ana Cardona's powerful new sculpture is generating a great amount of energee at the art museum! The 10-foot sement kactus rises from the floor in graceful lines taking senter staje. The public, of course, will deside for themselves. However, this reporter feels Ana Cardona's work has opened up a whole new categorry of sculpture art.

1. __energy__
2. __cement__
3. __cactus__
4. __graceful__
5. __center__
6. __stage__
7. __decide__
8. __category__

Now proofread your paragraph. Fix any mistakes.

Go for the Goal
Take your Final Test. Then fill in your Scoreboard. Send your mistakes to the Word Locker.

SCOREBOARD
number correct	number wrong

★ ★ ★ ★ ★ ★ ★ ★ **All-Star Words** ★ ★ ★ ★ ★ ★ ★ ★

gobble   college   damage   gasp   prince

Write a sentence for each All-Star Word. Then, read each sentence aloud to a partner, saying *blank* in place of the All-Star Word. See if your partner can complete each sentence with the correct missing word.

20   Lesson 4 ■ Hard and Soft **c** and **g**

 **Spelling Strategy**   To help students figure out whether a *c* or *g* is hard or soft, write List Words containing *c* on the board and invite the class to
• identify the letter that follows the *c*
• say the word and tell whether the *c* is hard or soft.
Follow the same procedure with List Words that contain *g*. Help students conclude that *c* and *g* are usually soft before *i, e,* and *y*.

Flex Your Spelling Muscles   *Page 20*
As students complete the **Writing** activity, encourage them to brainstorm ideas, write a first draft, revise, and proofread their work. The **Proofreading** exercise will help them prepare to proofread their paragraphs. To publish their writing, students may want to
• illustrate their paragraphs
• make a speech about which sculpture to see.

✍ Writer's Corner

Invite students to look in an encyclopedia or to use a library card catalog to help them gather information about sculpture. Suggest that students write a summary of the information they found the most interesting. Then students can illustrate their writing and create a classroom display.

Go for the Goal/Final Test
1. The source of solar **energy** is the sun.
2. The **graceful** skater glided across the ice.
3. Leo couldn't **decide** between the two jackets.
4. Don't stand so close to the **edge!**
5. Write your name in the **center** of the page.
6. Draw a **circle** around your name.
7. **Celery** is a crunchy green vegetable.
8. The train porter helped us with our **baggage.**
9. Is Smith a **common** name in the United States?
10. Thank you for all these lovely **gifts.**
11. Dad had to **force** the cabin door open.
12. Ruby got nervous when she walked on **stage.**
13. The **prices** in this store are outrageous!
14. He took care of my pet **gerbil** while I was away.
15. Look at the orange flower on that **cactus** plant.
16. Lisa had a **strange** feeling about the visitor.
17. Doesn't Jason's uncle drive a **cement** truck?
18. Apples and pears belong in the fruit **category.**
19. Ed decided the lamp looked best in the **corner.**
20. Although our dog is huge, she is very **gentle.**

Remind students to complete the Scoreboard and write any misspelled words in their Word Locker.

★★ **All-Star Words**   You may want to point out that the All-Star Words follow the spelling rule. With a volunteer, model the activity using a List Word.

25

Lesson 5

Objective

To spell words with two- and three-letter consonant blends

Correlated Phonics Lessons

MCP Phonics, Level D, Lessons 9–12

Warm Up   *Page 21*

Students may enjoy reading to find out which sport used to be called *baggataway.* Afterward, ask students whether they have ever played lacrosse, and invite them to tell what they know about the histories of other sports.

Call on volunteers to name the beginning consonant sounds in each boldfaced word.

On Your Mark/Warm Up Test

1. Did Juan buy a pair of woolen **gloves?**
2. A jet flies at great **speed.**
3. Taking photographs requires a lot of **skill.**
4. **Screens** on the windows will keep the flies out.
5. **Protect** yourself by driving defensively.
6. We planted flowers in **front** of the house.
7. The man's **craft** is making leather belts.
8. The **brains** of birds are very small.
9. I was **scared** when the dog barked!
10. Please put everything back in its **proper** place.
11. **Trace** the picture carefully.
12. I had a pleasant **dream** last night.
13. The students formed a **straight** line.
14. I got a **splinter** from that broken pencil.
15. We all heard the **screech** of the owl.
16. Write your answers in the **spaces.**
17. We will **stuff** the pillow with feathers.
18. The **greedy** dog ate the food in the cat's dish.
19. **Sprinkle** cheese on the pizza.
20. Do you think the rules are too **strict?**

Pep Talk/Game Plan   *Pages 22–23*

Introduce the spelling rule and have students read the List Words aloud. You may also want to point out that some words, such as *screech,* sound like the sound they are associated with. Then encourage students to look back at their Warm Up Tests and apply the spelling rule to any misspelled words.

As students work through the **Spelling Lineup, Rhyming,** and **Puzzle** exercises, remind them to look back at their List Words or in their dictionaries if they need help.

 See **Categorizing,** page 15

Name _____

Beginning Consonant Blends

LESSON 5

Warm Up

What sport was once called "baggataway"?

Lacrosse

North American Indians originally called this sport "baggataway." Today it's called *lacrosse.* Lacrosse is played by two teams on a grassy area a little larger than a football field. Each team has ten players. They wear heavy **gloves,** helmets, and shoulder pads to **protect** themselves. Each player carries a stick called a *crosse.* It is usually made of wood with a small pocket at the end. The pocket has a **screen** made of loose net so that the players can catch and throw the ball into it. Only the goalkeepers can touch the ball with their hands. The object of the game is to score goals. The team scoring the most goals wins. It is a game that requires both **speed** and **skill.**

The game was first used by Canadian Indians to train warriors. There were very few rules. Later, the French settlers gave it the name *lacrosse.* They added a few rules to make it safer to play. In 1867, it was adopted as the national game of Canada. Today it is popular in places as far away as Australia.

 Say each of the boldfaced words. How many consonant sounds do you hear at the beginning of each word?

On Your Mark

Take your Warm Up Test. Then check your spelling with the List Words on the next page.

21

Pep Talk

A **consonant blend** is two or more consonants that come together in a word. Their sounds blend together, but each sound is heard. Listen to the sounds of these consonant blends:

gloves
straight
screens
craft
protect

Listen for the consonant blend in each List Word.

LIST WORDS

1. gloves
2. speed
3. skill
4. screens
5. protect
6. front
7. craft
8. brains
9. scared
10. proper
11. trace
12. dream
13. straight
14. splinter
15. screech
16. spaces
17. stuff
18. greedy
19. sprinkle
20. strict

Game Plan

Spelling Lineup

Add a consonant blend to each group of letters to form a List Word.

1. strict
2. brains
3. stuff
4. screens
5. sprinkle
6. skill
7. scared
8. greedy
9. splinter
10. screech
11. trace
12. craft
13. front
14. gloves
15. protect
16. speed
17. straight
18. spaces
19. proper
20. dream

Rhyming
Use the clues to write List Words. Each List Word must rhyme with the underlined word.

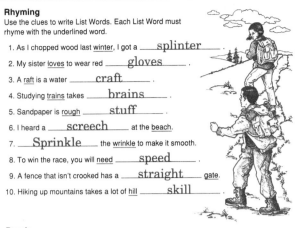

1. As I chopped wood last <u>winter</u>, I got a __splinter__
2. My sister <u>loves</u> to wear red __gloves__ .
3. A <u>raft</u> is a water __craft__ .
4. Studying <u>trains</u> takes __brains__ .
5. Sandpaper is <u>rough</u> __stuff__ .
6. I heard a __screech__ at the <u>beach</u>.
7. __Sprinkle__ the <u>wrinkle</u> to make it smooth.
8. To win the race, you will <u>need</u> __speed__ .
9. A fence that isn't crooked has a __straight__ <u>gate</u>.
10. Hiking up mountains takes a lot of <u>hill</u> __skill__ .

Puzzle
Fill in the crossword puzzle by writing a List Word to answer each clue.

ACROSS
2. wire window coverings
3. to watch over or keep safe
5. afraid
7. not willing to share
8. harsh or stiff

DOWN
1. to copy a picture
2. not crooked or bent
3. correct or suitable
4. the part that faces forward
6. a sleeping person's mind picture

Flex Your Spelling Muscles
Writing
What is your most favorite sport? What is your least favorite sport? Write a paragraph that explains why you prefer one sport over the other. Use as many List Words as you can.

Proofreading
The article below has ten mistakes. Use the proofreading marks to fix each mistake. Write the misspelled words correctly on the lines.

> **Proofreading Marks**
> ◯ spelling mistake
> ≡ capital letter

Native American Kickball
Kickball races were once popular among Native americans in the Southwest and are still held by many groups in mexico. The players kicked a ball made of bone, wood, woven grass, or stone for many miles. some even raced barefoot with nothing to (protekt) their feet. They moved the ball in (frunt) of them with great (skile) and (spead) they had to keep the ball going as (strayht) as possible in order to win. Sometimes they could kick the ball across flat (spases) to gain more ground and move ahead.

1. __protect__   4. __speed__
2. __front__   5. __straight__
3. __skill__   6. __spaces__

Now proofread what you wrote about your favorite sport. Fix any mistakes.

Go for the Goal
Take your Final Test. Then fill in your Scoreboard. Send your mistakes to the Word Locker.

SCOREBOARD
| number correct | number wrong |

★ ★ ★ ★ ★ ★ ★ ★ **All-Star Words** ★ ★ ★ ★ ★ ★ ★ ★

glow   crazy   program   scramble   strength

Write each All-Star Word. Then write a clue to go with it. Read each clue aloud to a partner. Ask your partner for the All-Star Word that goes with the clue.

⊙ **Spelling Strategy**   With a partner, students can take turns saying the List Words aloud to each other. The partner who is listening repeats the word and spells it, snapping a finger or tapping a foot when he or she says the letters for the consonant blend. Before students begin, remind them that the /k/ sound in some of the List Words (for example, *screens, craft*) is spelled with the letter *c*.

Flex Your Spelling Muscles   *Page 24*
As students complete the **Writing** activity, encourage them to brainstorm ideas, write a first draft, revise, and proofread their work. The **Proofreading** exercise will help them prepare to proofread their paragraphs. To publish their writing, students may want to
• use their paragraphs to hold a debate on the best sport
• create a sports magazine.

✐ Writer's Corner
> Students may enjoy writing fan letters to sports figures they admire. A reference librarian can help them locate appropriate addresses. Tell students that although some celebrities send publicity materials to fans, not all will respond.

Go for the Goal/Final Test
1. I *dream* of becoming a great scientist one day.
2. Please use *proper* manners at the table!
3. Children *trace* letters to learn how to print.
4. Is your little brother *scared* of the dark?
5. There were no *spaces* left on the card.
6. The nurse removed a *splinter* from my foot.
7. Max went *straight* home after school.
8. We heard the *screech* of the tires.
9. The rules were *strict* but fair.
10. Grandma will *stuff* the turkey with bread crumbs.
11. Please *sprinkle* some water on the plants.
12. The *greedy* child refused to share his popcorn.
13. Every spring we put *screens* in our windows.
14. The horse galloped at a frightening *speed.*
15. Use my *gloves* to keep your hands warm.
16. Joanna has enormous *skill* as a carpenter.
17. Dinosaurs were huge animals with tiny *brains.*
18. Mother lions will fight to *protect* their young.
19. Is the *front* of the building painted?
20. Robin learned the *craft* of shoeing horses.

Remind students to complete the Scoreboard and write any misspelled words in their Word Locker.

★★ **All-Star Words**   You may want to point out that the All-Star Words follow the spelling rule and model how to write a clue.

Lesson 6 • Instant Replay

Objective
To review spelling words with consonant sounds, short-vowel sounds, long-vowel sounds, hard and soft *c* and *g,* and beginning consonant blends

Time Out   *Pages 25–28*
Check Your Word Locker Based on your observations, note which words are giving students the most difficulty and offer assistance for spelling them correctly. Here are some frequently misspelled words to watch for: *straight, category,* and *until.*

To give students extra help and practice in taking standardized tests, you may want to have them take the Review Test for this lesson on pages 30–31. After scoring the tests, return them to students so that they can record their misspelled words in their Word Locker.

After practicing their troublesome words, students can work through the exercises for **Lessons 1–5.** Before they begin each exercise, you may want to go over the spelling rule.

 Take It Home Invite students to listen for the List Words in **Lessons 1–5** in conversations at home. Suggest that they keep a record of how often each word is used. For a complete list of the words, encourage them to take their *Spelling Workout* books home. Students can also use Take It Home Master 1 on pages 32–33 to help them do the activity. In class, they can share their lists and draw conclusions about the words that were used most often.

Name _____

Instant Replay • Lessons 1–5

LESSON 6

Time Out
Take another look at consonant sounds, short- and long-vowel sounds, the hard and soft sounds of **c** and **g,** and beginning consonant blends.

Check Your Word Locker
Look at the words in your Word Locker. Which words for Lessons 1 through 5 did you have the most trouble with? Write them here.

_____

Practice writing your troublesome words with a partner. Try writing the letters of each word in the air. Your partner can spell the word aloud as you write.

Lesson 1

In most words you can hear the sound of each consonant, as in <u>later</u>. Some words have double consonants that stand for one sound, as in <u>letters</u>.

List Words

banner
hammer
twelve
dollar
silent
wild
swift
bottles
pineapple
film

Write the List Word that belongs in each group.

1. nickel, quarter, ___dollar___
2. quiet, hushed, ___silent___
3. wrench, pliers, ___hammer___
4. apple, peach, ___pineapple___
5. quick, fast, ___swift___
6. jars, packages, ___bottles___
7. free, untamed, ___wild___
8. camera, movie, ___film___
9. four, eight, ___twelve___
10. flag, shield, ___banner___

25

Lesson 2

Vowels can stand for short sounds, as in <u>contest</u> and <u>judge</u>.

List Words

dentist
lifted
practice
solid
clasp
adopt
judge
shrimp
trust
pencil

Write two List Words next to each short-vowel sound. If a word has two short vowel sounds, use the stressed one.

/a/ as in <u>hat</u>   1. ___practice___   ___clasp___
/e/ as in <u>egg</u>   2. ___dentist___   ___pencil___
/ă/ as in <u>hop</u>   3. ___solid___   ___adopt___
/i/ as in <u>hit</u>   4. ___lifted___   ___shrimp___
/u/ as in <u>up</u>   5. ___judge___   ___trust___

Lesson 3

Vowels can also stand for long sounds, as in <u>these</u> and <u>stove</u>.

List Words

deny
safely
locate
costume
equal
idea
clover
rodent
tuba
pride

Write a List Word to complete each sentence.

1. A ___tuba___ is a musical instrument.
2. Ramon was filled with ___pride___ when he won.
3. Anna wore a chicken ___costume___ to the party.
4. Please help me ___locate___ my lost book.
5. I can't ___deny___ I'm happy it's summer.
6. We split the melon into ___equal___ halves.
7. People say a four-leaf ___clover___ is lucky.
8. Juan has a clever ___idea___ for a story.
9. A field mouse is a ___rodent___.
10. Drive ___safely___ to avoid accidents.

26 Lesson 6 ■ Instant Replay

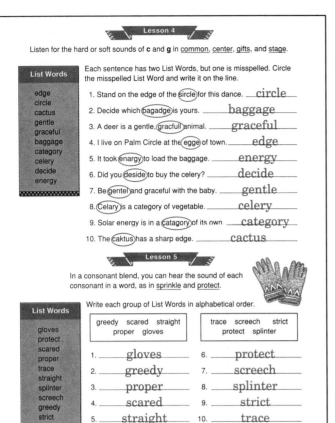

Listen for the hard or soft sounds of **c** and **g** in <u>common</u>, <u>center</u>, <u>gifts</u>, and <u>stage</u>.

List Words

edge
circle
cactus
gentle
graceful
baggage
category
celery
decide
energy

Each sentence has two List Words, but one is misspelled. Circle the misspelled List Word and write it on the line.

1. Stand on the edge of the (sircle) for this dance. _circle_
2. Decide which (bagadge) is yours. _baggage_
3. A deer is a gentle, (gracfull) animal. _graceful_
4. I live on Palm Circle at the (egge) of town. _edge_
5. It took (enargy) to load the baggage. _energy_
6. Did you (deside) to buy the celery? _decide_
7. Be (gentel) and graceful with the baby. _gentle_
8. (Celary) is a category of vegetable. _celery_
9. Solar energy is in a (catagory) of its own. _category_
10. The (caktus) has a sharp edge. _cactus_

In a consonant blend, you can hear the sound of each consonant in a word, as in <u>sprinkle</u> and <u>protect</u>.

List Words

gloves
protect
scared
proper
trace
straight
splinter
screech
greedy
strict

Write each group of List Words in alphabetical order.

greedy scared straight proper gloves	trace screech strict protect splinter

1. _gloves_   6. _protect_
2. _greedy_   7. _screech_
3. _proper_   8. _splinter_
4. _scared_   9. _strict_
5. _straight_   10. _trace_

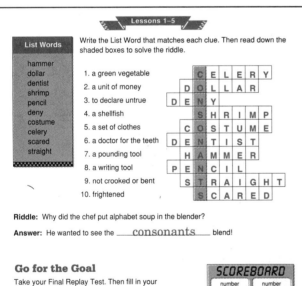

List Words

hammer
dollar
dentist
shrimp
pencil
deny
costume
celery
scared
straight

Write the List Word that matches each clue. Then read down the shaded boxes to solve the riddle.

1. a green vegetable — C E L E R Y
2. a unit of money — D O L L A R
3. to declare untrue — D E N Y
4. a shellfish — S H R I M P
5. a set of clothes — C O S T U M E
6. a doctor for the teeth — D E N T I S T
7. a pounding tool — H A M M E R
8. a writing tool — P E N C I L
9. not crooked or bent — S T R A I G H T
10. frightened — S C A R E D

Riddle: Why did the chef put alphabet soup in the blender?

Answer: He wanted to see the _consonants_ blend!

Go for the Goal

Take your Final Replay Test. Then fill in your Scoreboard. Send any misspelled words to your Word Locker.

SCOREBOARD

number correct	number wrong

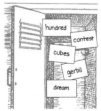

Clean Out Your Word Locker
Look in your Word Locker. Cross out each word you spelled correctly on your Final Replay Test. Circle the words you're still having trouble with. Add the words you circled to your Spelling Notebook. What do you notice about the words? Watch for those words as you write.

Go for the Goal/Final Replay Test   *Page 28*

1. Aunt Helen bought two **bottles** of orange juice.
2. We decided to **adopt** a stray puppy.
3. The cows chewed the **clover** in the meadow.
4. Our dog is **gentle** with young children.
5. The rules in this club are **strict.**
6. I saved a **dollar** by buying this shirt on sale.
7. Uncle Ken studied many years to be a **dentist.**
8. I can't **deny** that I'm thrilled to win the contest.
9. We waited at the **edge** of the road for the bus.
10. Does a triangle have three **straight** sides?
11. We heard the crows **screech** as they flew by.
12. Luis traced a coin to make a **circle.**
13. I'm happy that your dog returned home **safely.**
14. Every afternoon I **practice** the piano.
15. Sam is making a robot **costume** for the play.
16. Let's cut the **pineapple** into slices for dessert.
17. We designed a **banner** for the school soccer team.
18. We **lifted** the rug so that we could wash the floor.
19. Please break the chalk into two **equal** pieces.
20. Dad wears rubber **gloves** when he washes the car.
21. That **greedy** dog ate all the food!
22. Swans are **graceful** as they glide across the water.
23. A **tuba** is a very large instrument.
24. The **judge** wanted to ask another question.
25. I will be happy to sharpen your **pencil** for you.
26. We watched an old **silent** movie.
27. Lions and tigers are **wild** animals.
28. We tried to **locate** the train station on our map.
29. A **rodent** has made a nest in the attic.
30. Write each word in the correct **category.**
31. It takes **energy** and training to run a marathon.
32. **Cactus** plants grow in desert regions.
33. The puppy was **scared** by the loud thunder.
34. Will you show me how to **trace** a design?
35. Tony chopped the **celery** for the salad.
36. **Twelve** people attended the meeting last night.
37. Deer are **swift** runners.
38. Barbara will stir-fry the **shrimp** and broccoli.
39. Karen turned her clever **idea** into a fine cartoon.
40. The workers loaded the **baggage** into the plane.
41. Can you **decide** which sport is your favorite?
42. Grandma removed the **splinter** from my finger.
43. A mother bear will fight to **protect** her baby.
44. Mr. Cho taught the **proper** way to use chopsticks.
45. Al felt great **pride** when he solved the problem.
46. I know I can **trust** you to take good care of my cat.
47. The old coin was made of **solid** gold!
48. The **clasp** on the necklace is broken.
49. Did you buy **film** for the camera?
50. Use a **hammer** to pound the nail into the board.

Clean Out Your Word Locker Before writing each word, students can say the word and identify any short-vowel sounds, long-vowel sounds, or consonant blends they hear.

Name _____

Instant Replay Test

Side A

Read each set of words. Fill in the circle next to the word
that is spelled correctly.

1. (a) soled   (c) solud
    (b) saulid   (d) solid

2. (a) decied   (c) decide
    (b) desied   (d) deside

3. (a) wild   (c) whild
    (b) wiled   (d) whilde

4. (a) stricked   (c) strick
    (b) strickt   (d) strict

5. (a) ekwual   (c) equel
    (b) equal   (d) equall

6. (a) strate   (c) straght
    (b) straight   (d) streight

7. (a) sielent   (c) silent
    (b) sighlent   (d) silant

8. (a) baggage   (c) bagage
    (b) baggadge   (d) bagedge

9. (a) sircle   (c) surcle
    (b) circkle   (d) circle

10. (a) pencil   (c) pensle
    (b) pencill   (d) pensil

Instant Replay Test

Side B

Read each set of words. Fill in the circle next to the word that is spelled correctly.

11. ⓐ safeley   ⓒ safely
    ⓑ safly   ⓓ saifly

12. ⓐ pinapple   ⓒ pineappel
    ⓑ pineapple   ⓓ pienapple

13. ⓐ pracktice   ⓒ practice
    ⓑ practiss   ⓓ practise

14. ⓐ costume   ⓒ costuem
    ⓑ costoom   ⓓ costewm

15. ⓐ judje   ⓒ judg
    ⓑ juge   ⓓ judge

16. ⓐ screach   ⓒ skreech
    ⓑ screech   ⓓ schreech

17. ⓐ roadent   ⓒ roedent
    ⓑ rodant   ⓓ rodent

18. ⓐ category   ⓒ cadegory
    ⓑ catagory   ⓓ categorey

19. ⓐ doller   ⓒ dollor
    ⓑ dollar   ⓓ dolar

20. ⓐ gready   ⓒ greedy
    ⓑ gredey   ⓓ greedey

TAKE IT HOME

Your child has learned to spell many new words and would like to share them with you and your family. Here are some great activities that will help your child review the words in Lessons 1–5 as your family has fun, too!

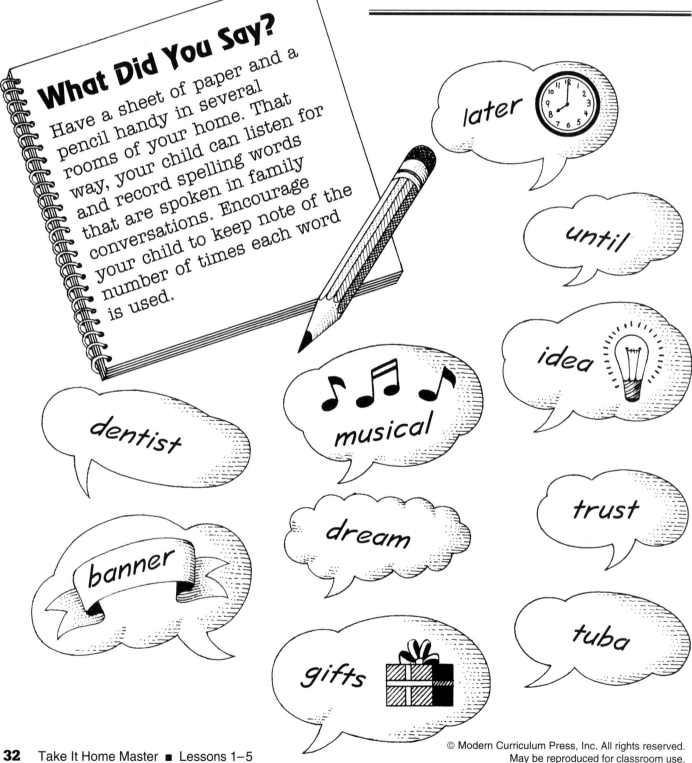

What Did You Say?

Have a sheet of paper and a pencil handy in several rooms of your home. That way, your child can listen for and record spelling words that are spoken in family conversations. Encourage your child to keep note of the number of times each word is used.

later

until

idea

musical

dentist

trust

dream

banner

tuba

gifts

Word Search

How many words can you and your child find in this puzzle?
Remember to read across and down.

musical	opened	deny	decide	stamp
banner	celery	dream	later	adopt

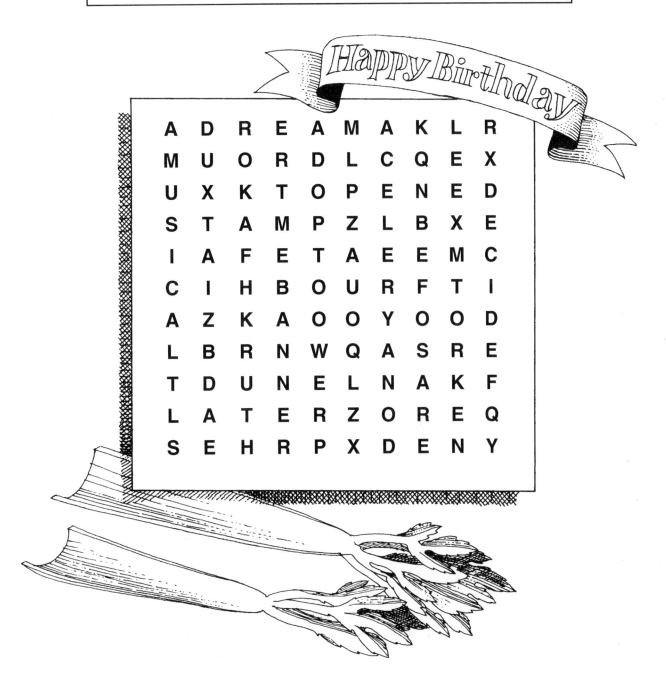

A D R E A M A K L R
M U O R D L C Q E X
U X K T O P E N E D
S T A M P Z L B X E
I A F E T A E E M C
C I H B O U R F T I
A Z K A O O Y O O D
L B R N W Q A S R E
T D U N E L N A K F
L A T E R Z O R E Q
S E H R P X D E N Y

Lesson 7

Objective
To spell words with consonant blends in an initial, medial, or final position

Correlated Phonics Lessons
MCP Phonics, Level D, Lessons 9–12

Warm Up   Page 29
In this selection, students read to find out about a two-headed animal. After reading, invite students to discuss which part of "Double Header" they liked the best.

Encourage students to look back at the boldfaced words. Ask volunteers to say each word and identify the consonant blends and their locations in the words.

On Your Mark/Warm Up Test
1. The cat slowly *crept* around the corner.
2. We could hear the snow *crunch* under our feet.
3. I was awakened at dawn by the *sounds* of birds.
4. Street lights turn on automatically at *dusk.*
5. José will get a *refund* on his game tickets.
6. The *colder* days show that winter is coming.
7. The dog ran away when it saw the *skunk.*
8. Who will *unfold* the flag?
9. You take a *risk* riding your bike at night.
10. May I have a glass of *milk* with my lunch?
11. The soldiers came to a *halt* outside the castle.
12. Is that program on at a *different* time?
13. People are *protesting* the cuts in bus service.
14. The weather report said a *twister* is coming!
15. An *independent* person will do things alone.
16. I haven't been *absent* from school this year.
17. This material will *stretch* enough to fit the chair.
18. We are *printing* the newspaper on colored paper.
19. Eileen *blended* yellow and red to make orange.
20. Does this *product* come with a battery?

Pep Talk/Game Plan   Pages 30–31
Introduce the spelling rule and have students read the List Words aloud. You may also want to discuss the meanings of words that may be unfamiliar to students (*risk, halt, protesting*). Then encourage students to look back at their Warm Up Tests and apply the spelling rule to any misspelled words.

As students work through the **Spelling Lineup, Vocabulary,** and **Synonyms** exercises, remind them to look back at their List Words or in their dictionaries if they need help.

 See **Charades/Pantomime,** page 15

Name _____

Consonant Blends   LESSON 7

Warm Up
What problems might a two-headed snake have?

Double Header
You may have heard the saying that "two heads are better than one." This is definitely not true when it comes to a two-headed snake. **Different** kinds of animals have been born with two heads. For an unknown reason, a large number of these two-headed animals have been snakes.

It might seem that there would be some advantages in being a two-headed snake. You might think that a snake with two heads would have better hearing. However, a snake does not hear **sounds** as we do, since it has no ears. A snake cannot hear the **crunch** of a footstep. It feels the vibrations. Two heads would not help the snake's speech, either. A snake has no vocal cords and can only make hissing noises.

Two heads can only bring problems. Each head would want to be **independent.** Think about what would happen if one head wanted to go, and the other head wanted to stay where it was. Everything would come to a **halt.** The heads would spend all their time **protesting,** and the snake wouldn't get anywhere.

Say each boldfaced word in the selection. Listen for the consonant blends. What do you notice about where the blends are in the words?

On Your Mark
Take your Warm Up Test. Then check your spelling with the List Words on the next page.

29

Pep Talk
Remember, when two or more consonants come together in a word, their sounds may blend together. In a **consonant blend,** you hear each letter. A blend may be found anywhere in a word. Listen for the consonant blends in the List Words.

crept
colder
risk
skunk

LIST WORDS
1. crept
2. crunch
3. sounds
4. dusk
5. refund
6. colder
7. skunk
8. unfold
9. risk
10. milk
11. halt
12. different
13. protesting
14. twister
15. independent
16. absent
17. stretch
18. printing
19. blended
20. product

Game Plan
Spelling Lineup
Add one or two consonant blends to each group of letters to form a List Word.

1. differe n t
2. s t r etch
3. refu n d
4. twi s t er
5. du s k
6. prote s t ing
7. unfo l d
8. p r oduct
9. sou n d s
10. indepe n d ent
11. s k unk
12. abse n t
13. c r unch
14. ha l t
15. ble n d ed
16. mi l k
17. p r inting
18. co l d er
19. c r ept
20. ri s k

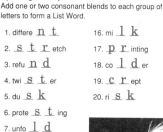

30   Lesson 7 ■ Consonant Blends

34

Vocabulary

Write the List Word that matches each clue.

1. noises
   __sounds__

2. a part of the day just before dark
   __dusk__

3. to chew with lots of noise
   __crunch__

4. not present
   __absent__

5. black and white animal
   __skunk__

6. something to drink that's white
   __milk__

7. any item bought at a store
   __product__

8. not ruled or controlled by others
   __independent__

Synonyms

Write the List Word that means the same or almost the same as each word given.

1. danger — __risk__
2. extend — __stretch__
3. crawled — __crept__
4. repay — __refund__
5. evening — __dusk__
6. complaining — __protesting__
7. cooler — __colder__
8. missing — __absent__
9. unusual — __different__
10. mixed — __blended__

11. open — __unfold__
12. tornado — __twister__
13. stop — __halt__
14. writing — __printing__

Lesson 7 ■ Consonant Blends   31

Flex Your Spelling Muscles

Writing

In what situations might a two-headed snake have difficulty making decisions? Write a conversation that the two heads might have about deciding what to eat or where to go. Use as many List Words as you can.

Proofreading

The following paragraph has ten mistakes. Use the proofreading marks to fix the mistakes. Then write the misspelled List Words correctly on the lines.

Proofreading Marks
◯ spelling mistake
⊙ add period
˅ add apostrophe

When (dusc) falls, the spotted (scunk) looks for food. Its an (indepedant) animal that might take over another animal's home. If a dog (krept) up on a spotted skunk it would be taking a (risc.) You'd hear some (prootesing) howls when the skunk sprayed the dog with a terrible smelling liquid.

1. __dusk__   4. __crept__
2. __skunk__   5. __risk__
3. __independent__ 6. __protesting__

Now proofread your snake's conversation. Fix any mistakes.

Go for the Goal

Take your Final Test. Then fill in your Scoreboard. Send your mistakes to the Word Locker.

SCOREBOARD
| number correct | number wrong |

★ ★ ★ ★ ★ ★ ★ ★ **All-Star Words** ★ ★ ★ ★ ★ ★ ★ ★

harvest   slender   stumble   branch   bask

Say each All-Star Word to your partner. Have your partner write the words and circle the consonant blends. Then switch roles and repeat the activity.

32   Lesson 7 ■ Consonant Blends

⊙ **Spelling Strategy** You may want to write words on the board that contain consonant blends found in the List Words (for example, li*st*, *cr*eam, be*nt*, so*ld*ier, la*nd*ing). Say the words and have the class listen for the consonant blends. Then ask volunteers to come to the board, circle the consonant blend in each word, and write a List Word that contains the same blend.

Flex Your Spelling Muscles   *Page 32*

As students complete the **Writing** activity, encourage them to brainstorm ideas, write a first draft, revise, and proofread their work. The **Proofreading** exercise will help them prepare to proofread their conversations. To publish their writing, students may want to

- create a cartoon strip
- perform their conversation with a partner.

✍ Writer's Corner

Students may enjoy reading *Snakes Are Hunters* by Patricia Lauber or a similar book. Invite them to write a summary of the book that can be used by classmates looking for research material or for an interesting book to read.

Go for the Goal/Final Test

1. The company said it would **refund** my money.
2. It is an **independent** station.
3. I was **absent** from school last week.
4. This **product** will make your dishes sparkle!
5. I love to **crunch** on cold carrot sticks.
6. Can you **unfold** the map completely?
7. There is almost no **risk** of injury when you walk.
8. Listen to the croaking **sounds** of all the frogs.
9. Please do not **stretch** my new sweatshirt.
10. The cat **crept** out of the room.
11. The two voices **blended** together beautifully.
12. We must try to **halt** the spread of air pollution.
13. Cars should turn on their headlights at **dusk.**
14. Today is much **colder** than yesterday.
15. Is there more **milk** in the refrigerator?
16. If there's a **twister,** you'll hear an alarm.
17. The store is **printing** new advertisements.
18. The citizens were **protesting** unfair taxes.
19. I knew I smelled a **skunk** nearby!
20. Here is a **different** book by the same writer.

Remind students to complete the Scoreboard and write any misspelled words in their Word Locker.

★★ **All-Star Words**   You may want to point out that the All-Star Words follow the spelling rule and remind students that a consonant blend can occur at the beginning, the end, or in the middle of a word.

Lesson 8

Objective
To spell words with *r*-controlled vowels

Correlated Phonics Lessons
MCP Phonics, Level D, Lessons 17–21

Warm Up   *Page 33*
Students may enjoy reading about transforming garbage into art. Afterward, invite them to suggest ideas for creating art from discarded objects or from trash.

Encourage students to look back at the boldfaced words. Ask volunteers to say each word and identify the sound that the vowel or vowels and *r* stand for.

On Your Mark/Warm Up Test
1. Keli bought a *carton* of milk at the store.
2. Is the *heart* one of the body's largest muscles?
3. Ted's school has won many *sports* championships.
4. Alwanda wants to be an *artist.*
5. Allan has a *spare* pencil that Cody may borrow.
6. This room is really *dirty!*
7. Chi and Anna went down to the *shore.*
8. Park the bicycles next to the *curb.*
9. The band is performing at the county *fair.*
10. Will there be enough *sherbet* for dessert?
11. Sherry will be using those *boards* for shelves.
12. That little dog seems *fearless.*
13. I have been keeping a *journal* for years.
14. The bus driver spoke *cheerfully* to everyone.
15. The *garbage* will be picked up tomorrow.
16. The liver is an important body *organ.*
17. There was one *error* on your spelling test.
18. *Sparks* flew when the pipe hit the sidewalk.
19. The *harbor* in Baltimore was important in 1812.
20. My father sneezes whenever I wear *perfume.*

Pep Talk/Game Plan   *Pages 34–35*
Introduce the spelling rule and have students read the List Words aloud. Encourage students to look back at their Warm Up Tests and apply the spelling rule to any misspelled words.

As students work through the **Spelling Lineup, Hidden Words,** and **Vocabulary** exercises, remind them to look back at their List Words or in their dictionaries if they need help. For the **Spelling Lineup,** provide an example of words that have different letters that spell the same vowel sound (*spare/fair*).

 See **Student Dictation,** page 14

Vowels with r

Warm Up
How can you turn garbage into art?

Recycling for Art
Before you toss out that milk **carton** or that pair of **dirty** old shoes, think about keeping them. What for? Art, of course!

Believe it or not, **garbage** could transform you into an **artist.** With a little imagination and careful hunting, you can make found objects or discarded materials into artistic treasures. The best part is that you are also recycling!

Recycling for art is not a new idea. Artists have been working with used materials for hundreds of years. Sculptors have used everything from broken tea cups to **spare** tires. And painters have created masterpieces, on everything from old **boards** to discarded clothing. Scientists have even discovered that underneath some very famous paintings, completely different pictures have been painted! Very often artists could not afford the price of new canvas, so they simply painted over old ones.

The challenge for you is to find objects no one wants, and make them into something someone would want. And if the idea of turning junk into art bothers you, don't think of it as art. Think of it as just another way to clean up!

 Look back at the boldfaced words. Say each word. What do you notice about the way the vowels sound in each word?

On Your Mark
Take your Warm Up Test. Then check your spelling with the List Words on the next page.

Pep Talk
When the letter **r** comes after a vowel or vowels, it sometimes changes the vowel sound. Say each pair of words. Notice how the **r** changes the sound that the vowel or vowels make.

heat—heart
spot—sports
cub—curb

Game Plan
Spelling Lineup
Say each word below. Then write each List Word under the word with the same vowel sound. If a List Word has two syllables, use the vowel sound in the stressed syllable. Remember that some words use different letters to spell the same sound.

LIST WORDS
1. carton
2. heart
3. sports
4. artist
5. spare
6. dirty
7. shore
8. curb
9. fair
10. sherbet
11. boards
12. fearless
13. journal
14. cheerfully
15. garbage
16. organ
17. error
18. sparks
19. harbor
20. perfume

part		short	
1. carton		12. sports	
2. heart		13. shore	
3. artist		14. boards	
4. garbage		15. organ	
5. sparks		**care**	
6. harbor		16. spare	
fur		17. fair	
7. dirty		18. error	
8. curb		**year**	
9. sherbet		19. fearless	
10. journal		20. cheerfully	
11. perfume			

Hidden Words

Each word below is hidden in a List Word. Write the List Word on the line. Circle the letters that spell the hidden word.

1. ports — s(ports)
2. cart — (cart)on
3. fume — per(fume)
4. park — (spark)s
5. air — f(air)
6. full — cheer(full)y
7. hear — (hear)t
8. oar — b(oar)ds
9. less — fear(less)
10. arbor — h(arbor)

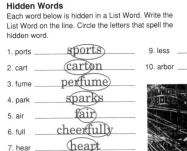

Vocabulary

Write the List Word that matches each definition.

1. something extra — spare
2. festival — fair
3. trash — garbage
4. a musical instrument — organ
5. not clean — dirty
6. a person who draws or paints — artist
7. edge of the street — curb
8. not afraid — fearless
9. a dessert like ice cream — sherbet
10. mistake — error
11. land at the edge of the sea — shore
12. diary — journal

Lesson 8 ■ Vowels with r   35

Flex Your Spelling Muscles

Writing

Imagine you are exhibiting your own works of "garbage art." Write an advertisement to tell about your show. Make it sound like something everyone would want to see. Use as many List Words as you can.

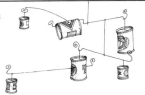

Proofreading

The editorial below has nine mistakes. Use the proofreading marks to fix the mistakes. Then write the misspelled List Words on the lines.

Proofreading Marks
◯ spelling mistake
∧ add something

What is the problem with garbaje? There is just too much of it. Who likes to look at dirtee beaches, or smell a polluted harber? Who wants to see a milk cartone lying on the cerb? It is time for people to stop this mess and be fare to our planet.

1. garbage
2. dirty
3. harbor
4. carton
5. curb
6. fair

Now proofread your advertisement. Fix any mistakes.

Go for the Goal

Take your Final Test. Then fill in your Scoreboard. Send your mistakes to the Word Locker.

SCOREBOARD
number correct   number wrong

★ ★ ★ ★ ★ ★ ★ ★ **All-Star Words** ★ ★ ★ ★ ★ ★ ★ ★

starve   nurse   nervous   forth   hearth

With a partner, write a story using words or phrases that mean the same or almost the same as the All-Star Words. Trade stories with other students. Replace the words and phrases with the All-Star Words. Which way does the story sound the best?

36   Lesson 8 ■ Vowels with r

Flex Your Spelling Muscles   *Page 36*

As students complete the **Writing** activity, encourage them to brainstorm ideas, write a first draft, revise, and proofread their work. The **Proofreading** exercise will help them prepare to proofread their advertisements. To publish their writing, students may want to
• create a bulletin-board display
• take a vote on which advertisement is the best.

✍ Writer's Corner

Students can learn how to recycle household items into decorative objects by requesting *Raft of Crafts* from Johnson Wax, Consumer Services Dept., P.O. Box 567, Dept. N–85, Racine, WI 53403. Students should write their request on a postcard.

Go for the Goal/Final Test

1. Do you like the smell of this **perfume?**
2. The wind fanned the **sparks** from the fire.
3. The patient needed an **organ** transplant.
4. Paul whistled **cheerfully** as he did his chores.
5. The **fearless** police officer saved the child.
6. The **sherbet** is made with fresh lemons.
7. The child sat on the **curb.**
8. Wash those **dirty** hands!
9. The **artist** donated one of her paintings.
10. The **heart** is a symbol of love.
11. The **carton** of juice tipped and spilled.
12. Many boys and girls play on **sports** teams.
13. Dad had to put the **spare** tire on the car.
14. Waves were crashing on the **shore.**
15. The judges at the **fair** selected the winner.
16. We walked on the **boards** that led to the beach.
17. Luis kept a **journal** of the events.
18. By mistake, I threw the shirt in the **garbage.**
19. Do you think I made an **error?**
20. Did they go down to the **harbor** to see the boats?

Remind students to complete the Scoreboard and write any misspelled words in their Word Locker.

★★ **All-Star Words**   You may want to point out that the All-Star Words follow the spelling rule and model writing a sentence in which a synonym is used for a List Word.

Lesson 9

Objective
To spell words with consonant digraphs

Correlated Phonics Lessons
MCP Phonics, Level D, Lessons 13–15

Warm Up   *Page 37*
In "Flash!," students read to find out what to do if lightning strikes. After reading, ask students whether they have ever been in a storm with lightning and, if so, what it was like.

Call on volunteers to say each boldfaced word and name the consonants that make one sound.

On Your Mark/Warm Up Test
1. Listen to the *thunder!*
2. Jennifer lives *farther* from school than Ann does.
3. If the batter *reaches* first base, he will be safe.
4. Susan would like a *chicken* sandwich for lunch.
5. In some states, the *wheat* fields stretch for miles.
6. Will we have our party next *Thursday?*
7. David felt *foolish* when he missed the bus.
8. In winter, we all *gather* around the fireplace.
9. Is Sarah's *brother* in the class play?
10. I'd like to rest *awhile* before the next race.
11. Clean the *chimney* before you use the fireplace.
12. Crease the paper *sharply* before you tear it.
13. The dog's *leash* is hanging by the door.
14. Don't *bother* your sister while she's reading.
15. The store expects a new *shipment* of shoes today.
16. I am allergic to pillows stuffed with real *feathers.*
17. Please *charge* the call to this phone number.
18. Pat will *shovel* the snow off the porch.
19. Watch the cat clean its *whiskers.*
20. *Crush* the cans before you put them in the trash.

Pep Talk/Game Plan   *Pages 38–39*
Introduce the spelling rule and have students read the List Words aloud. You may also want to point out the two different *th* sounds in the List Words—as in *thaw: thunder, Thursday;* as in *mother: farther, gather, brother, bother, feathers.* Then encourage students to look back at their Warm Up Tests and apply the spelling rule to any misspelled words.

As students work through the **Spelling Lineup, Sentence Completion,** and **Rhyming** exercises, remind them to look back at their List Words or in their dictionaries if they need help.

 See **Categorizing,** page 15

38

Name _____

Consonant Digraphs

LESSON 9

Warm Up
What should you do if lightning strikes?

Flash!
Flash! Crackle! Boom! The lightning **reaches** across the sky. The softball game has come to a stop. Then the **thunder** sounds **sharply** in your ears. Everyone runs for cover.

Air is always full of electricity. When a storm develops, the electricity changes into positive and negative charges. Because opposites attract, the positive and negative meet. The path of electricity between them is lightning. It can move across the sky or go straight to the ground.

What should you do if you're outside when a storm with lightning strikes? Scientists say to look for shelter, but choose carefully. Don't **bother** to **gather** your belongings. Don't be **foolish** and stand under a tree. Lightning usually strikes the highest point around, such as a tree or **chimney.** Stay close to the ground if you can't find a building. Get down on your hands and knees if you have to. One of the safest places is in a car.

After **awhile** the lightning stops, but now it's pouring rain. No one wants to play "water" sports, so the game is called off until **Thursday.**

 Look back at the boldfaced words. Say each word. Can you find two consonants together in each word that make only one sound?

On Your Mark
Take your Warm Up Test. Then check your spelling with the List Words on the next page.

37

LIST WORDS

1. thunder
2. farther
3. reaches
4. chicken
5. wheat
6. Thursday
7. foolish
8. gather
9. brother
10. awhile
11. chimney
12. sharply
13. leash
14. bother
15. shipment
16. feathers
17. charge
18. shovel
19. whiskers
20. crush

Pep Talk
Consonant digraphs are two consonants together that make a completely new sound. A consonant digraph may be found anywhere in a word. Listen for the sounds of these consonant digraphs.
/sh/ as in <u>sh</u>arply, fooli<u>sh</u>
/hw/ as in <u>wh</u>iskers, <u>wh</u>eat
/ch/ as in <u>ch</u>icken, rea<u>ch</u>es
The consonant digraph **th** has two different sounds.
/th/ as in <u>th</u>under
/th/ as in bo<u>th</u>er

Game Plan
Spelling Lineup
Write each List Word under the correct heading.

/hw/ as in <u>wh</u>ale	/ch/ as in pea<u>ch</u>
1. wheat	12. reaches
2. awhile	13. chicken
3. whiskers	14. chimney
/th/ as in <u>th</u>imble	15. charge
4. thunder	**/th/ as in mo<u>th</u>er**
5. Thursday	16. farther
/sh/ as in di<u>sh</u>	17. gather
6. foolish	18. brother
7. sharply	19. bother
8. leash	20. feathers
9. shipment	
10. shovel	
11. crush	

38 Lesson 9 ■ Consonant Digraphs

Sentence Completion

Write a List Word to complete each sentence.

1. The driver turned the corner _____sharply_____ to avoid the dog.
2. Smoke goes up the _____chimney_____ of our fireplace.
3. The _____chicken_____ stays in her nest to guard her eggs.
4. Jason felt a little _____foolish_____ wearing such a silly costume.
5. The spelling books will arrive in next month's _____shipment_____ .
6. Hand Gretta a _____shovel_____ so she can dig, too.
7. The oil on a duck's _____feathers_____ helps it keep dry.
8. My cat has long, white _____whiskers_____ .
9. Kim's house is _____farther_____ from town than mine is.
10. Keep your dog on a _____leash_____ at all times.

Rhyming

Write the List Word that rhymes with each word given.

1. beaches _____reaches_____
2. rather _____gather_____
3. father _____bother_____
4. large _____charge_____
5. sheet _____wheat_____
6. hush _____crush_____
7. another _____brother_____
8. under _____thunder_____

Flex Your Spelling Muscles

Writing

A thunder and lightning storm can be exciting and a little scary. Write a description of any kind of storm you have experienced. Include lots of vivid details. Use as many List Words as you can.

Proofreading

The newspaper report below has ten mistakes. Use the proofreading marks to fix the mistakes. Then write the misspelled List Words on the lines.

Proofreading Marks	
◯	spelling mistake
≡	capital letter
⚎	take out something

Strange weather hit our ~~our~~ area last (Thurzday). The day was warm until about noon when dark clouds began to (gathur) heavy rain fell for (awile) until there was a loud crash of (thundur) Suddenly, the rain turned to hail! this was the first hail storm our area has seen since 1963. The ~~the~~ hail came down so hard that one woman said it knocked the (fithers) off her prize (chikin!)

1. _____Thursday_____   4. _____thunder_____
2. _____gather_____   5. _____feathers_____
3. _____awhile_____   6. _____chicken_____

Now proofread your description. Fix any mistakes.

Go for the Goal

Take your Final Test. Then fill in your Scoreboard. Send your mistakes to the Word Locker.

SCOREBOARD

number correct	number wrong

★ ★ ★ ★ ★ ★ ★ ★ **All-Star Words** ★ ★ ★ ★ ★ ★ ★ ★

whether   arithmetic   thankful   champion   shelter

Write a sentence for each All-Star Word. Leave a blank where the word would be written. Trade papers with your partner. See if you can complete each other's sentences.

⊙ **Spelling Strategy**   To give students practice with consonant digraphs, invite them to get together with a partner and take turns pronouncing each List Word. As students say the words, they can stress the consonant digraphs (*wh*eat, *ch*icken) and identify the letters that stand for the sounds they hear.

Flex Your Spelling Muscles   *Page 40*

As students complete the **Writing** activity, encourage them to brainstorm ideas, write a first draft, revise, and proofread their work. The **Proofreading** exercise will help them prepare to proofread their descriptions. To publish their writing, students may want to
• illustrate their descriptions for a class book
• record them with sound effects of a storm.

✍ Writer's Corner

Invite students to do library research to find out about a weather hazard that threatens your region. Have them prepare a poster that gives tips for staying safe at home or at school when bad weather strikes. Give students copies to take home.

Go for the Goal/Final Test

1. The nest was lined with soft *feathers.*
2. That's a rooster, not a *chicken.*
3. Most flour is made from *wheat.*
4. On *Thursday* nights the stores stay open late.
5. The caterer will *charge* the meal to my company.
6. This machine can *crush* rocks.
7. I will help you dig if you give me a *shovel.*
8. Father shaved his *whiskers.*
9. I felt *foolish* in my silly costume.
10. Please help me *gather* the beads that spilled.
11. The bus stop is *farther* than I thought.
12. This dress *reaches* almost to the floor.
13. Is your *brother* in high school now?
14. The sound of *thunder* scares many dogs.
15. After they had walked *awhile,* they grew tired.
16. You can see the *chimney* from here.
17. Knock *sharply* on the door!
18. I keep my dog on a *leash* whenever it's outside.
19. If my radio starts to *bother* you, let me know.
20. When will the *shipment* of new cars arrive?

Remind students to complete the Scoreboard and write any misspelled words in their Word Locker.

★★ **All-Star Words**   You may want to point out that the All-Star Words follow the spelling rule and review writing cloze sentences.

Lesson 10

Objective
To spell words containing silent letters

Correlated Phonics Lessons
MCP Phonics, Level D, Lessons 26–27

Warm Up   *Page 41*
In this selection, students read to find out about a mysterious "ghost galleon." After reading, invite students to discuss why divers were thrilled to find the long-lost ship.

Encourage students to look back at the boldfaced words. Ask volunteers to say each word and identify the letter that is not pronounced.

On Your Mark/Warm Up Test
1. Did Kim wear a **ghost** costume to the party?
2. Not everyone has a "green **thumb.**"
3. I wish I had **known** it was raining!
4. We **often** go to the library after school.
5. Gary's **folks** came from Poland.
6. Keep your **wrist** steady when you hit the ball.
7. **Halfway** around the track, the runner fell.
8. Everyone wanted to **listen** to the new record.
9. Lucy scraped her **knuckle** while fixing her bike.
10. Please help me **comb** the back of my hair.
11. The junkyard is filled with old **wrecks.**
12. Did you enjoy your **flight** to Denver?
13. An **honest** person makes a good friend.
14. She lives on the **island** of Manhattan.
15. Is next **Wednesday** your birthday?
16. This cold wind makes me **numb!**
17. Uncle Lamar used a **wrench** to turn the bolt.
18. The mouse nibbled the **crumb** of bread.
19. Hand cream may help **soften** your dry skin.
20. Becky will **answer** right away.

Pep Talk/Game Plan   *Pages 42–43*
Introduce the spelling rule and have students read the List Words aloud. At this point, you may wish to clarify for students that some people pronounce the *t* in *often.* Then encourage students to look back at their Warm Up Tests and apply the spelling rule to any misspelled words.

As students work through the **Spelling Lineup, Rhyming,** and **Puzzle** exercises, remind them to look back at their List Words or in their dictionaries if they need help.

 See **Charades/Pantomime,** page 15

Name _____

Silent Letters

Warm Up
What is the "ghost galleon"?

Ghost Ship

Savage winds ripped her sails. Fierce waves spilled over her decks. A thundering crack was heard. Suddenly the towering mainmast broke and collapsed into the sea. The *Santa Margarita* was helpless, at the mercy of the wind and sea. In a short while, the mighty ship was gone, and over 120 people had drowned. In one of the most mysterious **wrecks** of all time, the *Santa Margarita* disappeared in 1622. Since then she has been **known** as the "ghost" galleon.

It wasn't until 358 years later, in 1980, that the *Santa Margarita* was found. Pieces of the ship's cargo were found under the sand and water near an **island** in the Florida Keys. When the treasure-hunting divers saw the ship's cargo, they quickly changed her nickname to the "gold-chain wreck." The name referred to the great amount of gold scattered on the ocean floor when the ship sank. Divers found a tangled mass of gold chains. When they untangled it, 43 glittering chains reached a total length of 180 feet! Each link was as thick as the **knuckle** of your **thumb.** In the 1600's, people often carried gold in the form of chains. Links could be unhooked and used like coins.

 Say each of the boldfaced words in the selection. Which letters do not make a sound?

On Your Mark
Take your Warm Up Test. Then check your spelling with the List Words on the next page.

41

Pep Talk

Some words contain **silent letters.** We don't hear the sounds of those letters when we say the words. Study the silent letters in these words.

known	wrist	folks
honest	halfway	flight
	often	

Be extra careful when you spell such words. Now study the silent letters in the remaining List Words.

Game Plan
Spelling Lineup
Write each List Word under the correct heading.

LIST WORDS
1. ghost
2. thumb
3. known
4. often
5. folks
6. wrist
7. halfway
8. listen
9. knuckle
10. comb
11. wrecks
12. flight
13. honest
14. island
15. Wednesday
16. numb
17. wrench
18. crumb
19. soften
20. answer

silent **b**
1. thumb
2. comb
3. numb
4. crumb

silent **w**
11. wrist
12. wrecks
13. wrench
14. answer

silent **h**
5. ghost
6. honest

silent **l**
15. folks
16. halfway

silent **gh**
7. flight

silent **d**
17. Wednesday

silent **k**
8. known
9. knuckle

silent **t**
18. often
19. listen
20. soften

silent **s**
10. island

42   Lesson 10 ■ Silent Letters

Rhyming

Write the List Word that rhymes with each word given.

1. bench ___wrench___   4. fist ___wrist___
2. kite ___flight___   5. bone ___known___
3. decks ___wrecks___   6. roast ___ghost___

Puzzle

Fill in the crossword puzzle by writing a List Word to answer each clue.

ACROSS
2. day of the week
4. people
6. part of the way
10. a spirit
11. land in the middle of water
13. understood or realized
15. tool used on the hair
16. tiny bit
17. to make soft

DOWN
1. destroys
3. response to a question
5. many times
6. truthful
7. trip on a plane
8. one of the fingers
9. part of each finger
12. to try to hear
14. without feeling

Crossword answers: WEDNESDAY, FOLKS, HALFWAY, GHOST, ISLAND, KNOWN, COMB, CRUMB, SOFTEN, WRENCH, ANSWER, HONEST, LIGHT, THUMB, KNUCKLE, NUMB

Lesson 10 ■ Silent Letters   43

Flex Your Spelling Muscles

Writing
Imagine what it would be like to find a shipwreck full of treasure. Write a newspaper article that reports the discovery.

Proofreading
This story has eight mistakes. Fix the mistakes with the proofreading marks. Then write the misspelled List Words correctly on the lines.

Proofreading Marks
◯ spelling mistake
∧ add something

Imagine being on a haunted ship! Well, (lissen) to this. There may reportedly be more than one (goast) on the Queen Mary, an ocean liner docked in Long Beach, California. Several crew members say they have sighted ghosts in different parts of the ship. Others have heard noises, like the clanging of a (rentch) banging on pipes. Some (focks) have seen moving lights. How scary! I would take (flihte) (hafwaiy) out the door in a moment if I saw a ghost.

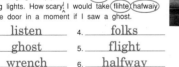

1. ___listen___   4. ___folks___
2. ___ghost___   5. ___flight___
3. ___wrench___   6. ___halfway___

Now proofread your newspaper article. Fix any mistakes.

Go for the Goal
Take your Final Test. Then fill in your Scoreboard. Send your mistakes to the Word Locker.

SCOREBOARD
number correct   number wrong

★ ★ ★ ★ ★ ★ ★ ★ **All-Star Words** ★ ★ ★ ★ ★ ★ ★ ★

daughter   bomb   knowledge   whistle   wrinkle

Draw a picture to give a clue for each All-Star Word. Trade drawings with a partner. Write the All-Star Word that goes with each picture.

◎ **Spelling Strategy**   In a group, students can choose *b, h, gh, k, s, w, l, d,* or *t* and list words in which that letter or pair of letters is silent, including List Words. Invite students to share their lists with other groups.

Flex Your Spelling Muscles   *Page 44*

As students complete the **Writing** activity, encourage them to brainstorm ideas, write a first draft, revise, and proofread their work. The **Proofreading** exercise will help them prepare to proofread their newspaper articles. To publish their writing, students may want to
• create a magazine called "Undersea Adventures"
• use their articles to create a TV news broadcast.

✍ **Writer's Corner** _____

Students might enjoy reading about marine exploration in books such as *Sunken Treasure* by Gail Gibbons. Encourage them to write reviews of the books they especially enjoyed.

Go for the Goal/Final Test

1. Our *flight* to Rome took six hours.
2. I have a bad bruise on my *knuckle.*
3. When I build a fort, Keith *wrecks* it.
4. I'll *comb* my hair before you take my picture.
5. If the phone rings, please *answer* it.
6. Should I use a *wrench* to loosen the bolt?
7. We ate every *crumb* of Jody's birthday cake.
8. Now we'll *soften* the butter in the microwave.
9. I have *known* Joanie for two years.
10. I heard a scary *ghost* story yesterday.
11. Karen made a puppet on her *thumb.*
12. We eat at that restaurant *often.*
13. The *folks* in our small town are very friendly.
14. My watch fell off my *wrist.*
15. Zoe was *halfway* to school when the bell rang!
16. Please *listen* carefully to the directions.
17. What is your *honest* opinion on the matter?
18. We'll take this boat to get to the *island.*
19. Next *Wednesday* is my best friend's birthday.
20. My hand felt *numb* because it was so cold.

Remind students to complete the Scoreboard and write any misspelled words in their Word Locker.

★★ **All-Star Words**   You may want to point out that the All-Star Words follow the spelling rule and model drawing a picture for a clue.

Lesson 11

Objective
To spell words with the /f/ sound represented by *f, ff, ph,* and *gh*

Correlated Phonics Lesson
MCP Phonics, Level D, Lesson 24

Warm Up   *Page 45*
Students may be interested in learning what it takes to move 230 elephants to a new home. After reading, discuss why the Indonesians moved the elephants and how they managed it successfully.

Encourage students to look back at the boldfaced words. Ask volunteers to say each word and identify the letter or letters that make the /f/ sound.

On Your Mark/Warm Up Test
1. Nancy has a *photo* of her new sister.
2. We made *graphs* to show the plants' growth.
3. Bob *laughs* whenever he sees that movie.
4. The smoke made everyone *cough.*
5. Did the girls' basketball team win a *trophy?*
6. Jim *roughly* pushed us aside.
7. Bruce decided that he'd had *enough* popcorn.
8. The English *alphabet* has twenty-six letters.
9. The book you want is on the top *shelf.*
10. We will go home right *after* the movie.
11. It's so cold I feel as if I'm frozen *stiff!*
12. *Elephants* are intelligent animals.
13. A *giraffe* can stand twelve feet high!
14. *Geography* is Leon's favorite subject.
15. My brother's son is my *nephew.*
16. We studied each *phase* of the animal's life.
17. Since the kitten was an *orphan,* we adopted it.
18. A *dolphin* swam alongside the ship.
19. The museum knew the statue was a *phony.*
20. Is an *autograph* of a president valuable?

Pep Talk/Game Plan   *Pages 46–47*
Introduce the spelling rule and have students read the List Words aloud. Encourage students to look back at their Warm Up Tests and apply the spelling rule to any misspelled words.

As students work through the **Spelling Lineup, Dictionary,** and **Puzzle** exercises, remind them to look back at their List Words or in their dictionaries if they need help.

 See **Variant Spellings,** page 14

/f/ Sound

Warm Up
How do you move 230 elephants with a total weight of more than 600 tons?

Big Move

Can you imagine moving more than 600 tons? Actually, the 600 tons moved themselves. In Indonesia, 230 **elephants** had to be moved because there wasn't **enough** food. Eventually, the elephants would have destroyed nearby crops in their search for food. So the government relocated them to a place where they'd find enough food.

Moving was a tough job. The 30-mile trip took two months and one thousand people. The people first changed the **geography,** or surface, of the land. They cut roads into thick jungles and swamps. **After** the elephants traveled the roads, deep canals were dug behind them so the animals could not turn back. The work was rough, but worth it. The elephants are now happy and eating well.

The herders say they've always called the elephants by their proper name, "mbah." That means grandma or grandpa. Indonesian animal experts say this name keeps the elephants calm while moving. It appears that even elephants like respect!

 Look back at the boldfaced words. Listen for the /f/ sound in each word. How many different spellings for the /f/ sound do you find?

On Your Mark
Take your Warm Up Test. Then check your spelling with the List Words on the next page.

45

Pep Talk
The sound /f/ is usually spelled with f, as in <u>after</u>. It can also be spelled with ff, as in <u>stiff</u>. Sometimes the /f/ sound is spelled with **ph,** as in <u>photo</u> and <u>graphs</u>. The /f/ sound can also be spelled with **gh,** as in <u>cough</u> and <u>laughs</u>.

LIST WORDS
1. photo
2. graphs
3. laughs
4. cough
5. trophy
6. roughly
7. enough
8. alphabet
9. shelf
10. after
11. stiff
12. elephants
13. giraffe
14. geography
15. nephew
16. phase
17. orphan
18. dolphin
19. phony
20. autograph

Game Plan
Spelling Lineup
Write each List Word under the correct heading.

/f/ spelled **ph**	/f/ spelled **gh**
1. photo	13. laughs
2. graphs	14. cough
3. trophy	15. roughly
4. alphabet	16. enough
5. elephants	
6. geography	/f/ spelled **f**
7. nephew	17. shelf
8. phase	18. after
9. orphan	
10. dolphin	/f/ spelled **ff**
11. phony	19. stiff
12. autograph	20. giraffe

46   Lesson 11 ■ /f/ Sound

42

Dictionary
Write the List Word that would come between these entry words in the dictionary.

The words found in a dictionary are called **entry words.** They are arranged in alphabetical order.

1. monkey—open ___nephew___
2. rusty—spread ___shelf___
3. elk—garage ___enough___
4. silver—taste ___stiff___
5. fresh—germ ___geography___
6. glass—heavy ___graphs___
7. phonograph—question ___photo___
8. other—pheasant ___phase___
9. duty—elf ___elephants___
10. brand—desire ___cough___
11. air—artist ___alphabet___
12. attract—baby ___autograph___

Puzzle
This is a crossword puzzle without word clues. Study the length and the letters already done for each List Word. Then complete the puzzle.

Lesson 11 ■ /f/ Sound 47

Flex Your Spelling Muscles

Writing
Draw pictures of elephants, giraffes, dolphins, or other animals. Use your List Words to write captions that go with the pictures.

Proofreading
Look for the nine mistakes in this article. Use the proofreading marks to fix the mistakes. Then write the misspelled words on the lines.

Proofreading Marks
◯ spelling mistake
≡ capital letter
∧ add something

how many wild animals are in trouble today? Elefant herds have been greatly reduced and young elephants have been made orfans because of ivory hunting. some animals, like the jirafe, are forced out of their homes by people looking for new places to build and farm. Dolfins get caught in fishermen's nets along with the fish. when will people learn to share the earth with animals?

1. ___Elephant___   3. ___giraffe___
2. ___orphans___   4. ___dolphins___

Now proofread your picture captions. Fix any mistakes.

Go for the Goal
Take your Final Test. Then fill in your Scoreboard. Send your mistakes to the Word Locker.

SCOREBOARD
number correct | number wrong

★ ★ ★ ★ ★ ★ ★ ★ **All-Star Words** ★ ★ ★ ★ ★ ★ ★

affection phrase earmuffs perfect tough

Write a paragraph using the All-Star Words, but leave three or four letters out of each word. Trade papers with a partner. Fill in the missing letters.

48 Lesson 11 ■ /f/ Sound

Flex Your Spelling Muscles   *Page 48*
As students complete the **Writing** activity, encourage them to brainstorm ideas, write a first draft, revise, and proofread their work. The **Proofreading** exercise will help them prepare to proofread their captions. To publish their writing, students may want to
• create a wildlife book
• use the pictures for a bulletin-board display.

✍ **Writer's Corner** _____

Students may enjoy interviewing local veterinarians to learn how to transport animals safely and without stress to the vet's office or to a new home. Students can take notes during the interviews and then use the notes to help them create a brochure for pet owners.

Go for the Goal/Final Test
1. My brother always *laughs* at my jokes.
2. The engine ran *roughly* until it warmed up.
3. There is *enough* room in my car for more people.
4. A *dolphin* is a very intelligent animal.
5. What *phase* is the moon in?
6. Quick, let's take a *photo!*
7. We learned how to make *graphs* in math class.
8. I asked the senator for her *autograph.*
9. Not every *alphabet* has twenty-six letters.
10. The doctor gave me something for my *cough.*
11. The dictionary is on the top *shelf.*
12. The farmer fed the calf, who was an *orphan.*
13. Save the cookies until *after* dinner.
14. These pearls are *phony,* but they are still pretty.
15. In *geography* we are learning the state capitals.
16. The *stiff* leather gets softer as you use it.
17. Our team won a *trophy* in the state finals.
18. Those *elephants* certainly eat a lot of hay.
19. My *nephew* Peter has a birthday this week.
20. Each *giraffe* has a different pattern of spots.

Remind students to complete the Scoreboard and write any misspelled words in their Word Locker.

★★ **All-Star Words** You may want to point out that the All-Star Words follow the spelling rule and model writing a sentence with an incomplete List Word.

43

Lesson 12 • Instant Replay

Objective
To review spelling words with consonant blends, vowels with *r,* consonant digraphs, silent letters, and the /f/ sound

Time Out   *Pages 49–52*
Check Your Word Locker Based on your observations, note which words are giving students the most difficulty and offer assistance for spelling them correctly. Here are some frequently misspelled words to watch for: *stretch, sherbet, chimney, answer, known, nephew, enough,* and *cough.*

To give students extra help and practice in taking standardized tests, you may want to have them take the Review Test for this lesson on pages 46–47. After scoring the tests, return them to students so that they can record their misspelled words in their Word Locker.

After practicing their troublesome words, students can work through the exercises for **Lessons 7–11.** Before they begin each exercise, you may want to go over the spelling rule. For the exercise on page 52, point out to students that the List Words should be capitalized because they are part of a title or a particular singing group.

Take It Home Invite students to collect phrases they hear at home that contain List Words from **Lessons 7–11** (new, improved *product; chicken* soup; *Thursday* night). For a complete list of the words, encourage them to take their *Spelling Workout* books home. Students can also use Take It Home Master 2 on pages 48–49 to help them do the activity. They can bring their lists to school and see whether any of their classmates heard the same phrases they did.

Name _____

Time Out
Take another look at consonant blends and digraphs, vowels with /r/, silent letters, and how to spell the sound /f/.

Check Your Word Locker
Look at the words in your Word Locker. Write your most troublesome words for Lessons 7 through 11.

_____

Practice writing your troublesome words with a partner. Try writing the letters for each word in a tray of sand, salt, or sugar. Your partner can check your spelling as you write.

Lesson 7

In a **consonant blend,** you can hear the sound of each letter. A blend may be found anywhere in a word, as in <u>twister</u>, <u>colder</u>, and <u>sounds</u>.

List Words

crept
crunch
dusk
refund
skunk
milk
halt
stretch
blended
product

Write a List Word to complete each sentence.

1. Bob ___blended___ the ingredients.
2. A ___skunk___ is black and white.
3. The sky begins to darken at ___dusk___ .
4. The store would not ___refund___ my money.
5. Thin the batter with a cup of ___milk___ .
6. Bike riders must ___halt___ at stop signs.
7. The rabbit ___crept___ into my garden.
8. Try to ___stretch___ the hat to fit.
9. My report was the ___product___ of hard work.
10. I heard the ___crunch___ of snow under my boots.

49

Lesson 8

When the letter **r** comes after a vowel, it often changes the sound the vowel stands for.
cub—curb   spots—sports

List Words

heart
artist
dirty
sherbet
journal
garbage
organ
error
harbor
perfume

Write the List Word that belongs in each group.

1. diary, autobiography, ___journal___
2. ice cream, pudding, ___sherbet___
3. musician, dancer, ___artist___
4. soiled, messy, ___dirty___
5. ocean, river, ___harbor___
6. valentine, love, ___heart___
7. piano, violin, ___organ___
8. trash, wastepaper, ___garbage___
9. mistake, blunder, ___error___
10. lipstick, powder, ___perfume___

Lesson 9

Sometimes two consonants together form a consonant digraph, making a new sound, as in <u>awhile</u>, <u>foolish</u>, <u>gather</u>, and <u>charge</u>.

List Words

thunder
chicken
wheat
brother
chimney
leash
shipment
feathers
shovel
whiskers

Add a consonant digraph to each group of letters to form a List Word.

1. _c h_ imney
2. fea _t h_ ers
3. _t h_ under
4. _c h_ icken
5. bro _t h_ er
6. _w h_ iskers
7. e _q u_ ipment
8. _c h_ icken
9. _w h_ eat
10. _s h_ ovel

Lesson 10

Some words contain silent letters. Be careful when you spell them. Look for the silent letters in <u>gh</u>ost, num<u>b</u>, and We<u>d</u>nesday.

List Words

known
folks
wrist
knuckle
comb
flight
wrench
crumb
soften
answer

Write each group of List Words in alphabetical order.

| wrist | flight | soften |
| wrench | folks | |

1. flight
2. folks
3. soften
4. wrench
5. wrist

| known | crumb | comb |
| knuckle | answer | |

6. answer
7. comb
8. crumb
9. known
10. knuckle

Lesson 11

The sound /f/ can be spelled in four different ways, as in a<u>f</u>ter, sti<u>ff</u>, <u>ph</u>ony, and lau<u>gh</u>s.

List Words

cough
trophy
roughly
enough
shelf
stiff
giraffe
nephew
orphan
dolphin

Build List Words by adding or subtracting letters.

1. knew – kn + neph   nephew
2. tough – t + c   cough
3. stick – ck + ff   stiff
4. though – th + en   enough
5. than – t + orp   orphan
6. girl – l + affe   giraffe
7. thin – t + dolp   dolphin
8. shed – d + lf   shelf
9. tropical – ical + hy   trophy
10. route – te + ghly   roughly

Lesson 12 ■ Instant Replay   51

Lessons 7–11

List Words

crept
crunch
dusk
heart
dirty
garbage
thunder
chicken
chimney
comb
flight
answer
trophy
giraffe
dolphin

Write a List Word to complete each song title or singing group.

1. "Take Out the __Garbage__," by the Trash Trio
2. "Let's Do the __Chicken__," by the Cluck Clucks
3. "Clean Up Your Act," by the __Dirty__ Shirts
4. "Take a __Flight__ with Me," by the Airplanes
5. "Share My Popcorn," by the __Crunch__ Bunch
6. "True or False?" by the __Answer__ Dancers
7. "Night Is Falling," by the __Dusk__ Duo
8. "My __Heart__ Beats for You," by the Valentines
9. "__Comb__ Your Hair," by the Brush Brothers
10. "__Thunder__ and Lightning," by the Boomers
11. "I'd Dive for You," by the __Dolphin__ Duet
12. "Up in Smoke," by Jimmy __Chimney__
13. "Head in the Clouds," by Ginny __Giraffe__
14. "A __Trophy__ for Sophie," by the Winners
15. "You __Crept__ into My Heart," by the Sneakers

Go for the Goal

Take your Final Replay Test. Then fill in your Scoreboard. Send any misspelled words to the Word Locker.

| SCOREBOARD | |
| number correct | number wrong |

Clean Out Your Word Locker
Look in your Word Locker. Cross out each word you spelled correctly on your Final Replay Test. Circle the words you're still having trouble with. Add the words you circled to your Spelling Notebook. What do you notice about the words? Watch for those words as you write.

Go for the Goal/Final Replay Test   *Page 52*

1. A *skunk* uses its scent to defend itself.
2. We *blended* the milkshake ingredients.
3. Your *heart* pumps blood throughout your body.
4. Three large ships were anchored in the *harbor.*
5. *Thunder* told us a storm was coming.
6. The cat cleaned its *whiskers.*
7. Each summer, my *folks* have a huge picnic.
8. Carlos guessed the right *answer.*
9. Scientists recorded the voice of the *dolphin.*
10. Karen's cold gave her a *cough.*
11. Beat the egg whites until they are *stiff.*
12. I hope I made *enough* sandwiches.
13. I wear my watch on my left *wrist.*
14. Only a *crumb* of bread was left on the plate.
15. Did you put the dog's *leash* back in the closet?
16. The store is expecting a *shipment* of dresses.
17. Pablo Picasso was a famous modern *artist.*
18. The *garbage* truck collected our trash.
19. We *crept* upstairs as quietly as we could.
20. I like to eat cereal with *milk* and fruit.
21. I heard a *crunch* when I bit into the apple.
22. The guard told the visitors to *halt.*
23. Put your *dirty* clothes in the washing machine.
24. Does Uncle Bert play the *organ?*
25. Grandma made rice and *chicken.*
26. The *chimney* on the old house needed repairs.
27. I scraped my *knuckle* when I fell.
28. This cream may *soften* your dry skin.
29. Don't play *roughly* with the puppy!
30. Ms. Manuelo took her *nephew* to the game.
31. The *giraffe* is the tallest animal of all.
32. The character Oliver Twist is an *orphan.*
33. Who made the first airplane *flight?*
34. I have *known* my friend Elaine for many years.
35. *Wheat,* oats, and barley are all nutritious grains.
36. Jen's *brother* is the pitcher on our baseball team.
37. Dad made homemade *sherbet* for dessert.
38. Don't make an *error* when you spell this word.
39. Every night, just at *dusk,* the nightingale sings.
40. This exercise will *stretch* your muscles.
41. We returned the bike for a full *refund.*
42. This *product* will remove stains easily.
43. Tim kept a daily *journal* throughout his trip.
44. This *perfume* smells wonderful!
45. Blue jays have beautiful *feathers.*
46. I offered to help Uncle Pete *shovel* the snow.
47. Loosen the bolt with a *wrench.*
48. I have to *comb* the tangles out of my hair.
49. The librarian put the book back on the *shelf.*
50. My dog won a *trophy* at the dog show.

Clean Out Your Word Locker After they write each word, students can underline any consonant blend, consonant digraph, or silent letter in the word.

45

Name _____

Instant Replay Test

Side A

Read each set of phrases. Fill in the circle next to the phrase with an underlined word that is spelled correctly.

1.   ⓐ garbedge disposal   © large garbbage bags
     ⓑ a garbage can   ⓓ a garbadge truck

2.   ⓐ will hault   © must halt
     ⓑ haulte now   ⓓ to hawlt

3.   ⓐ peacock fethers   © owl featheres
     ⓑ eagle feathers   ⓓ hawk fetheres

4.   ⓐ the young orfan   © a baby orphin
     ⓑ the tall orffan   ⓓ the healthy orphan

5.   ⓐ creaped quickly   © creeped along
     ⓑ crept forward   ⓓ creept quietly

6.   ⓐ a plastic shuvel   © his aluminum shovel
     ⓑ that metal shovle   ⓓ this child's shovvel

7.   ⓐ delicious crumbe   © the last crumb
     ⓑ that tiny crumm   ⓓ a bread crum

8.   ⓐ your durty face   © a dirtty room
     ⓑ his derty hands   ⓓ the dirty laundry

9.   ⓐ most dolfin fins   © the dollphin pool
     ⓑ the dolphin tricks   ⓓ the dolphen pups

10. ⓐ fresh sherbet   © lime surebet
     ⓑ dish of sherburt   ⓓ half-gallon of shurbet

Name _____

Instant Replay Test

Side B

Read each set of phrases. Fill in the circle next to the phrase with an underlined word that is spelled correctly.

11. (a) a tall <u>chimeny</u>
     (b) the brick <u>chimny</u>
     (c) that stone <u>chimney</u>
     (d) smoke from the <u>chimeney</u>

12. (a) its <u>flight</u> south
     (b) a smooth <u>fligt</u>
     (c) an airplane <u>flighte</u>
     (d) the <u>fliet</u> home

13. (a) a hungry <u>girraffe</u>
     (b) the exhausted <u>girafe</u>
     (c) the tallest <u>giraph</u>
     (d) a newborn <u>giraffe</u>

14. (a) this new <u>product</u>
     (b) an improved <u>prodduct</u>
     (c) an effective <u>produckt</u>
     (d) a cleaning <u>producked</u>

15. (a) first place <u>trophey</u>
     (b) the shiny <u>troughy</u>
     (c) a team <u>trofey</u>
     (d) the bronze <u>trophy</u>

16. (a) an immediate <u>refunnd</u>
     (b) an instant <u>refunned</u>
     (c) a mail-in <u>refund</u>
     (d) will <u>refunde</u>

17. (a) your youngest <u>brothur</u>
     (b) my twin <u>brother</u>
     (c) his older <u>bruther</u>
     (d) my other <u>brotherr</u>

18. (a) farm <u>folkes</u>
     (b) young <u>foakls</u>
     (c) adult <u>fokes</u>
     (d) city <u>folks</u>

19. (a) your swollen <u>nuckle</u>
     (b) his tiny <u>knukle</u>
     (c) my thumb <u>knuckel</u>
     (d) her scraped <u>knuckle</u>

20. (a) a trip <u>journal</u>
     (b) his daily <u>jurnal</u>
     (c) my private <u>jornal</u>
     (d) a <u>journel</u> entry

2

TAKE IT HOME

Your child has learned to spell many new words in Lessons 7–11 and would enjoy sharing them with you and your family. Here are some ideas that will make reviewing those words fun for everyone.

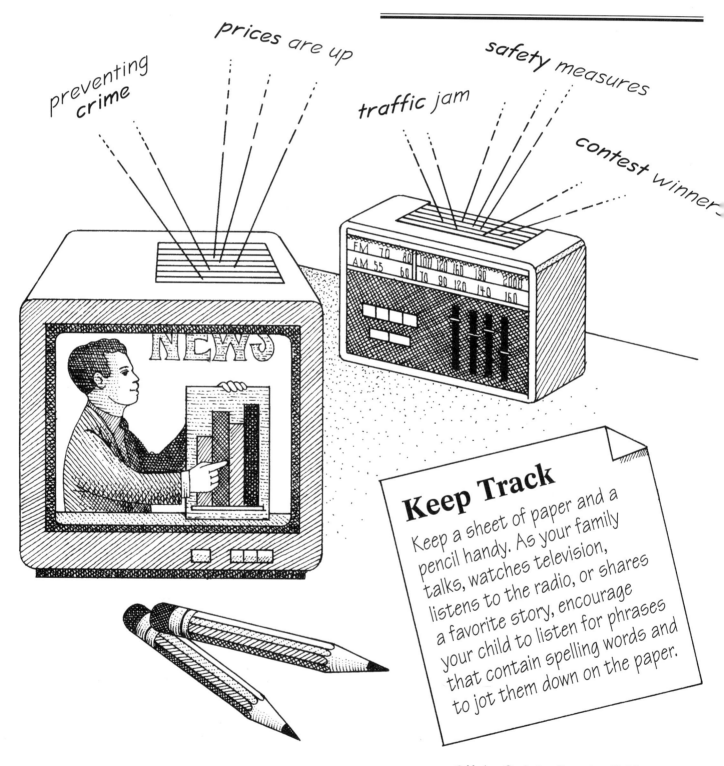

preventing crime

prices are up

traffic jam

safety measures

contest winners

Keep Track

Keep a sheet of paper and a pencil handy. As your family talks, watches television, listens to the radio, or shares a favorite story, encourage your child to listen for phrases that contain spelling words and to jot them down on the paper.

Alphabet Soup

Can you and your child make a spelling word by unscrambling the letters floating in each bowl of alphabet soup?

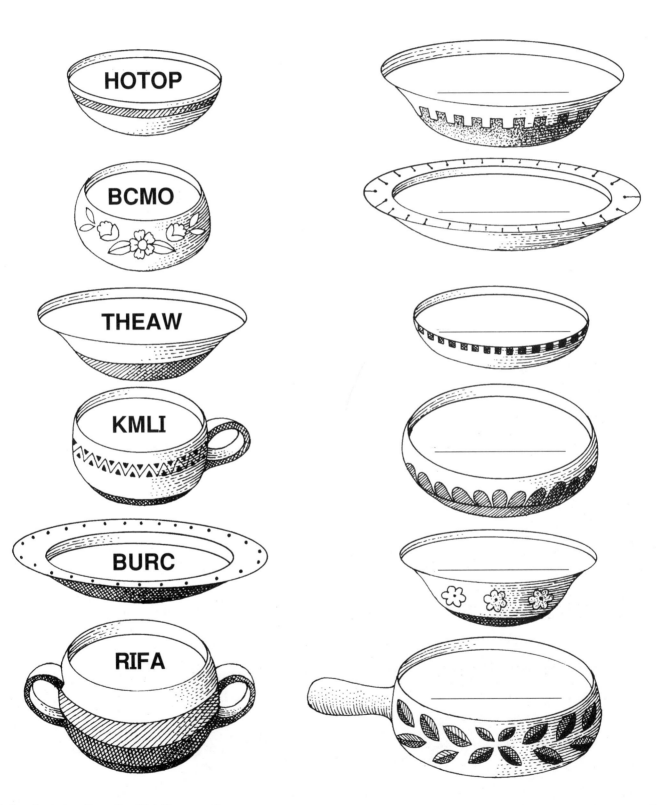

HOTOP

BCMO

THEAW

KMLI

BURC

RIFA

Lesson 13

Objective

To spell words with the suffixes *ed, er,* and *ing*, in which the root words do not change

Correlated Phonics Lessons

MCP Phonics, Level D, Lessons 30–31

Warm Up   *Page 53*

In this selection, students read to find out about the youngest person in America's space program. After reading, invite students to talk about careers they are interested in.

Ask volunteers to say each boldfaced word and identify the root word and suffix.

On Your Mark/Warm Up Test

1. Did you enjoy *watching* the football game?
2. The students were busy *checking* their answers.
3. After *finishing* her work, Rosa had a snack.
4. To be a good *learner,* you must listen well.
5. *Bending* and stretching is one way to exercise.
6. Rachel *cleaned* her desk.
7. Blake *sorted* the socks.
8. I *missed* my parents when they were in Europe.
9. Who's your favorite *singer?*
10. Brian *guessed* how many beans were in the jar.
11. What an excellent *teacher* Mr. West is!
12. A fast *walker* can reach the zoo in five minutes.
13. Tim *remembered* to take his books.
14. The ducklings were *following* their mother.
15. The fielder *tossed* the ball to home plate.
16. The leaves are *turning* yellow and orange.
17. Are you still *wishing* for a puppy?
18. The spaceship was *landing* on Mars.
19. The runner who was *leading* won the race.
20. The *catcher* spoke to the pitcher.

Pep Talk/Game Plan   *Pages 54–55*

Introduce the spelling rule and have students read the List Words aloud. Encourage students to look back at their Warm Up Tests and apply the spelling rule to any misspelled words.

As students work through the **Spelling Lineup, Classification,** and **Dictionary** exercises, remind them to look back at their List Words or in their dictionaries if they need help. For the **Dictionary** exercise, have students locate a pair of guide words in their dictionaries and note how the words indicate the first and last entries on the page.

 See **Questions/Answers,** page 15

50

Name _____

Suffixes ed, er, and ing

LESSON 13

Warm Up

Who is the youngest person ever to enter America's space program?

Space Fever

Almost everyone knows that Neil Armstrong was the first person to walk on the moon and that Alan Shepard was the first American astronaut. Do you remember when Sally Ride became the first American woman in space?

There's another important first that should be **remembered.** That's the first teenager in America's space program, Jackie Parker. She became a flight controller for NASA when she was only 19 years old. Jackie was responsible for **watching** and **checking** computers during space launches.

In school, Jackie was a quick **learner, finishing** high school in only two years. Then she went on to college and studied computer science. She completed college in record time, too. **Following** college she went to flight school. After only one week she was flying solo.

Jackie Parker has some advice for those who'd like to follow in her footsteps. "If you believe in yourself, you can do anything."

 Look back at the boldfaced words. What do you notice about their spelling? Did the root words change when an ending, or suffix, was added?

On Your Mark

Take your Warm Up Test. Then check your spelling with the List Words on the next page.

53

Pep Talk

You can add the suffixes **ed, er,** or **ing** to some words without changing the spelling of the root word. Study these examples:

clean + **ed** = cleaned
wish + **ing** = wishing
learn + **er** = learner
sing + **er** = singer

Find the unchanged root word in each List Word.

LIST WORDS

1. watching
2. checking
3. finishing
4. learner
5. bending
6. cleaned
7. sorted
8. missed
9. singer
10. guessed
11. teacher
12. walker
13. remembered
14. following
15. tossed
16. turning
17. wishing
18. landing
19. leading
20. catcher

Game Plan

Spelling Lineup

Write each List Word under the correct heading.

Root + **er**

1. learner
2. singer
3. teacher
4. walker
5. catcher

Root + **ed**

6. cleaned
7. sorted
8. missed
9. guessed
10. tossed
11. remembered

Root + **ing**

12. watching
13. checking
14. finishing
15. bending
16. following
17. turning
18. wishing
19. landing
20. leading

54   Lesson 13 ■ Suffixes ed, er, and ing

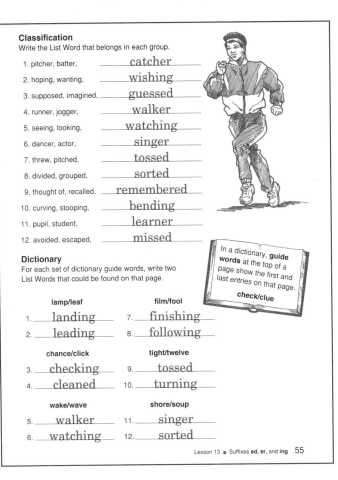

Classification
Write the List Word that belongs in each group.

1. pitcher, batter, _____ catcher
2. hoping, wanting, _____ wishing
3. supposed, imagined, _____ guessed
4. runner, jogger, _____ walker
5. seeing, looking, _____ watching
6. dancer, actor, _____ singer
7. threw, pitched, _____ tossed
8. divided, grouped, _____ sorted
9. thought of, recalled, _____ remembered
10. curving, stooping, _____ bending
11. pupil, student, _____ learner
12. avoided, escaped, _____ missed

Dictionary
For each set of dictionary guide words, write two List Words that could be found on that page.

In a dictionary, **guide words** at the top of a page show the first and last entries on that page.
check/clue

lamp/leaf
1. landing
2. leading

film/fool
7. finishing
8. following

chance/click
3. checking
4. cleaned

tight/twelve
9. tossed
10. turning

wake/wave
5. walker
6. watching

shore/soup
11. singer
12. sorted

Lesson 13 ■ Suffixes **ed, er,** and **ing**   55

Flex Your Spelling Muscles

Writing
Imagine that you are the first astronaut to land on an unknown planet. Write a journal entry to describe what you see and hear. Use List Words.

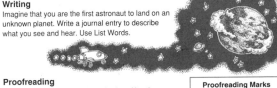

Proofreading
The paragraph below has ten mistakes. Use the proofreading marks to fix the mistakes. Then write the misspelled List Words correctly on the lines.

Proofreading Marks
◯ spelling mistake
≡ capital letter
⚇ take out something

Yesterday I went to an air show with my friend david and his mother, who is a teachr. We were waching six jets jets streak across the sky, one folowing the other. Suddenly, the plane that was leeding began to turn. The others followed. we stared in amazement as the jets did loops and dips. When the pilots came in for the landng, the crowd cheered! We wouldn't have mised that that show for anything!

1. teacher
2. watching
3. following
4. leading
5. landing
6. missed

Now proofread your journal entry. Fix any mistakes.

Go for the Goal
Take your Final Test. Then fill in your Scoreboard. Send your mistakes to the Word Locker.

SCOREBOARD
number correct	number wrong

★ ★ ★ ★ ★ ★ ★ ★ **All-Star Words** ★ ★ ★ ★ ★ ★ ★ ★

gulped   performer   mending   sinking   soared

Write a paragraph using all five words, but leave a blank for each word's suffix. Then trade papers with a partner. Finish each other's words.

56   Lesson 13 ■ Suffixes **ed, er,** and **ing**

⊚ **Spelling Strategy**   Write two columns on the board, one containing root words for three of the List Words and the other containing the suffixes *ing, ed,* and *er*. Then invite students to work with a partner to
• copy the columns
• draw connecting lines to make List Words
• write each List Word and use it in an oral sentence.
Continue until all the List Words have been written.

Flex Your Spelling Muscles   *Page 56*
As students complete the **Writing** activity, encourage them to brainstorm ideas, write a first draft, revise, and proofread their work. The **Proofreading** exercise will help them prepare to proofread their journal entries. To publish their writing, students may want to
• create a captain's log
• use their journal entries to make a postcard.

✎ **Writer's Corner**

Students might enjoy watching a film such as *Sally's Ride: The Flight of STS-7,* which can be purchased through Ricon Enterprises (713-683-0105). Afterward, invite students to write an answer to these questions: "Would you make a good astronaut? Why or why not?"

Go for the Goal/Final Test
1. Hiroshi is the **catcher** for our baseball team.
2. The tadpole was slowly **turning** into a frog.
3. Erika **missed** her friend who had moved away.
4. What a quick **learner** you are!
5. The **walker** stopped to enjoy the view.
6. I hope that he **remembered** to take his umbrella.
7. When the **singer** took a bow, everyone clapped.
8. We were **wishing** that the storm would end.
9. Would you mind **watching** the baby for a while?
10. **Bending** the metal bar took great strength.
11. He **cleaned** the stains in the sink.
12. Watching the moon **landing** was very exciting!
13. Keshia **guessed** what was in the box.
14. The little chicks were **following** the hen.
15. Is Dan **checking** the address?
16. I **tossed** the trash into the wastebasket.
17. At halftime, the Jets were **leading** the Giants.
18. Our **teacher** took us on a field trip.
19. Maria **sorted** the papers into two neat piles.
20. The students were **finishing** their spelling test.

Remind students to complete the Scoreboard and write any misspelled words in their Word Locker.

★★ **All-Star Words**   You may want to point out that the All-Star Words follow the spelling rule and remind students that *ed, er,* and *ing* are suffixes.

51

Lesson 14

Objective

To spell words with the suffixes *ed, er,* and *ing:* doubling the final consonant of the root word

Correlated Phonics Lesson

MCP Phonics, Level D, Lesson 33

Warm Up   Page 57

In "Blazing Paddles," students read about a race in Hawaii that involves giant canoes. Suggest that students compare these canoes to other types of boats they may be familiar with.

Encourage students to look back at the boldfaced words. Ask volunteers to say each word and tell how the spelling of the root word has changed.

On Your Mark/Warm Up Test

1. As I hiked, I was ***beginning*** to feel tired.
2. Did I hear you ***humming*** a tune?
3. The second baseman ***dropped*** the ball.
4. The puppy was ***sitting*** near the door.
5. A skater was ***slipping*** and sliding on the ice.
6. She yelled at the ***joggers,*** "Watch out for the car!"
7. After ***grabbing*** his jacket, Dan ran out the door.
8. The cork was ***bobbing*** in the waves.
9. Laurie ***tripped*** over the box.
10. A Chinese jacket is ***padded*** with cotton.
11. Try ***skimming*** the paragraph to find the answer.
12. I was ***scrubbing*** the floor when the phone rang.
13. All three ***winners*** walked on stage.
14. The hikers were ***outfitted*** with new boots.
15. Tony ***wrapped*** the present in colorful paper.
16. The audience would not stop ***clapping.***
17. John is ***dragging*** the trash can up the driveway.
18. The two neighbors are ***chatting*** in the yard.
19. Tara will finish because she's not a ***quitter.***
20. Did Stacie use a ***trimmer*** to cut the hedges?

Pep Talk/Game Plan   Pages 58–59

Introduce the spelling rule and have students read the List Words aloud. You may also want to go over the meanings of words that may be unfamiliar to students: *bobbing, skimming, outfitted.* Then encourage students to look back at their Warm Up Tests and apply the spelling rule to any misspelled words.

As students work through the **Spelling Lineup,** **Synonyms,** and **Rhyming** exercises, remind them to look back at their List Words or in their dictionaries if they need help.

 See **Spelling Aloud,** page 14

52

Name _____

Suffixes ed, er, and ing: Doubling Final Consonants

LESSON **14**

Warm Up

What kind of race uses giant canoes?

Blazing Paddles

The sky is bright and sunny. Light winds ripple the blue-green water. Six anxious competitors are **sitting** inside a giant canoe, ready to paddle. A gunshot pierces the silence. The blast marks the **beginning** of a 41-mile race from the Hawaiian island of Molokai to the island of Oahu. In moments, canoes are **skimming** across the water.

The Molokai Outrigger Canoe Race is not just a race. It has historical significance as well. Many years ago, hundreds of giant canoes could be seen in the Hawaiian Islands. Each boat was carved from a single tree—usually the Koa tree. The canoes were **outfitted** to be used as fishing boats, battleships, and even ferries. Over time, these giant boats were replaced by more efficient means of transportation.

Yet the tradition of the canoe continues with the annual outrigger race. Regardless of the outcome, all of us are **winners** because the race preserves an important part of Hawaiian culture.

 Look back at the boldfaced words. What do you notice about the spelling of the root words?

On Your Mark

Take your Warm Up Test. Then check your spelling with the List Words on the next page.

57

Pep Talk

When a short-vowel word ends in a single consonant, the consonant is usually doubled before adding a suffix that begins with a vowel.
hum + **ing** = humming
When a word has more than one syllable, the final consonant is usually doubled if the last syllable has a short vowel followed by a single consonant.
outfit + **ed** = outfitted

LIST WORDS

1. beginning
2. humming
3. dropped
4. sitting
5. slipping
6. joggers
7. grabbing
8. bobbing
9. tripped
10. padded
11. skimming
12. scrubbing
13. winners
14. outfitted
15. wrapped
16. clapping
17. dragging
18. chatting
19. quitter
20. trimmer

Game Plan

Spelling Lineup

Write each List Word under the correct suffix. Then circle the root word in each List Word.

ing	ed
1. beginning	12. dropped
2. humming	13. tripped
3. sitting	14. padded
4. slipping	15. outfitted
5. grabbing	16. wrapped
6. bobbing	**er or ers**
7. skimming	17. joggers
8. scrubbing	18. winners
9. clapping	19. quitter
10. dragging	20. trimmer
11. chatting	

58 Lesson 14 ■ Suffixes **ed, er,** and **ing:** Doubling Final Consonants

Synonyms

Write the List Word that means the same or almost the same as the word or phrase given.

1. dressed	outfitted	9. cushioned	padded
2. washing	scrubbing	10. reaching for	grabbing
3. covered	wrapped	11. reading quickly	skimming
4. starting	beginning	12. floating	bobbing
5. let go of	dropped	13. singing	humming
6. being seated	sitting	14. applauding	clapping
7. runners	joggers	15. hair cutter	trimmer
8. not losers	winners	16. stumbled	tripped

Rhyming

Write the List Words whose root words rhyme with the words given.

that
1. chatting

dim
6. skimming
7. trimmer

sum
11. humming

stop
2. dropped

strap
8. wrapped
9. clapping

hip
12. slipping
13. tripped

hit
3. sitting
4. outfitted

5. quitter

wag
10. dragging

Lesson 14 ■ Suffixes **ed, er,** and **ing**: Doubling Final Consonants   59

Flex Your Spelling Muscles

Writing

Pretend that you are a newspaper reporter covering a canoe race in Hawaii. The canoes are <u>skimming</u> over the water. Who will the <u>winners</u> be? In your report, help people "see" what is happening.

Proofreading

The paragraphs below have eleven mistakes. Use the proofreading marks to fix the mistakes. Then write the misspelled List Words correctly on the lines.

Proofreading Marks	
⟋	spelling mistake
⊙	add period
¶	indent paragraph

¶ Skeming along the ocean waters is a 50-foot-long cedar canoe. Siting inside are seventeen people, who are testing the craft. It is the first canoe the people of their village have built in many years.

The canoe is sliping into the bay while people on shore are claping and chatting excitedly. Draging the canoe onto land, the villagers feel proud. No other village has built such a magnificent canoe.

1. Skimming
2. Sitting
3. slipping
4. clapping
5. chatting
6. Dragging

Now proofread your news report. Fix any mistakes.

Go for the Goal

Take your Final Test. Then fill in your Scoreboard. Send your mistakes to the Word Locker.

SCOREBOARD

number correct	number wrong

★ ★ ★ ★ ★ ★ ★ ★ **All-Star Words** ★ ★ ★ ★ ★ ★ ★ ★

snapping   stepped   patrolling   dimmed   mugger

With a partner, identify the root word in each All-Star Word. Then look up the root words in a dictionary. Use the definitions to help you write each All-Star Word in a sentence.

60   Lesson 14 ■ Suffixes **ed, er,** and **ing**: Doubling Final Consonants

---

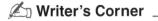

Spelling Strategy   Write several List Words on the board (*beginning, padded, scrubbing, quitter*). Then write short-vowel words that have two final consonants and a suffix: *gasped, adjusted, twisting, walker.* With a partner, students can identify the root words in each list and compare their spellings when a suffix is added. Help students conclude that when a short-vowel word ends in a single consonant, the consonant doubles when a suffix is added.

Flex Your Spelling Muscles   *Page 60*

As students complete the **Writing** activity, encourage them to brainstorm ideas, write a first draft, revise, and proofread their work. The **Proofreading** exercise will help them prepare to proofread their reports. To publish their writing, students may want to
• combine their reports into a class newspaper
• read their reports aloud as news broadcasts.

✍ Writer's Corner

Suggest that students read about other Hawaiian traditions in books such as *The Hawaiians of Old* by Elizabeth P. Dunford. Students can write a paragraph about their favorite tradition and create an illustration to go with it.

Go for the Goal/Final Test

1. Uncle Jack used the hedge *trimmer.*
2. Did you think the movie's *beginning* was boring?
3. The girls don't want a *quitter* on their team.
4. We left the show *humming* the songs we'd heard.
5. "Quit *chatting!*" ordered the teacher.
6. Dana *dropped* one of her books.
7. The dog is *dragging* its leash behind it.
8. Shane enjoys *sitting* in the sand.
9. The audience is *clapping* for the play.
10. The puppy was *slipping* on the newly waxed floor.
11. The packages are *wrapped* and ready to mail.
12. The *joggers* stopped to drink at the fountain.
13. The band was *outfitted* in their new uniforms.
14. Rob and I were *grabbing* for the last sandwich.
15. The boat was *bobbing* in the harbor.
16. Who are the *winners* of the art contest?
17. The acrobat *tripped* and lost her balance.
18. Adam is *skimming* the sports page.
19. Did you try *scrubbing* the pot with cleanser?
20. The goalie's pants were thickly *padded.*

Remind students to complete the Scoreboard and write any misspelled words in their Word Locker.

★★ **All-Star Words**   You may want to point out that the All-Star Words follow the spelling rule and remind students that the spellings of the root words changed because a suffix was added.

Lesson 15

Objective
To spell words with the suffixes *ed, er,* and *ing:* dropping the final *e* of the root word

Correlated Phonics Lesson
MCP Phonics, Level D, Lesson 32

Warm Up   Page 61
Students may enjoy reading about a snack that has been popular for hundreds of years. Afterward, invite students to discuss their favorite nutritious snacks.

Ask volunteers to say each boldfaced word and tell how the spelling of the root word has changed.

On Your Mark/Warm Up Test
1. Please plan on **coming** home in time for dinner.
2. Shannon **loved** the scary monster movie.
3. Will you help by **raking** the lawn?
4. The waiter **served** the salads first.
5. Columbus **proved** that the earth is round.
6. Megan is good at **sharing** with others.
7. Alanna and Nick **traded** baseball cards.
8. The **mover** loaded the chair into the big van.
9. Cam **saved** his sister a seat in the theater.
10. Will Mr. Cass be **giving** swimming lessons?
11. Amanda is a careful bike **rider.**
12. The audience applauded the graceful **dancer.**
13. Max **promised** to clean his room on Saturday.
14. What a **surprising** ending that story had!
15. The gymnast is **bouncing** on the trampoline.
16. Mike is **writing** an article for our school paper.
17. Mom **sliced** the pizza while it was still hot.
18. The price of this car has been greatly **reduced.**
19. The lake does not look the way I **pictured** it.
20. The weight lifters are **comparing** their muscles.

Pep Talk/Game Plan   Pages 62–63
Introduce the spelling rule and have students read the List Words aloud. Encourage students to look back at their Warm Up Tests and apply the spelling rule to any misspelled words.

As students work through the **Spelling Lineup, Suffixes,** and **Vocabulary** exercises, remind them to look back at their List Words or in their dictionaries if they need help. For the **Spelling Lineup,** ask students which suffix can form present-tense verbs (*ing*), which can form past-tense verbs (*ed*), and which can change a verb to a noun that names a kind of person (*er*).

 See **Words in Context,** page 14

Suffixes *ed, er,* and *ing:* Dropping the Final *e*

LESSON
15

Warm Up
What snack food has been popular for hundreds of years?

Pop Quiz
What food explodes as it cooks? Do you give up? It's popcorn.

Long before the Pilgrims landed in the New World, the North American Indians had been **sharing** this explosive treat among themselves. For hundreds of years, people **loved** eating it plain and hot. In the 1900s, movie houses began selling it. The theater owners **served** it spiced with butter and salt. That made popcorn eaters so thirsty that they bought something to drink, too.

Today, popcorn can be bought in shops, flavored with anything from grapes to onions. Plain or fancy, it is becoming one of America's best loved treats—happily eaten by nearly everyone, from the ballet **dancer** to the furniture **mover.** Every year, we eat millions of pounds of the fluffy stuff! Unlike most snack foods, this one is good for you and very low in calories—as long as you eat it plain.

 Look at the root words in the boldfaced words. What do you notice about their spelling?

On Your Mark
Take your Warm Up Test. Then check your spelling with the List Words on the next page.

Pep Talk
When a word ends in silent **e**, usually drop the **e** before adding a suffix that begins with a vowel.
trade + **ed** = traded
move + **er** = mover
surprise + **ing** = surprising

LIST WORDS
1. coming
2. loved
3. raking
4. served
5. proved
6. sharing
7. traded
8. mover
9. saved
10. giving
11. rider
12. dancer
13. promised
14. surprising
15. bouncing
16. writing
17. sliced
18. reduced
19. pictured
20. comparing

Game Plan
Spelling Lineup
Write the List Words that tell about action that is happening in the present. Circle the suffix in each word.

1. com**ing**   5. surpris**ing**
2. rak**ing**   6. bounc**ing**
3. shar**ing**   7. writ**ing**
4. giv**ing**   8. compar**ing**

Write the List Words that tell about action that happened in the past. Circle the suffix in each word.

9. lov**ed**   14. promis**ed**
10. serv**ed**   15. slic**ed**
11. prov**ed**   16. reduc**ed**
12. trad**ed**   17. pictur**ed**
13. sav**ed**

Write the List Words that name people and what they do. Circle the suffix in each word.

18. mov**er**   20. danc**er**
19. rid**er**

54

Dear Popcorn Institute,

My name is David Van Loon.
I am 8 years old. ~~I am~~
Could you send me some information
on Popcorn?

Thanks!

Suffixes

Write List Words by combining the root words and suffixes.

1. bounce + ing = __bouncing__   6. love + ed = __loved__
2. write + ing = __writing__   7. serve + ed = __served__
3. compare + ing = __comparing__   8. ride + er = __rider__
4. prove + ed = __proved__   9. share + ing = __sharing__
5. give + ing = __giving__

Vocabulary

Write the List Word that best completes each sentence.

1. The __mover__ put furniture in the van.
2. Tom is __raking__ up the leaves in the yard.
3. Leah __saved__ twenty dollars to buy a new purse.
4. The magician was __surprising__ everyone with magic tricks.
5. I __promised__ Pete I would help him paint the fence.
6. The football player __reduced__ his weight by fifteen pounds.
7. My grandparents are __coming__ to visit us in July.
8. Mom __traded__ in her old car for a brand new one.
9. The __dancer__ leaped gracefully.
10. I am __comparing__ the two shirts to see which one I like better.
11. I never met Richard, but I __pictured__ him to be tall and thin.
12. Anna __sliced__ the loaf of bread into several pieces.

Lesson 15 ■ Suffixes **ed, er,** and **ing:** Dropping the Final **e**   63

Flex Your Spelling Muscles

Writing

Some people love popcorn. What is your favorite snack? Write a description of it, using as many List Words as you can.

Proofreading

The advertisement below has twelve mistakes. Use the proofreading marks to fix the mistakes. Then write the misspelled List Words correctly on the lines.

Proofreading Marks	
◯	spelling mistake
∧	add something
⌄	add apostrophe

A snack that's beyond ⃝comparing,
One youre sure to enjoy ⃝shairing.
Its a ⃝moveer in the store!
You're sure to shout, "Lets have more!"
So if youve ⃝promisde yourself a treat,
Or ⃝pichtured something great to eat,
Go ahead and munch on our Yummies—
What a thrill youll be ⃝giveing your tummies!

1. __comparing__   4. __promised__
2. __sharing__   5. __pictured__
3. __mover__   6. __giving__

Now proofread your description of your favorite snack. Fix any mistakes.

Go for the Goal

Take your Final Test. Then fill in your Scoreboard. Send your mistakes to the Word Locker.

SCOREBOARD
number correct	number wrong

★ ★ ★ ★ ★ ★ ★ ★ **All-Star Words** ★ ★ ★ ★ ★ ★ ★ ★

driving   stared   shaking   rising   skater

Write a sentence using each All-Star Word, but draw a picture clue where the word would be written. Trade papers with a partner. See if you can guess each other's words.

◎ **Spelling Strategy**   Invite students to work with a partner to write each List Word as a word equation (*share - e + ing = sharing, dance - e + er = dancer*). Encourage students to tell whether the suffixes indicate the present tense, the past tense, or a noun that names a kind of person.

Flex Your Spelling Muscles   *Page 64*

As students complete the **Writing** activity, encourage them to brainstorm ideas, write a first draft, revise, and proofread their work. The **Proofreading** exercise will help them prepare to proofread their descriptions. To publish their writing, students may want to
• create a "tasty treats" catalog
• read their descriptions aloud as TV advertisements.

✍ **Writer's Corner** _____

> Students can learn more facts about popcorn by writing to the Popcorn Institute, 401 N. Michigan Ave., Chicago, IL 60611-4267. You may want to have a class popcorn party at which students can share what they learned about this popular food.

Go for the Goal/Final Test

1. The comedian *loved* to make people laugh.
2. The waiter *served* our dinner and left the check.
3. The teacher is *sharing* his ideas with the class.
4. Has the *mover* rolled up the carpet yet?
5. The professor is *giving* a science lecture.
6. What a fantastic *dancer* Mario is!
7. It was *surprising* to find them in the gym.
8. *Writing* is my favorite classroom activity.
9. The manager of the store *reduced* the prices.
10. The lawyers were *comparing* notes.
11. I never *pictured* Kyla as an astronaut.
12. The baker *sliced* the bread.
13. Logan was *bouncing* the ball down the court.
14. The mechanic *promised* to fix the car today.
15. Did the *rider* fall off the horse?
16. The accountant *saved* us hundreds of dollars.
17. The photographers *traded* cameras for one day.
18. The bus driver *proved* she could drive well.
19. The children are *raking* leaves in the backyard.
20. The doctor is *coming* to examine the injury.

Remind students to complete the Scoreboard and write any misspelled words in their Word Locker.

★★ **All-Star Words**   You may want to point out that the All-Star Words follow the spelling rule and model how to draw a picture clue for a List Word.

55

Lesson 16

Objective
To spell words with the suffixes *ed, es,* and *ing:* changing the root words that end in *y*

Correlated Phonics Lesson
MCP Phonics, Level D, Lesson 35

Warm Up   *Page 65*
Students can find out why a scientist might want to "go fly a kite." After reading, ask students to brainstorm other innovative uses for kites.

Encourage students to look back at the boldfaced words. Ask volunteers to say each word, identify the root word, and tell how it has changed.

On Your Mark/Warm Up Test
1. A champion always *tries* to excel.
2. Paula *carried* the grocery bags for her neighbor.
3. What a lot of *worries* you have!
4. Why are you *buying* two dozen eggs?
5. We're *satisfied* with the results we got.
6. "I am *relying* on you to be on time," said Dad.
7. If he *denies* what I said, I can prove it.
8. Andrea carefully *copied* the words from the board.
9. The thirsty guests *emptied* the pitcher of juice.
10. Berta was *hurrying* to catch the bus.
11. The campers were awakened by the *cries* of wolves.
12. No one knows where my dog *buries* her bones.
13. When 5 is *multiplied* by 4, the product is 20.
14. Joel always *replies* to my letters.
15. The supermarket *supplied* the fruit we ate.
16. While the paint is *drying,* clean the brushes.
17. *Petrified* wood is as hard as stone.
18. Please hand me the big *frying* pan.
19. Have you *applied* for that summer job?
20. All the gerbils are *scurrying* around the cage.

Pep Talk/Game Plan   *Pages 66–67*
Introduce the spelling rule and have students read the List Words aloud. Encourage students to look back at their Warm Up Tests and apply the spelling rule to any misspelled words.

As students work through the **Spelling Lineup, Puzzle,** and **Root Words** exercises, remind them to look back at their List Words or in their dictionaries if they need help.

 See **Change or No Change,** page 15

Suffixes ed, es, and ing: Words Ending with y

LESSON 16

Warm Up
Why would a scientist want to fly a kite during a lightning storm?

Go Fly a Kite
Almost 250 years ago, Benjamin Franklin flew a kite in a lightning storm. His paper-and-string aircraft **carried** a key as part of an experiment with electricity. Franklin should have been full of **worries** and **petrified** with fright. We all know that his kite could have been **frying,** instead of flying!

Today, the kite is still being used as a scientific instrument. More and more, scientists are **relying** on kites to gather information. Satellites don't provide detailed pictures, and planes can't stay in one spot. But kites, which can remain stationary in the atmosphere, are often used to collect data about temperature, water vapor, radiation, and the ozone layer.

While Ben Franklin's key weighed only a few ounces, today's kites are being prepared to launch a much bigger cargo. Scientists are planning kites **supplied** with meteorological equipment weighing from twenty to thirty pounds! If you have any doubts about how remarkable that is, try to picture a kite carrying a couple of bowling balls, sailing as high as a jet. Rest easy though, the experiments will be held far out of the way of passing jets!

 Look back at each boldfaced word. Identify the root word. Did it change when a suffix was added?

On Your Mark
Take your Warm Up Test. Then check your spelling with the List Words on the next page.

65

Pep Talk
When a word ends in **y** preceded by a consonant, change the **y** to **i** before adding a suffix other than **ing**.

worry + **es** = worries
dry + **ing** = drying
copy + **ed** = copied
fry + **ing** = frying

Game Plan
Spelling Lineup
Write each List Word under the correct suffix.

LIST WORDS
1. tries
2. carried
3. worries
4. buying
5. satisfied
6. relying
7. denies
8. copied
9. emptied
10. hurrying
11. cries
12. buries
13. multiplied
14. replies
15. supplied
16. drying
17. petrified
18. frying
19. applied
20. scurrying

es
1. tries
2. worries
3. denies
4. cries
5. buries
6. replies

ing
7. buying
8. relying
9. hurrying
10. drying
11. frying
12. scurrying

ed
13. carried
14. satisfied
15. copied
16. emptied
17. multiplied
18. supplied
19. petrified
20. applied

66   Lesson 16 ■ Suffixes **ed, es,** and **ing:** Words Ending with y

---

56

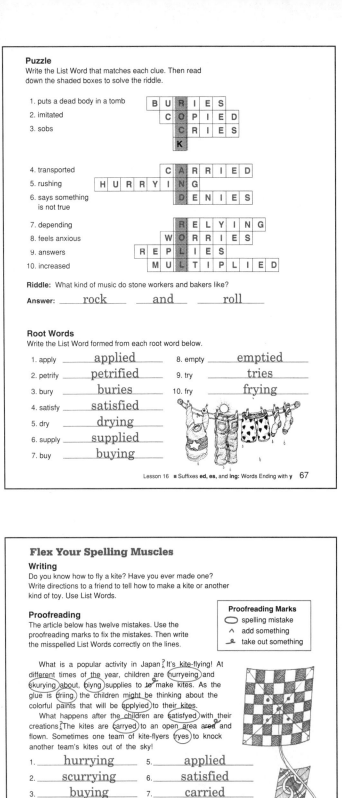

Puzzle

Write the List Word that matches each clue. Then read down the shaded boxes to solve the riddle.

1. puts a dead body in a tomb — B U R I E S
2. imitated — C O P I E D
3. sobs — C R I E S
   K

4. transported — C A R R I E D
5. rushing — H U R R Y I N G
6. says something is not true — D E N I E S

7. depending — R E L Y I N G
8. feels anxious — W O R R I E S
9. answers — R E P L I E S
10. increased — M U L T I P L I E D

Riddle: What kind of music do stone workers and bakers like?

Answer: __rock__ __and__ __roll__

Root Words

Write the List Word formed from each root word below.

1. apply — applied
2. petrify — petrified
3. bury — buries
4. satisfy — satisfied
5. dry — drying
6. supply — supplied
7. buy — buying

8. empty — emptied
9. try — tries
10. fry — frying

Lesson 16 ■ Suffixes *ed*, *es*, and *ing*: Words Ending with *y* 67

Flex Your Spelling Muscles

Writing

Do you know how to fly a kite? Have you ever made one? Write directions to a friend to tell how to make a kite or another kind of toy. Use List Words.

Proofreading

The article below has twelve mistakes. Use the proofreading marks to fix the mistakes. Then write the misspelled List Words correctly on the lines.

Proofreading Marks
- ⬭ spelling mistake
- ∧ add something
- ⤴ take out something

   What is a popular activity in Japan? It's kite-flying! At different times of the year, children are *hurryeing* and *skurying* about, *biyng* supplies to *to* make kites. As the glue is *driing*, the children might be thinking about the colorful paints that will be *applyied* to their kites.
   What happens after the children are *satisfyed* with their creations? The kites are *carryed* to an open area *area* and flown. Sometimes one team of kite-flyers *tryes* to knock another team's kites out of the sky!

1. hurrying   5. applied
2. scurrying   6. satisfied
3. buying   7. carried
4. drying   8. tries

Now proofread your directions. Fix any mistakes.

Go for the Goal

Take your Final Test. Then fill in your Scoreboard. Send your mistakes to the Word Locker.

SCOREBOARD
| number correct | number wrong |

★ ★ ★ ★ ★ ★ ★ **All-Star Words** ★ ★ ★ ★ ★ ★ ★

dairies   horrified   pitying   magnifying   mysteries

With a partner, write a mystery story using all five words. Get together with another pair of students and compare stories.

68   Lesson 16 ■ Suffixes *ed*, *es*, and *ing*: Words Ending with *y*

◎ **Spelling Strategy** Invite students to get together with a partner and take turns writing each List Word. The partner who writes the word

- circles the suffix
- points to the *y* or *i*
- explains why the *y* was or was not changed to *i*.

Flex Your Spelling Muscles   *Page 68*

As students complete the **Writing** activity, encourage them to brainstorm ideas, write a first draft, revise, and proofread their work. The **Proofreading** exercise will help them prepare to proofread their directions. To publish their writing, students may want to create a class book titled "Great Toys to Make for Fun."

✍ Writer's Corner _____

You may want to bring in directions for making a kite and have students follow the instructions to make their own kites. Suggest that students think of interesting names (i.e., *High Flyer, Wind Sailor*) to paint or write on their kites.

Go for the Goal/Final Test

1. Manuela *applied* for the manager's job.
2. The baby *tries* to talk, but she just babbles.
3. Our class is *buying* a gift for the custodian.
4. I'm *hurrying* as fast as I can!
5. Susan *multiplied* the numbers in her head.
6. I am *frying* the fish in a heavy skillet.
7. The pack mules *carried* the heaviest loads.
8. Jamie was *relying* on her mother to wake her up.
9. The coach *supplied* the players with team shirts.
10. Could you tell if the wood was *petrified?*
11. Mice were *scurrying* through the attic.
12. My dad *worries* when I am late and don't call.
13. He *denies* that he owes the teacher homework.
14. My dog *buries* his bones but never digs them up.
15. I washed my clothes and am *drying* them now.
16. Our curiosity was *satisfied* by Tim's letter.
17. We *emptied* the dishwasher before we left.
18. Will you pick the baby up if she *cries?*
19. Cynthia *copied* the instructions neatly.
20. I received ten *replies* to my invitations.

Remind students to complete the Scoreboard and write any misspelled words in their Word Locker.

★★ **All-Star Words** You may want to point out that the All-Star Words follow the spelling rule and discuss possible storylines for a mystery.

Lesson 17

Objective
To spell words with comparative suffixes *er* and *est:* changing root words ending in *y*

Correlated Phonics Lessons
MCP Phonics, Level D, Lessons 31, 35

Warm Up   Page 69
In this selection, students discover which fruit is more than just a delicious food. After reading, invite students to invent new apple recipes.

Encourage students to look back at the boldfaced words. Ask volunteers to say each word and tell which letter in the root word was changed.

On Your Mark/Warm Up Test
1. My explanation just made Mom *angrier.*
2. Those were the *angriest* words he ever spoke.
3. Elena was *happier* when her cat came home.
4. That was the *happiest* time Paul had known.
5. Eric finds multiplication *easier* than division.
6. Was the last test problem the *easiest?*
7. Inez arrived *earlier* than the other guests.
8. The *earliest* bus left at 5:00 in the morning.
9. The first comic was *funnier* than the second one.
10. What's the *funniest* joke you ever heard?
11. I think tulips are *prettier* than roses.
12. The *prettiest* view of town is from the hilltop.
13. It's *lonelier* on the beach than in the city.
14. My *loneliest* night was when I camped by myself.
15. Last year's snowfall was *heavier* than usual.
16. This bag of groceries is the *heaviest* of all.
17. The gold lace made the costume look *fancier.*
18. Grandpa made the *fanciest* birthday cake ever!
19. A watermelon is *juicier* than an apple.
20. The ripest pear will be the *juiciest.*

Pep Talk/Game Plan   Pages 70–71
Introduce the spelling rule and have students read the List Words aloud. Encourage students to look back at their Warm Up Tests and apply the spelling rule to any misspelled words.

As students work through the **Spelling Lineup, Suffixes,** and **Synonyms** exercises, remind them to look back at their List Words or in their dictionaries if they need help. For the **Spelling Lineup,** ask students which suffix is used when an adjective compares two things (*er*), and which is used when it compares two or more things (*est*).

 See **Words in Context,** page 14

58

Name _____

Suffixes er and est: Words Ending with y
LESSON 17

Warm Up
Which fruit is more than just a delicious food?

An Apple a Day
What do McIntosh, Granny Smith, and Cortland have in common? They're all apples. Some fruits may be **fancier.** Others may be **prettier,** but few can be enjoyed in more ways than the apple. Apples can be made into apple pie, applesauce, and apple butter. The **juiciest** ones can be squeezed into apple juice or apple cider. Of course, the **easiest** way to enjoy an apple is to eat it raw.

Apples are more than just a delicious food. They're part of our language. A person can describe someone special as "the apple of my eye." We call New York City "The Big Apple." We call the lump in a person's throat his or her "Adam's apple."

More than 100 years ago there were not many apple orchards in the United States. Then a man named John Chapman traveled across the country planting apple seeds. A **happier** or friendlier person than John Chapman would have been hard to find. People liked him and began to call him Johnny Appleseed. Thanks to John, apple picking is one of America's busiest farm industries.

> Look back at the root word in each boldfaced word. How did each root word change?

On Your Mark
Take your Warm Up Test. Then check your spelling with the List Words on the next page.

69

Pep Talk
Adjectives ending in **er** compare two things. Adjectives ending in **est** compare three or more things. To add **er** or **est** to an adjective that ends in **y**, change the **y** to **i** first.

happy + **er** = happier
happy + **est** = happiest

Game Plan
Spelling Lineup
Write the List Words that compare two things. Circle the suffix at the end of each word.

1. angri(er)   6. pretti(er)
2. happi(er)   7. loneli(er)
3. easi(er)   8. heavi(er)
4. earli(er)   9. fanci(er)
5. funni(er)   10. juici(er)

Write the List Words that compare three or more things. Circle the suffix at the end of each word.

11. angri(est)   19. fanci(est)
12. happi(est)   20. juici(est)
13. easi(est)
14. earli(est)
15. funni(est)
16. pretti(est)
17. loneli(est)
18. heavi(est)

LIST WORDS
1. angrier
2. angriest
3. happier
4. happiest
5. easier
6. easiest
7. earlier
8. earliest
9. funnier
10. funniest
11. prettier
12. prettiest
13. lonelier
14. loneliest
15. heavier
16. heaviest
17. fancier
18. fanciest
19. juicier
20. juiciest

70 Lesson 17 ■ Suffixes **er** and **est**: Words Ending with **y**

Suffixes

Fill in the chart by adding **er** and **est** to the root words to make List Words. Write the List Words on the lines.

	+ er	+ est
1. juicy	juicier	juiciest
2. lonely	lonelier	loneliest
3. easy	easier	easiest
4. angry	angrier	angriest
5. funny	funnier	funniest
6. early	earlier	earliest
7. heavy	heavier	heaviest
8. pretty	prettier	prettiest
9. fancy	fancier	fanciest
10. happy	happier	happiest

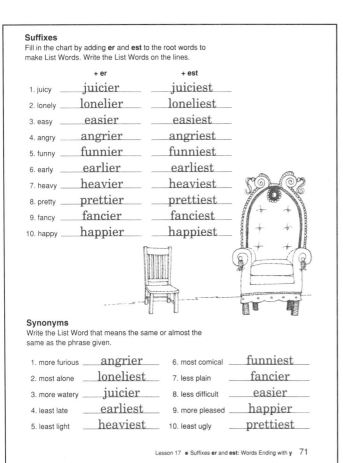

Synonyms

Write the List Word that means the same or almost the same as the phrase given.

1. more furious	angrier	6. most comical	funniest
2. most alone	loneliest	7. less plain	fancier
3. more watery	juicier	8. less difficult	easier
4. least late	earliest	9. more pleased	happier
5. least light	heaviest	10. least ugly	prettiest

Flex Your Spelling Muscles

Writing

Some people eat an apple a day. Write a short poem to describe your favorite fruit. Is it <u>juicier</u> and <u>tastier</u> than an apple? Is it <u>prettier</u> than a strawberry or <u>heavier</u> than a cantaloupe?

Proofreading

The paragraph below has ten mistakes. Use the proofreading marks to fix the mistakes. Then write the misspelled List Words correctly on the lines.

The best apple pies are made with the juicyest apples, not with watery or mushy ones. making an apple pie will be easyer if the Crust is prepared ahead of time. But remember—the more shortening in a crust, the heaver it will be. A top crust can be made fansier and prettyer with cutouts. tough crusts make cooks the angrest. Flaky crusts make cooks—and pie-eaters—happyer.

Now proofread your poem. Fix any mistakes.

Proofreading Marks
 spelling mistake
≡ capital letter
/ make small letter

1. juiciest
2. easier
3. heavier
4. fancier
5. prettier
6. angriest
7. happier

Go for the Goal

Take your Final Test. Then fill in your Scoreboard. Send your mistakes to the Word Locker.

SCOREBOARD
number correct | number wrong

★ ★ ★ ★ ★ ★ ★ ★   **All-Star Words**   ★ ★ ★ ★ ★ ★ ★ ★

tastier   loveliest   clumsier   luckiest   curlier

Write each All-Star Word and a clue to go with it. Then get together with a partner and read your clues aloud to each other. Can you guess the All-Star Word that goes with each clue?

◎ **Spelling Strategy**   Make two columns on the board, one labeled *er* and one *est,* and ask a volunteer to come to the front of the class. Tell the volunteer a root word contained in a List Word and have him or her add *er* or *est* to the root, writing the complete word in the appropriate column. Invite other students to come to the board. Continue this procedure until all the List Words have been written.

Flex Your Spelling Muscles   *Page 72*

As students complete the **Writing** activity, encourage them to brainstorm ideas, write a first draft, revise, and proofread their work. The **Proofreading** exercise will help them prepare to proofread their poems. To publish their writing, students may want to
• record their poems
• create a poetry book titled "Fruitful Thoughts."

✎ Writer's Corner

To find out about the many different varieties of apples, students can request the pamphlet *Delectably Nutritious Apples* from the International Apple Institute, 6707 Old Dominion Dr., Ste. 320, McLean, VA 22101. Include a long, self-addressed stamped envelope.

Go for the Goal/Final Test

1. This play is **funnier** that the first one we read.
2. It was **easier** to ski downhill the second time.
3. That ring is mother's **fanciest** piece of jewelry.
4. After we lost, I was **angrier** than the coach.
5. Courtney is **happiest** when she is painting.
6. The small oranges are **juicier** than the big ones.
7. I have never seen a **prettier** stage set.
8. What is the **loneliest** moment you have ever had?
9. Mr. Wang was the **angriest** person in the room.
10. Paul is **happier** about moving than I am.
11. Which peach is the **juiciest?**
12. These weights are **heavier** than they look.
13. Matt won the contest for the **funniest** costume.
14. **Earlier** in the day, I thought it would rain.
15. The **easiest** way to get there is to take the bus.
16. That is the **prettiest** garden I've ever seen!
17. The **earliest** I ever got up was 5:00 A.M.
18. Emily was **lonelier** than she expected at camp.
19. This hat is **fancier** than the feathered one.
20. The **heaviest** box is the one with all my books.

Remind students to complete the Scoreboard and write any misspelled words in their Word Locker.

★★ **All-Star Words**   You may want to point out that the All-Star Words follow the spelling rule and model writing a clue for a List Word.

Lesson 18 • Instant Replay

Objective

To review spelling words with the suffixes *ed, er,* and *ing; ed, er,* and *ing:* doubling final consonants; *ed, er,* and *ing:* dropping the final *e; ed, es,* and *ing:* words ending with *y; er* and *est:* words ending with *y*

Time Out   *Pages 73–76*

Check Your Word Locker Based on your observations, note which words are giving students the most difficulty and offer assistance for spelling them correctly. Here are some frequently misspelled words to watch for: *guessed, beginning, writing, multiplied, earlier, juicier,* and *angriest.*

To give students extra help and practice in taking standardized tests, you may want to have them take the Review Test for this lesson on pages 62–63. After scoring the tests, return them to students so that they can record their misspelled words in their Word Locker.

After practicing their troublesome words, students can work through the exercises for **Lessons 13–17.** Before they begin each exercise, you may want to go over the spelling rule.

Take It Home Suggest that students locate the List Words in **Lessons 13–17** in magazine and newspaper ads. For a complete list of the words, encourage students to take their *Spelling Workout* books home. Students can also use Take It Home Master 3 on pages 64–65 to help them do the activity. Encourage students to bring in their collages to share with the class. Students can identify List Words in one another's pictures.

Name _____

Instant Replay • Lessons 13–17

Time Out
Take another look at root words and suffixes.

Check Your Word Locker
Look at the words in your Word Locker. Write your most troublesome words for Lessons 13 through 17.

_____

Practice spelling your troublesome words with a partner. Take turns writing a word equation for each word.
apply – **y** + **i** + **ed** = applied

Lesson 13

You can add the suffixes **ed, er,** or **ing** to some words without changing the spelling of the root, as in sorted, learner, and checking.

List Words		
watching	Write a List Word that means the same as each word or phrase.	
finishing	1. vocalist	singer
singer	2. threw	tossed
guessed	3. touch down	landing
teacher	4. recalled	remembered
walker	5. viewing	watching
remembered	6. ending	finishing
tossed	7. figured out	guessed
wishing	8. hoping	wishing
landing	9. instructor	teacher
	10. jogger	walker

Lesson 18 ■ Instant Replay **73**

Lesson 14

When a short-vowel word or final syllable ends in a single consonant, the consonant is usually doubled when a suffix that begins with a vowel is added, as in slipping and quitter.

List Words		
	Write the List Word that belongs in each group.	
beginning	1. talking, speaking,	chatting
humming	2. stumbled, fell,	tripped
joggers	3. runners, racers,	joggers
tripped	4. opening, starting,	beginning
scrubbing	5. covered, sealed,	wrapped
outfitted	6. pulling, towing,	dragging
wrapped	7. dressed, equipped,	outfitted
clapping	8. cheering, applauding,	clapping
dragging	9. singing, whistling,	humming
chatting	10. washing, rinsing,	scrubbing

Lesson 15

When a word ends in silent **e**, the **e** is usually dropped before a suffix that begins with a vowel is added, as in sharing and served.

List Words		
	Write each List Word under the correct category.	

One Syllable		Two Syllables	
loved	1. loved	5. dancer
proved	2. proved	6. promised
saved	3. saved	7. bouncing
dancer	4. sliced	8. pictured
promised			
surprising	**Three Syllables**		
bouncing	9. surprising	10. comparing	
sliced			
pictured			
comparing			

74 Lesson 18 ■ Instant Replay

60

Lesson 16

When a word ends in a consonant and **y**, the **y** is changed to **i** before a suffix other than **ing** is added, as in supplied and denies.

List Words
worries
buying
satisfied
copied
emptied
cries
multiplied
replies
petrified
scurrying

Write a List Word to complete each sentence.

1. Four ___multiplied___ by two is eight.
2. I saw Jo ___buying___ a new baseball.
3. I expect the ___replies___ to my letters to come soon.
4. The truck ___emptied___ a load of sand.
5. The delicious meal ___satisfied___ my hunger.
6. Al ___copied___ his story.
7. The baby ___cries___ when she's tired.
8. Aunt Jan ___worries___ if I'm late.
9. I watched a cat ___scurrying___ up a tree.
10. ___Petrified___ wood is as hard as rock.

Lesson 17

When the suffixes **er** or **est** are added to an adjective ending in **y**, the **y** changes to **i**, as in prettier and earliest.

List Words
angriest
happier
easiest
earlier
funnier
prettiest
lonelier
heaviest
fancier
juiciest

Write the List Word that contains the root word given.

1. early ___earlier___ 8. juicy ___juiciest___
2. angry ___angriest___ 9. easy ___easiest___
3. happy ___happier___ 10. lonely ___lonelier___
4. funny ___funnier___
5. heavy ___heaviest___
6. pretty ___prettiest___
7. fancy ___fancier___

Lesson 18 ■ Instant Replay 75

Lessons 13–17

List Words
remembered
beginning
scrubbing
funnier
dancer
sliced
buying
replies
angriest
easiest

Write the List Word that matches each clue.

1. simplest ___easiest___
2. more humorous ___funnier___
3. brought back to mind ___remembered___
4. rubbing to remove dirt ___scrubbing___
5. answers ___replies___
6. person who moves to music ___dancer___
7. cut into strips ___sliced___
8. the start, or first part ___beginning___
9. getting with money ___buying___
10. maddest ___angriest___

Go for the Goal

Take your Final Replay Test. Then fill in your Scoreboard. Send any misspelled words to your Word Locker.

SCOREBOARD
number correct	number wrong

Clean Out Your Word Locker
Look in your Word Locker. Cross out each word you spelled correctly on your Final Replay Test. Circle the words you're still having trouble with. Add the words you circled to your Spelling Notebook. What do you notice about the words? Watch for those words as you write.

Go for the Goal/Final Replay Test   *Page 76*

1. That is the **angriest** person I've ever seen!
2. The big gold bow made the gift look **fancier.**
3. I thought the store opened **earlier** than that.
4. Rita **worries** about being late for supper.
5. Jamal **multiplied** the numbers and got 56.
6. The trees became **petrified** over time.
7. Grandmother **loved** to play with the girls.
8. Our class is **comparing** bacteria to viruses.
9. I plan on **surprising** Gina with a big party.
10. The story's **beginning** is set in Rome.
11. I spent an afternoon **chatting** with Grandpa.
12. The hikers were **outfitted** in foul-weather gear.
13. Michelle **wrapped** the gift in tissue paper.
14. Drivers must watch carefully for **joggers.**
15. Joe finally **proved** his point to me.
16. A **bouncing** baseball is often difficult to catch.
17. Can you name a great American **dancer?**
18. We heard the excited **cries** of the spectators.
19. The squirrels were **scurrying** along the branch.
20. His joke was **funnier** the first time he told it.
21. This is the **juiciest** watermelon I've ever had!
22. I feel **lonelier** now that Jason has moved away.
23. Are you **satisfied** with the meal you ordered?
24. The **replies** to our survey came in quickly.
25. Mom **sliced** tomatoes and put them in the salad.
26. Chris **promised** to send me a photograph.
27. Muriel is **humming** my favorite song.
28. We began **clapping** for the talented dancer.
29. How funny it was when the clown **tripped!**
30. I finally **remembered** the wildflower's name.
31. The plane will be **landing** at four o'clock.
32. Amy earns money as a dog **walker.**
33. We'll be **finishing** the story tomorrow.
34. The workers were **dragging** the barrels away.
35. Dad is **scrubbing** the dirty floors with a brush.
36. Would you like to be a **singer** in the choir?
37. Wayne **tossed** his dirty shirt into the washer.
38. The contestant **guessed** the right answer.
39. Debby **saved** money to buy a new bicycle.
40. The city looks just as I **pictured** it would.
41. We'll be **buying** a new house next year.
42. Mark **emptied** the pitcher of orange juice.
43. I **copied** the movements of the dance teacher.
44. This is the **prettiest** flower in the garden.
45. The baby seemed **happier** after her nap.
46. I was **watching** a television show about dolphins.
47. The **teacher** corrected the spelling tests.
48. I am **wishing** for a puppy for my birthday.
49. This is the **easiest** test I've ever taken.
50. Which box is the **heaviest** one?

Clean Out Your Word Locker Before writing each word, students can say the word and identify the root and the suffix.

61

Instant Replay Test

Side A

Read each sentence and set of words. Fill in the circle next to the word that is spelled correctly to complete the sentence.

1. Skiers are often _____ with goggles.
   - ⓐ outfitted
   - ⓒ outffited
   - ⓑ outfidded
   - ⓓ outfited

2. Tina is _____ Dad a magazine subscription.
   - ⓐ buing
   - ⓒ buying
   - ⓑ bying
   - ⓓ bieing

3. The principal informed us of the _____ news.
   - ⓐ serprising
   - ⓒ surprizing
   - ⓑ surprising
   - ⓓ surpriseing

4. Joey is _____ his homework before soccer practice.
   - ⓐ finishin
   - ⓒ finnishing
   - ⓑ finishing
   - ⓓ finiching

5. Squirrels were _____ around the oak trees.
   - ⓐ scurying
   - ⓒ skurrying
   - ⓑ schurying
   - ⓓ scurrying

6. The present was _____ with a huge, satin bow.
   - ⓐ wrappt
   - ⓒ wrapped
   - ⓑ rapped
   - ⓓ wrapt

7. This patient would prefer the _____ appointment.
   - ⓐ earlier
   - ⓒ erlier
   - ⓑ earlyer
   - ⓓ earleyer

8. We received six _____ to our invitation.
   - ⓐ replys
   - ⓒ replize
   - ⓑ replise
   - ⓓ replies

Instant Replay Test

Side B

Read each sentence and set of words. Fill in the circle next to the word that is spelled correctly to complete the sentence.

9. Tyrone's grandfather _____ my exact weight!
   - ⓐ gessed
   - ⓒ guessed
   - ⓑ guesd
   - ⓓ guesst

10. The audience was _____ with pleasure.
    - ⓐ cllaping
    - ⓒ claping
    - ⓑ clapping
    - ⓓ clapeing

11. This episode is _____ than the last one was.
    - ⓐ phunier
    - ⓒ funnier
    - ⓑ funnyer
    - ⓓ funier

12. The scientist _____ his theory.
    - ⓐ prooved
    - ⓒ proved
    - ⓑ pruved
    - ⓓ proovd

13. The singer _____ all six verses of the song.
    - ⓐ rememberd
    - ⓒ remmembered
    - ⓑ remembered
    - ⓓ rememberred

14. I'm unable to lift the _____ weight.
    - ⓐ heaviest
    - ⓒ heavviest
    - ⓑ heviest
    - ⓓ heavyest

15. Kim _____ all her earnings.
    - ⓐ saived
    - ⓒ sayved
    - ⓑ savved
    - ⓓ saved

TAKE IT HOME

Your child has learned to spell many new words and would like to share them with you and your family. Here are some engaging activities that will help your child review the spelling words in Lessons 13–17.

Ad Words

Here's another way to recycle those old magazines and newspapers. Encourage your child to cut out magazine and newspaper ads that contain spelling words. Your child may also enjoy creating a collage with the ads.

"More **satisfied joggers** are **buying** our **fancier** running shoes!"

Ad Game

With your child, use as many spelling words as you can to create captions or ads for the products pictured below. Remember, ads can be serious, humorous, outrageous, or just plain silly—so have some fun!

Lesson 19

Objective
To spell words with vowel digraphs *ee, ea, oa, oe,* and *ue*

Correlated Phonics Lessons
MCP Phonics, Level D, Lessons 41–44

Warm Up   Page 77
In "Camping Anyone?," students discover what it can be like to experience the "Great Outdoors." Invite students to describe their own camping trips and to share their most memorable moments.

Encourage students to look back at the boldfaced words. Ask volunteers to say each word and identify the vowel sounds they hear.

On Your Mark/Warm Up Test
1. Please arrive **between** five and six o'clock.
2. Two **eastern** states are Maine and Vermont.
3. A cool **breeze** is welcome on a hot day.
4. The only **clues** they found were footprints.
5. Has Lisa **hoed** the weeds in the garden?
6. A dictionary will tell you a word's **meaning.**
7. Carlos **tiptoes** down the stairs.
8. Amanda had a good **reason** for being late.
9. Are you **treating** us to the movie, too?
10. The campers **roasted** marshmallows over the fire.
11. Jefferson believed in **freedom** of speech.
12. Lisa **loaned** her new record to Teresa.
13. The jet began to **approach** the landing strip.
14. Did you **measure** two cups of flour?
15. Stephanie **glued** a label onto the package.
16. I'd like ham **instead** of chicken in my sandwich.
17. What powerful wings the bald **eagle** has!
18. Dave **boasted** that he would win the race.
19. The **fleet** of ships sailed out of the harbor.
20. The horse galloped through the **meadow.**

Pep Talk/Game Plan   Pages 78–79
Introduce the spelling rule and have students read the List Words aloud. At this point, you may want to point out that *fleet* can be a noun ("a group of ships or trucks") or an adjective ("swift"). Encourage students to look back at their Warm Up Tests and apply the spelling rule to any misspelled words.

As students work through the **Spelling Lineup, Dictionary,** and **Vocabulary** exercises, remind them to look back at their List Words or in their dictionaries if they need help.

 See **Letter Cards,** page 15

Name _____

Vowel Digraphs
ee, ea, oa, oe, and ue
LESSON 19

Warm Up
What is the "Great Outdoors" like?

Camping Anyone?
Millions of people go camping every year. Camping can cost a great deal of money, or it can cost very little. For example, you can make a simple tent by throwing a blanket over a line tied **between** two trees, or you can buy an expensive tent with double walls and screens. It doesn't matter how much or how little you spend. The most important thing is to have fun!

Sleeping bags are an important piece of camping equipment. There are many different kinds to choose from. Some sleeping bags are made to keep the chill off when there's a cool **breeze.** Others are lined with a special material that will keep you warm in freezing temperatures. Whatever kind of sleeping bag you choose, make sure it's appropriate for the climate.

It has been said that you haven't lived until you've **roasted** a marshmallow over a crackling fire, or smelled a fresh **meadow** in the early morning hours. It's all part of the camping experience. So, if you feel like **treating** someone you know to something special, take them camping. Remember, there's nothing better than the "Great Outdoors!"

 Say the boldfaced words in the selection. What sounds do the vowel pairs make in these words?

On Your Mark
Take your Warm Up Test. Then check your spelling with the List Words on the next page.

Pep Talk
Vowel digraphs are two vowels together that stand for one vowel sound. The vowel digraphs **ee** and **ea** can make the /ē/ sound, as in fleet and reason. Sometimes the vowel digraph **ea** makes the /e/ sound, as in measure.

The vowel digraphs **oa** and **oe** make the /ō/ sound, as in loaned and hoed. The vowel digraph **ue** makes the /ōō/ sound, as in clues.

LIST WORDS
1. between
2. eastern
3. breeze
4. clues
5. hoed
6. meaning
7. tiptoes
8. reason
9. treating
10. roasted
11. freedom
12. loaned
13. approach
14. measure
15. glued
16. instead
17. eagle
18. boasted
19. fleet
20. meadow

Game Plan
Spelling Lineup
Write each List Word under the correct heading.

/ē/ spelled **ee**		/ō/ spelled **oa**	
1. between	12.	roasted
2. breeze	13.	loaned
3. freedom	14.	approach
4. fleet	15.	boasted

/ōō/ spelled **ue**		/ō/ spelled **oe**	
5. clues	16.	hoed
6. glued	17.	tiptoes

/ē/ spelled **ea**		/e/ spelled **ea**	
7. eastern	18.	measure
8. meaning	19.	instead
9. reason	20.	meadow
10. treating		
11. eagle		

78 Lesson 19 ■ Vowel Digraphs ee, ea, oa, oe, and ue

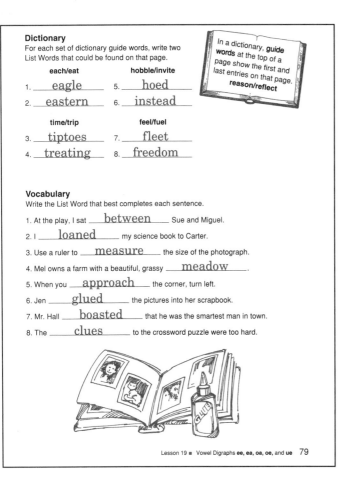

Dictionary

For each set of dictionary guide words, write two List Words that could be found on that page.

In a dictionary, guide words at the top of a page show the first and last entries on that page.
reason/reflect

each/eat
1. eagle
2. eastern

hobble/invite
5. hoed
6. instead

time/trip
3. tiptoes
4. treating

feel/fuel
7. fleet
8. freedom

Vocabulary

Write the List Word that best completes each sentence.

1. At the play, I sat __between__ Sue and Miguel.
2. I __loaned__ my science book to Carter.
3. Use a ruler to __measure__ the size of the photograph.
4. Mel owns a farm with a beautiful, grassy __meadow__.
5. When you __approach__ the corner, turn left.
6. Jen __glued__ the pictures into her scrapbook.
7. Mr. Hall __boasted__ that he was the smartest man in town.
8. The __clues__ to the crossword puzzle were too hard.

Flex Your Spelling Muscles

Writing

Do you like to hike or camp? Write a persuasive paragraph that will convince people of the joys of the "Great Outdoors." Use as many List Words as you can.

Proofreading

This poem has twelve mistakes. Use the proofreading marks to fix the mistakes. Then write the misspelled List Words on the lines.

Proofreading Marks
◯ spelling mistake
^ add something

There's always a good reeson
To camp in any season.
To feel a forest breaze
To hear wind in the trees,
Gives freedom a new meisure
To those who seek its treasure.
Be the one insteda who bowsted
Of food that's gently rowsted
On a fire burning bright
Near a meadoe green and light.

1. reason
2. breeze
3. freedom
4. measure
5. instead
6. boasted
7. roasted
8. meadow

Proofread your persuasive paragraph about the outdoors. Fix any mistakes.

Go for the Goal

Take your Final Test. Then fill in your Scoreboard. Send your mistakes to the Word Locker.

SCOREBOARD
number correct | number wrong

★ ★ ★ ★ ★ ★ ★ ★ **All-Star Words** ★ ★ ★ ★ ★ ★ ★ ★

cheat   forehead   sneeze   groan   dues

Try to use all five All-Star Words in a single sentence. Then get together with a partner and compare sentences.

⊚ **Spelling Strategy**   Write cloze sentences on the board for three or four List Words (for example, "We had a picnic in the _____"). For each sentence, provide a clue to the missing List Word by saying the appropriate vowel sound (/ē/, /e/, /ō/, or /ōō/) aloud (in this case, /e/ for *meadow*). After students guess the missing words, call on volunteers to write additional cloze sentences and provide the vowel-sound clues.

Flex Your Spelling Muscles   *Page 80*

As students complete the **Writing** activity, encourage them to brainstorm ideas, write a first draft, revise, and proofread their work. The **Proofreading** exercise will help them prepare to proofread their paragraphs. To publish their writing, students may want to create a brochure about the world's greatest campsites.

✍ Writer's Corner

The word *orienteering* means "finding one's way in an unfamiliar area by using a map and compass." Students can request an orienteering map and booklet by writing to Silva Orienteering Services— USA, Dept. FS, P.O. Box 1604, Binghamton, NY 13902. Enclose a long, self-addressed stamped envelope.

Go for the Goal/Final Test

1. She lost the mittens that I *loaned* her.
2. What a silly *reason* they gave for being late!
3. Steve used the *clues* to solve the puzzle.
4. Wildflowers grow in the *meadow.*
5. Will you play baseball *instead* of soccer?
6. Sara *boasted* that her ideas were the best.
7. We *roasted* a turkey for Thanksgiving dinner.
8. Do you know the *meaning* of this word?
9. Philadelphia is a large *eastern* city.
10. Did you *measure* the length of the pool?
11. Nicole *tiptoes* around while the baby sleeps.
12. Jason gave the trapped bird its *freedom.*
13. The gentle *breeze* stirred the curtains.
14. We watched the *fleet* of sailboats far out at sea.
15. Has John *glued* his model plane together?
16. The shed is *between* the house and the barn.
17. The farmer *hoed* her bean field.
18. The timid deer would not let us *approach* it.
19. The *eagle* lived up on a rocky cliff.
20. Thank you for *treating* me so kindly.

Remind students to complete the Scoreboard and write any misspelled words in their Word Locker.

★★ **All-Star Words**   You may want to point out that the All-Star Words follow the spelling rule and model writing a sentence using all the words.

Lesson 20

Objective
To spell words with vowel digraphs *ie* and *ei,* and apply a spelling rule

Correlated Phonics Lessons
MCP Phonics, Level D, Lessons 41–42, 44–45

Warm Up   *Page 81*
In this selection, students read to find out how runners can protect their feet. After reading, ask students what kind of exercise they like and how it affects their bodies.

Encourage students to look back at the boldfaced words. Ask volunteers to say each word and identify the vowel sound they hear.

On Your Mark/Warm Up Test
1. I watered the plant, but it *died* anyway.
2. The *fields* were planted with corn.
3. Jamie had a *brief* wait before the bus arrived.
4. Did aspirin give you *relief* from your headache?
5. I jumped when I heard the siren's *shriek!*
6. Do you *weigh* more than you did last summer?
7. I *believe* that he's telling the truth.
8. The kids rode a *sleigh* through the snow.
9. Be sure you *receive* the correct change.
10. Tomorrow my brother will be *eighteen* years old.
11. I tried to *seize* the ball from the other player.
12. She introduced herself to her new *neighbors.*
13. A *receipt* is proof that you paid for something.
14. A loudspeaker *amplifies* sound.
15. We use the pool *chiefly* in the summertime.
16. The *freighter* carried goods from many nations.
17. When you lie to people, you *deceive* them.
18. Could you *perceive* anything through the fog?
19. What delicious *pies* that bakery makes!
20. A balanced *diet* is important to good health.

Pep Talk/Game Plan   *Pages 82–83*
Introduce the spelling rule and have students read the List Words aloud. Encourage students to look back at their Warm Up Tests and apply the spelling rule to any misspelled words.

As students work through the **Spelling Lineup, Missing Vowels,** and **Puzzle** exercises, remind them to look back at their List Words or in their dictionaries if they need help. For the **Spelling Lineup,** help students notice that the *ie* in *diet* has two sounds.

 See **Tape Recording,** page 15

Vowel Digraphs *ie* and *ei*   LESSON 20

Warm Up
What should runners do to take care of their feet?

Tenderfeet
It seems everywhere you look, people are running. You see them on smooth streets, rough roads, sandy beaches, and grassy **fields.** Running can be good for your health. Doctors **believe** it can strengthen your heart. However, running **amplifies** the wear and tear on your feet.

Pressure equal to three times what you **weigh** pushes on each foot as it hits the ground. This means that when a 90-pound person runs, each foot is being pushed to the ground by 270 pounds of pressure. That's quite a jolt for those bones and muscles! No wonder our feet may need help.

Here are some tips for tending your toes:
- Wash your feet every day. Make sure they are dried well before you put on your shoes.
- Wear socks made of cotton or wool.
- Make sure your running shoes fit well and give your feet good support.
- Make sure your shoes are tied snugly, but not tightly.
- If you notice any foot problems, see a doctor.

Pass these tips on to friends and **neighbors.** Their feet will be glad you did.

 Look back at the boldfaced words. Notice that each word contains the vowel digraph **ie** or **ei.** Say each word. How many different vowel sounds do you hear?

On Your Mark
Take your Warm Up Test. Then check your spelling with the List Words on the next page.

81

Pep Talk
The vowel digraph **ie** can make the /ī/ sound you hear in pies or the /ē/ sound you hear in brief. The vowel digraph **ei** can make the /ā/ sound you hear in sleigh or the /ē/ sound you hear in seize.

It may help to remember this rhyme when spelling **ie** and **ei:**
   I before **E**
   except after **C**
   or when sounded like **A**
   as in neighbors or weigh!

LIST WORDS
1. died
2. fields
3. brief
4. relief
5. shriek
6. weigh
7. believe
8. sleigh
9. receive
10. eighteen
11. seize
12. neighbors
13. receipt
14. amplifies
15. chiefly
16. freighter
17. deceive
18. perceive
19. pies
20. diet

Game Plan
Spelling Lineup
Write each List Word under the correct heading.

/ā/ spelled **ei**
1. weigh
2. sleigh
3. eighteen
4. neighbors
5. freighter

/ē/ spelled **ie**
6. fields
7. brief
8. relief
9. shriek
10. believe
11. chiefly

/ī/ spelled **ie**
12. died
13. amplifies
14. pies

/ē/ spelled **ei**
15. receive
16. seize
17. receipt
18. deceive
19. perceive

Write the List Word in which **ie** together has two sounds, the /ī/ sound and the /e/ sound.
20. diet

Missing Vowels

Add **ie** or **ei** to each group of letters to form a List Word. Then write the whole word on the line.

1. p_i_e_s   pies
2. dec_e_i_ve   deceive
3. ch_i_e_fly   chiefly
4. _e_i_ghteen   eighteen

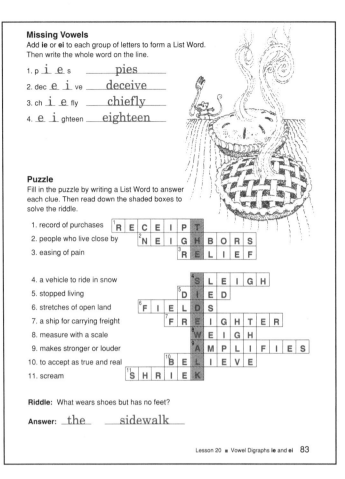

Puzzle

Fill in the puzzle by writing a List Word to answer each clue. Then read down the shaded boxes to solve the riddle.

1. record of purchases — R E C E I P T
2. people who live close by — N E I G H B O R S
3. easing of pain — R E L I E F
4. a vehicle to ride in snow — S L E I G H
5. stopped living — D I E D
6. stretches of open land — F I E L D S
7. a ship for carrying freight — F R E I G H T E R
8. measure with a scale — W E I G H
9. makes stronger or louder — A M P L I F I E S
10. to accept as true and real — B E L I E V E
11. scream — S H R I E K

Riddle: What wears shoes but has no feet?

Answer: the   sidewalk

Flex Your Spelling Muscles

Writing

Have you ever seen or heard about a bed race or a soap box derby? Use the List Words to describe an unusual or funny race that you may have seen or heard about.

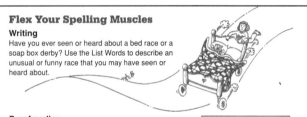

Proofreading

The following article has nine mistakes. Use the proofreading marks to fix the mistakes. Then write the misspelled List Words on the lines.

If you (perceev) that you need more exercise, you probably do. Many people (beleeve) there are more choices in exercise programs today. Those who want to (resieve) the best in fitness can do walking, running, aerobics, and step classes. When you combine exercise with (dyet), you can be sure you will look and feel better. Some people feel better after a (breif) time, while others need a little longer because they want to lose weight, as well as feel fit. So (sieze) the moment. Get in shape!

Now proofread your description. Fix any mistakes.

Proofreading Marks
◯ spelling mistake
∧ add something

1. perceive
2. believe
3. receive
4. diet
5. brief
6. seize

Go for the Goal

Take your Final Test. Then fill in your Scoreboard. Send your mistakes to the Word Locker.

SCOREBOARD

number correct	number wrong

★ ★ ★ ★ ★ ★ ★ ★ **All-Star Words** ★ ★ ★ ★ ★ ★ ★ ★

ceiling   hygiene   veil   achieve   allies

With your partner, write a definition for each All-Star Word. Then look up the words in your dictionary. Do your definitions match?

◉ **Spelling Strategy** Say each List Word and call on a volunteer to write it on the board. Then have the class tell you whether the word is spelled correctly. If it is, circle the vowel digraph *ie* or *ei*. If it isn't, erase the incorrect letters and fill in the correct ones. Encourage students to practice the words that gave them the most difficulty until they become more proficient at spelling them.

Flex Your Spelling Muscles   *Page 84*

As students complete the **Writing** activity, encourage them to brainstorm ideas, write a first draft, revise, and proofread their work. The **Proofreading** exercise will help them prepare to proofread their descriptions. To publish their writing, students may want to
• read their descriptions aloud as sports broadcasts
• create a class book titled "They're Off!"

✎ Writer's Corner

Encourage students to learn more about the feet by reading a book such as *The Story of Your Foot* by Alvin and Virginia B. Silverstein. Suggest that students jot down useful information as they read and use it to create a pamphlet on foot care, which they can donate to their nurse's or doctor's office.

Go for the Goal/Final Test

1. The vet put our dog on a high protein **diet.**
2. My aunt's **pies** won first prize at the fair.
3. Many young trees **died** during the cold winter.
4. The highway was bordered by **fields** of daisies.
5. The principal made a **brief** speech to welcome us.
6. Dogs don't **perceive** colors the way we do.
7. Some advertisements **deceive** the public.
8. What a **relief** it was to sit down at last!
9. A **freighter** carries goods to different ports.
10. The owl's **shriek** surprised us.
11. The auditorium was used **chiefly** for concerts.
12. It's easy to **believe** someone you trust.
13. This speaker **amplifies** the singers' voices.
14. Two horses pulled the **sleigh** through the snow.
15. You'll need the **receipt** if you return the toy.
16. Did Joe **receive** a phone call from his mother?
17. All the **neighbors** were invited to the party.
18. You have to wait until you're **eighteen** to vote.
19. I'll **weigh** these apples before I buy them.
20. Enemies tried to **seize** the castle.

Remind students to complete the Scoreboard and write any misspelled words in their Word Locker.

★★ **All-Star Words** You may want to point out that the All-Star Words follow the spelling rule and model creating a definition for a List Word.

Lesson 21

Objective
To spell words in which *au* and *aw* spell the /ô/ sound

Correlated Phonics Lesson
MCP Phonics, Level D, Lesson 48

Warm Up   *Page 85*
In "Little Lumberjacks," students find out which animal is a fantastic dam-builder. After reading, invite students to share additional information they might know about beavers.

Encourage students to look back at the boldfaced words. Ask volunteers to say each word and identify the vowel sound or sounds they hear.

On Your Mark/Warm Up Test
1. The cat sharpened its **claws** on the tree trunk.
2. It wasn't his **fault** that he was late.
3. The big snowstorm is **causing** a lot of damage.
4. Daylight's first appearance is called **dawn.**
5. We stuffed a scarecrow with **straw.**
6. These **drawings** are incredibly detailed!
7. Did you watch the rocket **launch** on television?
8. Dad makes a great tomato **sauce** for spaghetti.
9. The roots of your teeth are buried in your **jaw.**
10. Does he believe that ghosts can **haunt** a house?
11. Kay was so sleepy that she began to **yawn.**
12. We saw a deer and her **fawns** grazing in a field.
13. I felt **awkward** when I was learning to skate.
14. A beaver will **gnaw** at a tree until it falls.
15. Everyone in the **audience** loved the play.
16. Don't **scrawl** your name; print it neatly.
17. The man was a **fraud** and not a real doctor.
18. How **gaunt** he looks after his illness!
19. Which **restaurant** has the best enchiladas?
20. Sarah bought a beautiful silk **shawl.**

Pep Talk/Game Plan   *Pages 86–87*
Introduce the spelling rule and have students read the List Words aloud. You may also want to make sure students know the meanings of *awkward, gnaw, scrawl,* and *gaunt* and point out the silent *g* in *gnaw.* Then encourage students to look back at their Warm Up Tests and apply the spelling rule to any misspelled words.

As students work through the **Spelling Lineup, Synonyms,** and **Puzzle** exercises, remind them to look back at their List Words or in their dictionaries if they need help.

 See **Picture Clues,** page 15

70

Name _____

Vowel Digraphs <u>au</u> and <u>aw</u>
LESSON 21

Warm Up
How can a little animal build a dam?

Little Lumberjacks
The first time you see a beaver, you may think it looks a little strange. A beaver has a stout little body, small head, tiny **claws,** and a tail that looks like a ping-pong paddle. A beaver may look **awkward,** but in the water it is a fast, graceful, and strong swimmer.

Beavers are nature's best builders of dams. In spring and summer, the beavers **gnaw** on trees and branches. Their strong teeth can cut through a thick tree in minutes. They **launch** the cut logs into a stream. Then they push the logs into place. The wood is then packed with mud and **straw.**

Beavers usually make their homes in the ponds that form behind the dams. A beaver lodge has many underwater entrances. Inside is a dry place where the beavers live and store food inside for the winter. When the cold weather comes, they go inside and rest. But they must keep chewing on wood. If they don't, their teeth would keep growing and become too long, **causing** them harm. As soon as the spring thaw comes, the beavers go back to work. You can see why a busy person is often described as being "busy as a beaver."

 Each boldfaced word in the selection is spelled with **au** or **aw.** Say each word. What do you notice about the sound each makes?

On Your Mark
Take your Warm Up Test. Then check your spelling with the List Words on the next page.

85

Pep Talk
Be careful when you spell words with the /ô/ sound you hear in <u>fault</u> and <u>dawn</u>. The vowel digraphs **au** and **aw** make the /ô/ sound, and sound alike.

Game Plan
Spelling Lineup
Write each List Word under the correct heading.

LIST WORDS
1. claws
2. fault
3. causing
4. dawn
5. straw
6. drawings
7. launch
8. sauce
9. jaw
10. haunt
11. yawn
12. fawns
13. awkward
14. gnaw
15. audience
16. scrawl
17. fraud
18. gaunt
19. restaurant
20. shawl

/ô/ spelled **aw**	/ô/ spelled **au**
1. claws	12. fault
2. dawn	13. causing
3. straw	14. launch
4. drawings	15. sauce
5. jaw	16. haunt
6. yawn	17. audience
7. fawns	18. fraud
8. awkward	19. gaunt
9. gnaw	20. restaurant
10. scrawl	
11. shawl	

86 Lesson 21 ■ Vowel Digraphs au and aw

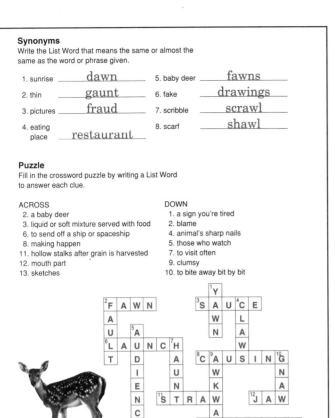

Synonyms

Write the List Word that means the same or almost the same as the word or phrase given.

1. sunrise ___dawn___
2. thin ___gaunt___
3. pictures ___fraud___
4. eating place ___restaurant___
5. baby deer ___fawns___
6. fake ___drawings___
7. scribble ___scrawl___
8. scarf ___shawl___

Puzzle

Fill in the crossword puzzle by writing a List Word to answer each clue.

ACROSS
2. a baby deer
3. liquid or soft mixture served with food
6. to send off a ship or spaceship
8. making happen
11. hollow stalks after grain is harvested
12. mouth part
13. sketches

DOWN
1. a sign you're tired
2. blame
4. animal's sharp nails
5. those who watch
7. to visit often
9. clumsy
10. to bite away bit by bit

Crossword answers:
2. FAWN
3. SAUCE
6. LAUNCH
8. CAUSING
11. STRAW
12. JAW
13. DRAWINGS
Down: 1. YAWN, 2. FAULT, 4. CLAWS, 5. AUDIENCE, 7. HAUNT, 9. AWKWARD, 10. GNAW

Flex Your Spelling Muscles

Writing

Have you ever watched a wild animal at work or at play? It might have been at the zoo, at the movies, or even in the woods. Write a description of what you saw. Use as many List Words as you can.

Proofreading

This description has twelve mistakes. Use the proofreading marks to fix the mistakes. Then write the misspelled List Words on the lines.

Proofreading Marks	
◯	spelling mistake
≡	capital letter
^	add something

Do you know what is fun to do? Watch the otters at the High desert museum. The museum is not far from bend, Oregon. These otters love an (awdience) They are up at (dahwn) playing and swimming. They (lanche) themselves down hills and slide into the water, making people laugh. can you guess what happens then? They do it all over again. it's also fun to watch an otter eat. It floats, holding food in its (claus.) It's like a show at a (restawrant.)

1. ___audience___
2. ___dawn___
3. ___launch___
4. ___claws___
5. ___restaurant___

Now proofread your animal description. Fix any mistakes.

Go for the Goal

Take your Final Test. Then fill in your Scoreboard. Send your mistakes to the Word Locker.

SCOREBOARD
| number correct | number wrong |

★ ★ ★ ★ ★ ★ ★ **All-Star Words** ★ ★ ★ ★ ★ ★ ★

drawn   saucer   automatic   author   lawyer

Write a sentence using each word, but leave a blank for the All-Star Word that completes the sentence. Trade papers with your partner. See if you can complete each other's sentences.

⊙ **Spelling Strategy**   Write each List Word on the board, leaving a blank for the vowel digraph *au* or *aw* (c __ sing, sh __ l). For each word, have the class ask, "Is it spelled with *au* or *aw*?" Then call on a volunteer to name the missing letters and complete the word on the board. Encourage the class to look in their *Spelling Workout* books to check the spelling.

Flex Your Spelling Muscles   *Page 88*

As students complete the **Writing** activity, encourage them to brainstorm ideas, write a first draft, revise, and proofread their work. The **Proofreading** exercise will help them prepare to proofread their descriptions. To publish their writing, students may want to illustrate their descriptions and use them to create a classroom display.

✍ **Writer's Corner**

Students might enjoy watching a video called *The Beaver,* which can be purchased from AIMS Media, Inc. (800-367-2467). Suggest that they write a paragraph about the video, detailing the most interesting facts they learned. Encourage students to share their paragraphs with one another.

Go for the Goal/Final Test

1. The museum has many old ***drawings*** of ships.
2. Everyone in the ***audience*** stood and applauded.
3. The young colt was ***awkward*** when it first stood.
4. Did they ***launch*** the new ship in the harbor?
5. Cats sharpen their ***claws*** on rough surfaces.
6. Did you make the ***shawl*** you're wearing?
7. The ***scrawl*** on the paper is actually a signature.
8. Abe Lincoln was a tall, ***gaunt*** man.
9. Do you like cheese ***sauce*** on your broccoli?
10. People say that ghosts ***haunt*** that old house.
11. The accident was no one's ***fault.***
12. Rodents must ***gnaw*** or their teeth grow too long.
13. A leak is ***causing*** the cracks in the ceiling.
14. The person who sold the fake diamond is a ***fraud.***
15. My ***straw*** hat protects me from the sun.
16. Chewing this tough meat makes my ***jaw*** hurt.
17. What expensive food this ***restaurant*** has!
18. My ***yawn*** made everyone else yawn, too!
19. Let's leave at ***dawn*** and get an early start.
20. Watch how the mother deer protects her ***fawns.***

Remind students to complete the Scoreboard and write any misspelled words in their Word Locker.

★★ **All-Star Words**   You may want to point out that the All-Star Words follow the spelling rule and review how to write a cloze sentence.

Lesson 22

Objective
To spell words containing *oi, oy, ai,* or *ay*

Correlated Phonics Lessons
MCP Phonics, Level D, Lessons 41, 50–51, 53

Warm Up   Page 89

In "End of the Trail," students learn about a ghost town that was preserved as a museum. Afterward, invite students to discuss whether they would have enjoyed living in the Wild West.

Encourage students to look back at the boldfaced words. Ask volunteers to say each word and identify the letters that spell the /ā/ or /oi/ sound.

On Your Mark/Warm Up Test

1. The hikers' *voices* echoed in the mountains.
2. Be careful not to *sprain* your ankle.
3. What frightening *noises* those are!
4. The *disloyal* knight betrayed his king.
5. The store will *employ* Becky this summer.
6. This belt is too big for my *waist.*
7. The earthquake *destroyed* many buildings.
8. The sleeves of this old jacket have begun to *fray.*
9. Is Dad *broiling* the hamburgers?
10. The sign was *swaying* in the wind.
11. The museum *displays* many famous paintings.
12. The newspaper *praised* the astronauts' courage.
13. If she breaks her promise, she'll *disappoint* me.
14. The *railroad* tracks run through the town.
15. The British *royalty* live in Buckingham Palace.
16. My mother was *appointed* to the city council.
17. Did you borrow this red *crayon* from Mary?
18. When the soup is *boiling,* turn down the stove.
19. This bread has *soybean* flour in it.
20. Our picnic lunch became *spoiled* in the sun.

Pep Talk/Game Plan   Pages 90–91

Introduce the spelling rule and have students read the List Words aloud. Explain the meaning of *fray* ("to wear down so as to become ragged"), and point out that *crayon* has two pronunciations (*krā´ ən, krā´ än*). Then encourage students to look back at their Warm Up Tests and apply the spelling rule to any misspelled words.

As students work through the **Spelling Lineup, Rhyming,** and **Classification** exercises, remind them to look back at their List Words or in their dictionaries if they need help.

 See **Categorizing,** page 15

Vowel Digraphs ai, ay; Diphthongs oi, oy
LESSON 22

Warm Up
How can a town be turned into a museum?

End of the Trail

The front door of Butch Cassidy's cabin stands open. A stagecoach is parked outside the General Store. No horses are restlessly pawing the gray dust. No **voices** can be heard from the well-traveled trail. In fact, the only **noises** that can be heard are the whispering breezes and chirping insects.

You may think this is a ghost town, but it's really a museum called Old Trail Town. It stands outside Cody, Wyoming. The town, which stands on five acres, was established by Bob and Terry Edgar. Among the **displays** are old cabins and treasures from the long-ago days of the Wild West.

Years ago, Bob noticed many old cabins standing empty on the range. "Some were falling in. Others were being **destroyed** by grazing cattle," he said. He decided to save them as a part of American history.

After working hard and sacrificing time and money, the Edgars' dream came to life. They should be **praised** for preserving a long-ago way of life. People are interested in seeing how cowhands and pioneers really lived. As Bob says, "The main thing is to enjoy the place and remember it."

Say each boldfaced word in the selection. How are the words with the /ā/ sound spelled? How are the words with the /oi/ sound spelled?

On Your Mark
Take your Warm Up Test. Then check your spelling with the List Words on the next page.

89

Pep Talk
The vowel digraphs **ai** and **ay** make the /ā/ sound you hear in waist and fray. Diphthongs are different from digraphs in that the two vowels blend together to make one sound. The diphthongs **oi** and **oy** make the /oi/ sound you hear in voices and employ.

Game Plan
Spelling Lineup
Write each List Word under the correct heading.

LIST WORDS

1. voices
2. sprain
3. noises
4. disloyal
5. employ
6. waist
7. destroyed
8. fray
9. broiling
10. swaying
11. displays
12. praised
13. disappoint
14. railroad
15. royalty
16. appointed
17. crayon
18. boiling
19. soybean
20. spoiled

/ā/ spelled **ai**
1. sprain
2. waist
3. praised
4. railroad

/ā/ spelled **ay**
12. fray
13. swaying
14. displays
15. crayon

/oi/ spelled **oi**
5. voices
6. noises
7. broiling
8. disappoint
9. appointed
10. boiling
11. spoiled

/oi/ spelled **oy**
16. disloyal
17. employ
18. destroyed
19. royalty
20. soybean

Rhyming

Write the List Word that rhymes with each word given.

1. train   <u>sprain</u>
2. grazed   <u>praised</u>
3. day   <u>fray</u>
4. annoy   <u>employ</u>
5. toiled   <u>spoiled</u>
6. playing   <u>swaying</u>
7. paste   <u>waist</u>
8. replays   <u>displays</u>

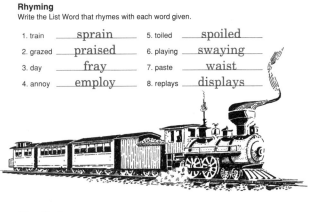

Classification

Write the List Word that belongs in each group.

1. pen, pencil,   <u>crayon</u>
2. baking, boiling,   <u>broiling</u>
3. bang, crash,   <u>noises</u>
4. soprano, alto,   <u>voices</u>
5. dissatisfy, fail,   <u>disappoint</u>
6. rice, potato,   <u>soybean</u>
7. queens, kings,   <u>royalty</u>
8. untrue, unfaithful,   <u>disloyal</u>
9. moving, rocking,   <u>swaying</u>
10. chosen, assigned,   <u>appointed</u>

Lesson 22 ■ Vowel Digraphs **ai, ay;** Diphthongs **oi, oy**   91

Flex Your Spelling Muscles

Writing

Cowhands worked hard at herding cattle, and riding and mending fence. Yet, they had fun, too. Write a paragraph telling what you think it was like to be an Old West cowhand. Use as many List Words as you can.

Proofreading

The paragraph below has twelve mistakes. Fix the mistakes with the proofreading marks. Then write the misspelled List Words on the lines.

Proofreading Marks	
◯	spelling mistake
⊙	add period
ℛ	take out something

The pioneers who came west in covered wagons are to be praysed. Even with an appoynted leader, they had to use all all their skills just to survive. Long days were spent riding in in the swaiying wagons in boyling hot or icy cold weather. Accidents could and did happen! A wagon wheel could be destroied by by the rough terrain or someone could have a sprained ankle with with no one to treat it. When the ralroad came, traveling west became easier, but still an adventure.

1. <u>praised</u>
2. <u>appointed</u>
3. <u>swaying</u>
4. <u>boiling</u>
5. <u>destroyed</u>
6. <u>railroad</u>

Now proofread your paragraph about cowhands. Fix any mistakes.

Go for the Goal

Take your Final Test. Then fill in your Scoreboard. Send your mistakes to the Word Locker.

SCOREBOARD

number correct	number wrong

★ ★ ★ ★ ★ ★ ★ ★ **All-Star Words** ★ ★ ★ ★ ★ ★ ★ ★

entertain   delay   embroider   loyal   raisin

Write a sentence for each word, but leave a blank in place of the All-Star Word. Then write a wrong All-Star Word in each blank. Trade papers with a partner. Try to write the correct All-Star Words in the sentences.

92   Lesson 22 ■ Vowel Digraphs **ai, ay;** Diphthongs **oi, oy**

◉ **Spelling Strategy**   To help students recognize the sounds that *ai, ay, oi,* and *oy* stand for, write /ā/ and /oi/ on the board as separate column headings. Invite the class to tell you which column each List Word belongs in, then write the word in that column. Finally, call on volunteers to come to the board, say each word aloud, and circle the letters that spell /ā/ or /oi/.

Flex Your Spelling Muscles   *Page 92*

As students complete the **Writing** activity, encourage them to brainstorm ideas, write a first draft, revise, and proofread their work. The **Proofreading** exercise will help them prepare to proofread their paragraphs. To publish their writing, students may want to
• create a bulletin board titled "Wild West Days"
• read their work aloud, role-playing a cowhand.

✍ Writer's Corner

Students might enjoy finding out more about the Wild West by requesting a brochure from the Buffalo Bill Historical Center, Education Department, Box 1000, Cody, WY 82414.

Go for the Goal/Final Test

1. Are some countries ruled by *royalty?*
2. The farmer *displays* his vegetables at the fair.
3. Loud *noises* came from the lion's den.
4. The drought *destroyed* many farm crops.
5. Could you hand me the *soybean* oil?
6. The baby drew on the wall with a red *crayon.*
7. The cook was *broiling* lamb chops.
8. The *voices* of my friends greeted me.
9. How many workers does that factory *employ?*
10. You'll *disappoint* us if you miss the party.
11. The dancers were *swaying* to the music.
12. Tie the sash around your *waist.*
13. How painful that ankle *sprain* was!
14. My grandfather works for the *railroad.*
15. The eggs were *boiling* in a big pan.
16. The teacher *praised* us for our hard work.
17. The old shirt had begun to *fray* around the collar.
18. Dogs are rarely *disloyal* to their masters.
19. A sudden rainstorm *spoiled* our baseball game.
20. I have been *appointed* secretary of my class.

Remind students to complete the Scoreboard and write any misspelled words in their Word Locker.

★★ **All-Star Words**   You may want to point out that the All-Star Words follow the spelling rule and model writing a sentence with an inappropriate List Word.

Lesson 23

Objective

To spell words in which *ou* and *ow* spell the vowel sounds /ou/, /ō/, /ô/, and /u/

Correlated Phonics Lessons

MCP Phonics, Level D, Lessons 52–53

Warm Up — *Page 93*

In this selection, students learn about a type of bird that can be as small as a sparrow or as large as an average-sized dog. After reading, invite students to compare owls with other kinds of birds they are familiar with.

Ask volunteers to say each boldfaced word and name the letters that stand for the /ō/ or /ou/ sound.

On Your Mark/Warm Up Test

1. Do you get eight ***hours*** of sleep every night?
2. Janie made a birdhouse for the ***sparrows.***
3. The new road goes through several ***towns.***
4. ***Powerful*** river currents pushed the canoes along.
5. The recipe calls for a small ***amount*** of onion.
6. Sharon solved the math problem ***without*** help.
7. Lin ***allows*** his cat to sleep at the foot of his bed.
8. A rain ***shower*** cooled the hot summer air.
9. The waiter ***brought*** the sandwiches to our table.
10. The mayor ***sought*** a solution to the problem.
11. The raccoon took a nap in a ***hollow*** tree trunk.
12. The runner quickly ***swallowed*** some water.
13. Mexico is our ***southern*** neighbor.
14. Ten times one hundred equals a ***thousand.***
15. I sat at my desk and ***thought*** about the problem.
16. Chi had ***trouble*** with the last part of the test.
17. Is this ***bouquet*** of roses for you?
18. ***Although*** it was nearly spring, it snowed.
19. What a great view you get from this ***mountain!***
20. New England clam ***chowder*** is delicious.

Pep Talk/Game Plan — *Pages 94–95*

Introduce the spelling rule and have students read the List Words aloud. At this point, you may want to mention that *bouquet* has two pronunciations: *bō kā'* and *boo kā'.* Encourage students to look back at their Warm Up Tests and apply the spelling rule to any misspelled words.

As students work through the **Spelling Lineup, Puzzle,** and **Dictionary** exercises, remind them to look back at their List Words or in their dictionaries if they need help.

for ESL students — See **Rhymes and Songs,** page 14

Name ______________________________

LESSON 23

ou and ow

Warm Up

What bird can be as small as a sparrow or as big as a dog?

Night Prowlers

Owls may not be as well known to people as other birds. This may happen because owls prefer the night **hours.** Even if we don't see them often, owls can be found around the world. There are more than 130 different kinds. Some are as small as **sparrows,** like the elf or pygmy owls. Others are very large. The great horned owl stands two feet tall and has a four-foot wing span. That's about as big as an average dog!

Owls often live in nests left behind by other birds. Other times they use **hollow** trees or logs for homes. When they live near **towns,** owls may move into buildings, such as barns.

Most owls sleep during the day. When dusk comes, they glide silently through the air, looking around for food. Usually, a rat, mole, or field mouse will do. Owls can see even with a small **amount** of light. They can spot food in the darkest places. Their keen eyes are fixed in their sockets and do not move. But owls have long, thin necks that allow them to turn their heads in almost a complete circle. Owls' hearing is as sharp as their sight, **although** some people may not believe this. After all, if owls can hear so well, why do they always say "whoo"?

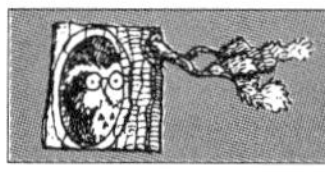

Look back at the boldfaced words. Say each word. Listen for the /ō/ and /ou/ sounds. What do you notice about the way these sounds are spelled?

On Your Mark

Take your Warm Up Test. Then check you spelling with the List Words on the next page.

93

Pep Talk

The diphthongs **ou** and **ow** can make the /ou/ sound, as in without and towns.
The letters **ow** can also be a vowel digraph, making the /ō/ sound, as in hollow.
The letters **ou** can make the /ō/ sound in although, the /ô/ sound in thought, or the /u/ sound, as in southern.

LIST WORDS

1. hours
2. sparrows
3. towns
4. powerful
5. amount
6. without
7. allows
8. shower
9. brought
10. sought
11. hollow
12. swallowed
13. southern
14. thousand
15. thought
16. trouble
17. bouquet
18. although
19. mountain
20. chowder

Game Plan

Spelling Lineup

Write each List Word under the correct heading.

/ou/ spelled **ou**

1. hours
2. amount
3. without
4. thousand
5. mountain

/ou/ spelled **ow**

6. towns
7. powerful
8. allows
9. shower
10. chowder

/ō/ spelled **ou**

11. bouquet
12. although

/ō/ spelled **ow**

13. sparrows
14. hollow
15. swallowed

/ô/ spelled **ou**

16. brought
17. sought
18. thought

/u/ spelled **ou**

19. southern
20. trouble

94 Lesson 23 ■ **ou and ow**

Puzzle

Read each clue. Write the List Word that means the same or almost the same as each word given. Then read down the shaded boxes to solve the riddle.

1. minus   W I T H O U T
2. problem   T R O U B L E

3. rain   S H O W E R
4. permits   A L L O W S
5. 1,000   T H O U S A N D

6. sum   A M O U N T

7. idea   T H O U G H T
8. empty   H O L L O W
9. soup   C H O W D E R
10. hill   M O U N T A I N

Riddle: Did you hear about the joke the owl told?

Answer: It was a hoot.

Dictionary

For each set of dictionary guide words, write the List Words that could be found on that page. Write the words in alphabetical order.

*In a dictionary, **guide words** at the top of a page show the first and last entries on that page. **maybe/mountain***

alter/cat
1. although
2. amount
3. bouquet
4. brought

skip/thorn
5. sought
6. southern
7. sparrows
8. swallowed

Flex Your Spelling Muscles

Writing

Write a poem about two kinds of birds, such as sparrows and hawks. Tell how they are alike and how they are different. Use some List Words in your poem.

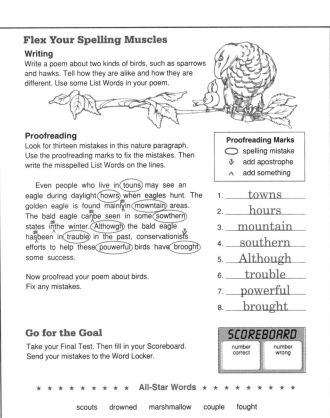

Proofreading

Look for thirteen mistakes in this nature paragraph. Use the proofreading marks to fix the mistakes. Then write the misspelled List Words on the lines.

Proofreading Marks
- ◯ spelling mistake
- ⩒ add apostrophe
- ∧ add something

Even people who live in touns may see an eagle during daylight howrs when eagles hunt. The golden eagle is found mainlyin mowntain areas. The bald eagle canbe seen in some southern states inthe winter. Althowgh the bald eagle hasbeen in trouble in the past, conservationists efforts to help these powerful birds have brooght some success.

Now proofread your poem about birds. Fix any mistakes.

1. towns
2. hours
3. mountain
4. southern
5. Although
6. trouble
7. powerful
8. brought

Go for the Goal

Take your Final Test. Then fill in your Scoreboard. Send your mistakes to the Word Locker.

SCOREBOARD
number correct	number wrong

★ ★ ★ ★ ★ ★ ★ ★ **All-Star Words** ★ ★ ★ ★ ★ ★ ★ ★

scouts   drowned   marshmallow   couple   fought

Work with your partner to write a story using the All-Star Words. Trade stories with other students. How were the words used in the story?

◎ **Spelling Strategy** To give students practice spelling the List Words, invite them to get together with a partner and take turns
- writing each List Word
- underlining the diphthong *ou* or *ow*
- telling the sound the diphthong makes
- pronouncing the complete word.

Flex Your Spelling Muscles   *Page 96*

As students complete the **Writing** activity, encourage them to brainstorm ideas, write a first draft, revise, and proofread their work. The **Proofreading** exercise will help them prepare to proofread their poems. To publish their writing, students may want to
- trade poems and read each other's work aloud
- create a class poetry book titled "Birds of a Feather."

✍ Writer's Corner

Students might enjoy watching a video about owls and hawks called *Hunters of the Wind, Hunters of the Night,* distributed through Centre Productions, Inc. (800–824–1166). Invite them to make posters to advertise a second showing of the film, which can be arranged for another class.

Go for the Goal/Final Test

1. Over thirty kinds of **sparrows** live in America.
2. What a **powerful** singing voice Tina has!
3. Sean was lonely **without** his best friend Dario.
4. He took a **shower** after working out in the gym.
5. During the storm, we **sought** shelter in the cabin.
6. The children **swallowed** their food in a hurry.
7. The hospital bill came to three **thousand** dollars.
8. I had **trouble** fitting in the last puzzle piece.
9. **Although** it was supposed to rain, the sun shone.
10. Mrs. Arnez puts vegetables in her **chowder.**
11. She spends two **hours** on homework every day.
12. What picturesque little **towns** these are!
13. The **amount** you owe for the book is four dollars.
14. He **allows** his students to check their own tests.
15. All the guests **brought** birthday gifts for Cara.
16. Rabbits were living in the **hollow** log.
17. Is Australia in the **Southern** Hemisphere?
18. Chan **thought** he had written an excellent story.
19. The word **bouquet** is a synonym for *smell.*
20. We will hike up Shawnee **Mountain.**

Remind students to complete the Scoreboard and write any misspelled words in their Word Locker.

★★ **All-Star Words** You may want to point out that the All-Star Words follow the spelling rule and offer assistance as needed as students brainstorm story ideas.

Lesson 24 • Instant Replay

Objective
To review spelling words with vowel digraphs *ee, ea, oa, oe, ue, ie, ei, au, aw, ai, ay;* diphthongs *oi, oy; ou* and *ow*

Time Out   *Pages 97–100*
Check Your Word Locker Based on your observations, note which words are giving students the most difficulty and offer assistance for spelling them correctly. Here are some frequently misspelled words to watch for: *instead, believe, relief, receipt, restaurant, audience,* and *disappoint.*

To give students extra help and practice in taking standardized tests, you may want to have them take the Review Test for this lesson on pages 78–79. After scoring the tests, return them to students so that they can record their misspelled words in their Word Locker.

After practicing their troublesome words, students can work through the exercises for **Lessons 19–23.** Before they begin each exercise, you may want to go over the spelling rule.

🏠 Take It Home Invite students to listen for and use List Words from **Lessons 19–23** during dinner time conversations. For a complete list of the words, encourage them to take their *Spelling Workout* books home. Students can also use Take It Home Master 4 on pages 80–81 to help them do the activity. Invite them to share the words they used with the class.

Time Out
Take another look at vowel digraphs and diphthongs.

Check Your Word Locker
Look at the words in your Word Locker. Write your most troublesome words for Lessons 19 through 23.

_____

Practice writing your troublesome words with a partner. Form the letters of each word using clay or pipe cleaners, while your partner spells the words aloud.

Lesson 19

The vowel digraphs **ee** and **ea** can spell /ē/, as in <u>fleet</u> and <u>reason</u>; **ea** can spell /e/, as in <u>instead</u>; **oa** and **oe** spell /ō/, as in <u>boasted</u> and <u>tiptoes</u>; and **ue** spells /o͞o/, as in <u>dues</u>.

List Words
breeze
hoed
meaning
roasted
freedom
approach
measure
glued
eagle
meadow

Add and subtract letters to form List Words.

1. fued – f + gl =   glued
2. tasted – t + ro =   roasted
3. each – ch + gle =   eagle
4. house – use + ed =   hoed
5. approve – ve + ach =   approach
6. freeze – f + b =   breeze
7. lining – li + mea =   meaning
8. meant – nt + dow =   meadow
9. random – ran + free =   freedom
10. treasure – tr + m =   measure

97

Lesson 20

The vowel digraph **ie** can spell /ī/, as in <u>died</u>, or /ē/, as in <u>fields</u>. The digraph **ei** can spell /ē/, as in <u>seize</u>, or /ā/, as in <u>weigh</u>.

List Words
brief
shriek
believe
sleigh
receive
neighbors
receipt
amplifies
chiefly
freighter

Write the List Word that belongs in each group.

1. canoe, sailboat,   freighter
2. scream, yell,   shriek
3. sled, ski,   sleigh
4. friends, partners,   neighbors
5. mainly, mostly,   chiefly
6. short, small,   brief
7. feel, think,   believe
8. increases, boosts,   amplifies
9. get, obtain,   receive
10. check, ticket,   receipt

Lesson 21

The vowel digraphs **au** and **aw** both spell /ô/, as in <u>haunt</u> and <u>claws</u>.

List Words
fault
drawings
launch
sauce
awkward
gnaw
audience
scrawl
gaunt
restaurant

Write each List Word under the correct category.

one syllable
1.   fault
2.   launch
3.   sauce
4.   gnaw
5.   scrawl
6.   gaunt

two syllables
7.   drawings
8.   awkward

three syllables
9.   audience
10.   restaurant

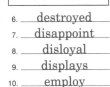

Lesson 22

Vowel digraphs **ai** and **ay** spell /ā/, as in waist and fray.
Diphthongs **oi** and **oy** spell /oi/, as in voices and employ.

List Words

sprain
disloyal
employ
destroyed
displays
disappoint
railroad
royalty
soybean
spoiled

Write each group of List Words in alphabetical order.

sprain royalty railroad soybean spoiled	disloyal employ destroyed displays disappoint

1. railroad
2. royalty
3. soybean
4. spoiled
5. sprain
6. destroyed
7. disappoint
8. disloyal
9. displays
10. employ

Lesson 23

The diphthongs **ou** and **ow** spell /ou/, as in amount and towns.
These letters can also be vowel digraphs. Listen for the /ō/ sound
in hollow and although and the /u/ sound in trouble.

List Words

hours
sparrows
powerful
shower
brought
hollow
swallowed
bouquet
mountain
chowder

Write a List Word to match each definition.

1. a very high hill — mountain
2. units of sixty minutes — hours
3. strong or forceful — powerful
4. a light rainfall — shower
5. carried or delivered — brought
6. having empty space inside — hollow
7. a thick soup — chowder
8. gray and brown songbirds — sparrows
9. a bunch of flowers — bouquet
10. passed down the throat — swallowed

Lesson 24 ■ Instant Replay 99

Lessons 19–23

List Words

breeze
roasted
eagle
believe
neighbors
freighter
drawings
scrawl
restaurant
employ
railroad
royalty
hours
mountain
chowder

Write a List Word to complete each book title or author's name.

1. "_Believe_ in Yourself" by Faith Builder
2. "Famous _Railroad_ Trips" by Choo Choos
3. "At Sea on a _Freighter_" by C. U. Later
4. "A Cook's Guide to Soups" by Clem _Chowder_
5. "Make Better _Drawings_" by U. B. Artist
6. "_Roasted_ Chicken Recipes" by Chef Cluck
7. "Flying High" by I. M. N. _Eagle_
8. "Counting the _Hours_" by Telly Time
9. "Visit Your _Neighbors_" by N. E. Juan Home
10. "Improve Your Handwriting" by I. _Scrawl_
11. "Great Meals at a _Restaurant_" by Bertha D. Diner
12. "Swaying in the _Breeze_" by Leaves R. Falling
13. "My Life in the _Royalty_" by Ima King
14. "People Want to Work for You!" by U. _Employ_
15. "Climb the Tallest _Mountain_" by Hi Hills

Go for the Goal

Take your Final Replay Test. Then fill in your
Scoreboard. Send any misspelled words to your
Word Locker.

SCOREBOARD

number correct	number wrong

Clean Out Your Word Locker

Look in your Word Locker. Cross out each word you
spelled correctly on your Final Replay Test. Circle the
words you're still having trouble with. Add the words
you circled to your Spelling Notebook. What do you
notice about the words? Watch for those words as
you write.

100 Lesson 24 ■ Instant Replay

1. Wildflowers bloom in the **meadow.**
2. The laws guarantee our **freedom** of speech.
3. The plane will descend and **approach** the runway.
4. Two white horses pulled the **sleigh.**
5. This **freighter** will leave tomorrow for Europe.
6. Did your **neighbors** move to Boston?
7. Beavers **gnaw** on the trunks of trees.
8. The Riverside Inn is my favorite **restaurant.**
9. My uncle was pale and **gaunt** during his illness.
10. Don't **sprain** your back when you move the sofa.
11. Our plans were **spoiled** by the sudden storm.
12. Some Chinese recipes call for **soybean** oil.
13. It took two **hours** to complete my report.
14. What is the highest **mountain** in the world?
15. How delicious that **chowder** smells!
16. The **sparrows** ate seeds at our bird feeder.
17. Carmela **brought** a visitor to school today.
18. Princess Anne is a member of the British **royalty.**
19. Dogs rarely are **disloyal** to their owners.
20. Be careful when you cross the **railroad** tracks!
21. Long, skinny legs make colts seem **awkward.**
22. We watched the rocket **launch** on television.
23. Do you have a recipe for spaghetti **sauce?**
24. Today I received a **brief** letter from Joan.
25. The **shriek** of the train whistle startled me.
26. When I paid for the hat, I was given a **receipt.**
27. The workers in this factory are **chiefly** women.
28. Use a teaspoon to **measure** the cinnamon.
29. Yesterday a baby **eagle** was born at the zoo.
30. A strong **breeze** will make the kite fly.
31. The dictionary told me the **meaning** of the word.
32. Mother **glued** the broken chair back together.
33. I **believe** that voting is our civic duty.
34. The **audience** waited for the curtain to rise.
35. If you **scrawl** your name, it may be hard to read.
36. The steel mills **employ** many people.
37. I'm sure that the movie won't **disappoint** you.
38. That storm in Florida was so **powerful!**
39. Tom bought a **bouquet** of roses for his wife.
40. Milk passes through a **hollow** straw.
41. Insects have **destroyed** many of the plants.
42. Chang **displays** his photographs at a gallery.
43. I'm afraid it's my **fault** that the book was lost.
44. Your **drawings** of wildflowers are beautiful.
45. A megaphone **amplifies** the cheerleader's voice.
46. You'll probably **receive** the package tomorrow.
47. Jim **hoed** the garden, and Ann planted the corn.
48. We **roasted** the potatoes over the campfire.
49. The dog **swallowed** every bit of his food.
50. A light **shower** fell in the late afternoon.

Clean Out Your Word Locker   After writing each
word, students can say the word and point to the
letters that stand for a vowel sound or sounds they
learned in **Lessons 19–23.**

77

Name _____

Instant Replay Test

Side A

Read each set of words. Fill in the circle next to the word that is spelled wrong.

1. ⓐ displays   ⓒ launch
   ⓑ disloyal   ⓓ shreak

2. ⓐ without   ⓒ sprein
   ⓑ eagle   ⓓ spoiled

3. ⓐ aproach   ⓒ sauce
   ⓑ railroad   ⓓ fault

4. ⓐ dawn   ⓒ mountin
   ⓑ meadow   ⓓ glued

5. ⓐ roasted   ⓒ gnaw
   ⓑ soybean   ⓓ distroyed

6. ⓐ brief   ⓒ freedom
   ⓑ gawnt   ⓓ swallowed

7. ⓐ drawings   ⓒ howed
   ⓑ boiling   ⓓ audience

8. ⓐ disapoint   ⓒ meaning
   ⓑ believe   ⓓ eastern

9. ⓐ chiefly   ⓒ disloyal
   ⓑ hours   ⓓ boquet

10. ⓐ frieghter ⓒ displays
    ⓑ sleigh   ⓓ clues

78

Name _____

Instant Replay Test

Side B

Read each set of words. Fill in the circle next to the word
that is spelled wrong.

11.   ⓐ hollow   ⓒ employ
     ⓑ fault   ⓓ powerfull

12.   ⓐ neighbers   ⓒ amplifies
     ⓑ shower   ⓓ sparrows

13.   ⓐ receive   ⓒ receit
     ⓑ meaning   ⓓ employ

14.   ⓐ sleigh   ⓒ scraul
     ⓑ hollow   ⓓ chiefly

15.   ⓐ hours   ⓒ disloyal
     ⓑ roasted   ⓓ mesure

16.   ⓐ believe   ⓒ fault
     ⓑ restaraunt   ⓓ spoiled

17.   ⓐ roylty   ⓒ swallowed
     ⓑ freedom   ⓓ audience

18.   ⓐ breaze   ⓒ drawings
     ⓑ brief   ⓓ soybean

19.   ⓐ chowder   ⓒ awkword
     ⓑ glued   ⓓ gnaw

20.   ⓐ believe   ⓒ died
     ⓑ broght   ⓓ sparrows

4 TAKE IT HOME

Your child has learned to spell many new words and would enjoy sharing them with you and your family. These activity ideas can make sharing the words in Lessons 19–23 fun for the whole family.

Sound Bites!

Here's a "tasteful" idea! Help your child listen for and use spelling words during dinner time conversations. It's a sure-fire recipe for spelling success! Start things off by using a word that interests you. (For example, "I remember the first time I met our new *neighbors*.") What words hold special meanings or memories for your child? Encourage your child to use and jot down those words.

Spell-and-Step

Which words in the box complete this word ladder? Afterward, you might enjoy using some of the leftover words to build a ladder of your own.

shower	roasted	eastern	deceive	neighbor
diet	hoed	noises	awkward	employ
sleigh	hours	eighteen	shriek	approach
amount	receipt	dawn	disloyal	eagle

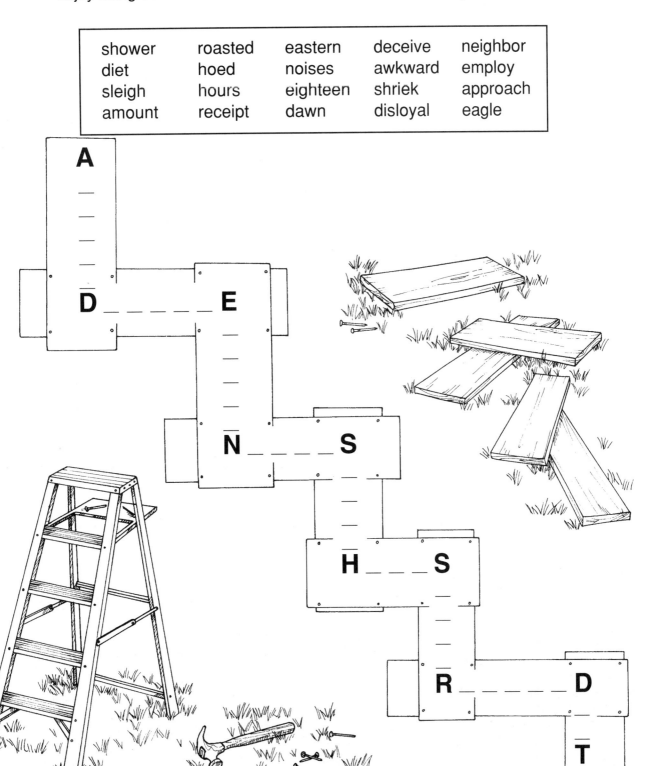

A _ _ _ _ _

D _ _ _ _ _ _ E

N _ _ _ _ _ S

H _ _ _ _ S

R _ _ _ _ _ _ D

T

Lesson 25

Objective
To spell regular plural nouns

Correlated Phonics Lesson
MCP Phonics, Level D, Lesson 56

Warm Up   *Page 101*
Invite students to read the selection to find out how to keep a bicycle in tip-top shape. Afterward, ask them to share their favorite bicycle-care tips.

Encourage students to look back at the boldfaced words. Have volunteers say each word and identify the letter or letters added to make the plural.

On Your Mark/Warm Up Test
1. Are the **axes** sharp enough to cut the trees?
2. The company's **bosses** work on Saturdays.
3. Nicole wears gold **chains** around her neck.
4. Bryant bought a new pair of jogging **shoes.**
5. Grandma signed her letter, "Hugs and **kisses."**
6. Lisa used two different **waxes** to polish her car.
7. Three **foxes** headed toward the chicken coop.
8. Your **splashes** are getting us wet.
9. Don't leave a campfire until the **ashes** are cold.
10. We heard several loud **crashes** of thunder.
11. Keep **matches** away from young children.
12. I usually eat two **sandwiches** for lunch.
13. The dentist gave us all new **toothbrushes.**
14. My brother has blond hair and dark **eyelashes.**
15. The Girl Scouts wear badges on green **sashes.**
16. Have they finished digging the drainage **ditches?**
17. The **flashes** of lightning scared me!
18. New England has many picturesque **churches.**
19. Two long **paces** cover about six feet.
20. The song includes many **clashes** of the cymbals.

Pep Talk/Game Plan   *Pages 102–103*
Introduce the spelling rule and invite students to read the List Words aloud. Encourage students to look back at their Warm Up Tests and apply the spelling rule to any misspelled words.

As students work through the **Spelling Lineup, Classification,** and **Definitions** exercises, remind them to look back at their List Words or in their dictionaries if they need help. If students do not understand the pun in the **Definitions** exercise, explain the two meanings of *spoke:* "part of a bicycle wheel" and the past tense of *speak.*

 See **Comparing/Contrasting,** page 15

Plurals

Warm Up
How do you keep a bike in tip-top shape?

Clean Machine
You have to work hard to keep a bike in tip-top shape. The best time to care for a bike is before anything goes wrong. Wash your bike with soap and water and dry it with towels. Pay attention to the reflectors. The cleaner they are, the easier they are for a driver of a car to see. To protect the shine, apply a coat of car wax. Some **waxes** can be applied in the sun.

To keep your bike safe, keep its chain in good condition. Old **toothbrushes** are great for removing grime. Oil the chain with bike chain oil. Don't use too much oil! Oily **chains** become gummy and collect dirt. If your bike has hand brakes, check each brake shoe. These are the rubber pads that grip the tires. Use rubbing alcohol to wipe the **shoes** clean. Make sure the brakes work well too, so you won't ride into any **ditches** and can avoid **crashes.**

Once your bike is in good working order, take it out for a test run.

 Look back at the boldfaced words. What letter or letters are added to each word to make it plural?

On Your Mark
Take your Warm Up Test. Then check your spelling with the List Words on the next page.

101

Pep Talk
You make most singular words plural by adding just **s** to the singular form.
shoe + **s** = shoes
If a singular word ends in **x, ss, sh,** or **ch,** you usually add **es** to make it mean more than one.
fox + **es** = foxes

Game Plan
Spelling Lineup
Finish spelling each List Word.

LIST WORDS
1. axes
2. chains
3. bosses
4. shoes
5. kisses
6. waxes
7. foxes
8. splashes
9. ashes
10. crashes
11. matches
12. sandwiches
13. toothbrushes
14. eyelashes
15. sashes
16. ditches
17. flashes
18. churches
19. paces
20. clashes

1. __kisses__
2. __ashes__
3. __waxes__
4. __axes__
5. __ditches__
6. __chains__
7. __matches__
8. __sashes__
9. __shoes__
10. __sand__wiches
11. __tooth__brushes
12. __crashes__
13. __bosses__
14. __flashes__
15. __eye__lashes
16. __foxes__
17. __paces__
18. __churches__
19. __clashes__
20. __splashes__

102   Lesson 25 ■ Plurals

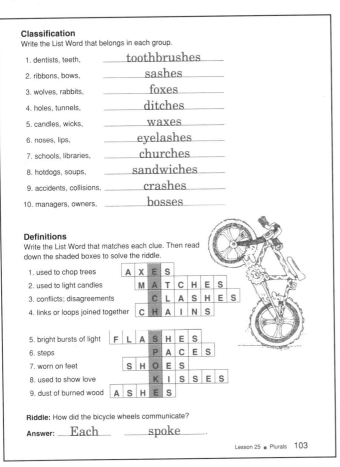

Classification
Write the List Word that belongs in each group.

1. dentists, teeth, **toothbrushes**
2. ribbons, bows, **sashes**
3. wolves, rabbits, **foxes**
4. holes, tunnels, **ditches**
5. candles, wicks, **waxes**
6. noses, lips, **eyelashes**
7. schools, libraries, **churches**
8. hotdogs, soups, **sandwiches**
9. accidents, collisions, **crashes**
10. managers, owners, **bosses**

Definitions
Write the List Word that matches each clue. Then read down the shaded boxes to solve the riddle.

1. used to chop trees — A X E S
2. used to light candles — M A T C H E S
3. conflicts; disagreements — C L A S H E S
4. links or loops joined together — C H A I N S
5. bright bursts of light — F L A S H E S
6. steps — P A C E S
7. worn on feet — S H O E S
8. used to show love — K I S S E S
9. dust of burned wood — A S H E S

Riddle: How did the bicycle wheels communicate?

Answer: Each _____ spoke _____.

Lesson 25 ■ Plurals 103

Flex Your Spelling Muscles

Writing

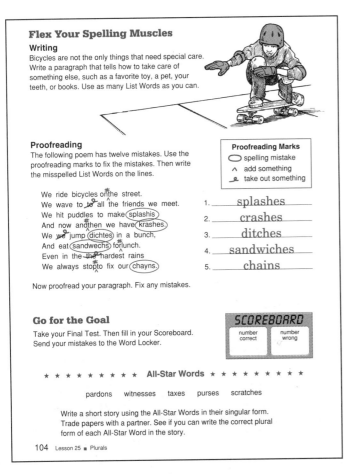

Bicycles are not the only things that need special care. Write a paragraph that tells how to take care of something else, such as a favorite toy, a pet, your teeth, or books. Use as many List Words as you can.

Proofreading
The following poem has twelve mistakes. Use the proofreading marks to fix the mistakes. Then write the misspelled List Words on the lines.

Proofreading Marks
◯ spelling mistake
∧ add something
⌲ take out something

We ride bicycles on the street.
We wave to to all the friends we meet.
We hit puddles to make ⟨splashis⟩
And now and then we have ⟨krashes.⟩
We we jump ⟨dichtes⟩ in a bunch,
And eat ⟨sandwechs⟩ for lunch.
Even in the the hardest rains
We always stop to fix our ⟨chayns.⟩

1. _____ splashes _____
2. _____ crashes _____
3. _____ ditches _____
4. _____ sandwiches _____
5. _____ chains _____

Now proofread your paragraph. Fix any mistakes.

Go for the Goal
Take your Final Test. Then fill in your Scoreboard. Send your mistakes to the Word Locker.

SCOREBOARD

number correct	number wrong

★ ★ ★ ★ ★ ★ ★ ★ **All-Star Words** ★ ★ ★ ★ ★ ★ ★ ★

pardons   witnesses   taxes   purses   scratches

Write a short story using the All-Star Words in their singular form. Trade papers with a partner. See if you can write the correct plural form of each All-Star Word in the story.

104 Lesson 25 ■ Plurals

Spelling Strategy
Write these List Words on the board: *chain, wax, kiss, clash, shoe,* and *ditch.* Call on volunteers to come to the board and
- circle the letter or letter pair at the end of each word
- say each word aloud in the singular and the plural, emphasizing the plural ending
- make the word plural by adding *s* or *es.*

Help the class conclude that most singular words add *s* to make the plural, unless the word ends in *x, ss, sh,* or *ch,* in which case *es* is added.

Flex Your Spelling Muscles   Page 104
As students complete the **Writing** activity, encourage them to brainstorm ideas, write a first draft, revise, and proofread their work. The **Proofreading** exercise will help them prepare to proofread their paragraphs. To publish their writing, students may want to make a class book titled "Taking Care of Something Special."

✍ Writer's Corner
Students might enjoy watching *Bicycle Safety and General Maintenance,* which can be purchased from Champions on Film and Video (800–521–2832). Invite them to make posters summarizing what they learned.

Go for the Goal/Final Test
1. My *shoes* gave me terrible blisters!
2. The two *crashes* you heard were falling branches.
3. *Ditches* by the side of the road drain off water.
4. That pink pillow *clashes* with the orange chair.
5. Mr. Espinosa sharpens knives and *axes.*
6. Where does the family of *foxes* have its den?
7. Did you also paint the window *sashes?*
8. Mom *kisses* me goodbye every morning.
9. There are two red *toothbrushes* in the bathroom.
10. The horse's *paces* are very smooth.
11. Those *chains* keep the gate to the pen shut.
12. You can smell the old *ashes* in the fireplace.
13. Some *waxes* are self-polishing.
14. My mother's last two *bosses* praised her work.
15. Your *splashes* have made the floor wet.
16. Use long wooden *matches* to light the stove.
17. A camel's *eyelashes* protect its eyes from sand?
18. Those *flashes* are light from the airport beacon.
19. Do you want tuna fish or ham *sandwiches.*
20. Not all *churches* have tall steeples.

Remind students to complete the Scoreboard and write any misspelled words in their Word Locker.

★★ All-Star Words
You may want to point out that the All-Star Words follow the spelling rule and help students brainstorm story ideas.

83

Lesson 26

Objective
To spell plural nouns that end with *y*

Correlated Phonics Lesson
MCP Phonics, Level D, Lesson 56

Warm Up   *Page 105*
In this selection, students discover when it's okay to "pig out." After reading, ask students how they would like to celebrate National Pig Day.

Encourage students to look back at the boldfaced words. Ask volunteers to say each word, identify the final letter in the singular form, and tell how the plural is spelled.

On Your Mark/Warm Up Test
1. Most school *holidays* fall on Mondays.
2. On graduation day, we went to several *parties.*
3. Maricella likes to read mystery *stories.*
4. They covered the food to keep the *flies* off it.
5. They have *birthdays* on the same day.
6. Please make ten *copies* of this letter.
7. What are the class secretary's *duties?*
8. Several *ladies* are visiting my mother.
9. Each state is divided into several *counties.*
10. Have astronauts explored the moon's *valleys?*
11. Kevin helped his mother unpack *groceries.*
12. Are your *hobbies* stamp collecting and skiing?
13. The *libraries* need more money to buy books.
14. Work crews repaired the state's *highways.*
15. This flashlight needs new *batteries.*
16. There were no *injuries* from the car accident.
17. What a fancy dessert *cherries* jubilee is!
18. Some *melodies* are easy to remember.
19. Our company conducts *surveys* for stores.
20. We visited *communities* hurt by the storm.

Pep Talk/Game Plan   *Pages 106–107*
Introduce the spelling rule and have students read the List Words aloud. You may also want to ask students to spell the singular form of each word and explain how the plural is formed. Then encourage students to look back at their Warm Up Tests and apply the spelling rule to any misspelled words.

As students work through the **Spelling Lineup,** **Rhyming,** and **Classification** exercises, remind them to look back at their List Words or in their dictionaries if they need help.

 See **Change or No Change,** page 15

84

Plurals of Words That End in y   LESSON 26

Warm Up
When is it okay to "pig out?"

Pig Out
Most of the time, "pigging out" is considered bad manners and unhealthy. There is one day a year, however, when not pigging out is impolite. That day is March 1, National Pig Day.

Most **holidays** were begun to recall historic events. This one, though, was begun by two sisters from Texas who happened to love pigs. When these girls were very young, they had read many children's **stories** about pigs and piglets. For **birthdays,** they exchanged such gifts as glass piggybanks. **Stories** of their pig-presents spread. Soon, friends, families, and neighboring **communities** began to share in the celebration. Their pig **parties** got larger and larger. Finally, the sisters were able to have their Pig Day registered as a real holiday.

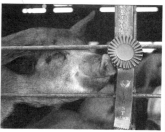

Today, the holiday is celebrated by pig lovers everywhere. Some people bake pig-shaped cookies or cakes. Others have piggyback races or play pig-tail. That's a game in which each player races to braid a piece of rope. You may even want to think of a special way to celebrate National Pig Day.

The singular form of each boldfaced word in the selection ends with the same letter. Which letter is it? How are the plurals spelled?

On Your Mark
Take your Warm Up Test. Then check your spelling with the List Words on the next page.

Pep Talk
If a word ends in **y** preceded by a vowel, add **s** to make the plural.

holiday + **s** = holidays

If a word ends in **y** preceded by a consonant, change **y** to **i** and add **es.**

copy + **es** = copies

Game Plan
Spelling Lineup
Complete each List Word by writing **y** and adding **s** to make the plural or by changing the **y** to **i** and adding **es** to make the plural.

LIST WORDS
1. holidays
2. parties
3. stories
4. flies
5. birthdays
6. copies
7. duties
8. ladies
9. counties
10. valleys
11. groceries
12. hobbies
13. libraries
14. highways
15. batteries
16. injuries
17. cherries
18. melodies
19. surveys
20. communities

1. groceries
2. flies
3. stories
4. duties
5. highways
6. copies
7. birthdays
8. hobbies
9. batteries
10. valleys
11. holidays
12. parties
13. injuries
14. surveys
15. melodies
16. communities
17. cherries
18. ladies
19. counties
20. libraries

Rhyming

Write the plural List Word whose singular form rhymes with the word given.

1. lobby ___hobbies___ 4. fruity ___duties___
2. byway ___highways___ 5. shy ___flies___
3. rally ___valleys___ 6. sloppy ___copies___

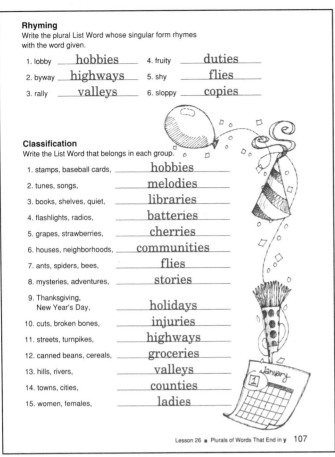

Classification

Write the List Word that belongs in each group.

1. stamps, baseball cards, ___hobbies___
2. tunes, songs, ___melodies___
3. books, shelves, quiet, ___libraries___
4. flashlights, radios, ___batteries___
5. grapes, strawberries, ___cherries___
6. houses, neighborhoods, ___communities___
7. ants, spiders, bees, ___flies___
8. mysteries, adventures, ___stories___
9. Thanksgiving, New Year's Day, ___holidays___
10. cuts, broken bones, ___injuries___
11. streets, turnpikes, ___highways___
12. canned beans, cereals, ___groceries___
13. hills, rivers, ___valleys___
14. towns, cities, ___counties___
15. women, females, ___ladies___

Flex Your Spelling Muscles

Writing

What event or day do you think should be celebrated? Use the List Words to write a paragraph to convince people that your holiday is important.

Proofreading

The article below has eleven mistakes. Use the proofreading marks to fix the mistakes. Then write the misspelled List Words on the lines.

> you've probably read or heard a lot of (storys) about pigs. Did any of them suggest having a pig as a pet? Although pigs are often thought to be filthy and dumb, (survays) have shown that they can be smart and clean. people in many (communitees) have even been able to teach their pet pigs to do tricks. The squeals of these pigs are (melodeys) to pig lovers everywhere and their (birthdais) are big (partees). now that you know more about pigs, would you like a pet pig?

Proofreading Marks
- ◯ spelling mistake
- ≡ capital letter
- ^ add something

1. ___stories___
2. ___surveys___
3. ___communities___
4. ___melodies___
5. ___birthdays___
6. ___parties___

Now proofread your paragraph. Fix any mistakes.

Go for the Goal

Take your Final Test. Then fill in your Scoreboard. Send your mistakes to the Word Locker.

SCOREBOARD
number correct	number wrong

★ ★ ★ ★ ★ ★ ★ ★ **All-Star Words** ★ ★ ★ ★ ★ ★ ★ ★

grizzlies   universities   deliveries   convoys   essays

Write a sentence for each word, but leave a blank for the All-Star Word that completes the sentence. Trade papers with your partner. Write the correct word in each sentence.

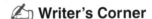

Spelling Strategy   Write these singular forms of List Words on the board: *fly, valley, hobby, highway, injury,* and *community.* With a partner, have students take turns spelling the plural of each word and explaining the rule to form the plural. Encourage students to think of other words that end with *y* and to form their plurals.

Flex Your Spelling Muscles   *Page 108*

As students complete the **Writing** activity, encourage them to brainstorm ideas, write a first draft, revise, and proofread their work. The **Proofreading** exercise will help them prepare to proofread their paragraphs. To publish their writing, students may want to
- create a flyer announcing their holidays
- combine their paragraphs into a booklet titled "Holiday Happenings."

✍ Writer's Corner

> Students can learn more about National Pig Day by writing to Ellen Stanley, 7006 Miami, Lubbock, TX 79413. Enclose a self-addressed stamped envelope.

Go for the Goal/Final Test

1. Ripe, sweet **cherries** are my favorite fruit.
2. I visited three **libraries** looking for that book.
3. **Flies** buzzed around my head as I tried to eat.
4. Do your relatives come to visit on **holidays?**
5. Two **communities** reported much flood damage.
6. This radio uses four *C* **batteries.**
7. **Ladies** and gentlemen, let's welcome our guest!
8. My **hobbies** are fishing and stamp collecting.
9. James carried the **groceries** to the car.
10. We flew over rivers and **valleys** on our way home.
11. Suffolk and Essex **counties** are in Massachusetts.
12. The musician signed both **copies** of the contract.
13. Do your new **duties** include filing?
14. Whose **birthdays** are national holidays?
15. Mother told us **stories** of her childhood.
16. The results of **surveys** are not always accurate.
17. She quit the game because of her **injuries.**
18. Some teenagers play loud music at their **parties.**
19. The **highways** were crowded with vacationers.
20. Some **melodies** remind me of my old friends.

Remind students to complete the Scoreboard and write any misspelled words in their Word Locker.

★★ **All-Star Words**   You may want to point out that the All-Star Words follow the spelling rule and review how to write a cloze sentence.

Lesson 27

Objective
To spell plural forms of irregular nouns and regular nouns that end in *f* or *fe*

Correlated Phonics Lessons
MCP Phonics, Level D, Lessons 57–58

Warm Up   **Page 109**
In "Smile!," students find out what they should do to keep their teeth healthy. Ask students which of the dental rules discussed in the selection they follow.

Have volunteers say each boldfaced word and identify its singular form.

On Your Mark/Warm Up Test
1. You must brush your **teeth** every day!
2. The **mice** were afraid of the cat.
3. How many **women** work in that hospital?
4. Please put the **knives** in the drawer.
5. Let's rake the **leaves** today.
6. Cut the apples into **halves.**
7. Will we need more than two **loaves** of bread?
8. We studied the **lives** of famous inventors.
9. We saw two baby **calves** in the field.
10. What enormous animals **moose** are!
11. The farmer has a large flock of **sheep.**
12. Pioneers often used **oxen** to move heavy loads.
13. Help **yourselves** to some crackers and cheese.
14. **Geese** lay larger eggs than chickens do.
15. How did the Cheyenne choose their **chiefs?**
16. **Buffaloes** used to roam across the prairies.
17. Have paper tissues replaced **handkerchiefs?**
18. They wore **scarves** to keep their necks warm.
19. Horses wear metal shoes to protect their **hoofs.**
20. Did you see any **bison** or other large animals?

Pep Talk/Game Plan   **Pages 110–111**
Introduce the spelling rule and have students read the List Words aloud, discussing the pluralization process for each word. (Please note that *hooves* is also an acceptable plural spelling of *hoof.*) Then encourage students to look back at their Warm Up Tests and apply the spelling rule to any misspelled words.

As students work through the **Spelling Lineup, Comparing Words,** and **Vocabulary** exercises, remind them to look back at their List Words or in their dictionaries if they need help. For the **Comparing Words** exercise, you can use this sentence to review analogies: *Sock is to foot as glove is to hand.*

 See **Picture Clues,** page 15

86

Name _____

Irregular Plurals: Plurals of Words That End in *f* or *fe*   LESSON 27

Warm Up
How can you help keep your teeth healthy?

Smile!
Babies are usually born without **teeth.** By the time children are about three years old, they have 28 teeth. One by one, these fall out and are replaced by 32 adult teeth. These should last people all their **lives.** Over half of the men and **women** in this country, however, lose some of their teeth because they haven't taken good care of them. Take care of **yourselves!** Follow these dental health rules today to give you a better chance of having your teeth tomorrow.
- Brush after meals.
- Drink lots of water.
- Use dental floss. Floss is a specially made string that helps remove food from between teeth.
- Avoid sugar, especially the kind that comes in cookies, in caramel, and in sugar-coated cereals.
- Visit your dentist regularly.

 Look back at the boldfaced words. Notice that all the words are plurals. What is the singular form of each word?

On Your Mark
Take your Warm Up Test. Then check your spelling with the List Words on the next page.

109

LIST WORDS

1. *teeth*
2. *mice*
3. *women*
4. *knives*
5. *leaves*
6. *halves*
7. *loaves*
8. *lives*
9. *calves*
10. *moose*
11. *sheep*
12. *oxen*
13. *yourselves*
14. *geese*
15. *chiefs*
16. *buffaloes*
17. *handkerchiefs*
18. *scarves*
19. *hoofs*
20. *bison*

Pep Talk
Most words ending in **f/fe** change the **f/fe** to **v** and add **es** to make plurals.
    calf—calves   knife—knives
A few words ending in **f** just add **s.**
    chief—chiefs   hoof—hoofs
Words ending in **o** add **s** or **es.**
    buffalo—buffaloes
Irregular plurals change their spelling or stay the same.
    mouse—mice   sheep—sheep

Game Plan
Spelling Lineup
Write the List Word that is the plural form of each word given.

1. hoof   hoofs   13. moose   moose
2. knife   knives   14. mouse   mice
3. sheep   sheep   15. loaf   loaves
4. chief   chiefs   16. goose   geese
5. ox   oxen   17. scarf   scarves
6. half   halves   18. tooth   teeth
7. bison   bison   19. calf   calves
8. leaf   leaves   20. woman   women
9. life   lives
10. handkerchief   handkerchiefs
11. buffalo   buffaloes
12. yourself   yourselves

110   Lesson 27 ■ Irregular Plurals: Plurals of Words That End in *f* or *fe*

Comparing Words

The first two underlined words in each sentence are related. Write a List Word that has the same relationship to the third underlined word.

1. Snow is to shovel as _____leaves_____ are to rake.
2. Feet are to people as _____hoofs_____ are to horses.
3. Patties are to hamburgers as _____loaves_____ are to bread.
4. Walk is to legs as chew is to _____teeth_____ .
5. Men are to boys as _____women_____ are to girls.
6. Scissors are to paper as _____knives_____ are to meat.
7. Calf is to calves as life is to _____lives_____ .
8. Belts are to waists as _____scarves_____ are to necks.
9. Hay is to horses as cheese is to _____mice_____ .
10. Puppies are to dogs as lambs are to _____sheep_____ .

Vocabulary

Write the List Word that matches each clue.

1. leaders of a group — chiefs
2. two parts of a whole — halves
3. birds that fly south in winter — geese
4. pieces of cloth used to blow your nose — handkerchiefs
5. the plural of yourself — yourselves
6. baby cows — calves

Flex Your Spelling Muscles

Writing

How do you feel about going to the dentist? Use the List Words to write a paragraph sharing your feelings.

Proofreading

This informational article has nine mistakes. Use the proofreading marks to fix the mistakes. Then write the misspelled List Words on the lines.

Proofreading Marks
◯ spelling mistake
∧ add something

Look at the teeth of people, dogs, sheep, and other animals. They differ because they chew different kinds of food. Sheep, (oxin,) (bisen,) (buffalows) and (mooses) have flat teeth for eating twigs, (leavss) grass, and hay. Dogs, cats, and tigers have sharp teeth for eating meat. People have both kinds of teeth. Sharks, whose teeth are as sharp as (knifes,) never run out of teeth because new ones grow in place of lost teeth.

1. _____oxen_____
2. _____bison_____
3. _____buffaloes_____
4. _____moose_____
5. _____leaves_____
6. _____knives_____

Now proofread your paragraph. Fix any mistakes.

Go for the Goal

Take your Final Test. Then fill in your Scoreboard. Send your mistakes to the Word Locker.

SCOREBOARD
number correct	number wrong

★ ★ ★ ★ ★ ★ ★ ★ **All-Star Words** ★ ★ ★ ★ ★ ★ ★ ★

beliefs   wives   patios   broccoli   deer

Use the All-Star Words to create a crossword puzzle. Then write a clue for each word. Swap papers with a partner. Can you fill in the puzzle with the correct All-Star Words?

◎ **Spelling Strategy**   Write *singular* and *plural* on the board at the top of two columns. Then write the singular form of *teeth* in the appropriate column. Ask a volunteer to come to the board, write the plural form of *tooth,* and explain the rule that applies to the pluralization process. Follow this procedure with the remainder of the List Words, helping students explain the rules as necessary.

Flex Your Spelling Muscles   *Page 112*

As students complete the **Writing** activity, encourage them to brainstorm ideas, write a first draft, revise, and proofread their work. The **Proofreading** exercise will help them prepare to proofread their paragraphs. To publish their writing, students may want to make a bulletin-board display titled "A Visit to the Dentist."

✍ Writer's Corner

> The class might enjoy watching a video about tooth care, such as *Teeth—Some Facts to Chew On,* distributed by Centron Films (800–621–2131). Invite students to use the information they learned to create a tooth-care poster to hang in the nurse's or doctor's office at your school.

Go for the Goal/Final Test

1. The hot *loaves* of bread burned my hands!
2. Men and *women* filled the audience.
3. Out in the meadow, the *sheep* grazed.
4. Horses wear iron shoes on their *hoofs.*
5. Were all of the Iroquois *chiefs* at the meeting?
6. *Buffaloes* have shaggy brown fur.
7. *Bison* roamed the plains.
8. *Oxen* are much larger than ordinary cows.
9. Did you put out *knives* as well as forks?
10. The *lives* of the early settlers are inspiring.
11. A large flock of *geese* flew over my house.
12. In what states are *moose* found?
13. These woolen *scarves* are soft and thick.
14. There are two *halves* in a whole.
15. The hungry *mice* nibbled the cheese.
16. The dentist cleaned my *teeth.*
17. Maple *leaves* have three points on them.
18. Mother cows take good care of their *calves.*
19. Can you finish the assignment by *yourselves?*
20. Do you sell *handkerchiefs* to match these ties?

Remind students to complete the Scoreboard and write any misspelled words in their Word Locker.

★★ **All-Star Words**   You may want to point out that the All-Star Words follow the spelling rule. Suggest that students create their puzzles by first arranging the All-Star Words, then drawing the puzzle squares to match that arrangement.

Lesson 28

Objective
To spell singular possessive nouns and contractions

Correlated Phonics Lessons
MCP Phonics, Level D, Lessons 59, 61

Warm Up   *Page 113*
In this selection, students find out what a "geoglyph" is and the best way to view one. After reading, you might ask, "If Native Americans created these drawings, why do you think they did so?"

Encourage students to look back at the boldfaced words. Ask volunteers to say each word and tell whether it is a possessive or a contraction.

On Your Mark/Warm Up Test
1. Lupe said **she'll** call if she's going to be late.
2. I **wouldn't** have gone if I'd still had my cold.
3. I hope **they'll** arrive on time.
4. **How's** the state going to get more tax money?
5. After the movie, **let's** go out for a pizza.
6. Christian asked, "**Where's** my baseball glove?"
7. If **we're** going to the show, we'd better leave.
8. Did you read about that **desert's** wildlife?
9. Each **person's** seat at the concert is reserved.
10. My **sister's** class took a trip to the museum.
11. She painted the **bicycle's** frame a bright blue.
12. **Arizona's** capital city is Phoenix.
13. The **child's** desk held his books and pencils.
14. Did you work in your **aunt's** store this summer?
15. My **cousin's** new painting is terrific!
16. **Florida's** coast has wonderful seashells.
17. I'll get to ride on my **uncle's** tractor.
18. Where is the **doctor's** telephone number?
19. Our apple tree **hasn't** blossomed yet.
20. What are each **season's** characteristics?

Pep Talk/Game Plan   *Pages 114–115*
Introduce the spelling rule and invite students to read the List Words aloud, discussing the placement and use of the apostrophe in each word. Then encourage students to look back at their Warm Up Tests and apply the spelling rule to any misspelled words.

As students work through the **Spelling Lineup, Vocabulary,** and **Puzzle** exercises, remind them to look back at their List Words or in their dictionaries if they need help.

 See **Questions/Answers,** page 15

Possessives and Contractions
LESSON 28

Warm Up
What is a geoglyph?

Grand Designs
If you ever fly over **Arizona's** deserts, look down. You may see block-long carvings of a rattlesnake or any of a dozen other designs. These carvings cover many flat areas between the Colorado River and Mexico. **They'll** be easier to figure out from above, in a plane. Some show horses, pumas, lizards, or people. Some carvings look more like doodles—just swirls and squares. **Wouldn't** you like to know who made these grand designs on the **desert's** floor? Scientists don't know for sure. Yet more than 250 of them exist. They're called geoglyphs by the scientists. Some people think the 1,000-year-old geoglyphs are examples of ancient Native American art. Perhaps we'll never know for sure just where they came from or what they mean.

 Look back at the boldfaced words. Notice that each word has an apostrophe. Can you identify which words are possessives and which words are contractions?

On Your Mark
Take your Warm Up Test. Then check your spelling with the List Words on the next page.

113

Pep Talk
Use an apostrophe to show where letters have been left out in a contraction.
she will—she'll   how is—how's
Use an apostrophe and **s** to show singular ownership.
the bike of my uncle—my uncle's bike

LIST WORDS
1. she'll
2. wouldn't
3. they'll
4. how's
5. let's
6. where's
7. we're
8. desert's
9. person's
10. sister's
11. bicycle's
12. Arizona's
13. child's
14. aunt's
15. cousin's
16. Florida's
17. uncle's
18. doctor's
19. hasn't
20. season's

Game Plan
Spelling Lineup
Write the List Word that is a contraction for each pair of words given.

1. has not ____ hasn't
2. how is ____ how's
3. she will ____ she'll
4. we are ____ we're
5. would not ____ wouldn't
6. where is ____ where's
7. they will ____ they'll
8. let us ____ let's

we are
we're

Write the List Words that show ownership.

9. desert's   15. aunt's
10. person's   16. cousin's
11. sister's   17. Florida's
12. bicycle's   18. uncle's
13. Arizona's   19. doctor's
14. child's   20. season's

114   Lesson 28 ■ Possessives and Contractions

88

Vocabulary

Write the List Word that goes with the underlined phrase in each sentence.

1. The hat that the child owns is pretty. — child's
2. The clothes of my sister are too big for me. — sister's
3. The house of my aunt is painted yellow. — aunt's
4. I know they will enjoy meeting you. — they'll
5. The nickname of Arizona is the Grand Canyon State. — Arizona's
6. Let us see if we can find some orange juice. — Let's
7. The newspaper has not arrived yet. — hasn't
8. I can't remember the name of the person. — person's
9. The office belonging to the doctor is on Elm Street. — doctor's
10. Where is the new playground being built? — Where's
11. The 30,000 lakes Florida has are different sizes. — Florida's

Puzzle

Fill in the crossword puzzle by writing a List Word to answer each clue. The apostrophes have been filled in for you.

ACROSS
1. how is
4. belonging to a bicycle
5. we are
6. of the desert

DOWN
2. she will
3. of the uncle

Flex Your Spelling Muscles

Writing

Imagine that you've discovered how the designs in Arizona's deserts came to be. Share your ideas in a news report. Use as many List Words as you can.

Proofreading

This article has eleven mistakes. Use the proofreading marks to fix the mistakes. Then write the List Words correctly on the lines.

Proofreading Marks
- ⊍ add apostrophe
- ^ add something
- ≡ capital letter

Wouldnt you know it, arizona was a big surprise! I went to visit my cousins ranch near flagstaff. I asked, "Wheres the desert?" He said, "Below us. Flagstaff is too high for a desert climate. We're in forests where each seasons weather is different." What a beautiful place! It should be on every persons list of places to go. some people like Florida's palm trees. I, however, like Arizonas pine trees.

1. Wouldn't
2. cousin's
3. Where's
4. season's
5. person's
6. Arizona's

Now proofread your news report. Fix any mistakes.

Go for the Goal

Take your Final Test. Then fill in your Scoreboard. Send your mistakes to the Word Locker.

SCOREBOARD

| number correct | number wrong |

★ ★ ★ ★ ★ ★ ★ ★ **All-Star Words** ★ ★ ★ ★ ★ ★ ★ ★

doesn't   shouldn't   principal's   factory's   there's

Write a sentence for each All-Star Word, and then erase the apostrophe. Trade papers with a partner, and add the apostrophe to the words.

⊚ **Spelling Strategy** To help students understand that every contraction is a short way of writing two words, invite them to get together with a partner and
- listen carefully as you say each List Word that is a contraction
- write the two words that form the contraction
- circle the letter or letters that are left out when the contraction is formed
- write the contraction.

Flex Your Spelling Muscles   *Page 116*

As students complete the **Writing** activity, encourage them to brainstorm ideas, write a first draft, revise, and proofread their work. The **Proofreading** exercise will help them prepare to proofread their news reports. To publish their writing, students may want to
- use their reports to create an art newsletter
- read their reports as radio broadcasts.

✍ Writer's Corner

Students might enjoy reading more about Native Americans in books such as *The Pueblo* by Charlotte Yue. Encourage them to write a review of a book they enjoyed and to form a group to share their reviews.

Go for the Goal/Final Test

1. I know **they'll** be very happy to see you.
2. The **doctor's** waiting room was almost empty.
3. I don't know a single **person's** name at the party.
4. Do you like this **season's** fashions?
5. When Misako sees you, **she'll** remember you.
6. Is there a leak in your **bicycle's** rear tire?
7. **Let's** all split a giant pizza!
8. The weather **hasn't** been too bad this winter.
9. **Where's** the new pool going to be built?
10. Many people enjoy **Arizona's** dry climate.
11. I **wouldn't** do that if I were you!
12. My **aunt's** husband was born in Saigon.
13. My **uncle's** hobby is fixing up old cars.
14. **How's** your family's puppy doing?
15. The **desert's** temperature drops at night.
16. My **cousin's** cat is named Mittens.
17. I think **we're** taking a bus that comes later.
18. I used my **sister's** desk when she outgrew it.
19. The Everglades are one of **Florida's** attractions.
20. Is that a **child's** sleeping bag or an adult's?

Remind students to complete the Scoreboard and write any misspelled words in their Word Locker.

★★ **All-Star Words** You may want to point out that the All-Star Words follow the spelling rule and model erasing the apostrophe in a List Word and then putting it back.

Lesson 29

Objective
To spell plural possessive nouns

Correlated Phonics Lesson
MCP Phonics, Level D, Lesson 60

Warm Up   Page 117
In this selection, students learn about a sturdy fabric that has been popular for more than a century. After reading, invite students to discuss whether they think people will be wearing denim a hundred years from now.

Encourage students to look back at the boldfaced words. Have volunteers say each word and explain how the possessive is formed.

On Your Mark/Warm Up Test
1. All the ***passengers'*** tickets were stamped.
2. Both ***armies'*** supplies are running out.
3. The flood swept away two ***families'*** homes!
4. The police discovered the two ***thieves'*** loot.
5. All the ***ranches'*** workers went to the big picnic.
6. Some ***benches'*** slats were broken.
7. Do you know the two ***umpires'*** names?
8. All ***airlines'*** flight attendants took safety courses.
9. Both ***dresses'*** hemlines were too short.
10. All the ***hostesses'*** uniforms were red and white.
11. Do both ***banjos'*** strings have to be replaced?
12. The three upright ***pianos'*** keys needed cleaning.
13. Mr. Allen joined a ***men's*** touch football game.
14. I bought a gift in the ***children's*** department.
15. Are the ***bodies'*** shapes similar in both cars?
16. The ***daisies'*** stems are quite strong.
17. The ***televisions'*** screens are all the same size.
18. The ***members'*** cars are parked in the big lot.
19. Did both ***governments'*** leaders speak English?
20. All the ***businesses'*** reports are being mailed.

Pep Talk/Game Plan   Pages 118–119
Introduce the spelling rule and have students read the List Words aloud. Encourage students to look back at their Warm Up Tests and apply the spelling rule to any misspelled words.

As students work through the **Spelling Lineup, Vocabulary,** and **Possessives** exercises, remind them to look back at their List Words or in their dictionaries if they need help.

 See **Words in Context,** page 14

Plurals and Plural Possessives
LESSON 29

Warm Up
What fabric never goes out of style?

Durable Denim
There is a kind of fabric that never goes out of style, and almost everyone has worn it at least once. Some people wear it every day. It's denim. This sturdy cloth has been meeting **families'** clothing needs for more than one hundred years.

In 1873, when Levi Strauss began making **men's** work clothes for miners, he needed a fabric that would be strong, and yet comfortable to wear. Cotton denim was the answer. It was a basic durable fabric that looked good.

Jeans, which are made of denim, have become an almost necessary piece of everyday clothing today. Denim is used not only for men's clothing, but women's clothing and **children's** clothing as well. Levi Strauss probably had no idea that after a century, denim would be the center of his **businesses'** success.

You might think that denim is strictly American, but the word *denim* comes from French. Weavers in Nîmes, a city in France, created this sturdy twilled cloth, woven so that the cloth's ribs were diagonal and parallel. This made the cloth strong, but flexible. The name *denim* comes from the twilled cloth of Nîmes, or as the French say *de Nîmes*. Somehow over time, the "de" and "Nîmes" were blended together to form the word *denim*.

 Look back at the boldfaced words. Notice that all the words are plural. How is the possessive of each word formed?

On Your Mark
Take your Warm Up Test. Then check your spelling with the List Words on the next page.

Pep Talk
Form the possessive of a plural ending in **s** by adding just an apostrophe, as in armies—armies'.
If the plural does not end in **s**, form its possessive by adding an apostrophe and **s**, as in men—men's.

Game Plan
Spelling Lineup
Write each List Word that was formed by adding an apostrophe and **s** to a plural word.

1. ___men's___   2. ___children's___

Write each List Word that was formed by adding just an apostrophe to a plural word.

3. ___dresses'___   15. ___bodies'___
4. ___armies'___   16. ___daisies'___
5. ___families'___   17. ___pianos'___
6. ___thieves'___   18. ___members'___
7. ___ranches'___   19. ___hostesses'___
8. ___benches'___   20. ___banjos'___
9. ___umpires'___
10. ___airlines'___
11. ___passengers'___
12. ___governments'___
13. ___businesses'___
14. ___televisions'___

LIST WORDS
1. passengers
2. armies
3. families
4. thieves
5. ranches
6. benches
7. umpires
8. airlines
9. dresses
10. hostesses
11. banjos
12. pianos
13. men's
14. children's
15. bodies
16. daisies
17. televisions
18. members
19. governments
20. businesses

90

Vocabulary

Write the List Word that best completes each sentence.

1. The cattle of the ranches are the __ranches'__ cattle.
2. The strings of the banjos are the __banjos'__ strings.
3. The barracks of the armies are the __armies'__ barracks.
4. The uniforms of the hostesses are the __hostesses'__ uniforms.
5. The parts of our bodies are our __bodies'__ parts.
6. The families of the passengers are the __passengers'__ families.
7. The pictures on the televisions are the __televisions'__ pictures.
8. The keys of the pianos are the __pianos'__ keys.
9. The paint of the benches is the __benches'__ paint.
10. The prices of the dresses are the __dresses'__ prices.
11. The stems of the daisies are the __daisies'__ stems.

Possessives

Circle the word in each pair of sentences that needs an apostrophe. Then write the word correctly.

1. The airlines have friendly attendants.
   Those (airlines) attendants have a lot of experience. __airlines'__
2. The decisions of the umpires are final.
   The (umpires) uniforms protect them from injury. __umpires'__
3. The businesses need more workers.
   The (businesses) workers put in long hours. __businesses'__
4. The (members) dues are paid every month.
   The club's members will all vote in the election. __members'__

Lesson 29 ■ Plurals and Plural Possessives   119

Flex Your Spelling Muscles

Writing

Imagine you are having a fashion show to exhibit the latest denim clothing. Use the List Words to write an ad telling people what you're showing.

Proofreading

Find the eleven mistakes in the article below. Use the proofreading marks to fix the mistakes. Then write the List Words correctly on the lines.

Proofreading Marks
- ⌄ add apostrophe
- ^ add something
- / make small letter

Thousands of years ago, Ønly the Chinese knew that silkworms spin the silk threads needed for making silk fabric. For a longtime, Several governments officials guarded thesecret. When other countries discovered this wonderful cloth, they wanted to make it themselves. Soon some traders discovered how to sneak silkworms out of China. The thieves idea was to carry the creatures out inthe hollows of bamboo canes. The idea worked! Soon other countries could Make silk fabric and produce mens, women's, and childrens clothing. Many families wardrobes could now include this fabric.

1. __governments'__
2. __thieves'__
3. __men's__
4. __children's__
5. __families'__

Now proofread your fashion ad. Fix any mistakes.

Go for the Goal

Take your Final Test. Then fill in your Scoreboard. Send your mistakes to the Word Locker.

SCOREBOARD

number correct	number wrong

★ ★ ★ ★ ★ ★ ★ ★ **All-Star Words** ★ ★ ★ ★ ★ ★ ★ ★

diaries'   fish's   classes'   spies'   species'

Work with your partner to write a short story, leaving blanks in place of the All-Star Words. Trade stories with other students. Write the All-Star Words in the appropriate places.

120   Lesson 29 ■ Plurals and Plural Possessives

◉ **Spelling Strategy** Write this sentence on the board, leaving out the apostrophes: *The hostesses speeches were interrupted by the mens songs.* Say the sentence aloud, circling the plurals as you do so. Then ask the class to use context to determine which of the plurals are plural possessives (*hostesses, mens*). Call on a volunteer to rewrite the sentence, adding the apostrophes. Ask students to think of other sentences that contain List Words and to write them on the board.

Flex Your Spelling Muscles   *Page 120*

As students complete the **Writing** activity, encourage them to brainstorm ideas, write a first draft, revise, and proofread their work. The **Proofreading** exercise will help them prepare to proofread their ads. To publish their writing, students may want to
• illustrate their ads
• use their ads to help them role-play a fashion show.

✍ Writer's Corner

The class can learn more about denim clothing by writing to Levi Strauss & Co., P.O. Box 7215, San Francisco, CA 94120. Encourage students to use the information they receive to help them design denim outfits for the 21st century.

Go for the Goal/Final Test

1. The **bodies'** temperatures were measured.
2. Many **daisies'** colors are yellow and white.
3. Are the **hostesses'** names on the work schedule?
4. All the **passengers'** seats had pillows on them.
5. The **businesses'** addresses are downtown.
6. Both **armies'** doctors worked day and night.
7. The two **banjos'** tuning pegs are the same.
8. Both **televisions'** antennas can be rotated.
9. All the **families'** homes are in the same village.
10. Both **pianos'** lids have been lowered.
11. Most **members'** names are in the guest book.
12. The police discovered the **thieves'** hiding places.
13. Both **governments'** laws were written years ago.
14. All the **ranches'** cattle brands are different.
15. The **men's** voices are much too loud!
16. Were all the **children's** permission slips signed?
17. Four **benches'** backs have to be repaired.
18. Did you compare the three **airlines'** prices?
19. Those **dresses'** colors are the most popular.
20. All the **umpires'** uniforms are black.

Remind students to complete the Scoreboard and write any misspelled words in their Word Locker.

★★ **All-Star Words** You may want to point out that the All-Star Words follow the spelling rule and help students brainstorm story ideas.

91

Lesson 30 • Instant Replay

Objective
To review spelling words that are plurals; plurals of words that end in *y*; irregular plurals: plurals of words that end in *f* or *fe*; possessives and contractions; plurals and plural possessives

Time Out   *Pages 121–124*
Check Your Word Locker Based on your observations, note which words are giving students the most difficulty and offer assistance for spelling them correctly. Here are some frequently misspelled words to watch for: *sandwiches, libraries, groceries, halves,* and *chiefs.*

To give students extra help and practice in taking standardized tests, you may want to have them take the Review Test for this lesson on pages 94–95. After scoring the tests, return them to students so that they can record their misspelled words in their Word Locker.

After practicing their troublesome words, students can work through the exercises for **Lessons 25–29.** Before they begin each exercise, you may want to go over the spelling rule.

 Take It Home Suggest that students and their families create a crossword puzzle using List Words in **Lessons 25–29.** For a complete list of the words, encourage students to take their *Spelling Workout* books home. Students can also use Take It Home Master 5 on pages 96–97 to help them do the activity. Encourage them to bring in their puzzles to share with the class.

Name_____

Time Out
Take another look at plurals, contractions, and possessives.

Check Your Word Locker
Look at the words in your Word Locker. Write your troublesome words for Lessons 25–29.

_____

Practice writing your troublesome words with a partner. Form the letters of each word using clay. Your partner can spell the word aloud as you form the letters.

 **Lesson 25**

Most plurals are formed by adding **s** to the singular form, as in <u>chains</u>. If a word ends in **x, ss, sh,** or **ch,** add **es** to form the plural, as in <u>foxes</u> and <u>bosses</u>.

List Words		Write a List Word to match each definition.
axes	1. bright bursts of light	flashes
waxes	2. cloths worn at waists	sashes
matches	3. sticks to light a fire	matches
sandwiches	4. hairs on eyelids	eyelashes
eyelashes	5. tools to chop wood	axes
sashes	6. holes in the ground	ditches
ditches	7. meals between bread	sandwiches
flashes	8. makes surfaces shiny	waxes
churches	9. places of worship	churches
paces	10. steps taken	paces

121

Lesson 26

If a word ends in **vowel-y**, add **s**, as in <u>valleys</u>. If it ends in **consonant-y**, change **y** to i and add **es**, as in <u>duties</u>.

List Words	Write a List Word to complete each sentence.
holidays	1. Libraries loan books.
flies	2. Flies are common insects.
groceries	3. School is closed on holidays.
libraries	4. Portable radios run on batteries.
batteries	5. I made a pie with fresh cherries.
injuries	6. Communities are made up of families.
cherries	7. Don sang three new melodies.
melodies	8. We were told to fill out surveys.
surveys	9. Helmets have prevented injuries.
communities	10. Those groceries will feed us for a week.

Lesson 27

If a word ends in **f** or **fe,** usually change the **f** or **fe** to **v** and add **es,** as in <u>scarves.</u> Some words change their vowel sound or spelling to make the plural form, as in <u>teeth.</u> Others have the same form for singular and plural, as in <u>bison.</u>

List Words	Write the List Words in alphabetical order.
mice	1. buffaloes
knives	2. halves
halves	3. hoofs
calves	4. knives
sheep	5. oxen 8. geese
oxen	6. calves 9. mice
geese	7. chiefs 10. sheep
chiefs	
buffaloes	
hoofs	

Lesson 28

Use apostrophes in contractions, as in where's and wouldn't. Singular possessives and those made from irregular plurals take 's, as in sister's and children's.

List Words

she'll
they'll
we're
bicycle's
Arizona's
cousin's
Florida's
uncle's
doctor's
hasn't

Write the List Word that is a part of each word given.

1. has _hasn't_
2. Arizona _Arizona's_
3. bicycle _bicycle's_
4. cousin _cousin's_
5. she _she'll_
6. Florida _Florida's_
7. we _we're_
8. uncle _uncle's_
9. doctor _doctor's_
10. they _they'll_

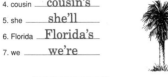

Lesson 29

Form the possessive of a plural word that ends in **s** by adding an apostrophe, as in dresses'.

List Words

passengers'
umpires'
airlines'
hostesses'
families'
banjos'
men's
children's
members'
businesses'

Circle the correct form of the List Word in each group. Then write the List Word on the line.

1. banjose' (banjos') _banjos'_
2. (businesses') business'es _businesses'_
3. mens' (men's) _men's_
4. hostes's (hostesses') _hostesses'_
5. umpirs' (umpires') _umpires'_
6. (members') membors' _members'_
7. (children's) childrens' _children's_
8. familie's (families') _families'_
9. (passengers') pasengers' _passengers'_
10. (airlines') airlineses' _airlines'_

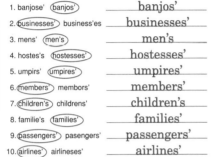

Lesson 30 ■ Instant Replay 123

Lessons 25–29

List Words

waxes
sandwiches
umpires'
communities
oxen
hostesses'
uncle's
doctor's

Write the List Word that matches each clue. Then read down the shaded boxes to solve the riddle.

1. lunch foods
2. belonging to sports figures
3. polishes
4. towns or cities
5. farm animals
6. belonging to a relative
7. belonging to a medical person
8. belonging to party givers

```
1 S A N D W I C H E S
2 U M P I R E S'
    3 W A X E S
4 C O M M U N I T I E S
    5 O X E N
  6 U N C L E'S
    7 D O C T O R S'
8 H O S T E S S E S'
```

Riddle: What do a baseball umpire and a jeweler have in common?

Answer: Each works on _diamonds_ !

Go for the Goal

Take your Final Replay Test. Then fill in your Scoreboard. Send any misspelled words to your Word Locker.

SCOREBOARD

number correct	number wrong

Clean Out Your Word Locker
Look in your Word Locker. Cross out each word you spelled correctly on your Final Replay Test. Circle the words you're still having trouble with. Add the words you circled to your Spelling Notebook. What do you notice about the words? Watch for those words as you write.

124   Lesson 30 ■ Instant Replay

Go for the Goal/Final Replay Test   *Page 124*

1. The *passengers'* tickets were collected.
2. The club built a parking lot for *members'* cars.
3. Kayla wrote a *children's* musical about a dragon.
4. My *cousin's* name is Tiffany.
5. *Arizona's* climate is hot and dry.
6. Jim *hasn't* finished cutting the grass.
7. My cat loves to play with catnip *mice.*
8. Are *buffaloes* still found in the Midwest?
9. What incredibly strong creatures *oxen* are!
10. Did he receive any *injuries* in the crash?
11. *Surveys* provide facts about people's opinions.
12. Several *communities* have soccer teams.
13. Will you visit your aunt during the *holidays?*
14. I need to buy new *batteries* for my flashlight.
15. Sharp *axes* are very dangerous!
16. Some *churches* have stained glass windows.
17. They walked twenty *paces* behind the queen.
18. The girls' dresses were tied with bright *sashes.*
19. Put the *matches* in that box so that they stay dry.
20. The little horse has long black *eyelashes.*
21. *Flies* buzzed against the window screen.
22. Angelo washed the *cherries* before eating them.
23. At some colleges, *libraries* stay open all night.
24. A flock of wild *geese* flew over the meadow.
25. The *chiefs* of all the tribes held a conference.
26. Female *sheep* are called *ewes.*
27. *We're* having the dress rehearsal for our play.
28. My *uncle's* best friend is a famous author.
29. The *bicycle's* rear tire is flat.
30. Are the *banjos'* cases in the music room?
31. Many *businesses'* booths gave out free samples.
32. The *airlines'* ticket prices are about the same.
33. The *hostesses'* names are on their name tags.
34. The *men's* soccer team left for the Olympics.
35. *Florida's* resorts are famous all over the world.
36. *She'll* be coming home soon.
37. Please rinse the *knives* and put them away.
38. The *calves* have soft brown coats.
39. We passed the time humming old *melodies.*
40. I carried the bags of *groceries* into the house.
41. The farmer dug irrigation *ditches* in the field.
42. *Flashes* of lightning lit up the night sky.
43. These *waxes* will restore the floor's shine.
44. Fold your paper into two equal *halves.*
45. Do you hear the clatter of horses' *hoofs?*
46. The boys said that *they'll* come to the meeting.
47. I decided to make a *doctor's* appointment.
48. Did you agree with the *umpires'* decisions?
49. The *families'* questionnaires were read carefully.
50. Denise will serve *sandwiches* at her party.

Clean Out Your Word Locker   Before writing each word, students can analyze the word and determine how the plural and/or the possessive is formed, or how a contraction is formed.

93

Instant Replay Test

Side A

Read each set of phrases. Fill in the circle next to the phrase with
an underlined word that is spelled wrong.

1. (a) those wet <u>matches</u>
   (b) three <u>businesses'</u> presidents
   (c) thirty <u>pases</u> away
   (d) the frightened <u>mice</u>

2. (a) some male <u>sheep</u>
   (b) the city's <u>liberries</u>
   (c) four <u>passengers'</u> wives
   (d) <u>Arizona's</u> weather conditions

3. (a) on federal <u>holidays</u>
   (b) when <u>he'll</u> call
   (c) the horse's <u>hoovs</u>
   (d) when <u>she'll</u> arrive

4. (a) the sharp <u>axxes</u>
   (b) some grazing <u>bison</u>
   (c) your <u>cousin's</u> knee
   (d) these sharp <u>knives</u>

5. (a) two <u>halfs</u>
   (b) these black <u>flies</u>
   (c) club <u>members'</u> husbands
   (d) two <u>umpires'</u> decisions

6. (a) although <u>they'll</u> wish
   (b) those popular <u>melodies</u>
   (c) the llama's <u>eyelashes</u>
   (d) twin <u>oxes</u>

7. (a) bags of <u>groceries</u>
   (b) results of <u>survays</u>
   (c) my <u>doctor's</u> advice
   (d) <u>Florida's</u> coast

8. (a) some dry <u>matches</u>
   (b) two <u>banjo's</u> strings
   (c) <u>men's</u> locker room
   (d) the <u>bicycle's</u> spoke

9. (a) these fresh <u>batteries</u>
   (b) honks of <u>geese</u>
   (c) slippery <u>waxes</u>
   (d) the <u>childrens'</u> concerns

10. (a) the <u>hostesses'</u> minds
    (b) <u>has'nt</u> rained
    (c) four young <u>sheep</u>
    (d) the exact <u>copies</u>

Instant Replay Test

Side B

Read each set of phrases. Fill in the circle next to the phrase with
an underlined word that is spelled wrong.

11.   ⓐ   the green <u>leaves</u>   ⓒ   when <u>we're</u> finished
      ⓑ   <u>flashes</u> of heat   ⓓ   my <u>uncles'</u> wife

12.   ⓐ   dangerous <u>ditches</u>   ⓒ   when <u>they'll</u> visit
      ⓑ   the hot <u>ashes</u>   ⓓ   three <u>familys'</u> apartments

13.   ⓐ   when <u>she'll</u> learn   ⓒ   with minor <u>injurys</u>
      ⓑ   the tribal <u>chiefs</u>   ⓓ   the female <u>geese</u>

14.   ⓐ   those new <u>batteries</u>   ⓒ   two newborn <u>calves</u>
      ⓑ   the <u>bicycles'</u> seat   ⓓ   my father's <u>bosses</u>

15.   ⓐ   steeples of <u>cherches</u>   ⓒ   <u>Arizona's</u> laws
      ⓑ   these tasty <u>cherries</u>   ⓓ   three <u>passengers'</u> suitcases

16.   ⓐ   although <u>we're</u> young   ⓒ   these car <u>waxes</u>
      ⓑ   <u>flashes</u> of light   ⓓ   his <u>doctors</u> office

17.   ⓐ   <u>Florida's</u> major cities   ⓒ   wool from <u>sheep</u>
      ⓑ   the <u>mens'</u> department   ⓓ   the scurrying <u>mice</u>

18.   ⓐ   some state <u>holidays</u>   ⓑ   several <u>comunities</u>
      ⓑ   the longest <u>eyelashes</u>   ⓓ   temple <u>members'</u> donations

19.   ⓐ   herds of <u>bufaloes</u>   ⓒ   soft organ <u>melodies</u>
      ⓑ   these annoying <u>flies</u>   ⓓ   when <u>they'll</u> receive

20.   ⓐ   these silk <u>sashes</u>   ⓒ   handles of <u>knives</u>
      ⓑ   grilled cheese <u>sandwitches</u>   ⓓ   unloading <u>groceries</u>

TAKE IT HOME

Your child has learned to spell many new words and would enjoy sharing them with you and your family. You'll find some great ideas on these pages for helping your child review the words in Lessons 25–29.

Across and Down

You and your child can create a crossword puzzle using some of the spelling words. Here's how:

• Lightly pencil in the grid below with some of the words.

• On a sheet of paper, write definitions for the words on the grid, indicating which are Across and which are Down. Encourage your child to use the dictionary in the Spelling Workout book.

• Number each word and its matching definition. Then erase the words on the grid.

• Invite the entire family to get together to complete the puzzle!

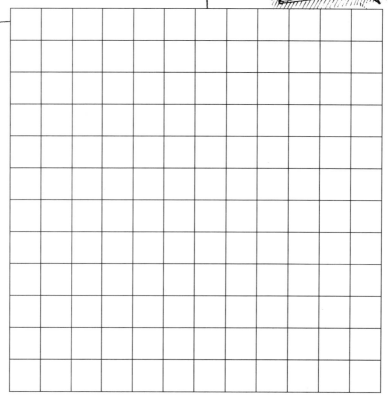

Silly Story Titles

With your child, make up silly story titles using as many spelling words as you can. Write the titles on the blank book spines below.

Lesson 31

Objective

To spell words with the prefixes *pre*, *re*, *im*, *non*, and *con*

Correlated Phonics Lessons

MCP Phonics, Level D, Lessons 64–68

Warm Up   *Page 125*

In this selection, students discover how the sun could be used as a giant night light. After reading, encourage students to discuss the advantages and disadvantages of lengthening daylight hours.

Ask volunteers to say each boldfaced word and identify its prefix.

On Your Mark/Warm Up Test

1. This *nonsense* must stop immediately!
2. She *prepaid* her airplane ticket.
3. The copilot took *control* of the plane.
4. Javier *returned* his library books on time.
5. Did their plan turn out to be *impractical?*
6. Shannon took a *nonstop* flight across the country.
7. In science class, we will *conduct* an experiment.
8. Solomon saw a *preview* of the new movie.
9. Your book *report* is due next week.
10. The *imperfect* diamond has many cracks.
11. The *nonprofit* organization rescues animals.
12. I need to buy some *refills* for my pen.
13. Who knows how to *construct* a doghouse?
14. The heavy piano seemed totally *immovable.*
15. As a *precaution,* always fasten your seat belt.
16. I *predict* that Dr. Wong will be very successful.
17. I tried to *convince* Megan to stay for dinner.
18. This formal business letter is too *impersonal.*
19. Is our city's air considered *impure?*
20. Dad had a bad *reaction* to the bee sting.

Pep Talk/Game Plan   *Pages 126–127*

Introduce the spelling rule and have students read the List Words aloud, helping them understand the meanings of the prefixes, the roots, and the complete words. Then encourage students to look back at their Warm Up Tests and apply the spelling rule to any misspelled words.

As students work through the **Spelling Lineup, Antonyms,** and **Puzzle** exercises, remind them to look back at their List Words or in their dictionaries if they need help.

 See **Spelling Aloud,** page 14

98

Name _____

Prefixes pre, re, im, non, and con

LESSON **31**

Warm Up

How can the sun light up the night?

Night Light

What if we could harness the sunlight and use it to light the night? It may seem like **nonsense,** but scientists **report** that they are trying to figure out a way to use the sun as a giant night light.

The idea is to **construct** a giant mirror, position it in space, and reflect light back to the dark side of the earth. Since the sun is always shining somewhere on the earth, reflecting light to the darkened side is possible. Put simply, it's the same as using a hand mirror to reflect sunlight to a dark corner of a room.

Russian scientists have considered this possibility for many years. In an experiment called Banner (*Znamya* in Russian), they are determining whether or not the idea is an **impractical** one. If successful, scientists **predict** that the extra light could save billions of dollars in electricity. Farmers with longer daylight hours could have more efficient planting and harvesting seasons. Building projects could be completed more quickly by working at night.

Of course, those of us who like to sleep will probably be calling the Russians to ask them to turn out that night light!

 Say the boldfaced words in the selection. These words have word parts that are added to the front of the words to make new words. These word parts are called **prefixes.** Can you name the prefix in each word?

On Your Mark

Take your Warm Up Test. Then check your spelling with the List Words on the next page.

125

Pep Talk

A **prefix** is a word part that is added to the beginning of a root to make a new word. Every prefix has a meaning, and it changes the meaning of the root.

pre means <u>before</u>, as in <u>pre</u>view
re means <u>again</u> or <u>back</u>, as in <u>re</u>fills
im and **non** mean <u>not</u>, as in <u>im</u>perfect
con means <u>with</u> or <u>together</u>, as in <u>con</u>struct

LIST WORDS

1. nonsense
2. prepaid
3. control
4. returned
5. impractical
6. nonstop
7. conduct
8. preview
9. report
10. imperfect
11. nonprofit
12. refills
13. construct
14. immovable
15. precaution
16. predict
17. convince
18. impersonal
19. impure
20. reaction

Game Plan

Spelling Lineup
Write each List Word under the correct heading.

words with the prefix **pre**
1. prepaid
2. preview
3. precaution
4. predict

words with the prefix **re**
13. returned
14. report
15. refills
16. reaction

words with the prefix **im**
5. impractical
6. imperfect
7. immovable
8. impersonal
9. impure

words with the prefix **con**
17. control
18. conduct
19. construct
20. convince

words with the prefix **non**
10. nonsense
11. nonstop
12. nonprofit

126   Lesson 31 ■ Prefixes pre, re, im, non, and con

Antonyms

Write the List Word that means the opposite of the word or words given.

1. personal _____ *impersonal*
2. movable _____ *immovable*
3. sense _____ *nonsense*
4. with stops _____ *nonstop*
5. perfect _____ *imperfect*
6. for profit _____ *nonprofit*

Puzzle

Fill in the crossword puzzle by writing the List Words that contain the roots given.

ACROSS
2. port   9. fills
5. pure   10. caution
7. dict

DOWN
1. trol   4. view
2. action 6. paid
3. turned 8. duct

Flex Your Spelling Muscles

Writing

A giant space mirror that creates more hours of daylight would be an amazing news story. Use the List Words to write a brief news report on this new invention.

Proofreading

Look for nine mistakes in this informational article. Use the proofreading marks to fix the mistakes. Then write the misspelled List Words on the lines.

Proofreading Marks	
◯	spelling mistake
⊿	take out something
⊙	add period

A practical way to use the heat from the sun is is already in use. People construkt flat metal plates on their roofs to collect and store energy from the sun in in the form of heat⊙ They can conduck the stored heat into their homes to warm themselves on cold or cloudy days. Some people predikt this energy method will will become even more popular in the future if we can convinse more people to try it⊙

1. _____ *construct*   3. _____ *predict*
2. _____ *conduct*   4. _____ *convince*

Now proofread your news report. Fix any mistakes.

Go for the Goal

Take your Final Test. Then fill in your Scoreboard. Send your mistakes to the Word Locker.

SCOREBOARD

number correct	number wrong

★ ★ ★ ★ ★ ★ ★ **All-Star Words** ★ ★ ★ ★ ★ ★ ★

nonfiction   contact   preset   recount   impatient

Write a sentence for each All-Star Word. Trade sentences with a partner. Circle the prefixes in the All-Star Words.

◎ **Spelling Strategy**   Invite students to work with a partner to practice spelling the List Words. One member of the pair writes the first ten words in the List Words box; the other member writes the remaining words. Then have partners trade papers and circle the prefixes in each other's words. Encourage students to get together with another set of partners to compare their work.

Flex Your Spelling Muscles   *Page 128*

As students complete the **Writing** activity, encourage them to brainstorm ideas, write a first draft, revise, and proofread their work. The **Proofreading** exercise will help them prepare to proofread their news reports. To publish their writing, students may want to
• read their news stories as TV broadcasts
• use their news stories to create a science journal.

✍ Writer's Corner

To learn more about solar energy, students might be interested in reading a book such as Catch a Sunbeam: *A Book of Solar Study and Experiments* by Florence Adams. Encourage groups of students to try one of the experiments described in the book and to write a report summarizing the results.

Go for the Goal/Final Test

1. Take your umbrella as a **precaution** against rain.
2. How can we treat this **impure** water?
3. Manuel Rodriguez will **conduct** the band tonight.
4. I donated money to a **nonprofit** organization.
5. That horse is galloping out of **control!**
6. We will **preview** the show before its opening.
7. The gardener **refills** the pot with fresh soil.
8. She **returned** from her trip at the end of June.
9. What was his **reaction** when he saw the gift?
10. We **predict** that Liz will finish the race first.
11. Her **report** said that the food had been shipped.
12. Tai tried to **convince** me that I wasn't tired.
13. It is **nonsense** to want an elephant as a pet.
14. What silly, **impractical** ideas that inventor has!
15. Let's **construct** a cage for our pet rabbit.
16. Rick is a shy, **impersonal** man with few friends.
17. I have an **imperfect** knowledge of the language.
18. Roberto found the huge rock **immovable.**
19. Is your subscription to the magazine **prepaid?**
20. We flew **nonstop** from Boston to Paris.

Remind students to complete the Scoreboard and write any misspelled words in their Word Locker.

★★ **All-Star Words**   You may want to point out that the All-Star Words follow the spelling rule and model the activity using a List Word.

Lesson 32

Objective

To spell words with the prefixes *ex, de, dis, un,* and *ad*

Correlated Phonics Lessons

MCP Phonics, Level D, Lessons 64, 66–67

Warm Up   *Page 129*

Students may never catch a cold again after reading "Don't Catch It!" Ask students which information in the selection they found the most interesting and useful.

Encourage students to look back at the boldfaced words. Ask volunteers to say the words and identify the prefixes.

On Your Mark/Warm Up Test

1. Poets use images to *express* their thoughts.
2. Chen will *design* the set for the school play.
3. This part of town is *unknown* to me.
4. It is often difficult to *admit* you are wrong.
5. Is any part of my explanation *unclear?*
6. Columbus was sent to *explore* distant islands.
7. Do you *disagree* with what she just said?
8. I will *defend* your right to offer an opinion.
9. Many of the characters in this book seem *unreal.*
10. José and Bob went on a grand *adventure.*
11. It's *unwise* to go without a coat on a cold day.
12. Will the detective *disclose* details of the case?
13. What good *advice* your aunt gave!
14. The teacher will *excuse* us when the bell rings.
15. I was *disinterested,* but Ana was excited.
16. You cannot trust a *dishonest* person.
17. I was *unprepared* for the difficult hike.
18. The spoiled food gave off an *unpleasant* smell.
19. We bought our tickets well in *advance.*
20. Is this word an adjective or an *adverb?*

Pep Talk/Game Plan   *Pages 130–131*

Introduce the spelling rule and invite students to read the List Words aloud, discussing the meanings of the prefixes, roots, and complete words. Then encourage students to look back at their Warm Up Tests and apply the spelling rule to any misspelled words.

As students work through the **Spelling Lineup, Word Parts,** and **Vocabulary** exercises, remind them to look back at their List Words or in their dictionaries if they need help.

You may also want to point out that *excuse* has two pronunciations, depending on which part of speech it is (*ek skyo͞oz'* for *v.; ek skyo͞os'* for *n.*).

 See **Questions/Answers,** page 15

Prefixes <u>ex</u>, <u>de</u>, <u>dis</u>, <u>un</u>, and <u>ad</u>   LESSON 32

Warm Up

How can you avoid catching a cold?

Don't Catch It!

With all the advances in medicine today, doctors still have not found a cure for an **unpleasant** illness that affects more of us than any other—the common cold. Every year, North Americans spend over a billion dollars on medicines to battle colds, but we still catch over 500 million colds a year! Most of those colds happen to children. But there are ways to **defend** ourselves. Let's **explore** one of them—knowing in **advance** how colds are spread.

Colds are not caused by going out without a hat or working too hard. Although many will **disagree,** people rarely catch colds by being near someone who is sneezing or coughing. Colds are caused by viruses, and there are at least 200 different types! These viruses almost always travel from the nose of a person with a cold to their hands. From there it goes to anything they touch. If someone else touches that same object, and then touches their nose or eyes, the virus can infect them.

The average person touches his or her eyes or nose about three times every hour! So it is very good **advice** to wash your hands often, and try not to touch your face. With your help, the common cold could become a little less common!

 | Take a look at the boldfaced words in the selection. What prefixes do you find?

On Your Mark

Take your Warm Up Test. Then check your spelling with the List Words on the next page.

129

Pep Talk

Here are more **prefixes** to add to the beginning of roots or root words. Each prefix has a meaning, and it changes the meaning of the root.
ex means <u>out of</u> or <u>from</u>, as in express
de means <u>down</u> or <u>away from</u>, as in defend
dis and **un** mean <u>not</u> or <u>the opposite of</u>, as in unclear
ad means <u>to</u>, <u>at</u>, or <u>toward</u>, as in advice

LIST WORDS

1. express
2. design
3. unknown
4. admit
5. unclear
6. explore
7. disagree
8. defend
9. unreal
10. adventure
11. unwise
12. disclose
13. advice
14. excuse
15. disinterested
16. dishonest
17. unprepared
18. unpleasant
19. advance
20. adverb

Game Plan

Spelling Lineup
Write each List Word under the correct heading.

words with the prefix **un**
1. unknown
2. unclear
3. unreal
4. unwise
5. unprepared
6. unpleasant

words with the prefix **dis**
10. disagree
11. disclose
12. disinterested
13. dishonest

words with the prefix **ex**
7. express
8. explore
9. excuse

words with the prefix **ad**
14. admit
15. adventure
16. advice
17. advance
18. adverb

words with the prefix **de**
19. design
20. defend

130   Lesson 32 ■ Prefixes ex, de, dis, un, and ad

Word Parts

Write List Words by adding prefixes to the roots or root words given.

1. fend	defend	8. agree	disagree	
2. verb	adverb	9. close	disclose	
3. plore	explore	10. honest	dishonest	
4. vice	advice	11. mit	admit	
5. vance	advance	12. clear	unclear	
6. press	express	13. cuse	excuse	
7. venture	adventure	14. sign	design	

Vocabulary

Write a List Word with the prefix **un** to complete each sentence. Use each word only once.

1. Some _____unreal_____ jewels look just like the real ones.

2. Tell whether you understood the directions or if you think they are _____unclear_____ .

3. Dr. Holmes is an _____unpleasant_____ person who rarely smiles.

4. We felt _____unprepared_____ for the difficult test.

5. The identity of the masked stranger is still _____unknown_____ .

6. We knew it would be _____unwise_____ to skate on the thin ice.

Lesson 32 ■ Prefixes **ex, de, dis, un,** and **ad**   131

Flex Your Spelling Muscles

Writing

What should you do to take care of a cold? Use the List Words to write a paragraph advising people how to take care of their colds.

Proofreading

The article below has eight mistakes. Use the proofreading marks to fix the mistakes. Then write the misspelled List Words on the lines.

Proofreading Marks	
◯	spelling mistake
¶	indent paragraph
∧	add something

¶Having a cold is certainly (unpleasant) especially if you are (unprepared) for that sudden sneeze. Here's some good (advies,) "Keep a handkerchief close by."

Handkerchiefs have been used for a long time. At first, they were made from grass mats. In China, silk tissue, or paper was used. In the 1600s, handkerchiefs of every size shape, and (dezin) could be found. Imagine using a handkerchief decorated with gem stones! Toward the 1800s, people became (disintarested) in these fancy pieces of cloth and began to use tissues.

1. unpleasant
2. unprepared
3. advice
4. design
5. disinterested

Now proofread your paragraph. Fix any mistakes.

Go for the Goal

Take your Final Test. Then fill in your Scoreboard. Send your mistakes to the Word Locker.

SCOREBOARD

number correct	number wrong

★ ★ ★ ★ ★ ★ ★ **All-Star Words** ★ ★ ★ ★ ★ ★ ★

define   unrelated   disgrace   advantage   exchange

Write a sentence for each word, and then erase the prefix. Trade papers with a partner, and add the correct prefix to the All-Star Words so that they make sense in the sentence.

132   Lesson 32 ■ Prefixes **ex, de, dis, un,** and **ad**

◎ **Spelling Strategy**   Write the prefixes *ex, de, dis, un,* and *ad* on the board. Then call out each root or root word contained in a List Word and ask the class to name the prefix it goes with. Call on a volunteer to write the complete List Word on the board as a word equation (*dis + interested = disinterested*).

Flex Your Spelling Muscles   *Page 132*

As students complete the **Writing** activity, encourage them to brainstorm ideas, write a first draft, revise, and proofread their work. The **Proofreading** exercise will help them prepare to proofread their paragraphs. To publish their writing, students may want to
- create a pamphlet called "Treating Colds"
- use their paragraphs to make a health poster.

✍ Writer's Corner

> You may want to invite the school nurse or a public health worker to talk to students about staying healthy during the cold and flu season. The class can write a list of questions to ask the guest speaker.

Go for the Goal/Final Test

1. We ordered a pizza in **advance.**
2. Are there still **unknown** regions of the earth?
3. The children **disagree** about which game to play.
4. It's **unwise** to skip breakfast.
5. I was **disinterested,** but Pia was very concerned.
6. I **admit** that I'm not a great skier.
7. Why won't you **disclose** where you hid the map?
8. Mr. Jackson circled the **adverb** in each sentence.
9. **Dishonest** people do not make good friends.
10. Are you prepared to **defend** your opinions?
11. A good writer tries to **express** ideas clearly.
12. My experience seems as **unreal** as a dream.
13. Are the directions still **unclear** to you?
14. The nervous speaker was **unprepared** to talk.
15. Jason found it **unpleasant** to handle a snake.
16. Please **excuse** me for being late.
17. What a terrific **adventure** our trip was!
18. Never **explore** caves without supervision!
19. Lea will **design** her dress for the dance.
20. Many people go to Kim for **advice.**

Remind students to complete the Scoreboard and write any misspelled words in their Word Locker.

★★ **All-Star Words**   You may want to point out that the All-Star Words follow the spelling rule and model writing a sentence using a List Word.

101

Lesson 33

Objective
To spell compound words

Warm Up   *Page 133*

In this selection, students read about a popular outdoor sport called *birling.* Afterward, invite students to read aloud the part of the selection they liked the best.

Encourage students to look back at the boldfaced words. Have volunteers say each word and identify the two words that make up the compound word.

On Your Mark/Warm Up Test

1. The plane flew one hundred miles **northwest.**
2. What a beautiful day to be **outdoors!**
3. **Everybody** voted in the school election.
4. Add one **teaspoon** of cinnamon to the batter.
5. We hiked as far as the **waterfall.**
6. Will this bus take us **downtown?**
7. The old **schoolhouse** is used as a museum.
8. To the **southeast** of the city is a large airport.
9. Mario works after school at a **supermarket.**
10. Their car is out front; **therefore,** they're home.
11. How much **homework** do you have to do tonight?
12. They planted flowers along the **sidewalk.**
13. We had scrambled eggs for **breakfast** today.
14. What an **outstanding** artist Ashley has become!
15. Button up your **overcoat** when the wind is strong.
16. Mr. Farooqui put his old **typewriter** in the attic.
17. I'll teach you how to pitch **horseshoes.**
18. Did the dentist cure your **toothache?**
19. My mother works in an **aircraft** factory.
20. Bill got a new **knapsack** for his birthday.

Pep Talk/Game Plan   *Pages 134–135*

Introduce the spelling rule and have students read the List Words aloud. Encourage students to look back at their Warm Up Tests and apply the spelling rule to any misspelled words.

As students work through the **Spelling Lineup, Definitions,** and **Classification** exercises, remind them to look back at their List Words or in their dictionaries if they need help. After students have completed the **Definitions** exercise, you may wish to explain the pun involved in the word *downfall.*

 See **Charades/Pantomime,** page 15

Compound Words   LESSON 33

Warm Up
What is *birling?*

Falling Off a Log

What's the favorite sport of lumberjacks? Its official name is *birling.* Most people know it as *logrolling.* Every year **outstanding** logrollers from all over North America come to Historyland in Hayward, Wisconsin, to take part in the world logrolling championship.

In the contest, two contestants step onto a floating log. They start the log rolling, then spin it rapidly with their feet. They can stop the log or start it spinning in the other direction. The idea is to throw your opponent off balance without falling off the log yourself. When the loser falls into the water, it's called "a wetting." The contest always ends with a big splash for **everybody!** It could even be called a **waterfall.**

Logrolling started in New England in the 1800s. The practice spread to the U.S. **northwest** and Canada. Lumberjacks would roll logs to break up jams. Then the logs could float freely down the river. Rolling logs was part of a lumberjack's everyday life. Today it is a popular sport played **outdoors** by both men and women. It's as easy as falling off a log, but it's a lot more fun!

> Look back at the boldfaced words. What two words make up each word?

On Your Mark
Take your Warm Up Test. Then check your spelling with the List Words on the next page.

Pep Talk
A **compound word** is made up of two or more words joined together to make a new word.
A *sidewalk* is a place to *walk* near the *side* of the road.
Study the List Words to find the words that make up each compound word.

LIST WORDS

1. *northwest*
2. *outdoors*
3. *everybody*
4. *teaspoon*
5. *waterfall*
6. *downtown*
7. *schoolhouse*
8. *southeast*
9. *supermarket*
10. *therefore*
11. *homework*
12. *sidewalk*
13. *breakfast*
14. *outstanding*
15. *overcoat*
16. *typewriter*
17. *horseshoes*
18. *toothache*
19. *aircraft*
20. *knapsack*

Game Plan
Spelling Lineup
Add a word to each word given to write a List Word.

1. knap __knapsack__
2. out __outdoors__
3. down __downtown__
4. north __northwest__
5. air __aircraft__
6. over __overcoat__
7. tea __teaspoon__
8. home __homework__
9. every __everybody__
10. tooth __toothache__

11. out __outstanding__
12. type __typewriter__
13. horse __horseshoes__
14. break __breakfast__
15. water __waterfall__
16. there __therefore__
17. school __schoolhouse__
18. super __supermarket__
19. south __southeast__
20. side __sidewalk__

Definitions

Write the List Word that matches each clue. Then read down the shaded boxes to solve the riddle.

1. a walkway next to the street
2. work done at home
3. a machine that makes printed letters
4. business section of a city
5. as a result
6. a canvas or leather bag
7. water that falls from a steep height
8. a place to learn

		S	I	D	E	W	A	L	K		
H	O	M	E	W	O	R	K				
	T	Y	P	E	W	R	I	T	E	R	
	D	O	W	N	T	O	W	N			
T	H	E	R	E	F	O	R	E			
K	N	A	P	S	A	C	K				
W	A	T	E	R	F	A	L	L			
S	C	H	O	O	L	H	O	U	S	E	

Riddle: What did the king find on the stairs?

Answer: his **downfall**

Classification

Write the List Word that belongs in each group.

1. lunch, dinner, **breakfast**
2. headache, earache, **toothache**
3. river, lake, **waterfall**
4. great, terrific, **outstanding**
5. cup, tablespoon, **teaspoon**
6. saddle, reins, **horseshoes**
7. store, shop, **supermarket**
8. all, everyone, **everybody**
9. jacket, parka, **overcoat**
10. helicopter, plane, **aircraft**

Flex Your Spelling Muscles

Writing

What exciting contests or events have you seen? Write a paragraph to describe the event. Use as many List Words as you can.

Proofreading

Find the ten mistakes in the poster below. Use the proofreading marks to fix the mistakes. Then write the misspelled List Words on the lines.

Proofreading Marks
○ spelling mistake
⊙ add period
/ make a small letter

Come one, come all to Idaho Spud Day. Visit downtown Shelley, Idaho, for The best potatoes in the northwest. There will be free spuds for everebody. Enjoy a fine breckfast, lunch, or dinner served outdores. Join us on the Third Saturday in September for a super day of fun.

1. downtown
2. northwest
3. everybody
4. breakfast
5. outdoors

Now proofread your paragraph. Fix any mistakes.

Go for the Goal

Take your Final Test. Then fill in your Scoreboard. Send your mistakes to the Word Locker.

SCOREBOARD

number correct	number wrong

★ ★ ★ ★ ★ ★ ★ ★ **All-Star Words** ★ ★ ★ ★ ★ ★ ★ ★

taxpayer   easygoing   sweatshirt   breakdown   westward

Write a sentence for each All-Star Word. Replace each All-Star Word with an equation that shows the two parts that make up a compound word. Trade papers with your partner and solve each other's equations.

⊚ **Spelling Strategy**   Call out one of the smaller words in each List Word and ask the class to name the other half of the word, referring to their *Spelling Workout* books if necessary. Then have students say the complete word and finger-write it in the air as they spell it aloud. Call on a volunteer to write the word on the board.

Flex Your Spelling Muscles   *Page 136*

As students complete the **Writing** activity, encourage them to brainstorm ideas, write a first draft, revise, and proofread their work. The **Proofreading** exercise will help them prepare to proofread their paragraphs. To publish their writing, students may want to
• give dramatic readings of their paragraphs
• create a bulletin-board display titled "Winning!"

✍ **Writer's Corner** _____

Invite students to bring in news stories about exciting sports competitions or other competitive events. Encourage them to write paragraphs telling why they would or would not like to participate in one of these activities.

Go for the Goal/Final Test

1. Do you use a *typewriter* or a computer?
2. Pack your flashlight in your *knapsack.*
3. We played hopscotch on the *sidewalk.*
4. To the *southeast,* we saw beautiful mountains.
5. Use a *teaspoon* to measure the baking powder.
6. What a surprise to see *everybody* here on time!
7. Jake finished his *homework* after dinner.
8. Grandma went to a one-room *schoolhouse.*
9. Is your new *overcoat* waterproof?
10. I'm writing a report on the history of *aircraft.*
11. Are *horseshoes* made of iron?
12. The new *supermarket* will open tomorrow.
13. Chandra took a picture of the *waterfall.*
14. Do grizzly bears roam free in the *northwest?*
15. Eat a nutritious *breakfast* every day.
16. We went *downtown* to go shopping.
17. Carlos woke up with a painful *toothache.*
18. Do you enjoy working *outdoors?*
19. The trip costs too much; *therefore,* we won't go.
20. Her photographs of birds are *outstanding!*

Remind students to complete the Scoreboard and write any misspelled words in their Word Locker.

★★ **All-Star Words**   You may want to point out that the All-Star Words follow the spelling rule and show students how to write an equation (for example, *knap + sack = knapsack*).

103

Lesson 34

Objective
To spell and identify antonyms and synonyms

Correlated Phonics Lessons
MCP Phonics, Level D, Lessons 76–77

Warm Up   *Page 137*
In "The Mail Must Go Through!," students find out why the Pony Express lasted only a short time. Ask students, "What do you think being a Pony Express rider was like? Would you like to have been one?"

Call on volunteers to say each boldfaced word and tell which one means the same as *trip* and which one means the opposite of *easy.*

On Your Mark/Warm Up Test
1. Joan finds swimming easy, but diving **difficult.**
2. For dinner they had a **tender** steak.
3. The principal gave a **lengthy** talk.
4. To reach a high object, use a **sturdy** stepladder.
5. Is he saving money to buy an **expensive** bike?
6. Erin **repaired** the flat tire on her bike.
7. What an **enormous** creature that dinosaur was!
8. What is the longest **journey** you have ever taken?
9. The runners were **weary** at the end of the race.
10. Just before the race, the drivers were **tense.**
11. When crossing a busy street, be **cautious.**
12. Mei Ling felt great **sorrow** when her cat died.
13. Luis was **vague** about the date of the party.
14. Was this **ancient** ruin a Roman temple?
15. The mountain climber's **courage** was admirable.
16. After a big lunch, we were **drowsy.**
17. He stared in **disbelief** at the magician's tricks.
18. I read about **current** events in the newspaper.
19. The workers **descend** into the mine in elevators.
20. The runner was **rapidly** taking the lead.

Pep Talk/Game Plan   *Pages 138–139*
Introduce the spelling rule and have students read the List Words aloud. Encourage students to look back at their Warm Up Tests and apply the spelling rule to any misspelled words.

As students work through the **Spelling Lineup, Puzzle,** and **Dictionary** exercises, remind them to look back at their List Words or in their dictionaries if they need help. For the **Spelling Lineup,** explain that the answers in the first column are synonyms for words in the sentences and the answers in the second column are antonyms.

 See **Student Dictation,** page 14

Synonyms and Antonyms   LESSON 34

Warm Up
Why was the Pony Express in business for only two years?

The Mail Must Go Through!

It's been over a hundred years since the Pony Express delivered mail. The Express was started in 1860 between Missouri and California. Riders made the **journey** on horseback. It was a **difficult** ride for both horse and rider so relay stations were set up ten to fifteen miles apart. Riders would pick up fresh horses at each station. The **lengthy** trip took eight days. Because it was so **expensive,** the Pony Express had only a brief life. Railroads could offer cheap rates and quicker delivery. After only two years, the Pony Express went out of business.

However, years later the Express was in business again but only for a short time. In California, a huge mud slide had closed the road to a mountain town called Little Norway. The only way mail could be delivered was by horseback. Each morning, the postmaster gave the first rider a pouch of mail. It took ten riders to make the long, forty-mile trip. Riders ranged in age from teenagers to a 72-year-old. Eventually the road was **repaired,** but for a brief time the Pony Express rode once again.

 Look back at the boldfaced words in the selection. Can you name the word that means almost the same as trip? Can you name the word that means the opposite of easy?

On Your Mark
Take your Warm Up Test. Then check your spelling with the List Words on the next page.

Pep Talk
A **synonym** is a word that means the same or almost the same as another word. The word long is a synonym for lengthy. An **antonym** is a word that means the opposite or almost the opposite of another word. The word brief is an antonym for lengthy.

LIST WORDS
1. difficult
2. tender
3. lengthy
4. sturdy
5. expensive
6. repaired
7. enormous
8. journey
9. weary
10. tense
11. cautious
12. sorrow
13. vague
14. ancient
15. courage
16. drowsy
17. disbelief
18. current
19. descend
20. rapidly

Game Plan
Spelling Lineup
Write the List Word that best completes each sentence.

1. A hard problem is __difficult__
2. A long book is __lengthy__
3. A huge elephant is __enormous__
4. A sleepy baby is __drowsy__
5. A costly ring is __expensive__
6. Sadness is also __sorrow__
7. An uptight person is __tense__
8. A long trip is a __journey__
9. A brave person has __courage__
10. A fixed watch is __repaired__

11. Go slowly, not __rapidly__
12. Don't be tough, be __tender__
13. Climb up, don't __descend__
14. Be energetic, not __weary__
15. A modern desk is not __ancient__
16. A weak floor is not __sturdy__
17. A clear idea is not __vague__
18. It isn't trust, it's __disbelief__
19. Reckless people aren't __cautious__
20. A past issue is not __current__

Puzzle

Fill in the crossword puzzle by writing a List Word to answer each clue. Write antonyms ACROSS. Write synonyms DOWN.

ACROSS (antonyms)
3. clear
6. happiness
9. broken
11. fear
13. modern
14. short

DOWN (synonyms)
1. recent
2. strong
4. nervous
5. costly
7. tired
8. hard
10. trip

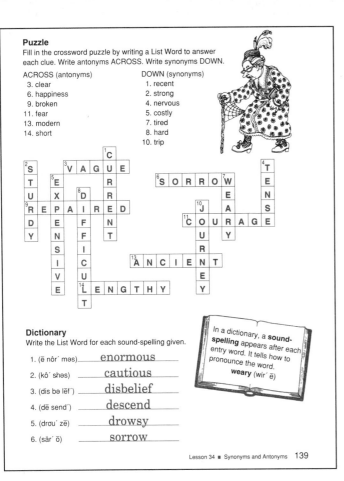

Crossword answers:
- 3. VAGUE
- 6. SORROW
- 9. REPAIRED
- 11. COURAGE
- 13. ANCIENT
- 14. LENGTHY
- 1. CURRENT
- 2. STURDY
- 4. TENSE
- 5. EXPENSIVE
- 7. WEARY
- 8. DIFFICULT
- 10. JOURNEY

Dictionary

Write the List Word for each sound-spelling given.

In a dictionary, a **sound-spelling** appears after each entry word. It tells how to pronounce the word.
weary (wir´ ē)

1. (ē nôr´ məs) __enormous__
2. (kô´ shəs) __cautious__
3. (dis bə lēf´) __disbelief__
4. (dē send´) __descend__
5. (drou´ zē) __drowsy__
6. (sär´ ō) __sorrow__

Lesson 34 ■ Synonyms and Antonyms 139

Flex Your Spelling Muscles

Writing

The Pony Express riders faced many dangers on their long rides. Use the List Words to write a newspaper ad asking for riders to sign up. Include some special skills or qualities a Pony Express rider might need.

Proofreading

There are eleven mistakes in this diary entry. Use the proofreading marks to fix the mistakes. Then write the misspelled List Words on the lines.

Proofreading Marks
◯ spelling mistake
⌄ add apostrophe
⟋ take out something

September 23, 1847

This journey seems more lengthee than I thought it would be be. Emmas horse has tennder feet and may have to to be left behind. Johns wagon has been repayred but the delay was espensive. We cant waste any more time because winter is rapidlee approaching.

1. __journey__
2. __lengthy__
3. __tender__
4. __repaired__
5. __expensive__
6. __rapidly__

Now proofread your newspaper ad. Fix any mistakes.

Go for the Goal

Take your Final Test. Then fill in your Scoreboard. Send your mistakes to the Word Locker.

SCOREBOARD
number correct | number wrong

★ ★ ★ ★ ★ ★ ★ ★ **All-Star Words** ★ ★ ★ ★ ★ ★ ★ ★

smooth   regular   familiar   intelligent   brilliant

With your partner, write a paragraph using an antonym for each All-Star Word. Trade papers with another team. Rewrite their paragraph, using the All-Star Words.

140 Lesson 34 ■ Synonyms and Antonyms

◉ Spelling Strategy

With a partner, students can take turns saying the List Words aloud. The partner who is listening
• repeats the word
• writes it while spelling it aloud
• names a synonym or an antonym for it.

Flex Your Spelling Muscles   Page 140

As students complete the **Writing** activity, encourage them to brainstorm ideas, write a first draft, revise, and proofread their work. The **Proofreading** exercise will help them prepare to proofread their newspaper ads. To publish their writing, students may want to
• compile a "Help Wanted" newsletter
• create recruitment posters for Pony Express riders.

✍ Writer's Corner

Students may be interested in requesting information about the Pony Express by writing to the Pony Express Museum, 11th & Charles, St. Joseph, MO 64501. Enclose a long, self-addressed stamped envelope.

Go for the Goal/Final Test

1. The temperature outside is falling *rapidly.*
2. Do you get *tense* before a big test?
3. *Current* weather trends indicate a hot summer.
4. We praised the *courage* of the firefighters.
5. We became *drowsy* during the long film.
6. How *weary* she was after her long hike!
7. An *enormous* clap of thunder shook the house.
8. My feet are too *tender* to walk without shoes.
9. Be *cautious* whenever you ride your bike.
10. Stephanie gave a *lengthy* explanation.
11. What an *expensive* mitt this is!
12. Our grandparents built *sturdy* furniture.
13. Has the shop *repaired* your bicycle yet?
14. She could see *sorrow* on the young child's face.
15. Lana has a *vague* memory of the house.
16. What *ancient* civilization built those temples?
17. This summer we will *journey* across the country.
18. How long will it take to *descend* the mountain?
19. He listened to the amazing story in *disbelief.*
20. This is the most *difficult* word on the test.

Remind students to complete the Scoreboard and write any misspelled words in their Word Locker.

★★ **All-Star Words** You may want to point out that the All-Star Words follow the spelling rule. Suggest that students use the classroom dictionary or a thesaurus if they need help thinking of antonyms.

105

Lesson 35

Objective
To spell homonyms

Correlated Phonics Lessons
MCP Phonics, Level D, Lessons 78–79

Warm Up   *Page 141*
In this selection, students learn fascinating facts about hair—including who had the world's tallest hairstyle. After reading, invite students to discuss different hairstyles and to invent silly or fantastic coiffures.

Ask volunteers to identify the pairs of boldfaced words that sound the same and to suggest words that sound like *tale* and *whose*.

On Your Mark/Warm Up Test
1. This is a *tale* about a giant.
2. The mouse has a long, pink *tail.*
3. There's a hole in the *heel* of my sock.
4. Keep the cut clean and it will *heal* quickly.
5. After a hard day, Kelly wanted *peace* and quiet.
6. Tim needed another *piece* of writing paper.
7. Do you have a *plain* white shirt to wear?
8. We boarded the *plane* to London.
9. Leave your dishes *there* by the sink.
10. They brought *their* dogs to the park on leashes.
11. Your answer showed good *sense.*
12. Of all the *scents,* I like that of roses best.
13. *Which* desk is yours?
14. The story was about a *witch* and three elves.
15. We saw the man *whose* picture was in the paper.
16. We already know *who's* playing the lead role.
17. Watch out or you'll *break* something!
18. Your bike also has a *brake* on the back wheel.
19. When are you going to cut your *hair?*
20. What a large animal a Belgian *hare* is!

Pep Talk/Game Plan   *Pages 142–143*
Introduce the spelling rule and have students read the List Words aloud. Explain to students how they can tell homonym pairs apart (context, spelling). Then encourage them to look back at their Warm Up Tests and apply the spelling rule to any misspelled words.

As students work through the **Spelling Lineup, Synonyms and Antonyms,** and **Homonyms** exercises, remind them to look back at their List Words or in their dictionaries if they need help. For the **Spelling Lineup,** remind students that rhyming words may have different spellings.

 See **Words in Context,** page 15

106

Name _____

Homonyms

Warm Up
Who holds the record for the world's tallest hair style?

A Hair-Raising Tale
It may seem like a tall tale, but according to the *Guinness Book of World Records,* in 1989, a woman named Colinda Sirls broke the record for the world's tallest hair style. Colinda's hair measured eight feet over her head! She called it the "flagpole" style. It's not clear exactly who she was trying to flag down, but it was definitely a signal to someone!

Hair as a transmitter of signals is common in the animal kingdom. Moose have hairs between **their** toes that turn green when sending signals to other moose during the mating season.

There are many animals **whose** hair serves as insulation, not only for the animals themselves, but also for their young. For example, the polar bear has a thick coat of fur that keeps it warm. A mother **hare** (rabbit) makes a nest of her own **hair** to shelter her young! Hair is also used as protection from enemies. A porcupine's quills are a type of hair. Porcupines are able to throw their quills into the bodies of attackers.

 Look back at the boldfaced words. Which words sound the same, but have different spellings and meanings? Do you know another word that sounds the same as <u>tale</u> or <u>whose</u>?

On Your Mark
Take your Warm Up Test. Then check your spelling with the List Words on the next page.

Pep Talk
Homonyms are words that sound the same, but have different meanings and spellings.
heel—the back of the foot
heal—to make someone well
The meaning of a sentence helps you know which homonym to use.

LIST WORDS

1. tale
2. tail
3. heel
4. heal
5. peace
6. piece
7. plain
8. plane
9. there
10. their
11. sense
12. scents
13. which
14. witch
15. whose
16. who's
17. break
18. brake
19. hair
20. hare

Game Plan
Spelling Lineup
Write the List Words that rhyme with each word given.

take		chain	
1. break		11. plain	
2. brake		12. plane	

mail		shoes	
3. tale		13. whose	
4. tail		14. who's	

tents		feel	
5. sense		15. heel	
6. scents		16. heal	

bear		pitch	
7. hair		17. which	
8. hare		18. witch	
9. there		grease	
10. their		19. peace	
		20. piece	

Synonyms and Antonyms

Write the List Word that means the same or almost the same as each word given.

1. rabbit _____ hare
2. portion _____ piece
3. story _____ tale
4. smells _____ scents
5. smash _____ break
6. cure _____ heal

Write the List Word that means the opposite of each word given.

1. fancy _____ plain
2. here _____ there
3. foolishness _____ sense
4. war _____ peace

Homonyms

Write two List Words that are homonyms to complete each sentence.

1. _____ Which _____ witch _____ fell off her broom?
2. _____ Who's _____ the lucky kid _____ whose _____ pony we can ride?
3. The bike won't stop if you _____ break _____ the _____ brake _____ .
4. _____ Their _____ seats for the game are over _____ there _____ .
5. Soaking my hurt _____ heel _____ should help it _____ heal _____ .
6. The _____ plane _____ we flew in was very _____ plain _____ .
7. The _____ hair _____ all over the floor is from my pet _____ hare _____ .
8. One folk _____ tale _____ tells how
the bear lost its _____ tail _____ .

Flex Your Spelling Muscles

Writing

Do you think hair fashions are funny, great, or not a subject you think about? Write your opinion in a paragraph and state your reasons. Use as many List Words as you can.

Proofreading

There are ten mistakes in this article. Use the proofreading marks to fix the mistakes. Circle the List Words that are used incorrectly. Then write the correct List Words on the lines.

Proofreading Marks	
≡	capital letter
∧	add something

This (tail) of the history of the beard will raise your hair . did you know that at one time, all men wore beards?Then Alexander the Great thought it made (scents) for soldiers to shave (there) beards so enemies could not grab them. Did you know that the Vandyke beard, (witch) was pointed, was popular in the 1600s? In the 1830s in america, men were not allowed to wear beards. Joseph Palmer, who's beard was bushy, was jailed for that reason. Newspaper stories forced his release to keep the (piece.)

1. _____ tale _____   4. _____ their _____
2. _____ hair _____   5. _____ which _____
3. _____ sense _____   6. _____ peace _____

Now proofread your opinion paragraph. Fix any mistakes.

Go for the Goal

Take your Final Test. Then fill in your Scoreboard. Send your mistakes to the Word Locker.

SCOREBOARD

number correct	number wrong

★ ★ ★ ★ ★ ★ ★ **All-Star Words** ★ ★ ★ ★ ★ ★ ★

flew   flue   flu   knead   need

Write a paragraph using each word. Then mix up the All-Star Words. Trade papers with a partner. Rewrite each other's paragraph, using the All-Star Words correctly.

◎ **Spelling Strategy**   To help students distinguish between the words in a homonym pair, write cloze sentences on the board for pairs of List Words. Next to each sentence, add letters as a clue. For example:
"Will that cut _____ ?" (ea)
"She broke the _____ on her shoe." (ee)
"The answer doesn't make _____ ." (ens)
"The house is full of the _____ of flowers. " (cen)
Invite the class to read each pair of sentences and to decide which List Words go in the blanks. Call on a volunteer to fill in the words.

Flex Your Spelling Muscles   *Page 144*

As students complete the **Writing** activity, encourage them to brainstorm ideas, write a first draft, revise, and proofread their work. The **Proofreading** exercise will help them prepare to proofread their paragraphs. To publish their writing, invite students to present their paragraphs to the class as short speeches.

✍ Writer's Corner

You may want to organize a trip to the library so that students can gather interesting information about animals' fur. Students can share what they learn by writing facts on a class collage.

Go for the Goal/Final Test

1. Make sure the **brake** is on before leaving the car.
2. My shoe has a nail in the **heel.**
3. The **plane** was delayed until the fog lifted.
4. Which of these **scents** do you like best?
5. *Cinderella* is a fairy **tale** I have always liked.
6. Here's a fable about a tortoise and a **hare.**
7. The good **witch** granted her three wishes.
8. Ask your parents if we can use **their** radio.
9. How long will it take this wound to **heal?**
10. Your plan makes good **sense** to me.
11. I'd like my **hair** cut a little shorter in front.
12. A raccoon has stripes on its **tail.**
13. Are those your books **there** on the table?
14. Jon knew **which** street was mine.
15. Look out or you'll **break** that window!
16. Perhaps one day the world will be at **peace.**
17. Choose the partner **whose** ticket matches yours.
18. Do you want your hamburger **plain** or with sauce?
19. Try to find out **who's** coming to the party.
20. Yes, you may have another **piece** of toast.

Remind students to complete the Scoreboard and write any misspelled words in their Word Locker.

★★ **All-Star Words**   You may want to point out that the All-Star Words follow the spelling rule. Help students brainstorm ways to use all the words in a paragraph.

Lesson 36 • Instant Replay

Objective
To review spelling words with the prefixes *pre, re, im, non, con, ex, de, dis, un,* and *ad;* compound words; synonyms and antonyms; homonyms

Time Out   *Pages 145–148*

Check Your Word Locker   Based on your observations, note which words are giving students the most difficulty and offer assistance for spelling them correctly. Here are some frequently misspelled words to watch for: *immovable, advice, weary, who's, their,* and *there.*

To give students extra help and practice in taking standardized tests, you may want to have them take the Review Test for this lesson on pages 110–111. After scoring the tests, return them to students so that they can record their misspelled words in their Word Locker.

After practicing their troublesome words, students can work through the exercises for **Lessons 31–35.** Before they begin each exercise, you may want to go over the spelling rule.

Take It Home   Suggest that students and their parents make up a humorous story using as many of the List Words in **Lessons 31–35** as possible. For a complete list of the words, encourage students to take their *Spelling Workout* books home. Students can also use Take It Home Master 6 on pages 112–113 to help them do the activity. Encourage them to bring their stories to class and combine them into a series of skits. After rehearsing, students may want to invite another class to a performance.

Instant Replay • Lessons 31–35

LESSON **36**

Time Out
Take another look at prefixes, compound words, synonyms and antonyms, and homonyms.

Check Your Word Locker
Look at the words in your Word Locker. Write your troublesome words for Lessons 31 through 35.

_____

Practice writing your troublesome words with a partner. Take turns dividing the words into syllables as your partner spells them aloud.

Lesson 31

Prefixes

pre = <u>before</u>, as in <u>preview</u>   **re** = <u>again</u> or <u>back</u>, as in <u>refills</u>
im = <u>not</u>, as in <u>impure</u>   **non** = <u>not</u>, as in <u>nonprofit</u>
con = <u>with</u> or <u>together</u>, as in <u>control</u>

List Words

nonsense
prepaid
impractical
nonstop
nonprofit
construct
immovable
predict
convince
reaction

Add a prefix to each word or word part to make a List Word.

1. **im** movable ___immovable___
2. **con** vince ___convince___
3. **non** sense ___nonsense___
4. **non** profit ___nonprofit___
5. **re** action ___reaction___
6. **non** stop ___nonstop___
7. **pre** paid ___prepaid___
8. **con** struct ___construct___
9. **pre** dict ___predict___
10. **im** practical ___impractical___

145

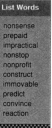

Lesson 32

Prefixes

ex = <u>out of</u> or <u>from</u>, as in <u>express</u>   **de** = <u>down</u> or <u>away from</u>, as in <u>defend</u>
dis = <u>opposite</u> or <u>not</u>, as in <u>dishonest</u>   **un** = <u>not</u>, as in <u>unreal</u>
ad = <u>to</u>, <u>at</u>, or <u>towards</u>, as in <u>admit</u>

List Words

express
design
unknown
explore
disagree
adventure
unwise
excuse
unprepared
admit

Write a List Word to match each definition.

1. to be against an idea ___disagree___
2. not ready ___unprepared___
3. not showing good sense ___unwise___
4. to state or say ___express___
5. decoration or pattern ___design___
6. to search carefully ___explore___
7. to take or accept as true ___admit___
8. undiscovered ___unknown___
9. to free from blame ___excuse___
10. an exciting experience ___adventure___

Lesson 33

A **compound word** is made up of two or more words, as in <u>homework</u> and <u>downtown</u>.

List Words

outdoors
everybody
supermarket
sidewalk
breakfast
outstanding
typewriter
toothache
aircraft
knapsack

Combine each word in the first box with a word in the second box to make a compound List Word. Then write the List Word.

out	type	every	side
super	break	out	tooth
	air	knap	

doors	fast	standing	body
walk	market	writer	ache
	sack	craft	

1. ___outdoors___   6. ___outstanding___
2. ___everybody___   7. ___typewriter___
3. ___supermarket___   8. ___toothache___
4. ___sidewalk___   9. ___aircraft___
5. ___breakfast___   10. ___knapsack___

Lesson 34

A **synonym** means the same or almost the same as another word.
An **antonym** means the opposite or almost opposite of another word.

Write a List Word to match each clue.

List Words

lengthy
expensive
repaired
enormous
journey
cautious
vague
ancient
courage
descend

Synonyms

1. careful   cautious
2. bravery   courage
3. fixed   repaired
4. voyage   journey
5. old   ancient

Antonyms

6. go up   descend
7. brief   lengthy
8. cheap   expensive
9. small   enormous
10. clear   vague

Lesson 35

Homonyms are words that sound alike, but have different meanings and spellings.

List Words

tale
tail
peace
piece
there
their
whose
who's
break
brake

Underline the List Word that completes each sentence. Then write that List Word on the line.

1. The dog wagged its (tale, <u>tail</u>).   tail
2. Grandma told us a (<u>tale</u>, tail).   tale
3. (<u>Whose</u>, Who's) coat is this?   Whose
4. (Whose, <u>Who's</u>) the best singer?   Who's
5. I'd like a (peace, <u>piece</u>) of toast.   piece
6. We work for world (<u>peace</u>, piece).   peace
7. Please put my books (<u>there</u>, their).   there
8. Put (<u>their</u>, there) books on the table.   their
9. Use the (break, <u>brake</u>) to stop.   brake
10. The cup could (<u>break</u>, brake).   break

Lesson 36 ■ Instant Replay   147

Lessons 31–35

List Words

nonsense
nonstop
construct
design
adventure
admit
supermarket
breakfast
toothache
expensive
repaired
ancient
tale
tail
brake

Write the List Words in alphabetical order.

1. admit
2. adventure
3. ancient
4. brake
5. breakfast
6. construct
7. design
8. expensive
9. nonsense
10. nonstop
11. repaired
12. supermarket
13. tail
14. tale
15. toothache

Go for the Goal

Take your Final Replay Test. Then fill in your Scoreboard. Send any misspelled words to your Word Locker.

SCOREBOARD

number correct	number wrong

Clean Out Your Word Locker
Look in your Word Locker. Cross out each word you spelled correctly on your Final Replay Test. Circle the words you're still having trouble with. Add the words you circled to your Spelling Notebook. What do you notice about the words? Watch for those words as you write.

1. **Whose** dog is that?
2. Put a **piece** of cheese on the cracker.
3. The title of that **tale** is *The Little Red Hen.*
4. Be careful not to **break** the glass in the frame.
5. She wrote a **lengthy** article about snakes.
6. It takes **courage** to be different from the group.
7. Did you enjoy your **journey** through the South?
8. Be **cautious** when you ride your skateboard.
9. For **breakfast,** Dad made blueberry pancakes.
10. Pack an extra pair of socks in your **knapsack.**
11. What an **outstanding** poem Taneesha wrote!
12. We'll buy a gallon of milk at the **supermarket.**
13. Songwriters **express** feelings through music.
14. It was **unwise** to leave your jacket home today.
15. We felt **unprepared** for the difficult hike.
16. Can you name the **adverb** in this sentence?
17. Please **excuse** me for being late today.
18. I love to read **nonsense** poems!
19. Did she **convince** you to sign her petition?
20. The movie got a positive **reaction** from critics.
21. Uncle Martin helped me **construct** a tree house.
22. I'd like to buy a ticket on a **nonstop** flight.
23. I **predict** that Adam will enjoy his new school.
24. The students had fun planning their **adventure.**
25. Will you tell us why you **disagree?**
26. The wallpaper was white with a floral **design.**
27. Let's go **outdoors** and play basketball.
28. If you have a **toothache,** see the dentist.
29. We saw a film in class about early **aircraft.**
30. The tickets for the trip are very **expensive.**
31. The **ancient** Vikings lived in Scandinavia.
32. Tonio **repaired** the broken chair with glue.
33. I have **vague** memories of my early childhood.
34. She hung **their** coats in the hall closet.
35. The rear **brake** on my bike needs to be fixed.
36. The horse has a beautiful white **tail.**
37. **There** aren't many days left until vacation.
38. Use the railing when you **descend** the stairs.
39. David lives in an **enormous** apartment building.
40. I **prepaid** the theater tickets months ago.
41. The heavy piano seemed **immovable** to the boys.
42. What an **impractical** plan this is!
43. I donated my old clothes to a **nonprofit** agency.
44. When did Lewis and Clark **explore** this region?
45. Are any western regions still **unknown?**
46. **Everybody** in the class did well on the test.
47. Ms. Yee taught me how to use a **typewriter.**
48. A clown sold balloons on the **sidewalk.**
49. **Who's** behind that funny mask?
50. The people worked hard for **peace** and justice.

Clean Out Your Word Locker   Before writing each word, students can identify its prefixes or tell whether it is a compound word or part of a homonym pair.

Instant Replay Test

Side A

Read each set of words. Fill in the circle next to the word that is spelled wrong.

1. (a) tale   (c) courage
    (b) overcoat   (d) advenchure

2. (a) brake   (c) supermarket
    (b) peace   (d) tipewriter

3. (a) enormos   (c) vague
    (b) toothache   (d) design

4. (a) who's   (c) reaction
    (b) exploar   (d) nonstop

5. (a) there   (c) breake
    (b) descend   (d) express

6. (a) expensive   (c) unwize
    (b) prepaid   (d) disagree

7. (a) ancient   (c) outstanding
    (b) impracticle   (d) outdoors

8. (a) excuse   (c) lenthy
    (b) journey   (d) aircraft

9. (a) peice   (c) adverb
    (b) courage   (d) nonprofit

10. (a) predict   (c) tail
    (b) sidewalk   (d) who'se

Name _____

Instant Replay Test

Side B

Read each set of words. Fill in the circle next to the word that is spelled wrong.

11. (a) disclose   (c) defend
     (b) nonsense   (d) nonproffit

12. (a) convinse   (c) express
     (b) excuse   (d) outstanding

13. (a) construct   (c) prepaid
     (b) cautios   (d) unknown

14. (a) reaction   (c) tail
     (b) expensive   (d) unprepaired

15. (a) adjust   (c) descent
     (b) thier   (d) nonstop

16. (a) design   (c) there
     (b) breckfast   (d) nonsense

17. (a) sidewalk   (c) outdoors
     (b) vague   (d) immoveable

18. (a) who's   (c) courage
     (b) tale   (d) napsack

19. (a) repared   (c) toothache
     (b) supermarket   (d) journey

20. (a) ancient   (c) brake
     (b) evrybody   (d) aircraft

6

TAKE IT HOME

Your child has learned to spell many new words and would enjoy sharing them with you and your family. Here are some ideas to help your child review the words in Lessons 31–35 and have fun, too.

And Then What Happened?

With your child, take turns using the spelling words to tell a humorous story—the sillier the better! At each turn, work one or more of the words into the story. For example, you might say, "One day I set out on an adventure, and the first thing I saw was a green **waterfall** with white polka dots. Suddenly, ..."

HONEY

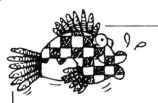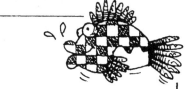

What a Card!

Cut out the word cards on this page and make more of your own using the spelling words. Then place the cards in two stacks. Take turns drawing one card from each stack and using the two words in a silly sentence.

supermarket	knapsack
advice	impractical
enormous	nonsense

Writing and Proofreading Guide

1. Choose a topic to write about.
2. Write your ideas. Don't worry about mistakes.
3. Now organize your writing so that it makes sense.
4. Proofread your work.
   Use these proofreading marks to make changes.

> **Proofreading Marks**
> ⬯ spelling mistake
> ≡ capital letter
> ⊙ add period
> ∧ add something
> ⸜ add apostrophe
> ⸛ take out something
> ¶ indent paragraph
> / make small letter

Isnt a (dolfin) one of the ~~the~~ most Intelligent sea mammals ?

5. Write your final copy.

   Isn't a dolphin one of the most intelligent sea mammals?

6. Share your writing.

Dolphins use sound to Communicate with each other.

Using Your Dictionary

The Spelling Workout Dictionary shows you many things about your spelling words.

The **sound-spelling or respelling** tells how to pronounce the word.

The **entry word** listed in alphabetical order is the word you are looking up.

The **part of speech** is given as an abbreviation.

im·prove (im proov′) **v.** I to make or become better [Business has *improved.*] 2 to make good use of [She *improved* her spare time by reading.] — **im·proved′, im·prov′ing**

Sample sentences or phrases show how to use the word.

Other **forms** of the word are given.

The **definition** tells what the word means. There may be more than one definition.

Pronunciation Key

SYMBOL	KEY WORDS	SYMBOL	KEY WORDS	SYMBOL	KEY WORDS	SYMBOL	KEY WORDS
a	ask, fat	o͝o	look, pull	b	bed, dub	t	top, hat
ā	ape, date	o͞o	ooze, tool	d	did, had	v	vat, have
ä	car, lot	ou	out, crowd	f	fall, off	w	will, always
				g	get, dog	y	yet, yard
e	elf, ten	u	up, cut	h	he, ahead	z	zebra, haze
ē	even, meet	u͡	fur, fern	j	joy, jump		
				k	kill, bake	ch	chin, arch
i	is, hit	ə	a in ago	l	let, ball	ŋ	ring, singer
i	ice, fire		e in agent	m	met, trim	sh	she, dash
			e in father	n	not, ton	th	thin, truth
ō	open, go		i in unity	p	put, tap	*th*	then, father
ô	law, horn		o in collect	r	red, dear	zh	s in pleasure
oi	oil, point		u in focus	s	sell, pass		

An Americanism is a word or usage of a word that was born in this country. An open star before an entry word or definition means that the word or definition is an Americanism.

These dictionary entries are taken, by permission, in abridged or modified form from *Webster's New World Dictionary.* Copyright © 1992 by Simon & Schuster Inc.

Aa

ab·sent (ab′sənt) *adj.* not present; away [No one in the class was *absent* that day.]

a·chieve (ə chēv′) *v.* **1** to do; succeed in doing; accomplish [She *achieved* a lot while she was mayor.] **2** to get or reach by trying hard; gain [He *achieved* his goal of graduating.] —**a·chieved, a·chiev′ing**

ad·just (ə just′) *v.* **1** to change or move so as to make fit [You can *adjust* the piano bench to suit your size.] **2** to arrange the parts of to make work correctly; regulate [My watch needs *adjusting*.] **3** to settle or put in order [We *adjust* our accounts at the end of the month.]

ad·mit (ad mit′) *v.* **1** to permit or give the right to enter [One ticket *admits* two persons.] **2** to have room for [The hall *admits* 500 people.] **3** to take or accept as being true; confess [Lucy will not *admit* her mistake.] —**ad·mit′ted, ad·mit′ting**

a·dopt (ə däpt′) *v.* **1** to choose and take into one's family by a legal process [They *adopted* their daughter when she was four months old.] **2** to take and use as one's own [He *adopted* her teaching methods for his own classroom.] **3** to choose or follow [We must *adopt* a new plan of action.] —**a·dop′tion** *n.*

ad·vance (ad vans′) *v.* **1** to go or bring forward; move ahead [On first down they *advanced* the football two yards.] **2** to cause to happen earlier [The test date was *advanced* from May 10 to May 5.] —**ad·vanced′, ad·vanc′ing** ◆*n.* a moving forward or ahead; progress [new *advances* in science].

ad·van·tage (ad van′tij) *n.* a more favorable position; better chance [My speed gave me an *advantage* over them.]

ad·ven·ture (ad ven′chər) *n.* **1** an exciting and dangerous happening [He told of his *adventures* in the jungle.] **2** an unusual experience that is remembered [Going to a circus is an *adventure* for a child.]

ad·verb (ad′vurb) *n.* a word used with a verb, adjective, or another adverb to tell when, where, how, what kind, or how much [In the sentence, "She runs fast," the word "fast" is an *adverb*.]

ad·vice (ad vīz′) *n.* opinion given as to what to do or how to do something [We followed her *advice* in selecting a new home.]

af·fec·tion (ə fek′shən) *n.* fond or tender feeling; warm liking.

af·ter (af′tər) *adv.* **1** behind; coming next [You go on ahead, and we'll follow *after*.] **2** following in time; later [They came at noon and left three hours *after*.] ◆*prep.* **1** behind [The soldiers marched one *after* the other.] **2** in search of [What are you *after*?] **3** later than [It's ten minutes *after* four.] **4** as a result of; because of [*After* what has happened, he won't go.]

air·craft (er′kraft) *n.* any machine or machines for flying [Airplanes, dirigibles, and helicopters are all *aircraft*.] —*pl.* **air′craft**

☆**air·line** (er′līn) *n.* a system or company for moving freight and passengers by aircraft.

al·low (ə lou′) *v.* **1** to let be done; permit; let [*Allow* us to pay. No smoking *allowed*.] **2** to let have [She *allows* herself no sweets.] **3** to let enter or stay [Dogs are not usually *allowed* on buses.] **4** to admit to be true or right [His claim for $50 was *allowed*.]

al·ly (al′ī) *n.* a country or person joined with another for a special purpose [England was our *ally* during World War II.] —*pl.* **al′lies**

al·pha·bet (al′fə bet) *n.* **1** the letters of a language, given in the regular order [The English *alphabet* goes from A to Z.] **2** any system of symbols used in writing [the Braille *alphabet*].

al·though (ôl thō′) *conj.* in spite of the fact that; even if; though: *sometimes spelled* **altho** [*Although* the sun is shining, it may rain later.]

al·ti·tude (al′tə tōod *or* al′tə tyōod) *n.* **1** height; especially, the height of a thing above the earth's surface or above sea level. **2** a high place.

a·mount (ə mount′) *v.* to add up; total [The bill *amounts* to $4.50.] ◆*n.* **1** the sum; total [The bill was $50, but he paid only half that *amount*.] **2** a quantity [a small *amount* of rain].

am·pli·fy (am′plə fī′) *v.* to make larger, stronger, louder, etc. —**am′pli·fied, am′pli·fy·ing**

an·cient (ān′chənt *or* ān′shənt) *adj.* **1** of times long past; belonging to the early history of people, before about 500 A.D. **2** having lasted a long time; very old [their *ancient* quarrel].

An·go·ra (aŋ gôr′ə) *n.* **1** a kind of cat with long, silky fur. **2** a kind of goat with long, silky hair. This hair, called **Angora wool**, is used in making mohair. **3** a long-eared rabbit (**Angora rabbit**) with long, silky hair. This hair is used to make a soft yarn which is woven into sweaters, mittens, etc.

an·gry (aŋ′grē) *adj.* **1** feeling or showing anger [*angry* words; an *angry* crowd]. **2** wild and stormy [an *angry* sea]. —**an′gri·er, an′gri·est**

aircraft

a	ask, fat
ā	ape, date
ä	car, lot
e	elf, ten
ē	even, meet
i	is, hit
ī	ice, fire
ō	open, go
ô	law, horn
oi	oil, point
oo	look, pull
ōō	ooze, tool
ou	out, crowd
u	up, cut
u	fur, fern
ə	a in ago
	e in agent
	e in father
	i in unity
	o in collect
	u in focus
ch	chin, arch
ŋ	ring, singer
sh	she, dash
th	thin, truth
th	then, father
zh	s in pleasure

151

an·swer (an′sər) *n.* **1** something said, written, or done in return to a question, argument, letter, action, etc.; reply; response [The only *answers* required for the test were "true" or "false." His *answer* to the insult was to turn his back.] **2** a solution to a problem, as in arithmetic. ◆*v.* **1** to give an answer; reply or react, as to a question or action. **2** to be responsible [You must *answer* for the children's conduct.]

Ant·arc·ti·ca (ant ärk′ti kə *or* ant är′ti kə) a large area of land, completely covered with ice, around the South Pole: *also called* **Antarctic Continent.**

an·to·nym (an′tə nim) *n.* a word opposite in meaning to another word ["Sad" is an *antonym* of "happy."]

a·part·ment (ə pärt′mənt) *n.* a group of rooms, or a single large room, to live in. It is usually a single suite in a building (called an **apartment house**) of several or many suites.

ap·pe·tiz·er (ap′ə tīz ər) *n.* a small bit of a tasty food or a drink for giving one a bigger appetite at the beginning of a meal [Olives, tomato juice, etc. are used as *appetizers.*]

ap·ply (ə plī′) *v.* **1** to put or spread on [*Apply* glue to the surface.] **2** to put into use [*Apply* your knowledge to this problem.] **3** to work hard and steadily [He *applied* himself to his studies.] **4** to have to do with or be suitable to [This rule *applies* to all of us.] —**ap·plied′, ap·ply′ing**

ap·point (ə point′) *v.* **1** to fix or set; decide upon [Let's *appoint* a time for our meeting.] **2** to name or choose for an office or position [Federal judges are *appointed* by the President.]

ap·proach (ə prōch′) *v.* **1** to come closer or draw nearer [We saw three riders *approaching.* Vacation time *approaches.*] **2** to go to someone with a plan or request [Have you *approached* the bank about a loan?] ◆*n.* a coming closer or drawing nearer [The first robin marks the *approach* of spring.]

A·pril (ā′prəl) *n.* the fourth month of the year, which has 30 days: abbreviated **Apr.**

a·rith·me·tic (ə rith′mə tik) *n.* the science or skill of using numbers, especially in adding, subtracting, multiplying, and dividing.

Ar·i·zo·na (ar′ə zō′nə) a State in the southwestern part of the U.S.: abbreviated **Ariz., AZ**

ar·mor (är′mər) *n.* **1** covering worn to protect the body against weapons [The knight's suit of *armor* was made of metal plate.] **2** any covering that protects, as the shell of a turtle or the metal plates on a warship.

ar·my (är′mē) *n.* **1** a large group of soldiers trained for war, especially on land; also, all the soldiers of a country. **2** a large group of persons organized to work for some cause [the Salvation *Army*]. **3** any large group of persons or animals [An *army* of workers was building the bridge.] —*pl.* **ar′mies**

ar·riv·al (ə rī′vəl) *n.* **1** the act of arriving [to welcome the *arrival* of spring]. **2** a person or thing that has arrived [They are recent *arrivals* to the U.S. from South America.]

ar·rive (ə rīv′) *v.* **1** to come to a place after a journey [When does the bus from Chicago *arrive* here?] **2** to come [The time has *arrived* to say goodbye.] —**ar·rived′, ar·riv′ing**

art·ist (ärt′ist) *n.* **1** a person who works in any of the fine arts, especially in painting, drawing, sculpture, etc. **2** a person who does anything very well.

ash·es (ash′əz) *n.pl.* the grayish powder or fine dust that is left after something has been burned.

A·sia (ā′zhə) the largest continent, about 17,000,000 square miles in area. The Pacific Ocean is on its east and it is separated from northern Europe by the Ural Mountains.

as·tro·naut (as′trə nôt *or* as′trə nät) *n.* a person trained to make rocket flights in outer space.

as·tron·o·my (ə strän′ə mē) *n.* the science that studies the motion, size, and makeup of the stars, planets, comets, etc.

au·di·ence (ô′dē əns *or* ä′dē əns) *n.* **1** a group of persons gathered together to hear and see a speaker, a play, a concert, etc. **2** all those persons who are tuned in to a radio or TV program.

aunt (ant *or* änt) *n.* **1** a sister of one's mother or father. **2** the wife of one's uncle.

Aus·tral·ia (ô strāl′yə *or* ä strāl′yə) **1** an island continent in the Southern Hemisphere, southeast of Asia. **2** a country made up of this continent and Tasmania.

au·thor (ôthər *or* a′ther) *n.* a person who writes something, as a book or story [She is the *author* of many mystery stories.]

au·to·graph (ôt′ə graf) *n.* something written in a person's own handwriting, especially that person's name. ◆*v.* to write one's name on [Please *autograph* this baseball.]

au·to·mat·ic (ôt′ə mat′ik *or* ät′ə mat′ik) *adj.* **1** done without thinking about it, as if mechanically or from force of habit; unconscious [Breathing is usually *automatic.*] **2** moving or working by itself [*automatic* machinery].

a·vi·a·tor (ā′vē āt′ər) *n.* a person who flies airplanes; pilot.

a·while (ə hwīl′ *or* ə wīl′) *adv.* for a while; for a short time [Sit down and rest *awhile.*]

astronaut

awk·ward (ôk′wərd *or* äk′wərd) *adj.* **1** not having grace or skill; clumsy; bungling [an *awkward* dancer; an *awkward* writing style] . **2** hard to use or manage; not convenient [an *awkward* tool]. **3** uncomfortable; cramped [sitting in an *awkward* position]. **4** embarrassed or embarrassing [an *awkward* remark]. —**awk′ward·ly** *adv.* —**awk′ward·ness** *n.*

ax *or* **axe** (aks) *n.* a tool for chopping or splitting wood. It has a long wooden handle and a metal head with a sharp blade. —*pl.* **ax′es**

bag·gage (bag′ij) *n.* the trunks, suitcases, etc. that a person takes on a trip; luggage.

bait (bāt) *n.* **1** food put on a hook or trap to attract and catch fish or animals. **2** anything used to tempt or attract a person. ◆*v.* **1** to put bait on a hook or trap. **2** to torment or tease by saying annoying or cruel things [They *baited* me by calling me "Fatty."]

bal·co·ny (bal′kə nē) *n.* **1** a platform with a low wall or railing, that juts out from the side of a building. **2** an upper floor of rows of seats, as in a theater. It often juts out over the main floor. —*pl.* **bal′co·nies**

bal·lot (bal′ət) *n.* **1** a piece of paper on which a person marks a choice in voting. **2** the act or a way of voting.

band·age (ban′dij) *n.* a strip of cloth, gauze, etc. used to cover a sore or wound or to bind up an injured part of the body. ◆*v.* to bind or cover with a bandage. —**band′aged, band′ag·ing**

☆**ban·jo** (ban′jō) *n.* a stringed musical instrument with a long neck and a round body covered on top with tightly stretched skins. It has, usually, four or five strings that are plucked with the fingers or a pick. —*pl.* **ban′jos** *or* **ban′joes**

ban·ner (ban′ər) *n.* **1** a piece of cloth with an emblem or words on it [The *banner* behind the President's desk bears the seal of the U.S.] **2** a flag [the Star-Spangled *Banner*]. **3** a headline across a newspaper page. ◆*adj.* top; leading [Our company had a *banner* year in sales.]

barge (bärj) *n.* a large boat with a flat bottom, for carrying goods on rivers or canals. ◆*v.* to enter in a clumsy or rude way [They *barged* in without knocking.] —**barged, barg′ing**

ba·rom·e·ter (bə räm′ə tər) *n.* **1** an instrument that measures the pressure of the air around us. It is used in forecasting changes in the weather and finding the height above sea level. **2** anything that shows changes in conditions [The stock market is a *barometer* of business.] —**bar·o·met·ric** (bar′ə met′rik) *adj.*

bar·rel (bar′əl) *n.* **1** a large, round container that has bulging sides and a flat top and bottom. It is usually made of wooden slats bound together by metal hoops. **2** the amount a barrel will hold: the standard barrel in the U.S. holds 31 1/2 gallons (119.2275 liters). ◆*v.* to put in barrels. —**bar′reled** *or* **bar′relled, bar′rel·ing** *or* **bar′rel·ling**

bask (bask) *v.* to warm oneself pleasantly [to *bask* in the sun].

bass (bas) *n.* a fish with spiny fins, found in both fresh and salt water and used for food. —*pl.* **bass** *or* **bass′es**

bat·ter·y (bat′ər ē) *n.* an electric cell or a group of connected cells that furnishes an electric current [*Batteries* are used in automobiles and flashlights.] —*pl.* **bat′ter·ies**

be·gin (bē gin′) *v.* to start being, doing, acting, etc.; get under way [Work *begins* at 8:00 A.M. My cold *began* with a sore throat.] —**be·gan′, be·gun′, be·gin′ning**

be·gin·ning (bē gin′iŋ) *n.* a start or starting; first part or first action [We came in just after the *beginning* of the movie. Going to the dance together was the *beginning* of our friendship.]

be·lief (bē lēf′) *n.* a feeling that something is true or real; faith [You cannot destroy my *belief* in the honesty of most people.] —*pl.* **be·liefs**

be·lieve (bē lēv′) *v.* **1** to accept as true or real [Can we *believe* that story?] **2** to have trust or confidence [I know you will win; I *believe* in you.] **3** to suppose; guess. —**be·lieved′, be·liev′ing** —**be·liev′a·ble** *adj.* —**be·liev′er** *n.*

bench (bench) *n.* **1** a long, hard seat for several persons, with or without a back. **2** a strong table on which work with tools is done [a carpenter's *bench*]. **3** the place where judges sit in a courtroom. **4** a seat where sports players sit when not on the field. —*pl.* **bench′es**

bend (bend) *v.* **1** to pull or press something hard or stiff into a curve or angle [*Bend* the branch down so we can reach the plums.] **2** to be curved in this way [The trees *bent* under the weight of the snow.] **3** to stoop [*Bend* over and touch your toes.] —**bent, bend′ing** ◆*n.* **1** the act of bending. **2** a bent or curving part.

banjo

a	ask, fat
ā	ape, date
ä	car, lot
e	elf, ten
ē	even, meet
i	is, hit
ī	ice, fire
ō	open, go
ô	law, horn
oi	oil, point
ഠഠ	look, pull
o͞o	ooze, tool
ou	out, crowd
u	up, cut
ʉ	fur, fern
ə	a in ago
	e in agent
	e in father
	i in unity
	o in collect
	u in focus
ch	chin, arch
ŋ	ring, singer
sh	she, dash
th	thin, truth
th	then, father
zh	s in pleasure

153

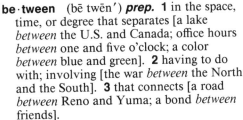

bison

be·tween (bē twēn′) **prep. 1** in the space, time, or degree that separates [a lake *between* the U.S. and Canada; office hours *between* one and five o'clock; a color *between* blue and green]. **2** having to do with; involving [the war *between* the North and the South]. **3** that connects [a road *between* Reno and Yuma; a bond *between* friends].

bev·er·age (bev′ər ij *or* bev′rij) **n.** any kind of drink (except water), as milk, coffee, or lemonade.

bi·cy·cle (bī′si kəl) **n.** a vehicle to ride on that has two wheels, one behind the other. It is moved by foot pedals and steered by a handlebar. ◆**v.** to ride a bicycle. —**bi′cy·cled, bi′cy·cling**

birth·day (burth′dā) **n. 1** the day on which a person is born or something is begun. **2** the anniversary of this day.

bi·son (bī′sən) **n.** a wild animal of the ox family, with a shaggy mane, short, curved horns, and a humped back. The American bison is often called a *buffalo*. —*pl.* **bi′son**

blend (blend) **v. 1** to mix different kinds together in order to get a certain flavor, color, etc. [to *blend* tea or paint]. **2** to come together or mix so that the parts are no longer distinct [The sky *blended* with the sea at the horizon.] **3** to go well together; be in harmony [Her blue sweater *blends* well with her gray skirt.] ◆**n.** a mixture of different kinds [a *blend* of coffee].

☆**bliz·zard** (bliz′ərd) **n.** a heavy snowstorm with very strong, cold winds.

board (bôrd) **n. 1** a long, flat, broad piece of sawed wood, used in building. **2** a flat piece of wood or other hard material made for a special use [a checker*board*; a bulletin *board*; an ironing *board*]. **3** a group of people who manage or control a business, school, department, etc. [*board* of education]. ◆**v. 1** to cover up with boards [The windows of the old house were *boarded* up.] **2** to get on a ship, airplane, bus, etc.

boast (bōst) **v. 1** to talk about with too much pride and pleasure; praise too highly; brag [We tired of hearing him *boast* of his bravery.] **2** to be proud of having [Our city *boasts* a fine new zoo.]

bob (bäb) **v. 1** to move with short, jerky motions [Our heads *bobbed* up and down as our car bounced over the ruts.] **2** to cut off short [to *bob* a dog's tail]. —**bobbed, bob′bing** ◆**n. 1** a short, jerky movement [She greeted us with a *bob* of her head.] **2** a style of short haircut for women or girls. **3** a hanging weight at the end of a plumb line. **4** a cork on a fishing line.

bod·y (bäd′ē) **n. 1** the whole physical part of a person or animal [Athletes have strong *bodies*.] **2** the main part of a person or animal, not including the head, legs, and arms [The boxer received many blows to the *body*.] **3** the main or central part of anything, as the trunk of a tree or the part of a car that holds the passengers. —*pl.* **bod′ies**

boil (boil) **v. 1** to bubble up and become steam or vapor by being heated [Water *boils* at 100°C.] **2** to heat a liquid until it bubbles up in this way [to *boil* water]. **3** to cook in a boiling liquid [to *boil* potatoes]. **4** to be stirred up, as with rage. ◆**n.** the condition of boiling [Bring the soup to a *boil*.]

bomb (bäm) **n.** a hollow case filled with an explosive or a poisonous gas: bombs are blown up by a fuse or timing device or by being dropped or thrown against something with force.

☆**boss** (bôs *or* bäs) **n. 1** a person who is in charge of workers, as an employer, a manager, or a foreman. **2** a person who controls a political group, as in a county. —*pl.* **bosses.** ◆ **v.** to act as boss of.

both·er (bä*th*′ər) **v. 1** to annoy; cause worry or trouble to; pester [Does the noise *bother* you?] **2** to take the time or trouble [Don't *bother* to answer this letter.] ◆**n.** something that annoys or causes worry or trouble [Flies are a *bother*.]

bot·tle (bät′l) **n. 1** a container, especially for liquids, usually made of glass or plastic. Bottles generally have a narrow neck and no handles. **2** the amount that a bottle holds [The baby drank a *bottle* of milk.] ◆**v. 1** to put into a bottle or into bottles. **2** to store under pressure in a tank [*bottled* gas]. —**bot′tled, bot′tling**

bounce (bouns) **v. 1** to hit against a surface so as to spring back; bound or rebound [to *bounce* a ball against a wall; to *bounce* up and down on a sofa]. **2** to move suddenly; jump; leap [I *bounced* out of bed when the alarm went off.] —**bounced, bounc′ing** ◆**n. 1** a springing or bounding; leap. **2** the ability to bound or rebound [This ball has lost its *bounce*.]

bounc·ing (boun′siŋ) **adj.** big, healthy, strong, etc. [It's a *bouncing* baby boy.]

bou·quet (bōō kā′ *or* bō kā′) **n. 1** a bunch of flowers. **2** (bōō kā′) a fragrant smell.

☆**box·car** (bäks′kär) **n.** a railroad car for carrying freight, with a roof and closed sides.

brain (brān) **n. 1** the gray and white tissue inside the skull of a person or of any animal with a backbone. It is the main part of the nervous system, by which one thinks and feels. **2** *often* **brains**, *pl.* intelligence; understanding.

brake (brāk) *n.* a device used to slow down or stop a car, machine, etc. It is often a block or band that is pressed against a wheel or other moving part. ◆*v.* to slow down or stop with a brake. —**braked, brak′ing**

branch (branch) *n.* any part of a tree growing from the trunk or from a main limb.

break (brāk) *v.* **1** to come or make come apart by force; split or crack sharply into pieces [*Break* an egg into the bowl. The rusty hinge *broke.*] **2** to force one's way [A firefighter *broke* through the door.] **3** to get out of working order; make or become useless [You can *break* your watch by winding it too tightly.] **4** to fail to carry out or follow [to *break* an agreement; to *break* the law] —**broke, bro′ken, break′ing** ◆*n.* **1** a broken place [The X-ray showed a *break* in the bone.] **2** an interruption [Recess is a relaxing *break* in our school day.]

break·down (brāk′doun) *n.* a failure to work properly [*breakdown* of a machine].

break·fast (brek′fəst) *n.* the first meal of the day. ◆*v.* to eat breakfast.

breeze (brēz) *n.* **1** a light and gentle wind. **2** a thing easy to do: *used only in everyday talk* [The test was a *breeze.*] ◆*v.* to move or go quickly, briskly, etc.: *slang in this meaning.* —**breezed, breez′ing**

brief (brēf) *adj.* **1** not lasting very long; short in time [a *brief* visit]. **2** using just a few words; not wordy; concise [a *brief* news report]. ◆*v.* to give the main points or necessary facts to [to *brief* pilots before a flight]. —**brief′ly** *adv.* —**brief′ness** *n.*

bril·liant (bril′yənt) *adj.* **1** very bright; glittering or sparkling [the *brilliant* sun on the water]. **2** outstanding or distinguished [a *brilliant* performance]

bring (briŋ) *v.* **1** to carry or lead here or to the place where the speaker will be [*Bring* it to my house tomorrow.] **2** to cause to happen or come [War *brings* death and hunger.]

broc·co·li (bräk′ə lē) *n.* a plant whose tender shoots and loose heads of tiny green buds are eaten as a vegetable.

broil (broil) *v.* **1** to cook or be cooked close to a flame or other high heat [to *broil* steaks over charcoal]. **2** to make or be very hot [a *broiling* summer day]. ◆*n.* the act or state of broiling.

broth·er (bruth′ər) *n.* **1** a boy or man as he is related to the other children of his parents. **2** a person who is close to one in some way; especially, a fellow member of the same race, religion, club, etc. —*pl.* **broth′ers**

brought (brôt *or* brät) *past tense and past participle of* **bring.**

buf·fa·lo (buf′ə lō) *n.* a wild ox, sometimes tamed as a work animal, as the water buffalo of India. The American bison is also commonly called a *buffalo.* —*pl.* **buf′fa·loes** *or* **buf′fa·los** *or* **buf′fa·lo**

bump (bump) *v.* **1** to knock against something; hit with a jolt [The bus *bumped* the car ahead of it. Don't *bump* into the wall.] **2** to move with jerks or jumps; jolt [The car *bumped* over the railroad tracks.] ◆*n.* **1** a knock or blow; light jolt. **2** a part that bulges out, causing an uneven surface. **3** a swelling caused by a blow.

bur·y (ber′ē) *v.* **1** to put a dead body into the earth, a tomb, or the sea [The Egyptians *buried* the Pharaohs in pyramids.] **2** to cover up so as to hide [He *buried* his face in his hands.] **3** to put away and forget [Let's *bury* our feud.] **4** to put oneself deeply into [She *buried* herself in her work.] —**bur′ies, bur′ied, bur′y·ing**

busi·ness (biz′nəs) *n.* **1** what one does for a living; one's work or occupation [Shakespeare's *business* was writing plays.] **2** what one has a right or duty to do [You had no *business* telling her I was here.] **3** the buying and selling of goods and services; commerce; trade. **4** a place where things are made or sold; store or factory [Nino owns three *businesses.*]—*pl.* **bus′i·ness·es**

but·ter·milk (but′ər milk) *n.* the sour liquid left after churning butter from milk.

buy (bī) *v.* to get by paying money or something else [The Dutch *bought* Manhattan Island for about $24.] —**bought, buy′ing**

byte (bīt) *n.* a series of computer bits, usually eight, used as a single piece of information.

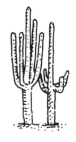

cactus

Cc

cab·in (kab′in) *n.* **1** a small house built in a simple, rough way, usually of wood [Lincoln was born in a log *cabin.*] **2** a room on a ship, especially one with berths for sleeping. **3** the space in an airplane where the passengers ride.

ca·boose (kə boos′) *n.* ☆a car for the crew on a freight train. It is usually the last car.

cac·tus (kak′təs) *n.* a plant with fleshy stems that bear spines or scales instead of leaves. Cactuses grow in hot, dry places and often have showy flowers. —*pl.* **cac′tus·es** *or* **cac·ti** (kak′tī)

cal·cu·la·tor (kal′kyoo lāt′ər) *n.* **1** a person who calculates. **2** a machine that adds, subtracts, etc. rapidly, now often by electronic means.

calf¹ (kaf) *n.* **1** a young cow or bull. **2** a young elephant, whale, hippopotamus, seal, etc. **3** *a shorter word for* **calfskin.** —*pl.* **calves**

a	ask, fat
ā	ape, date
ä	car, lot
e	elf, ten
ē	even, meet
i	is, hit
ī	ice, fire
ō	open, go
ô	law, horn
oi	oil, point
oo	look, pull
o͞o	ooze, tool
ou	out, crowd
u	up, cut
ʉ	fur, fern
ə	a in ago
	e in agent
	e in father
	i in unity
	o in collect
	u in focus
ch	chin, arch
ŋ	ring, singer
sh	she, dash
th	thin, truth
th	then, father
zh	s in pleasure

calf² (kaf) *n.* the fleshy back part of the leg between the knee and the ankle. —*pl.* **calves**

cam·el (kam′əl) *n.* a large, cud-chewing animal with a humped back, that is commonly used for riding and for carrying goods in Asian and North African deserts. When food and drink are scarce, it can keep going for a few days on the fat and water stored in its body tissue. The **Arabian camel** has one hump and the **Bac·tri·an** (bak′trē ən) **camel** has two.

can·di·date (kan′di dāt′) *n.* a person who seeks, or who has been suggested for, an office or award [a *candidate* for mayor].

car·di·nal (kärd′n əl) *adj.* **1** of most importance; chief [The *cardinal* points of the compass are north, south, east, and west.] **2** bright-red. ◆*n.* ☆ an American songbird that is bright red and has a black face.

car·go (kär′gō) *n.* the load of goods carried by a ship, airplane, truck, etc. —*pl.* **car′goes** or **car′gos**

car·ry (ker′ē) *v.* **1** to take from one place to another; transport or conduct [Please help me *carry* these books home. The large pipe *carries* water. Air *carries* sounds.] **2** to cause to go; lead [A love of travel *carried* them around the world.] **3** to bring over a figure from one column to the next in adding a row of figures. —**car′ried, car′ry·ing**

car·ton (kärt′n) *n.* a box or other container made of cardboard, plastic, etc.

cast (kast) *v.* **1** to throw out or down; toss; fling; hurl [to *cast* stones into the water; to *cast* a line in fishing]. **2** to deposit a ballot or vote. ◆*n.* a stiff plaster form for keeping a broken arm or leg in place while it is healing. —**cast, cast′ing**

catch·er (kach′ər *or* kech′ər) *n.* **1** one who catches. ☆**2** in baseball, the player behind home plate, who catches pitched balls that are not hit away by the batter.

cat·e·go·ry (kat′ə gôr′ē) *n.* a division of a main subject or group; class [Biology is divided into two *categories*, zoology and botany.] —*pl.* **cat′e·go′ries**

cause (kôz *or* käz) *n.* **1** a person or thing that brings about some action or result [A spark from the wire was the *cause* of the fire.] **2** a reason for some action, feeling, etc. [We had *cause* to admire the coach.] ◆*v.* to be the cause of; make happen; bring about [The icy streets *caused* some accidents.] —**caused, caus′ing** —**cause′less** *adj.*

cau·tious (kô′shəs *or* kä′shəs) *adj.* careful not to get into danger or make mistakes [a *cautious* chess player]. —**cau′tious·ly** *adv.*

ceil·ing (sēl′iŋ) *n.* the inside top part of a room, opposite the floor.

camel

cel·e·ry (sel′ər ē) *n.* a plant whose crisp, long stalks are eaten as a vegetable.

ce·ment (sə ment′) *n.* **1** a powder made of lime and clay, mixed with water and sand to make mortar or with water, sand, and gravel to make concrete. It hardens like stone when it dries. **2** any soft substance that fastens things together when it hardens, as paste or glue ◆*v.* to fasten together or cover with cement [to *cement* the pieces of a broken cup].

cen·ter (sen′tər) *n.* **1** a point inside a circle or sphere that is the same distance from all points on the circumference or surface. **2** the middle point or part; place at the middle [A vase of flowers stood at the *center* of the table.] ◆*v.* to place in or at the center [Try to *center* the design on the page.]

chain (chān) *n.* **1** a number of links or loops joined together in a line that can be bent [a *chain* of steel; a *chain* of daisies]. **2 chains,** *pl.* anything that binds or holds someone prisoner, as bonds or shackles. **3** a series of things joined together [a mountain *chain*; a *chain* of events]. ◆*v.* **1** to fasten or bind with chains [The prisoner was *chained* to the wall.] **2** to hold down; bind [I was *chained* to my job.]

cham·pi·on (cham′pē ən) *n.* a person, animal, or thing that wins first place or is judged to be best in a contest or sport [a tennis *champion*].

change (chānj) *v.* **1** to make or become different in some way; alter [Time *changes* all things. His voice began to *change* at the age of thirteen.] **2** to put or take one thing in place of another; substitute [to *change* one's clothes; to *change* jobs]. **3** to give or take one thing in return for another; substitute [Let's *change* seats. Can you *change* this dollar bill for four quarters?] —**changed, chang′ing** ◆*n.* **1** the act of changing in some way [There will be a *change* in the weather tomorrow.] **2** something put in place of something else [a fresh *change* of clothing]. **3** the money returned when one has paid more than the amount owed [If it costs 70 cents and you pay with a dollar, you get back 30 cents as *change*.]

charge (chärj) *v.* **1** to load or fill [to *charge* a gun with ammunition]. ☆**2** to supply with electrical energy [to *charge* a battery]. **3** to give a task, duty, etc. to; make responsible for [The nurse was *charged* with the care of the child.] **4** to set as a price; ask for payment [Barbers once *charged* a quarter for a haircut. We do not *charge* for gift wrappings.] —**charged, charg′ing**

chat (chat) *v.* to talk in an easy, relaxed way. —**chat′ted, chat′ting** ◆*n.* an easy, relaxed talk or conversation.

cheat (chēt) *v.* to act in a dishonest or unfair way in order to get what one wants [to *cheat* on a test].

check (chek) **n. 1** a test to find out if something is as it should be [Add the column of numbers again as a *check* on your answer.] **2** the mark √, used to show that something is right, or to call attention to something. **3** a piece of paper telling how much one owes, as for a meal at a restaurant. **4** a written order to a bank to pay a certain amount of money from one's account to a certain person. **5** a pattern of small squares like a checkerboard; also, any of the squares in such a pattern. ◆**v.** to prove to be right or find what is wanted by examining, comparing, etc. [These figures *check* with mine. *Check* the records for this information.]

cheer·ful (chir′fəl) **adj. 1** full of cheer; glad; joyful [a *cheerful* smile]. **2** bright and gay [a *cheerful* room]. **3** willing; glad to help [a *cheerful* worker]. —**cheer′ful·ly adv.** —**cheer′ful·ness n.**

chee·tah (chēt′ə) **n.** an animal found in Africa and southern Asia that is like the leopard but smaller. It can be trained to hunt.

cher·ry (cher′ē) **n. 1** a small, round fruit with sweet flesh covering a smooth, hard seed. Cherries are bright red, dark red, or yellow. **2** the tree that this fruit grows on. **3** bright red. —*pl.* **cher′ries**

Chi·ca·go (shi kä′gō) a city in northeastern Illinois, on Lake Michigan.

chick·en (chik′ən) **n. 1** a common farm bird raised for its eggs and flesh; hen or rooster, especially a young one. **2** the flesh of a chicken.

chief (chēf) **n.** the leader or head of some group [an Indian *chief*; the *chief* of a hospital staff]. —*pl.* **chiefs** ◆**adj. 1** having the highest position [the *chief* foreman]. **2** main; most important [Jill's *chief* interest is golf.]

chief·ly (chēf′lē) **adv.** most of all; mainly; mostly [A watermelon is *chiefly* water.]

child (chīld) **n. 1** a baby; infant. **2** a young boy or girl. **3** a son or daughter [Their *children* are all grown up.] —*pl.* **chil′dren**

chil·dren (chil′drən) **n.** *plural of* **child.**

chim·ney (chim′nē) **n. 1** a pipe or shaft going up through a roof to carry off smoke from a furnace, fireplace, or stove. Chimneys are usually enclosed with brick or stone. **2** a glass tube around the flame of a lamp. —*pl.* **chim′neys**

Chi·na (chī′nə) a country in eastern Asia. It has the most people of any country in the world.

☆**chow·der** (chou′dər) **n.** a thick soup made of fish or clams with onions, potatoes, milk or tomatoes, etc.

church (church) **n. 1** a building for holding religious services, especially one for Christian worship. **2** religious services [*Church* will be at 11 on Sunday.] —*pl.* **church′es**

cir·cle (sur′kəl) **n. 1** a closed curved line forming a perfectly round, flat figure. Every point on this line is the same distance from a point inside called the center. **2** the figure formed by such a line. **3** anything round like a circle or ring [a *circle* of children playing a game].

clap (klap) **v. 1** to make the sudden, loud sound of two flat surfaces being struck together **2** to strike the palms of the hands together, as in applauding. —**clapped, clap′ping** ◆**n. 1** the sudden, loud sound of clapping [a *clap* of thunder]. **2** a sharp blow; slap.

clash (klash) **n. 1** a loud, harsh noise, as of metal striking against metal with great force [the *clash* of a sword on a shield]. **2** a sharp disagreement; conflict [a *clash* of ideas]. —*pl.* **clash′es** ◆**v.** to strike with a clash [He *clashed* the cymbals together.]

clasp (klasp) **n. 1** a fastening, as a hook or catch, for holding two things or parts together [The *clasp* on my pocketbook is loose.] **2** a holding in the arms; embrace. **3** a holding with the hand; grip. ◆**v.** to fasten with a clasp.

class (klas) a group of students meeting together to be taught [Half the *class* missed school today.] —*pl.* **clas·ses**

claw (klô *or* klä) **n. 1** a sharp, curved nail on the foot of an animal or bird. **2** a foot with such nails [The eagle holds its victims in its *claws*]. **3** the grasping part on each front leg of a lobster, crab, or scorpion.

clean (klēn) **adj. 1** without dirt or impure matter [*clean* dishes; *clean* oil]. **2** without evil or wrongdoing [to lead a *clean* life]. **3** neat and tidy [to keep a *clean* desk]. ◆**v.** to make clean. [Please *clean* the oven.]

clerk (klurk) **n. 1** an office worker who keeps records, types letters, etc. [Some *clerks*, as a *clerk* of courts or a city *clerk*, have special duties.] ☆**2** a person who sells in a store; salesperson.

Cleve·land (klēv′lənd) a city in northeastern Ohio.

cli·mate (klī′mət) **n. 1** the average weather conditions of a place over a period of years [Arizona has a mild, dry *climate*, but its weather last week was stormy.] **2** a region with particular weather conditions [They went south to a warmer *climate*.]

clo·ver (klō′vər) **n.** a low-growing plant with leaves in three parts and small, sweet-smelling flowers. *Red clover* is grown for fodder; *white clover* is often found in lawns.

clue (klōō) **n.** a fact or thing that helps to solve a puzzle or mystery [Muddy footprints were a *clue* to the man's guilt.]

clum·sy (klum′zē) **adj.** not having good control in moving the hands or feet; awkward [The *clumsy* waiter dropped the dish.] —**clum′si·er, clum′si·est**

cheetah

a	ask, fat
ā	ape, date
ä	car, lot
e	elf, ten
ē	even, meet
i	is, hit
ī	ice, fire
ō	open, go
ô	law, horn
oi	oil, point
၊၊	look, pull
၊၊	ooze, tool
ou	out, crowd
u	up, cut
u	fur, fern
ə	a in ago
	e in agent
	e in father
	i in unity
	o in collect
	u in focus
ch	chin, arch
ŋ	ring, singer
sh	she, dash
th	thin, truth
th	then, father
zh	s in pleasure

cock·pit (käk′pit) *n.* in a small airplane, the space where the pilot and passengers sit. In a large plane, it is the space for the pilot and copilot.

col·an·der (kul′ən dər *or* käl′ən dər) *n.* a pan with holes in the bottom for draining off liquids, as in washing vegetables.

cold (kōld) *adj.* 1 having a temperature much lower than that of the human body; very chilly; frigid [a *cold* day; a *cold* drink]. 2 without the proper heat or warmth [Your bath will get *cold*.] 3 feeling chilled [If you are *cold*, put on your coat.] 4 without any feeling; unkind, unfriendly, or gloomy [a *cold* welcome; a *cold* stare]. —**cold′er, cold′est**

col·lege (käl′ij) *n.* a school that one can go to after high school for higher studies.

Co·lum·bus (kə lum′bəs) the capital of Ohio.

comb (kōm) *n.* a thin strip of hard rubber, plastic, metal, etc. with teeth. A comb is passed through the hair to arrange or clean it, or is put in the hair to hold it in place. ◆*v.* 1 to smooth, arrange, or clean with a comb. 2 to search carefully through [I *combed* the house for that book.]

come (kum) *v.* 1 to move from "there" to "here" [*Come* to me. Will you *come* to our party?] 2 to arrive or appear [Help will *come* soon.] —**came, come, com′ing**

com·ing (kum′iŋ) *adj.* that will come; approaching; on the way [Let's go this *coming* Friday.] ◆*n.* arrival; approach [Cold mornings warn of the *coming* of winter.]

com·mon (käm′ən) *adj.* 1 belonging equally to each or all [England, Canada, and the U.S. share a *common* language.] 2 belonging to all the people; public [a *common* park]. 3 of, from, by, or to all [the *common* good]. 4 often seen or heard; widespread; usual [Squirrels are *common* in these woods. That's a *common* saying.]

com·mu·ni·ty (kə myōo′ni tē) *n.* 1 all the people who live in a particular district, city, etc. [The new swimming pool is for the use of the entire *community*.] 2 a group of people living together and having similar interests and work [a college *community*]. —*pl.* **com·mu′ni·ties**

☆**com·mut·er** (kə myōot′ər) *n.* a person who travels daily by train, bus, car, etc. between home and work or school.

com·pare (kəm per′) *v.* 1 to describe as being the same; liken [The sound of thunder can be *compared* to the roll of drums.] 2 to examine certain things in order to find out how they are alike or different [How do the two cars *compare* in size and price?] 3 to equal or come close to by comparison [Few dogs can *compare* with the Great Dane in size.] —**com·pared′, com·par′ing**

com·put·er (kəm pyōot′ər) *n.* 1 a person who computes. 2 an electronic device used as a calculator or to store and select data.

con·duct (kän′dukt) *n.* the way one acts or behaves; behavior [The teacher praised the students for their good *conduct* in class.] ◆*v.* (kən dukt′) 1 to manage; direct; be the leader of [to *conduct* a meeting; to *conduct* an orchestra]. 2 to behave [They *conducted* themselves like adults.] 3 to be a means for carrying; transmit [Copper *conducts* electricity.]

cone (kōn) *n.* a solid object that narrows evenly from a flat circle at one end to a point at the other.

con·stel·la·tion (kän′stə lā′shən) *n.* a group of stars, usually named after something that it is supposed to suggest [Orion is a *constellation* seen in the winter sky.]

con·struct (kən strukt′) *v.* to make or build with a plan [to *construct* a house or a theory].

con·tact (kän′takt) *v.* to get in touch with; communicate with [*Contact* my cousin as soon as possible.]

con·test (kən test′) *v.* 1 to try to prove that something is not true, right, or lawful; dispute [to *contest* a will]. 2 to fight for; struggle to win or keep [to *contest* a prize]. ◆*n.* (kän′test) 1 a fight, struggle, or argument. 2 a race, game, etc. in which there is a struggle to be the winner.

con·ti·nent (kän′ti nənt) *n.* any of the main large land areas of the earth. The continents are Africa, Asia, Australia, Europe, North America, South America, and, sometimes, Antarctica. —**the Continent,** all of Europe except the British Isles.

con·tin·ue (kən tin′yōo) *v.* 1 to keep on being or doing [The rain *continued* for five days.] 2 to stay in the same place or position [The chairman will *continue* in office for another year.] 3 to go on or start again after a stop; resume [After a sip of water, the speaker *continued*.] 4 to go on or extend; stretch —**con·tin′ued, con·tin′u·ing**

con·trol (kən trōl′) *v.* 1 to have the power of ruling, guiding, or managing [A thermostat *controls* the heat.] 2 to hold back; curb [*Control* your temper!] —**con·trolled′, con·trol′ling** ◆*n.* power to direct or manage [He's a poor coach, with little *control* over the team.]

con·vince (kən vins′) *v.* to make feel sure; persuade [I'm *convinced* they are telling the truth.] —**con·vinced′, con·vinc′ing**

con·voy (kän′voi) *n.* a group of ships or vehicles traveling together in order to protect one another.

colander

constellation

cop·y (käp′ē) *n.* **1** a thing made just like another; imitation or likeness [four carbon *copies* of a letter]. **2** any one of a number of books, magazines, pictures, etc. with the same printed matter [a library with six *copies* of *Tom Sawyer*]. **3** a piece of writing that is to be set in type for printing [Reporters must write clear *copy*.] —*pl.* **cop′ies** ◆*v.* **1** to make a copy or copies of [*Copy* the questions that are on the chalkboard.] **2** to act or be the same as; imitate. —**cop′ied, cop′y·ing**

cor·al (kôr′əl) *n.* **1** a hard, stony substance made up of the skeletons of many tiny sea animals. Reefs of coral are found in tropical seas. **2** a piece of coral. ◆*adj.* **1** made of coral. **2** yellowish-red in color.

cor·ner (kôr′nər) *n.* **1** the place where two lines or surfaces come together to form an angle. **2** the space between such lines or surfaces [a lamp in the *corner* of a room]. **3** the place where two streets meet. **4** a place or region; quarter [every *corner* of America].

cos·tume (käs′tōōm *or* käs′tyōōm) *n.* **1** the way or style of dressing of a certain place or time or for a certain purpose [a Japanese *costume*; an eighteenth-century *costume*; a riding *costume*]. **2** clothing worn by an actor in a play or by a person at a masquerade [a pirate *costume*].

cot·tage (kät′ij) *n.* a small house [a peasant's *cottage*; a summer *cottage* at the beach].

cou·gar (kōō′gər) *n.* a large animal of the cat family, with a slender, tan body and a long tail.

cough (kôf *or* käf) *v.* **1** to force air from the lungs with a sudden, loud noise, as to clear the throat. **2** to get out of the throat by coughing [to *cough* up phlegm]. ◆*n.* **1** the act or sound of coughing. **2** a condition of coughing often [I have a bad *cough*.]

coun·ty (koun′tē) *n.* ☆**1** in the U.S., any of the sections into which a State is divided. Each county has its own officials. **2** any of the districts into which Great Britain and Ireland are divided. —*pl.* **coun′ties**

cou·ple (kup′əl) *n.* two things of the same kind that go together; pair [a *couple* of bookends].

cour·age (kʉr′ij) *n.* the quality of being able to control one's fear and so to face danger, pain, or trouble willingly; bravery.

cous·in (kuz′ən) *n.* **1** the son or daughter of one's uncle or aunt: *also called* **first cousin**. You are a *second cousin* to the children of your parents' first cousins, and you are a *first cousin once removed* to the children of your first cousins. **2** a distant relation.

crack (krak) *v.* **1** to make or cause to make a sudden, sharp noise, as of something breaking [The lion tamer *cracked* his whip.] **2** to break or split, with or without the parts falling apart [The snowball *cracked* the window. *Crack* the coconut open.] **3** to become harsh or change pitch suddenly [Her voice *cracked* when she sang the highest note.]

craft (kraft) *n.* **1** special skill or ability. **2** work that takes special skill, especially with the hands [the *craft* of weaving]. **3** the members of a skilled trade. **4** skill in fooling or tricking others; slyness.

crash (krash) *v.* **1** to fall, hit, or break with force and with a loud, smashing noise. **2** to fall to the earth so as to be damaged or smashed [The airplane *crashed*.] ◆*n.* **1** a loud, smashing noise. **2** the crashing of a car, airplane, etc.

cray·on (krā′ən *or* krā′än) *n.* a small stick of chalk, charcoal, or colored wax, used for drawing or writing. ◆*v.* to draw with crayons.

cra·zy (krā′zē) *adj.* mentally ill; insane. —**cra′zi·er, cra′zi·est**

cream (krēm) *n.* **1** the oily, yellowish part of milk that rises to the top and contains the butterfat. **2** any food that is made of cream or is like cream [ice *cream*]. **3** a smooth, oily substance used to clean and soften the skin.

creep (krēp) *v.* **1** to move along with the body close to the ground, as a baby on hands and knees. **2** to move in a slow or sneaking way [The cars *crept* along in the heavy traffic. The thieves *crept* into the store at night.] **3** to come on almost without being noticed [Old age *crept* up on her.] —**crept, creeping**

crept (krept) *v.* past tense and past participle of **creep**.

cries (krīz) **1** *the form of the verb* **cry** *used in the present with* he, she, *or* it. **2** *the plural of the noun* **cry**.

crime (krīm) *n.* **1** the doing of something that is against the law; serious wrongdoing that breaks the law. **2** an evil or foolish act; sin [It would be a *crime* to waste this food.]

cruise (krōōz) *v.* **1** to sail or drive from place to place, as for pleasure or in searching for something. **2** to move smoothly at a speed that is not strained [The airplane *cruised* at 300 miles per hour.] —**cruised, cruis′ing** ◆*n.* a ship voyage from place to place for pleasure.

crumb (krum) *n.* **1** a tiny piece broken off, as of bread or cake. **2** any bit or scrap [*crumbs* of knowledge].

crunch (krunch) *v.* **1** to chew with a noisy, crackling sound [to *crunch* raw carrots]. **2** to grind or move over with a noisy, crushing sound [The wheels *crunched* the pebbles in the driveway.]

costume

a	ask, fat
ā	ape, date
ä	car, lot
e	elf, ten
ē	even, meet
i	is, hit
ī	ice, fire
ō	open, go
ô	law, horn
oi	oil, point
ͻͻ	look, pull
ōō	ooze, tool
ou	out, crowd
u	up, cut
ʉ	fur, fern
ə	a in ago
	e in agent
	e in father
	i in unity
	o in collect
	u in focus
ch	chin, arch
ŋ	ring, singer
sh	she, dash
th	thin, truth
th	then, father
zh	s in pleasure

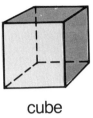

cube

crush (krush) *v.* **1** to press or squeeze with force so as to break, hurt, or put out of shape [She *crushed* the flower in her hand. His hat was *crushed* when he sat on it.] **2** to grind or pound into bits [This machine *crushes* rocks.] **3** to bring to an end by force; subdue; suppress [The government *crushed* the revolt.] ◆*n.* a crushing or squeezing; strong pressure.

cry (krī) *v.* **1** to make a loud sound with the voice; call out or shout [Lou *cried* out in fright when a face appeared at the window.] **2** to show sorrow, pain, etc. by sobbing or shedding tears. **3** to say loudly; shout; exclaim ["Help! Help!" the victim *cried*.] —**cried, cry′ing** ◆*n.* **1** a loud sound made by the voice; shout or call [I heard your *cry* for help.] **2** a fit of sobbing and weeping [I had a good *cry* and fell asleep.] **3** the sound an animal makes [the *cry* of a lost sheep]. —*pl.* **cries**

cube (kyo͞ob) *n.* **1** a solid with six square sides, all the same size. **2** anything with more or less this shape [an ice *cube*]. **3** the result got by multiplying a number by itself and then multiplying the product by the same number [The *cube* of 3 is 27 (3 × 3 × 3 = 27).] ◆*v.* to cut into cubes [I *cubed* the fruit for salad.] —**cubed, cub′ing**

curb (kʉrb) *n.* **1** a chain or strap passed around a horse's jaw and attached to the bit. It holds back the horse when the reins are pulled. **2** anything that checks or holds back [Fear of punishment is often a *curb* to wrongdoing.] **3** the stone or concrete edging along a street. ◆*v.* to hold back; keep in check [to *curb* one's appetite].

curl·y (kʉr′lē) *adj.* full of curls [*curly* hair]. —**curl′i·er, curl′i·est**

cur·rent (kʉr′ənt) *adj.* **1** of the present time; now going on; most recent [the *current* decade; *current* events]. **2** commonly known, used, or accepted [*current* gossip; a belief *current* in earlier times]. ◆*n.* **1** a flow of water or air in a definite direction; stream. **2** the flow of electricity in a wire or other conductor. **3** the general movement or drift, as of opinion. —**cur′rent·ly** *adv.*

dair·y (der′ē) *n.* **1** a building where milk and cream are kept and butter and cheese are made. **2** a farm (**dairy farm**) on which milk, butter, cheese, etc. are produced. **3** a store that sells milk, butter, cheese, etc. —*pl.* **dair′ies**

dai·sy (dā′zē) *n.* ☆**1** a common plant with flowers that have white or pink petals around a yellow center. **2** such a flower. —*pl.* **dai′sies**

dam·age (dam′ij) *n.* injury or harm to a person or thing that results in a loss of health, value, and so on [A poor diet can cause *damage* to your heart.]

danc·er (dan′sər) *n.* a person who dances.

daugh·ter (dôt′ər *or* dät′ər) *n.* a girl or woman as she is related to a parent or to both parents.

dawn (dôn *or* dän) *v.* **1** to begin to grow light as the sun rises [Day is *dawning*.] **2** to come into being; begin to develop [With the discovery of electricity, a new age *dawned*.] **3** to begin to be understood or felt [The meaning suddenly *dawned* on me.] ◆*n.* **1** the beginning of day; daybreak. **2** the beginning of anything [the *dawn* of the Space Age].

de·ceive (dē sēv′) *v.* to make someone believe what is not true; fool or trick; mislead [The queen *deceived* Snow White by pretending to be her friend.]

de·cide (dē sīd′) *v.* **1** to choose after some thought; make up one's mind [I can't *decide* what suit to wear.] **2** to end a contest or argument by giving one side the victory; settle [A jury will *decide* the case.] —**de·cid′ed, de·cid′ing**

deer (dir) *n.* a swift-running, hoofed animal. —*pl.* **deer** or **deers**

de·fend (dē fend′) *v.* **1** to keep safe from harm or danger; guard; protect [She learned karate to *defend* herself.] **2** to uphold something that is under attack; especially, to be the lawyer for a person accused or sued in a law court.

de·fine (dē fīn′) *v.* to tell the meaning or meanings of; explain [The dictionary *defines* "deficient" as "not having enough."]

de·lay (dē lā′) *v.* to put off to a later time; postpone [The bride's illness will *delay* the wedding.]

de·liv·er·y (dē liv′ər ē) *n.* the act of transferring or distributing [daily *deliveries* to customers]. —*pl.* **de·liv′er·ies**

den·tist (den′tist) *n.* a doctor whose work is preventing and taking care of diseased or crooked teeth, or replacing them with artificial teeth.

de·ny (dē nī′) *v.* **1** to say that something is not true or right; contradict [They *denied* that they had broken the window.] **2** to refuse to grant or give [We were *denied* permission to see the movie.] —**de·nies′, de·nied′, de·ny′ing**

de·scend (dē send′) *v.* **1** to move down to a lower place [to *descend* from a hilltop; to *descend* a staircase]. **2** to become lesser or smaller [Prices have *descended* during the past month.] **3** to come from a certain source [They are *descended* from pioneers.]

des·ert (dez′ərt) *n.* a dry sandy region with little or no plant life. ◆*adj.* **1** of or like a desert. **2** wild and not lived in [a *desert* island].

de·sign (dē zīn′) *v.* **1** to think up and draw plans for [to *design* a new model of a car]. **2** to arrange the parts, colors, etc. of [Who *designed* this book?] **3** to set apart for a certain use; intend [This chair was not *designed* for hard use.] ◆*n.* **1** a drawing or plan to be followed in making something [the *designs* for a house]. **2** the arrangement of parts, colors, etc.; pattern or decoration [the *design* in a rug]. **3** a plan or purpose [It was my *design* to study law.]

de·stroy (dē stroi′) *v.* to put an end to by breaking up, tearing down, ruining, or spoiling [The flood *destroyed* 300 homes.]

di·a·ry (dī′ə rē) *n.* a record written day by day of some of the things done, seen, or thought by the writer. —*pl.* **di′a·ries**

die (dī) *v.* **1** to stop living; become dead. **2** to stop going, moving, acting, etc. [The motor sputtered and *died*.] **3** to lose force; become weak, faint, etc. [The sound of music *died* away.] **4** to want greatly: *used only in everyday talk* [She's *dying* to know my secret.] —**died, dy′ing**

di·et (dī′ət) *n.* **1** what a person or animal usually eats or drinks; usual food [Rice is a basic food in the *diet* of many Asian peoples.] **2** a special choice as to kinds and amounts of food eaten, as for one's health or to gain or lose weight [a sugar-free *diet*; a reducing *diet*]. ◆*v.* to eat certain kinds and amounts of food, especially in order to lose weight.

dif·fer·ent (dif′ər ənt *or* dif′rənt) *adj.* **1** not alike; unlike [Cottage cheese is quite *different* from Swiss cheese.] **2** not the same; separate; distinct [There are three *different* colleges in the city.] **3** not like most others; unusual [Their house is really *different*.] —**dif′fer·ent·ly adv.**

dif·fi·cult (dif′i kult) *adj.* **1** hard to do, make, or understand; that takes much trouble, thought, or skill [This arithmetic problem is *difficult*.] **2** hard to please; not easy to get along with [a *difficult* employer].

dim (dim) *v.* to make or grow somewhat dark [Cars approaching each other should *dim* their headlights.] —**dimmed, dim′ming**

dirt·y (durt′ē) *adj.* **1** having dirt on or in it; not clean; soiled. **2** foul or indecent; not nice; mean [a *dirty* trick]. —**dirt′i·er, dirt′i·est** ◆*v.* to make or become dirty; soil. —**dirt′ied, dirt′y·ing** —**dirt′i·ness n.**

dis·a·gree (dis ə grē′) *v.* **1** to differ in opinion; often, to quarrel or argue [to *disagree* on politics]. **2** to be different; differ [His story of the accident *disagreed* with hers.] —**dis·a·greed′, dis·a·gree′ing**

dis·ap·point (dis ə point′) *v.* to fail to give or do what is wanted, expected, or promised; leave unsatisfied [I am *disappointed* in the weather. You promised to come, but *disappointed* us.]

dis·be·lief (dis bə lēf′) *n.* the state of not believing; lack of belief [The guide stared at me in *disbelief*.]

dis·close (dis klōz′) *v.* **1** to bring into view; uncover [I opened my hand and *disclosed* the new penny.] **2** to make known; reveal [to *disclose* a secret]. —**dis·closed′, dis·clos′ing**

dis·grace (dis grās′) *n.* loss of favor, respect, or honor; dishonor; shame [in *disgrace* for cheating]

dis·hon·est (dis än′əst) *adj.* not honest; lying, cheating, stealing, etc. —**dis·hon′est·ly adv.** —**dis·hon′es·ty n.**

dis·in·ter·est·ed (dis in′trəs təd) *adj.* **1** not having a selfish interest in the matter; impartial [A *disinterested* judge picked the winner.] **2** not interested; uninterested: *an older meaning that is being used again.*

dis·loy·al (dis loi′əl) *adj.* not loyal or faithful; faithless. —**dis·loy′al·ty n.**

dis·play (di splā′) *v.* **1** to put or spread out so as to be seen; exhibit [to *display* a collection of stamps]. **2** to do something that is a sign or example of; show; reveal [to *display* one's courage]. ◆*n.* a displaying or showing; exhibition [a *display* of jewelry; a *display* of strength].

ditch (dich) *n.* a long, narrow opening dug in the earth, as for carrying off water; trench [a *ditch* along the road]. —*pl.***ditch′es** ◆*v.* **1** to dig a ditch in or around. **2** to throw into a ditch.

doc·tor (däk′tər) *n.* **1** a person trained to heal the sick; especially, a physician or surgeon. **2** a person who has received the highest degree given by a university [Doctor of Philosophy]. ◆*v.* to try to heal [to *doctor* oneself].

does·n't (duz′ənt) does not.

dol·lar (däl′ər) *n.* ☆**1** a United States coin or piece of paper money, equal to 100 cents. The dollar is our basic unit of money; its symbol is $. **2** a unit of money in certain other countries, as Canada.

dol·phin (dôl′fin) *n.* a water animal related to the whale but smaller. The common dolphin has a long snout and many teeth.

☆**down·town** (doun′toun) *adj., adv.* in or toward the lower part or the main business section of a city or town. ◆*n.* this section of a city or town.

drag (drag) *v.* **1** to pull in a slow, hard way, especially along the ground; haul [He *dragged* the sled up the hill.] **2** to be pulled along the ground, floor, etc. [Her skirt *dragged* in the mud.] **3** to move or pass too slowly [Time *dragged* as we waited for recess.] **4** to search for something in a river, lake, etc. by dragging a net or hooks along the bottom. —**dragged, drag′ging**

a	ask, fat
ā	ape, date
ä	car, lot
e	elf, ten
ē	even, meet
i	is, hit
ī	ice, fire
ō	open, go
ô	law, horn
oi	oil, point
ᴏᴏ	look, pull
o͞o	ooze, tool
ou	out, crowd
u	up, cut
ʉ	fur, fern
ə	a in ago
	e in agent
	e in father
	i in unity
	o in collect
	u in focus
ch	chin, arch
ŋ	ring, singer
sh	she, dash
th	thin, truth
th	then, father
zh	s in pleasure

draw (drô *or* drä) *v.* to make a picture or design with a pencil, pen, or chalk. —**drew** (drōō), **draw′ing**

draw·ing (drô′iŋ *or* drä′iŋ) *n.* **1** the making of pictures, designs, etc., as with a pencil or pen. **2** such a picture, design, etc. **3** a lottery.

drawn (drôn *or* drän) *past participle of* **draw**.

dream (drēm) *n.* **1** a series of thoughts, pictures, or feelings that passes through the mind of a sleeping person. **2** a pleasant idea that one imagines or hopes for; daydream [to have *dreams* of glory]. ◆*v.* **1** to have a dream or dreams. **2** to imagine as possible; have any idea of [I wouldn't *dream* of going without you.] —**dreamed** or **dreamt** (dremt), **dream′ing** —**dream′er** *n.*

dress (dres) *n.* **1** the common outer garment worn by girls and women. It is usually of one piece with a skirt. **2** clothes in general [native *dress*; formal *dress*]. —*pl.***dress′es** ◆*v.* **1** to put clothes on; clothe. **2** to put medicine and bandages on a wound or sore. **3** to make ready for use; prepare [to *dress* a chicken; to *dress* leather]. ◆*adj.* worn on formal occasions [a *dress* suit].

drive (drīv) *v.* to control the movement of an automobile, horse and wagon, bus, or other vehicle [She *drives* a school bus.] —**drove, driv′ing**

drop (dräp) *n.* **1** a bit of liquid that is rounded in shape, as when falling [*drops* of rain]. **2** anything like this in shape [a chocolate *drop*]. **3** a very small amount [He hasn't a *drop* of courage.] ◆*v.* **1** to fall or let fall in drops [Tears *dropped* from the actor's eyes.] **2** to fall or let fall [Ripe fruit *dropped* from the trees. He *dropped* his lunch in the mud.] —**dropped** or *sometimes* **dropt, drop′ping**

drown (droun) *v.* to die from being under water, where the lungs can get no air [to fall overboard and *drown*]. —**drowned, drown′ing**

drow·sy (drou′zē) *adj.* **1** sleepy or half asleep. **2** making one feel sleepy [*drowsy* music]. —**drow′si·er, drow′si·est** —**drow′si·ly** *adv.* —**drow′si·ness** *n.*

dry (drī) *adj.* **1** not under water [*dry* land]. **2** not wet or damp; without moisture. **3** having little or no rain or water [a *dry* summer]. **4** with all its water or other liquid gone [a *dry* fountain pen; *dry* bread; a *dry* well]. —**dri′er, dri′est** —**dried, dry′ing** —**dry′ly** *adv.* —**dry′ness** *n.*

dues (dōōz *or* dyōōz) *pl.n.* money paid regularly for being a member of a club or institution [The *dues* are $25 per month.]

dusk (dusk) *n.* the dim part of twilight that comes before the dark of night.

du·ty (dōōt′ē *or* dyōōt′ē) *n.* **1** what a person should do because it is thought to be right, just, or moral [It is the *duty* of every citizen to vote.] **2** any of the things that are done as part of a person's work [the *duties* of a secretary]. —*pl.* **du′ties**

eagle

ea·gle (ē′gəl) *n.* a large, strong bird that captures and eats other birds and animals and has sharp eyesight. The **bald eagle** is the symbol of the U.S.

ear·ly (ur′lē) *adv., adj.* **1** ncar the beginning; soon after the start [in the *early* afternoon; *early* in his career]. **2** before the usual or expected time [The bus arrived *early*.] —**ear′li·er, ear′li·est** —**ear′li·ness** *n.*

ear·muffs (ir′mufs) *pl.n.* cloth or fur coverings worn over the ears to keep them warm in cold weather.

east·ern (ēs′tərn) *adj.* **1** in, of, or toward the east [the *eastern* sky]. **2** from the east [an *eastern* wind]. **3** Eastern, of the East.

eas·y (ē′zē) *adj.* **1** not hard to do, learn, get, etc. [an *easy* job; an *easy* book]. **2** without worry, pain, or trouble [an *easy* life]. **3** restful or comfortable [an *easy* chair]. —**eas′i·er, eas′i·est**

eas·y·go·ing (ē′zē gō′iŋ) *adj.* not worried, rushed, or strict about things.

edge (ej) *n.* **1** the sharp, cutting part [the *edge* of a knife]. **2** the line or part where something begins or ends; border or margin [the *edge* of a plate; the *edge* of the forest]. **3** the brink [on the *edge* of disaster]. —**edged, edg′ing**

ed·i·tor (ed′it ər) *n.* **1** a person who edits. ☆**2** the head of a department of a newspaper, magazine, etc.

eight·een (ā′tēn′) *n., adj.* eight more than ten; the number 18.

el·e·phant (el′ə fənt) *n.* a huge animal with a thick skin, two ivory tusks, and a long snout, or trunk. It is found in Africa and India and is the largest of the four-legged animals.

e·lev·en (ē lev′ən) *n., adj.* one more than ten; the number 11.

em·broi·der (em brōi′dər) *v.* to stitch designs on cloth with a needle and thread [Hal *embroidered* his initials on his shirt.]

e·mer·gen·cy (ē mur′jən sē) *n.* a sudden happening that needs action or attention right away [the *emergency* created by a hurricane]. —*pl.* **e·mer′gen·cies**

em·ploy (em plȯi′) *v.* **1** to hire and pay for the work or services of; have working for one [That company *employs* 50 people.] **2** to use [The baby *employed* clever tricks to get attention.] ◆*n.* the condition of being employed [Chan is no longer in our *employ*.]

emp·ty (emp′tē) *adj.* **1** having nothing or no one in it; not occupied; vacant [an *empty* jar; an *empty* house]. —**emp′ti·er, emp′ti·est** ◆*v.* **1** to make or become empty [The auditorium was *emptied* in ten minutes.] **2** to take out or pour out [*Empty* the dirty water in the sink.] **3** to flow out; discharge [The Amazon *empties* into the Atlantic.] —**emp′tied, emp′ty·ing** —**emp′ti·ly** *adv.* —**emp′ti·ness** *n.*

en·e·my (en′ə mē) *n.* a person, group, or country that hates another or fights against another; foe. —*pl.* **en′e·mies**

en·er·gy (en′ər jē) *n.* **1** power to work or be active; force; vigor [Eleanor Roosevelt was a woman of great *energy*.] **2** the power of certain forces in nature to do work [Electricity and heat are forms of *energy*.] **3** resources, as coal, oil, etc., used to produce such power; also, the supply of such resources that can be got [an *energy* shortage]. —*pl.* **en′er·gies**

e·nor·mous (ē nôr′məs) *adj.* much larger than usual; huge [an *enormous* stadium]. —**e·nor′mous·ly** *adv.* —**e·nor′mous·ness** *n.*

e·nough (ē nuf′) *adj.* as much or as many as needed or wanted; sufficient [There is *enough* food for all.] ◆*n.* the amount needed or wanted [I have heard *enough* of that music.] ◆*adv.* **1** as much as needed; to the right amount [Is your steak cooked *enough*?] **2** fully; quite [Oddly *enough*, she never asked me.]

en·ter·tain (en tər tān′) *v.* to keep interested and give pleasure to [She *entertained* us by playing the organ.]

e·qual (ē′kwəl) *adj.* **1** of the same amount, size, or value [The horses were of *equal* height.] **2** having the same rights, ability, or position [All persons are *equal* in a court of law in a just society.] ◆*n.* any person or thing that is equal [As a sculptor, she has few *equals*.] ◆*v.* to be equal to; match [His long jump *equaled* the school record. Six minus two *equals* four.] —**e′qualed** or **e′qualled, e′qual·ing** or **e′qual·ling** —**e′qual·ly** *adv.*

e·qua·tor (ē kwāt′ər) *n.* an imaginary circle around the middle of the earth, at an equal distance from the North Pole and South Pole.

er·ror (er′ər) *n.* **1** a belief, answer, act, etc. that is untrue, incorrect, or wrong; mistake [an *error* in multiplication]. **2** a play by a baseball fielder which is poorly made, but which would have resulted in an out if it had been properly made.

es·say (es′ā) *n.* a short piece of writing on some subject, giving the writer's personal ideas.

Eu·rope (yoor′əp) the continent between Asia and the Atlantic Ocean.

ev·er·y·bod·y (ev′rē bäd′ē *or* ev′rē bud′ē) *pron.* every person; everyone [*Everybody* loves a good story.]

ex·change (eks chānj′) *v.* to give in return for something else; trade [She *exchanged* the bicycle for a larger one.] —**ex·changed′, ex·chang′ing**

ex·cuse (ek skyōōz′) *v.* **1** to be a proper reason or explanation for [That was a selfish act that nothing will *excuse*.] **2** to think of a fault or wrongdoing as not important; overlook; forgive; pardon [Please *excuse* this interruption.] **3** to allow to leave or go [You may be *excused* from the table.] —**ex·cused′, ex·cus′ing** ◆*n.* (ek skyōōs′) a reason given to explain some action or behavior; apology [Ignorance of the law is no *excuse* for wrongdoing.]

ex·er·cise (ek′sər sīz) *n.* **1** active use of the body in order to make it stronger or healthier [Long walks are good outdoor *exercise*.] **2** *usually* **exercises**, *pl.* a series of movements done regularly to make some part of the body stronger or to develop some skill [These *exercises* will strengthen your legs.] **3** a problem to be studied and worked on by a student in order to get more skill [piano *exercises*]. ◆*v.* to put into use or do certain regular movements, in order to develop or train [*Exercise* your weak ankle. I *exercise* every morning.] —**ex′er·cised, ex′er·cis·ing**

ex·pen·sive (ek spen′siv) *adj.* costing much; having a high price [She wears *expensive* clothes.] —**ex·pen′sive·ly** *adv.*

ex·plore (ek splôr′) *v.* **1** to travel in a region that is unknown or not well known, in order to find out more about it [to *explore* a wild jungle]. **2** to look into or examine carefully [to *explore* a problem]. —**ex·plored′, ex·plor′ing** —**ex′plo·ra′tion** *n.* —**ex·plor′er** *n.*

ex·press (ek spres′) *v.* **1** to put into words; state [It is hard to *express* my feelings.] **2** to give or be a sign of; show [a frown that *expressed* doubt]. ☆**3** to send goods by a fast way. ◆*adj.* taking the shortest and fastest route; not making many stops [an *express* train or bus].

ex·tend (ek stend′) *v.* to make longer; stretch out [Careful cleaning *extends* the life of a rug.]

ex·tinct (ek stiŋkt′) *adj.* **1** no longer living; having died out [Dinosaurs are *extinct*.] **2** no longer burning or active [an *extinct* volcano].

ex·tin·guish·er (ek stiŋ′gwish ər) *n.* a person or thing that extinguishes; especially, a device for putting out a fire by spraying a liquid or gas on it.

eye·lash (ī′lash) *n.* **1** any of the hairs that grow along the edge of the eyelid. **2** a fringe of these hairs. —*pl.* **eye′lash·es**

equator

a	ask, fat
ā	ape, date
ä	car, lot
e	elf, ten
ē	even, meet
i	is, hit
ī	ice, fire
ō	open, go
ô	law, horn
oi	oil, point
oo	look, pull
ōō	ooze, tool
ou	out, crowd
u	up, cut
u	fur, fern
ə	a in ago
	e in agent
	e in father
	i in unity
	o in collect
	u in focus
ch	chin, arch
ŋ	ring, singer
sh	she, dash
th	thin, truth
th	then, father
zh	s in pleasure

fa·ble (fā′bəl) *n.* **1** a very short story that teaches a lesson. It is usually about animals who act and talk like people [Aesop's *fable* "The Grasshopper and the Ant" teaches the need to work hard and be thrifty.]

fac·to·ry (fak′tər ē *or* fak′trē) *n.* a building or group of buildings where products are made by machinery. —*pl.*fac′to·ries

fair (fer) *adj.* **1** beautiful [your *fair* city]. **2** light in color; blond [*fair* hair; *fair* skin]. **3** clear and sunny [*fair* weather]. **4** just and honest; according to what is right [a *fair* price; *fair* play]. —**fair′ness** *n.*

fame (fām) *n.* the condition of being well known or much talked about; great reputation [Marie Curie's scientific research brought her much *fame.*]

fa·mil·iar (fə mil′yər) *adj.* friendly; intimate; well-acquainted [a *familiar* face in the crowd].

fam·i·ly (fam′ə lē) *n.* **1** a group made up of two parents and all of their children. **2** the children alone [a widow who raised a large *family*]. **3** a group of people who are related by marriage or a common ancestor; relatives; clan. —*pl.* **fam′i·lies**

fan·cy (fan′sē) *n.* the power of picturing in the mind things that are not real, especially in a light and playful way; imagination ["Alice's Adventures in Wonderland" is the product of Lewis Carroll's *fancy.*] —*pl.* **fan′cies ◆adj. 1** having much design and decoration; not plain; elaborate [a *fancy* tie]. **2** of better quality than the usual; special [a *fancy* grade of canned pears]. —**fan′ci·er, fan′ci·est ◆v.** to have a liking for [He *fancies* Swiss chocolate.] —**fan′cied, fan′cy·ing**

far·ther (fär′thər) *the comparative of* **far. ◆adj.** more distant [My home is *farther* from school than yours.] **◆adv.** at or to a greater distance [I can swim *farther* than you can.]

fault (fôlt) *n.* **1** a thing that keeps something from being perfect; defect; flaw [His main *fault* is that he's lazy.] **2** an error; mistake. **3** blame; responsibility [It isn't my *fault* that we're late.]

fawn (fôn *or* fän) *n.* a young deer, less than one year old.

fear·less (fir′ləs) *adj.* having no fear; not afraid; brave. —**fear′less·ly** *adv.*

feath·er (feth′ər) *n.* any of the parts that grow out of the skin of birds, covering the body and filling out the wings and tail. Feathers are soft and light. —**feath′er·y** *adj.*

flamingo

fend·er (fen′dər) *n.* ☆**1** a metal piece over the wheel of a car to keep off splashing mud. **2** a metal piece at the front of a locomotive to throw off things that are hit.

field (fēld) *n.* **1** a wide piece of open land without many trees; especially, a piece of land for growing crops, grazing animals, etc. **2** a piece of land having a special use or producing a certain thing [a landing *field*; an oil *field*]. **3** an area where games or athletic events are held; also, the part of such an area where such events as high jump, long jump, pole vault, shot put, etc. are held. ◆*v.* to stop or catch and return a batted ball.

fight (fīt) *v.* to use fists, weapons, or other force in trying to beat or overcome someone or something [to *fight* a war]. —**fought, fight′ing**

film (film) *n.* **1** a thin skin or coating [a *film* of ice on the pond]. **2** a sheet or roll of material covered with a chemical substance that is changed by light, used for taking photographs or making movies. **3** a movie.

fin·ish (fin′ish) *v.* **1** to bring or come to an end; complete or become completed [Did you *finish* your work? The game *finished* early.] **2** to give final touches to; perfect [We *finished* the room by putting up molding.] **3** to use up; consume completely [*Finish* your milk.] ◆*n.* the kind of surface a thing has [an oil *finish* on wood].

fish (fish) *n.* an animal that lives in water and has a backbone, fins, and gills for breathing [The aquarium exhibits many *fishes.*] —*pl.* **fish′es**

fla·min·go (flə miŋ′gō) *n.* a wading bird that has a very long neck and legs, and pink or red feathers. It lives in tropical regions. —*pl.* **fla·min′gos** *or* **fla·min′goes**

flash (flash) *v.* **1** to send out a short and bright burst of light [Electric signs *flashed* all along the street.] **2** to sparkle or gleam [Her eyes *flashed* with anger.] **3** to come, move, or send swiftly or suddenly [The train *flashed* by. The news was *flashed* to Paris by radio.] ◆*n.* a short burst of light or of something bright [a *flash* of lightning; a *flash* of wit, hope, etc.] —*pl.* **flash′es**

fleet¹ (flēt) *n.* **1** a group of warships under one command [our Pacific *fleet*]. **2** any group of ships, trucks, buses, etc. moving together or under one control.

fleet² (flēt) *adj.* moving swiftly; swift.

flew (flōō) *past tense of* **fly¹.**

flies (flīz) **1** *the form of the verb* **fly¹,** *used in the present with* he, she, *or* it. **2** *the plural of* **fly¹** *and* **fly².**

flight (flīt) *n.* **1** the act or way of flying or moving through space. **2** a trip through the air, as by an airplane, bird, etc. [a 500-mile *flight*]. **3** a group of things flying together [a *flight* of wild swans].

Flor·i·da (flôr′i də) a State in the southeastern part of the U.S.: abbreviated **Fla., FL**

flu (flōō) *n.* a disease caused by a virus, like a bad cold only more serious.

flue (flōō) *n.* a tube, pipe, or shaft through which smoke, steam, or hot air can escape [the *flue* in a chimney].

fly¹ (flī) *v.* **1** to move through the air by using wings, as a bird. **2** to travel or carry through the air, as in an aircraft. **3** to pilot an aircraft. **4** to wave or float in the air, or cause to float in the air, as a flag or kite. **5** to move swiftly [The door *flew* open. Time *flies*.] —**flew, flown, fly′ing** ◆*n.* a baseball batted high in the air inside the foul lines. —*pl.* **flies**

fly² (flī) *n.* **1** a flying insect having one pair of wings, as the housefly and gnat. Some insects with two pairs of wings are called flies, as the mayfly. **2** an object used in fishing, made of bright feathers, silk, etc. tied to a fishhook to look like a fly. —*pl.* **flies**

folk (fōk) *n.* **folk** or **folks,** *pl.* people or persons [The farmer disliked city *folk*. *Folks* differ in customs.] —*pl.* **folk** or **folks** ◆*adj.* of the common people [a *folk* saying].

folk tale a story made and handed down by word of mouth among the common people: *also* **folk story.**

fol·low·ing (fä′lō iŋ) *adj.* going or coming after; next after [the *following* week]. ◆*n.* people who follow; followers. ◆*prep.* after [*Following* dinner we played cards.]

fond (fänd) *v.* loving and tender; affectionate [*fond* parents].

fool·ish (fōōl′ish) *adj.* without good sense; silly. —**fool′ish·ly** *adv.* —**fool′ish·ness** *n.*

force (fôrs) *n.* **1** power or energy that can do or make something [Electricity is a powerful natural *force*. The *force* of the high winds broke the windows.] **2** power or strength used against a person or thing [The police used *force* to scatter the crowd.] **3** the power to cause motion or to stop or change motion [the *force* of gravity]. ◆*v.* **1** to make do something by using strength or power of some kind [You shouldn't *force* a child to eat. The blizzard *forced* us to stay home.] **2** to break open or through by using strength [He *forced* the lock with a pick.] —**forced, forc′ing**

fore·head (fôr′hed *or* fär′hed) *n.* the part of the face above the eyebrows.

forth (fôrth) *adv.* **1** forward or onward [She never left the house from that day *forth*.] **2** out; into view [The bears came *forth* from their den.]

fought (fôt *or* fät) *past tense and past participle of* **fight.**

fox (fäks) *n.* **1** a wild animal of the dog family, with pointed ears, a bushy tail, and, usually, reddish-brown fur. —*pl.* **foxes**

France (frans) a country in western Europe.

fraud (frôd *or* fräd) *n.* **1** a cheating, tricking, or lying; dishonesty. **2** a person who cheats or is not what he or she pretends to be.

fray (frā) *v.* to wear down so as to become ragged and have loose threads showing [a coat *frayed* at the elbows].

free·dom (frē′dəm) *n.* **1** the condition of being free; liberty; independence. **2** a being able to use or move about in as one wishes [Has your dog been given *freedom* of the house?]

freight·er (frāt′ər) *n.* a ship for freight.

front (frunt) *n.* **1** the part that faces forward; most important side [The *front* of a house usually faces the street.] **2** the part ahead of the rest; first part; beginning [That chapter is toward the *front* of the book.] **3** outward look or behavior [I put on a bold *front* in spite of my fear.] **4** the land alongside a lake, ocean, street, etc. [docks on the water*front*].

fron·tier (frun tir′) *n.* **1** the line or border between two countries. ☆**2** the part of a settled country that lies next to a region that is still a wilderness. **3** any new field of learning or any part of it still to be explored [the *frontiers* of medicine].

fry (frī) *v.* to cook in hot fat over direct heat. —**fried, fry′ing** ◆*n.* ☆**1** a kind of picnic at which food is fried and eaten [a fish *fry*]. **2** **fries,** *pl.* things fried, as potatoes. —*pl.* **fries**

fun·ny (fun′ē) *adj.* **1** causing smiles or laughter; amusing; comical. **2** odd or unusual: *used only in everyday talk* [It's *funny* that he's late.] —**fun′ni·er, fun′ni·est** ◆☆*n.* *usually* **funnies,** *pl.* comic strips: *used only in everyday talk.* —*pl.* **fun′nies** —**fun′ni·ness** *n.*

Florida

gal·ax·y (gal′ək sē) *often* **Galaxy,** *another name for* **Milky Way.** ◆*n.* **1** any vast group of stars. **2** a group of very famous people. —*pl.* **gal′ax·ies**

gal·ley (gal′ē) *n.* **1** a large, low ship of long ago, having both sails and many oars. The oars were usually rowed by slaves or prisoners in chains. **2** the kitchen of a ship. —*pl.* **gal′leys**

gal·lon (gal′ən) *n.* a measure of liquids, equal to four quarts or eight pints. One gallon equals 3.785 liters.

gar·bage (gär′bij) *n.* spoiled or waste food that is thrown away.

gasp (gasp) *v.* to breathe in suddenly [She *gasped* in sudden surprise.]

a	ask, fat
ā	ape, date
ä	car, lot
e	elf, ten
ē	even, meet
i	is, hit
ī	ice, fire
ō	open, go
ô	law, horn
oi	oil, point
oo	look, pull
ōō	ooze, tool
ou	out, crowd
u	up, cut
ʉ	fur, fern
ə	a in ago
	e in agent
	e in father
	i in unity
	o in collect
	u in focus
ch	chin, arch
ŋ	ring, singer
sh	she, dash
th	thin, truth
th	then, father
zh	s in pleasure

giraffe

glove

gath·er (ga*th*′ər) **v. 1** to bring or come together in one place or group [The child *gathered* her toys together.   The families *gathered* for a reunion.] **2** to get or collect gradually; accumulate [to *gather* wealth; to *gather* one's strength; to *gather* news for a paper]. **3** to pick or glean [to *gather* crops]. —**gath′er·er** *n.*

gaunt (gônt *or* gänt) *adj.* **1** so thin that the bones show; worn and lean, as from hunger or illness. **2** looking gloomy and deserted [the *gaunt*, rocky coast of the island]. —**gaunt′ly** *adv.* —**gaunt′ness** *n.*

geese (gēs) *n. plural of* **goose**.

gen·tle (jent′l) *adj.* **1** mild, soft, or easy; not rough [a *gentle* touch; a *gentle* scolding]. **2** tame; easy to handle [a *gentle* horse]. **3** gradual; not sudden [a *gentle* slope]. —**gen′tler, gen′tlest** —**gen·tle·ness** *n.*

ge·og·ra·phy (jē ôg′rə fē *or* jē ä′grə fē) *n.* **1** the study of the surface of the earth and how it is divided into continents, countries, seas, etc.   Geography also deals with the climates, plants, animals, minerals, etc. of the earth. **2** the natural features of a certain part of the earth [the *geography* of Ohio]. —**ge·og′ra·pher** *n.*

ger·bil or **ger·bille** (jʉr′bəl) *n.* an animal like a mouse but with very long hind legs.   It is found in Africa and Asia.

ghost (gōst) *n.* **1** a pale, shadowy form that some people think they can see and that is supposed to be the spirit of a dead person. **2** a mere shadow or slight trace [not a *ghost* of a chance].

gift (gift) *n.* **1** something given to show friendship, thanks, support, etc.; a present [Christmas *gifts*; a *gift* of $5,000 to a museum]. **2** a natural ability; talent [a *gift* for writing catchy tunes].

gi·raffe (ji raf′) *n.* a large animal of Africa that chews its cud.   It has a very long neck and legs and a spotted coat, and is the tallest animal alive.

give (giv) *v.* **1** to pass or hand over to another [*Give* me your coat and I'll hang it up.] **2** to hand over to another to keep; make a gift of [My uncle *gave* a book to me for my birthday.] **3** to cause to have [Music *gives* me pleasure.] **4** to be the source of; supply [Cows *give* milk.] —**gave, giv′en, giv′ing**

gla·cier (glā′shər) *n.* a large mass of ice and snow that moves very slowly down a mountain or across land until it melts.   Icebergs are pieces of a glacier that have broken away into the sea.

glove (gluv) *n.* **1** a covering to protect the hand, with a separate part for each finger and the thumb [Surgeons wear rubber *gloves*.   Padded *gloves* are worn in playing baseball.] **2** a padded mitt worn in boxing: *also* **boxing glove.** ◆*v.* to put gloves on. —**gloved, glov′ing**

glow (glō) *v.* **1** to give off light because of great heat; be red-hot or white-hot [embers *glowing* in a fire]. **2** to give out light without flame or heat [Fireflies *glow* in the dark.]

glue (glo͞o) *n.* **1** a thick, sticky substance made by boiling animal hoofs and bones, used for sticking things together. **2** any sticky substance like this. ◆*v.* **1** to stick together with glue. **2** to keep or hold without moving [The exciting movie kept us *glued* to our seats.] —**glued, glu′ing** —**glue′y** *adj.*

gnaw (nô *or* nä) *v.* to bite and wear away bit by bit with the teeth [The rat *gnawed* the rope in two.   The dog *gnawed* on the bone.]

gob·ble (gäb′əl) *v.* to eat quickly and greedily [She *gobbled* half the pizza before I finished a single piece.] —**gob′bled, gob′bling**

goose (go͞os) *n.* a swimming bird that is like a duck but has a larger body and a longer neck; especially, the female of this bird.   The male is called a *gander*. —*pl.* **geese**

gov·ern·ment (guv′ərn mənt) *n.* **1** control or rule, as over a country, city, etc. **2** a system of ruling or controlling [a centralized *government*; democratic *governments*]. **3** all the people who control the affairs of a country, city, etc. [The French *government* moved to Vichy during World War II.] —☆**gov′ern·men′tal** *adj.*

grab (grab) *v.* **1** to seize or snatch suddenly. **2** to take by force or in a selfish way. —**grabbed, grab′bing** ◆*n.* **1** the act of grabbing [He made a *grab* for the handle.] **2** something grabbed.

grace·ful (grās′fəl) *adj.* having grace, or beauty of form or movement. —**grace′ful·ly** *adv.* —**grace′ful·ness** *n.*

gram (gram) *n.* the basic unit of weight in the metric system.   It is the weight of one cubic centimeter of distilled water at 4°C; one gram equals about 1/28 of an ounce.

graph (graf) *n.* a chart or diagram that shows the changes taking place in something, by the use of connected lines, a curve, etc. [a *graph* showing how sales figures vary during the year].

Greece (grēs) a country in southeastern Europe, on the Mediterranean.

greed·y (grēd′ē) *adj.* wanting or taking all that one can get with no thought of what others need [The *greedy* girl ate all the cookies.] —**greed′i·er, greed′i·est** —**greed′i·ly** *adv.* —**greed′i·ness** *n.*

grid·dle (grid′əl) *n.* a heavy, flat, metal plate or pan for cooking pancakes, etc.

griz·zly (griz′lē) *n.* a large, ferocious bear found in western North America. —*pl.* **griz′zlies**

groan (grōn) *v.* to make a deep sound showing sorrow, pain, annoyance, or disapproval [We *groaned* when our team lost.]

gro·cer·y (grō′sər ē) *n.* ☆**1** a store selling food and household supplies. **2 groceries**, *pl.* the goods sold by a grocer. —*pl.* **gro′cer·ies**

guess (ges) *v.* **1** to judge or decide about something without having enough facts to know for certain [Can you *guess* how old he is?] **2** to judge correctly by doing this [She *guessed* the exact number of beans in the jar.] **3** to think or suppose [I *guess* you're right.] *◆n.* a judgment formed by guessing; surmise [Your *guess* is as good as mine.] —**guess′er** *n.*

gulp (gulp) *v.* to swallow in a hurried or greedy way [She *gulped* her breakfast and ran to school.] —**gulped, gulp′ing**

hair (her) *n.* **1** any of the thin growths, like threads, that come from the skin of animals and human beings. **2** the whole number of these growths that cover a person's head, the skin of an animal, etc. [I must comb my *hair*.]

half (haf) *n.* **1** either of the two equal parts of something [Five is *half* of ten.] **2** either of two almost equal parts: *thought by some people to be not a proper use* [Take the smaller *half* of the pie.] **3** a half hour [It is *half* past two.]—*pl.* **halves** *◆adv.*

half·way (haf′wā′) *adj.* **1** at the middle between two points or limits [to reach the *halfway* mark]. **2** not complete; partial [to take *halfway* measures]. *◆adv.* **1** to the midway point; half the distance [They had gone *halfway* home.] **2** partially [The house is *halfway* built.]

halt (hôlt) *n., v.* stop [I worked all morning without a *halt*. Rain *halted* the game.]

halves (havz) *n. plural of* **half**.

ham·mer (ham′ər) *n.* **1** a tool for driving in nails, breaking stones, shaping metal, etc. It usually has a metal head and a handle. **2** a thing like this in shape or use, as the part that strikes against the firing pin of a gun or any of the parts that strike the strings of a piano. *◆v.* to hit with many blows [They *hammered* on the door with their fists.]

hand (hand) *n.* **1** the end of the arm beyond the wrist, including the palm, fingers, and thumb. **2** any of the pointers on a clock or watch. **3** a person hired to work with the hands [a farm *hand*; dock *hand*]. **4** help [Give me a *hand* with this job.] **5** a clapping of hands; applause [Give the dancer a big *hand*.] *◆v.* to give with the hand; pass [*Hand* me the book, please.]

hand·ker·chief (haŋ′kər chif) *n.* a small piece of cloth for wiping the nose, eyes, or face, or worn as a decoration. —*pl.* **hand′ker·chiefs**

hap·py (hap′ē) *adj.* **1** feeling or showing pleasure or joy; glad; contented [a *happy* child; a *happy* song]. **2** lucky; fortunate [The story has a *happy* ending.] —**hap′pi·er, hap′pi·est** —**hap′pi·ly** *adv.* —**hap′pi·ness** *n.*

har·bor (här′bər) *n.* **1** a place where ships may anchor and be safe from storms; port; haven. **2** any place where one is safe; shelter. *◆v.* to shelter or hide [to *harbor* an outlaw]

hare (her) *n.* a swift animal with long ears, a split upper lip, large front teeth used for gnawing, and long, powerful hind legs. Hares are related to rabbits but are usually larger.

har·vest (här′vəst) *n.* the act or process of gathering a crop of grain, fruit, or vegetables when it becomes ripe.

has·n't (haz′ənt) has not.

haunt (hônt *or* hänt) *v.* **1** to spend much time at; visit often [We like to *haunt* bookstores. A *haunted* house is one that is supposed to be visited by a ghost.] **2** to keep coming back to the mind [Memories *haunt* her.] *◆n.* a place often visited [They made the library their *haunt*.]

heal (hēl) *v.* to get or bring back to good health or a sound condition; cure or mend [The wound *healed* slowly. Time *heals* grief.]

heart (härt) *n.* **1** the hollow muscle that gets blood from the veins and sends it through the arteries by squeezing together and expanding. **2** the part at the center [*hearts* of celery; the *heart* of the jungle]. **3** the main or most important part [Get to the *heart* of the matter.] **4** the human heart thought of as the part that feels love, kindness, pity, sadness, etc. [a tender *heart*; a heavy *heart*].

hearth (härth) *n.* the stone or brick floor of a fireplace.

heav·y (hev′ē) *adj.* **1** hard to lift or move because of its weight; weighing very much [a *heavy* load]. **2** weighing more than is usual for its kind [Lead is a *heavy* metal.] **3** larger, deeper, greater, etc. than usual [a *heavy* vote; a *heavy* sleep; a *heavy* blow]. —**heav′i·er, heav′i·est** *◆adv.* in a heavy manner [*heavy*-laden].

heel (hēl) *n.* **1** the back part of the foot, below the ankle and behind the arch. **2** that part of a stocking or sock which covers the heel. **3** the part of a shoe that is built up to support the heel.

a	ask, fat
ā	ape, date
ä	car, lot
e	elf, ten
ē	even, meet
i	is, hit
ī	ice, fire
ō	open, go
ô	law, horn
oi	oil, point
oo	look, pull
o͞o	ooze, tool
ou	out, crowd
u	up, cut
u	fur, fern
ə	a in ago
	e in agent
	e in father
	i in unity
	o in collect
	u in focus
ch	chin, arch
ŋ	ring, singer
sh	she, dash
th	thin, truth
th	then, father
zh	s in pleasure

167

heron

horseshoe

herd (hurd) *n.* a number of cattle or other large animals feeding or living together [a *herd* of cows; a *herd* of elephants]. ◆*v.* **1** to form into a herd, group, or crowd. **2** to take care of a herd of animals.

her·on (her′ən) *n.* a wading bird with long legs, a long neck, and a long, pointed bill. Herons live in marshes or along river banks.

hes·i·tate (hez′i tāt′) *v.* **1** to stop or hold back, as because of feeling unsure [Never *hesitate* to speak the truth. He *hesitated* at the door before entering.] **2** to feel unwilling [I *hesitate* to ask you for money.] —**hes′i·tat·ed, hes′i·tat·ing**

high·way (hī′wā) *n.* a main road.

hob·by (häb′ē) *n.* something that one likes to do, study, etc. for pleasure in one's spare time [Her *hobby* is collecting coins.] —*pl.* **hob′bies**

hoe (hō) *n.* a garden tool with a thin, flat blade on a long handle. It is used for removing weeds, loosening the soil, etc. ◆*v.* to dig, loosen soil, etc. with a hoe. —**hoed, hoe′ing**

hol·i·day (häl′ə dā) *n.* **1** a day on which most people do not have to work, often one set aside by law [Thanksgiving is a *holiday* in all States.] **2** a religious festival; holy day [Easter is a Christian *holiday*.]

hol·low (häl′ō) *adj.* **1** having an empty space on the inside; not solid [a *hollow* log]. **2** shaped like a bowl; concave. **3** sunken in [*hollow* cheeks]. —**hol′low·ness *n.***

home·work (hōm′wurk) *n.* **1** lessons to be studied or schoolwork to be done outside the classroom. **2** any work to be done at home.

hom·o·nym (häm′ə nim) *n.* a word that is pronounced like another word but that has a different meaning and is usually spelled differently ["Bore" and "boar" are *homonyms*.]

hon·est (än′əst) *adj.* **1** that does not steal, cheat, or lie; upright or trustworthy [an *honest* person]. **2** got in a fair way, not by stealing, cheating, or lying [to earn an *honest* living]. **3** sincere or genuine [He made an *honest* effort.]

hoof (hoof *or* hoof) *n.* **1** the horny covering on the feet of cows, horses, deer, pigs, etc. **2** the whole foot of such an animal. —*pl.* **hoofs** or **hooves**

hor·ri·fy (hôr′ə fī) *v.* to fill with horror [He was *horrified* at the sight of the victims.] —**hor′ri·fied, hor′ri·fy·ing**

horse·shoe (hôrs′shoo) *n.* **1** a flat metal plate shaped like a U, nailed to a horse's hoof to protect it. **2** anything shaped like this. **3 horseshoes**, *pl.* a game in which the players toss horseshoes at a stake in the ground.

host·ess (hōs′təs) *n.* **1** a woman who has guests in her own home, or who pays for their entertainment away from home. **2** a

woman hired by a restaurant to welcome people and show them to their tables. —*pl.* **host′ess·es**

hour (our) *n.* **1** any of the 24 equal parts of a day; 60 minutes. **2** a particular time [At what *hour* shall we meet?] **3** often **hours**, *pl.* a particular period of time [the dinner *hour*; the doctor's office *hours*].

how (hou) *adv.* **1** in what way [*How* do you start the motor? She taught him *how* to dance.] **2** in what condition [*How* is your mother today?] **3** for what reason; why [*How* is it that you don't know?]

how's (houz) **1** how is. **2** how has. **3** how does.

hum (hum) *v.* **1** to make a low, steady, buzzing sound like that of a bee or a motor. **2** to sing with the lips closed, not saying the words. —**hummed, hum′ming**

☆**hum·ming·bird** (hum′iŋ burd′) *n.* a tiny bird with a long, thin bill, that it uses to suck nectar from flowers. Its wings move very fast, with a humming sound, and it can hover in the air.

hun·dred (hun′drəd) *n., adj.* ten times ten; the number 100.

hur·ri·cane (hur′ə kān) *n.* a very strong windstorm, often with heavy rain, in which the wind blows in a circle at 73 or more miles per hour. Hurricanes usually start in the West Indies and move northward.

hur·ry (hur′ē) *v.* **1** to move, send, or carry quickly or too quickly [You fell because you *hurried*. A taxi *hurried* us home.] **2** to make happen or be done more quickly [Please try to *hurry* those letters.] **3** to try to make move or act faster [Don't *hurry* me when I'm eating.] —**hur′ried, hur′ry·ing**

hy·giene (hī′jēn) *n.* the practice of keeping clean [good personal *hygiene*].

i·de·a (ī dē′ə) *n.* **1** something one thinks, knows, imagines, feels, etc.; belief or thought. **2** a plan or purpose [an *idea* for making money].

im·mov·a·ble (im moov′ə bəl) *adj.* **1** that cannot be moved; firmly fixed [The ancients thought the earth *immovable*.] **2** not changing; steadfast [an *immovable* purpose].

im·pa·tient (im pā′shənt) *adj.* not patient; not willing to put up with delay or annoyance [*impatient* customers standing in line].

im·per·fect (im pur′fikt) *adj.* **1** not perfect; having some fault or flaw. **2** lacking in something; not complete; unfinished [an *imperfect* knowledge of Russian]. —**im·per′fect·ly *adv.***

im·per·son·al (im pur′sən əl) *adj.* not referring to any particular person [The teacher's remarks about cheating were *impersonal* and meant for all the students.] —**im·per′son·al·ly** *adv.*

im·prac·ti·cal (im prak′ti kəl) *adj.* not practical; not useful, efficient, etc.

im·pure (im pyoor′) *adj.* **1** not clean; dirty [Smoke made the air *impure*.] **2** mixed with things that do not belong [*impure* gold]. **3** not decent or proper [*impure* thoughts].

in·de·pend·ent (in′dē pen′dənt) *adj.* **1** not ruled or controlled by another; self-governing [Many colonies became *independent* countries after World War II.] **2** not connected with others; separate [an *independent* grocer]. **3** not influenced by others; thinking for oneself [an *independent* voter]. —**in′de·pend′ent·ly** *adv.*

In·di·a (in′dē ə) **1** a large peninsula of southern Asia. **2** a country in the central and southern part of this peninsula.

in·ju·ry (in′jər ē) *n.* harm or damage done to a person or thing [*injuries* received in a fall; *injury* to one's good name]. —*pl.* **in′ju·ries**

in·stant (in′stənt) *n.* a very short time; moment [Wait just an *instant*.]

in·stead (in sted′) *adv.* in place of the other; as a substitute [If you have no cream, use milk *instead*.]

in·tel·li·gent (in tel′ə jənt) *adj.* having or showing intelligence, especially high intelligence.

is·land (ī′lənd) *n.* **1** a piece of land smaller than a continent and surrounded by water. **2** any place set apart from what surrounds it [The oasis was an *island* of green in the desert.]

It·a·ly (it′l ē) a country in southern Europe, including the islands of Sicily and Sardinia.

jag·uar (jag′wär) *n.* a large wildcat that looks like a large leopard. It is yellowish with black spots and is found from the southwestern U.S. to Argentina.

Jan·u·ar·y (jan′yoo er′ē) *n.* the first month of the year, which has 31 days: abbreviated **Jan.**

Ja·pan (jə pan′) a country east of Korea, made up of many islands.

jaw (jô *or* jä) *n.* **1** either of the two bony parts that form the frame of the mouth and that hold the teeth. **2** either of two parts that close to grip or crush something [A vise and a pair of pliers have *jaws*.] **3 jaws,** *pl.* the mouth; also, the entrance of a canyon, valley, etc.

jog (jäg) *v.* **1** to give a little shake to; jostle or nudge [*Jog* him to see if he's awake.] **2** to shake up or rouse, as the memory or the mind. —**jogged, jog′ging** ◆*n.* **1** a little shake or nudge. **2** a jogging pace; trot. —**jog′ger** *n.*

jour·nal (jur′nəl) *n.* **1** a daily record of what happens, such as a diary [She kept a *journal* of her trip.] **2** a written record of what happens at the meetings of a legislature, club, etc. **3** a newspaper or magazine.

jour·ney (jur′nē) *n.* a traveling from one place to another; trip. —*pl.* **jour′neys** ◆*v.* to go on a trip; travel. —**jour′neyed, jour′ney·ing**

judge (juj) *n.* **1** a public official with power to hear cases in a law court and decide what laws apply to them. **2** a person chosen to decide the winner in a contest or to settle an argument. ◆*v.* **1** to decide the winner of a contest or settle an argument [to *judge* a beauty contest]. **2** to form an opinion on something [Don't *judge* by first impressions.] —**judged, judg′ing** —**judge′ship′** *n.*

juic·y (joo′sē) *adj.* full of juice [a *juicy* plum]. —**juic′i·er, juic′i·est**

Ju·ly (joo lī′) *n.* the seventh month of the year, which has 31 days: abbreviated **Jul.**

June (joon) *n.* the sixth month of the year, which has 30 days: abbreviated **Jun.**

kayak

Kk

kay·ak (kī′ak) *n.* an Eskimo canoe made of a wooden frame covered with skins all around, except for an opening for the paddler.

kelp (kelp) *n.* a brown seaweed that is large and coarse.

kil·o·gram (kil′ə gram) *n.* a unit of weight, equal to 1,000 grams.

kil·o·li·ter (kil′ə lēt′ər) *n.* a unit of volume, equal to 1,000 liters or one cubic meter.

kiss (kis) *v.* **1** to touch with the lips as a way of showing love, respect, etc. or as a greeting. **2** to touch lightly [Her bowling ball just *kissed* the last pin.] ◆*n.* a touch or caress with the lips. —*pl.* **kiss′es**

knap·sack (nap′sak) *n.* a leather or canvas bag worn on the back, as by hikers, for carrying supplies.

knead (nēd) *v.* to keep pressing and squeezing dough or clay to make it ready for use [to *knead* bread dough].

knife (nīf) *n.* **1** a tool having a flat, sharp blade set in a handle, used for cutting. **2** a cutting blade that is part of a machine. —*pl.* **knives** ◆*v.* to cut or stab with a knife. —**knifed, knif′ing**

a	ask, fat
ā	ape, date
ä	car, lot
e	elf, ten
ē	even, meet
i	is, hit
ī	ice, fire
ō	open, go
ô	law, horn
oi	oil, point
oo	look, pull
o͞o	ooze, tool
ou	out, crowd
u	up, cut
u	fur, fern
ə	a in ago
	e in agent
	e in father
	i in unity
	o in collect
	u in focus
ch	chin, arch
ŋ	ring, singer
sh	she, dash
th	thin, truth
th	then, father
zh	s in pleasure

knives (nīvz) *n. plural of* **knife.**

know (nō) *v.* **1** to be sure of or have the facts about [Do you *know* why grass is green? She *knows* the law.] **2** to be aware of; realize [He suddenly *knew* he would be late.] **3** to have in one's mind or memory [The actress *knows* her lines.] **4** to be acquainted with [I *know* your brother well.] —**knew, known, know'ing**

knowl·edge (nä'lij) *n.* the fact or condition of knowing [*Knowledge* of the crime spread through the town.]

known (nōn) *past participle of* **know.**

knuck·le (nuk'əl) *n.* **1** a joint of the finger; especially, a joint connecting a finger to the rest of the hand. **2** the knee or hock joint of a pig, calf, etc., used as food. —☆**knuckle down,** to work hard. —**knuckle under,** to give in.

kook·a·bur·ra (kook'ə bur ə) *n.* an Australian bird related to the kingfisher. Its cry sounds like someone laughing loudly.

kookaburra

la·dy (lā'dē) *n.* **1** a woman, especially one who is polite and refined and has a sense of honor. **2** a woman belonging to a family of high social standing, as the wife of a lord. —*pl.* **la'dies**

land·ing (lan'diŋ) *n.* **1** a coming to shore or a putting on shore [the *landing* of troops]. **2** a place where a ship can land; pier or dock. **3** a platform at the end of a flight of stairs. **4** a coming down after flying, jumping, or falling.

late (lāt) *adj., n.* **1** happening or coming after the usual or expected time; tardy [*late* for school; a *late* train]. **2** happening or appearing just before now; recent [a *late* news broadcast]. —**lat'er** or **lat'ter, lat'est** or **last** ◆*adv.* **1** after the usual or expected time [Roses bloomed *late* last year.] **2** toward the end of some period [They came *late* in the day.] —**lat'er, lat'est** —**late'ness** *n.*

lat·i·tude (lat'ə tood *or* lat'ə tyood) *n.* **1** freedom from strict rules; freedom to do as one wishes [Our school allows some *latitude* in choosing courses.] **2** distance north or south of the equator, measured in degrees [Minneapolis is at 45 degrees north *latitude.*]

laugh (laf) *v.* **1** to make a series of quick sounds with the voice that show one is amused or happy or, sometimes, that show scorn. One usually smiles or grins when laughing. ◆*n.* the act or sound of laughing.

launch (lônch *or* länch) *v.* **1** to throw, hurl, or send off into space [to *launch* a rocket]. **2** to cause to slide into the water; set afloat [to *launch* a new ship]. **3** to start or begin [to *launch* an attack].

law·yer (lô'yər *or* lä'yər) *n.* a person whose profession is giving advice on law or acting for others in lawsuits.

lead (lēd) *v.* **1** to show the way for; guide [*Lead* us along the path. The lights *led* me to the house.] **2** to go or make go in some direction [This path *leads* to the lake. Drainpipes *lead* the water away.] **3** to be at the head of or be first [He *leads* the band. Their team was *leading* at the half.] —**led, lead'ing** ◆*n.* **1** the first place or position [The bay horse is in the *lead.*] **2** a clue [The police followed up every *lead.*]

lead·ing (lē'diŋ) *adj.* **1** that leads; guiding [A *leading* question guides one toward a certain answer.] **2** most important; playing a chief role [She played a *leading* part in our campaign.]

leaf (lēf) *n.* **1** any of the flat, green parts growing from the stem of a plant or tree. **2** a petal [a rose *leaf*]. **3** a sheet of paper in a book [Each side of a *leaf* is a page.] —*pl.* **leaves**

learn (lurn) *v.* **1** to get some knowledge or skill, as by studying or being taught [I have *learned* to knit. Some people never *learn* from experience.] **2** to find out about something; come to know [When did you *learn* of his illness?] **3** to fix in the mind; memorize [*Learn* this poem by tomorrow.] —**learned** (lurnd) or **learnt** (lurnt), **learn'ing** —**learn'er** *n.*

leash (lēsh) *n.* a strap or chain by which a dog, etc. is led or held. —*pl.* **leash'es** ◆*v.* to put a leash on.

leaves (lēvz) *n. plural of* **leaf.**

leg·end (lej'ənd) *n.* **1** a story handed down through the years and connected with some real events, but probably not true in itself [The story of King Arthur is a British *legend.*] **2** all such stories as a group [famous in Irish *legend*].

☆**length·y** (leŋkth'ē) *adj.* long or too long [a *lengthy* speech]. —**length'i·er, length'i·est** —**length'i·ly** *adv.*

leop·ard (lep'ərd) *n.* **1** a large, fierce animal of the cat family, having a tan coat with black spots. It is found in Africa and Asia. **2** *another name for* **jaguar.**

let's (lets) let us.

let·ter (let'ər) *n.* **1** any of the marks used in writing or printing to stand for a sound of speech; character of an alphabet. **2** a written message, usually sent by mail. ◆*v.* to print letters by hand [Will you *letter* this poster?]

li·brar·y (lī'brer'ē) *n.* **1** a place where a collection of books is kept for reading or borrowing. **2** a collection of books. —*pl.* **li'brar'ies**

life (līf) *n.* **1** the quality of plants and animals that makes it possible for them to take in food, grow, produce others of their kind, etc. and that makes them different from rocks, water, etc. [Death is the loss of *life*.] **2** a living thing; especially, a human being [The crash took six *lives*.] —*pl.* **lives**

life·boat (līf′bōt) *n.* **1** any of the small boats carried by a ship for use if the ship must be abandoned. **2** a sturdy boat kept on a shore, for use in rescuing people in danger of drowning.

lift (lift) *v.* **1** to bring up to a higher place; raise [Please *lift* that box onto the truck.] **2** to rise or go up [Our spirits *lifted* when spring came.] ◆*n.* **1** a ride in the direction one is going. **2** a device for carrying people up or down a slope [a ski *lift*].

lis·ten (lis′ən) *v.* to pay attention in order to hear; try to hear [*Listen* to the rain. *Listen* when the counselor speaks.] —**lis′ten·er** *n.*

li·ter (lēt′ər) *n.* the basic unit of capacity in the metric system, equal to 1 cubic decimeter. A liter is equal to a little more than a quart in liquid measure and to a little less than a quart in dry measure.

lives (līvz) *n.* *plural of* **life**.

loaf (lōf) *n.* **1** a portion of bread baked in one piece, usually oblong in shape. **2** any food baked in this shape [a meat *loaf*]. —*pl.* **loaves**

loan (lōn) *n.* **1** the act of lending [Thanks for the *loan* of your pen.] **2** something lent, especially a sum of money. ◆*v.* to lend, especially a sum of money or something to be returned.

loaves (lōvz) *n.* *plural of* **loaf**.

lo·cate (lō′kāt *or* lō kāt′) *v.* **1** to set up or place; situate [Their shop is *located* in the new mall.] **2** to find out where something is [Have you *located* the gloves that you lost?] —**lo′cat·ed, lo′cat·ing**

lock (läk) *n.* **1** a device for fastening a door, safe, etc. by means of a bolt. A lock can usually be opened only by a special key, etc. **2** an enclosed part of a canal, river, etc. with gates at each end. Water can be let in or out of it to raise or lower ships from one level to another. ◆*v.* to fasten or become fastened with a lock [I *locked* the door.] —**locked, lock′ing**

lo·co·mo·tive (lō′kə mō′tiv) *n.* a steam, electric, or diesel engine on wheels, that pulls or pushes railroad trains. ◆*adj.* moving or able to move from one place to another.

lodge (läj) *n.* **1** a place to live in; especially, a small house for some special purpose [a hunting *lodge*]. **2** the hut or tent of an American Indian. ◆*v.* **1** to provide with a place to live or sleep in for a time [She agreed to *lodge* the strangers overnight.] **2** to come to rest and stick firmly [A fish bone *lodged* in her throat.] —**lodged, lodg′ing**

lone·ly (lōn′lē) *adj.* **1** unhappy because one is alone or away from friends or family [Billy was *lonely* his first day at camp.] **2** without others nearby; alone [a *lonely* cottage]. **3** with few or no people [a *lonely* island]. —**lone′li·er, lone′li·est** —**lone′li·ness** *n.*

love (luv) *n.* **1** a deep and tender feeling of fondness and devotion [parents' *love* for their children; the *love* of Romeo and Juliet] . **2** a strong liking [a *love* of books]. **3** a person that one loves [my own true *love*]. ◆ *v.* to feel love for [to *love* one's parents; to *love* all people]. —**loved, lov′ing**

love·ly (luv′lē) *adj.* very pleasing in looks or character; beautiful [a *lovely* person]. —**love′li·er, love′li·est**

loy·al (loi′əl) *adj.* **1** faithful to one's country [a *loyal* citizen]. **2** faithful to one's family, duty, or beliefs [a *loyal* friend].

luck·y (luk′ē) *adj.* having good luck [She is *lucky* to go to Rome.] —**luck′i·er, luck′i·est**

lug·gage (lug′ij) *n.* the suitcases, trunks, etc. of a traveler; baggage.

manatee

Mm

mag·ni·fy (mag′nə fī) *v.* to make look or seem larger than is really so [to *magnify* an object with a lens]. —**mag′ni·fied, mag′ni·fy·ing**

mam·mal (mam′əl) *n.* any animal with glands in the female that produce milk for feeding its young. —**mam·ma·li·an** (mə mā′lē ən) *adj., n.*

mam·moth (mam′əth) *n.* a type of large elephant that lived long ago. Mammoths had a hairy skin and long tusks that curved upward. ◆*adj.* very big; huge.

man (man) *n.* an adult male human being. **2** any human being; person ["that all *men* are created equal"]. —*pl.* **men**

man·ag·er (man′ij ər) *n.* a person who manages a business, baseball team, etc.

man·a·tee (man′ ə tē) *n.* a large animal that lives in shallow tropical waters and feeds on plants. It has flippers and a broad, flat tail; sea cow.

March (märch) *n.* the third month of the year, which has 31 days: abbreviated **Mar.**

marsh·mal·low (märsh′mel′ō *or* märsh′mal′ō) *n.* a soft, white, spongy candy coated with powdered sugar.

mas·cot (mas′kät) *n.* a person, animal, or thing thought to bring good luck by being present [Our team's *mascot* is the lion.]

match¹ (mach) *n.* **1** a slender piece of wood or cardboard having a tip coated with a chemical that catches fire when rubbed on a certain surface. **2** a slowly burning cord or wick once used for firing a gun or cannon. —*pl.* **match′es**

a	ask, fat
ā	ape, date
ä	car, lot
e	elf, ten
ē	even, meet
i	is, hit
ī	ice, fire
ō	open, go
ô	law, horn
oi	oil, point
oo	look, pull
oo	ooze, tool
ou	out, crowd
u	up, cut
u	fur, fern
ə	a in ago
	e in agent
	e in father
	i in unity
	o in collect
	u in focus
ch	chin, arch
ŋ	ring, singer
sh	she, dash
th	thin, truth
th	then, father
zh	s in pleasure

match² (mach) *n.* **1** two or more people or things that go well together [That suit and tie are a good *match*.] **2** a game or contest between two persons or teams [a tennis *match*].

mead·ow (med′ō) *n.* **1** a piece of land where grass is grown for hay. **2** low, level grassland near a stream or lake.

mean·ing (mēn′iŋ) *n.* what is meant; what is supposed to be understood; significance [She repeated her words to make her *meaning* clear. What is the *meaning* of this poem?] ◆*adj.* that has some meaning [a *meaning* smile].

meas·ure (mezh′ər) *v.* **1** to find out the size, amount, or extent of, as by comparing with something else [*Measure* the child's height with a yardstick. How do you *measure* a person's worth?] **2** to set apart or mark off a certain amount or length of [*Measure* out three pounds of sugar.] **3** to be of a certain size, amount, or extent [The table *measures* five feet on each side.] —**meas′ured, meas′ur·ing** ◆*n.* the size, amount, or extent of something, found out by measuring [The *measure* of the bucket is 15 liters.] **2** the notes or rests between two bars on a staff of music. **3** rhythm or meter, as of a poem or song.

meat (mēt) *n.* **1** the flesh of animals used as food. Meat usually does not include fish and often does not include poultry. **2** the part that can be eaten [the *meat* of a nut].

med·i·cine (med′ə sən) *n.* **1** any substance used in or on the body to treat disease, lessen pain, heal, etc. **2** the science of treating and preventing disease. **3** the branch of this science that makes use of drugs, diet, etc., especially as separate from surgery.

mel·o·dy (mel′ə dē) *n.* **1** an arrangement of musical tones in a series so as to form a tune; often, the main tune in the harmony of a musical piece [The *melody* is played by the oboes.] **2** any pleasing series of sounds [a *melody* sung by birds]. —*pl.* **mel′o·dies**

mem·ber (mem′bər) *n.* **1** any of the persons who make up a church, club, political party, or other group. **2** a leg, arm, or other part of the body.

mem·o·ry (mem′ər ē) *n.* **1** the act or power of remembering [to have a good *memory*]. **2** all that one remembers. **3** something remembered [The music brought back many *memories*.] **4** the part of a computer that stores information. —*pl.* **mem′o·ries**

men (men) *n.* plural of man.

mend (mend) *v.* to put back in good condition; repair; fix [to *mend* a torn shirt]. —**mend′ed, mend′ing**

men·u (men′yōō) *n.* a list of the foods served at a meal [a restaurant's dinner *menu*].

me·ter (mēt′ər) *n.* **1** a measure of length that is the basic unit in the metric system. One meter is equal to 39.37 inches. **2** rhythm in poetry; regular arrangement of accented and unaccented syllables in each line. **3** rhythm in music; arrangement of beats in each measure [Marches are often in 4/4 *meter*, with four equal beats in each measure.]

Mi·am·i (mī am′ē) a city on the southeastern coast of Florida.

mice (mīs) *n.* *plural of* **mouse.**

mi·cro·wave (mī′krō wāv′) *n.* any radio wave within a certain range, usually between 300,000 and 300 megahertz. Those of a certain wavelength create great heat when they pass through substances such as food. A **microwave oven** uses these waves for fast cooking. Others are used to transmit signals to and from communications satellites.

mi·grate (mī′grāt) *v.* **1** to move from one place or country to another, especially in order to make a new home. **2** to move from one region to another when the season changes, as some birds do in the spring and fall. —**mi′grat·ed, mi′grat·ing** —**mi·gra′tion** *n.*

milk (milk) *n.* a white liquid formed in special glands of female mammals for suckling their young. The milk that is a common food comes from cows. ◆*v.* to squeeze milk out from a cow, goat, etc. —**milk′er** *n.* —**milk′ing** *n.*

mil·li·gram (mil′i gram) *n.* a unit of weight, equal to one thousandth of a gram.

mil·li·li·ter (mil′i lēt′ər) *n.* a unit of volume, equal to one thousandth of a liter.

mil·li·me·ter (mil′i mēt′ər) *n.* a unit of measure, equal to one thousandth of a meter (.03937 inch).

min·er·al (min′ər əl) *n.* **1** a substance formed in the earth by nature; especially, a solid substance that was never animal or vegetable [Iron, granite, and salt are *minerals*. Coal is sometimes called a *mineral*, too.] **2** any of certain elements, as iron or phosphorus, needed by plants and animals.

miss (mis) *v.* **1** to fail to hit, meet, reach, get, catch, see, hear, etc. [The arrow *missed* the target. We *missed* our plane. I *missed* you at the play last night.] **2** to let go by; fail to take [You *missed* your turn.] **3** to escape; avoid [He just *missed* being hit.]

mol·lusk or **mol·lusc** (mäl′əsk) *n.* an animal with a soft body that is usually protected by a shell, as the oyster, clam, snail, etc.

☆**moose** (mōōs) *n.* a large animal related to the deer, of the northern U.S. and Canada. The male has broad antlers with many points. —*pl.* **moose**

mollusk

moun·tain (mount′n) *n.* **1** a part of the earth's surface that rises high into the air; very high hill. **2 mountains,** *pl.* a chain or group of such high hills.

mouse (mous) *n.* **1** a small, gnawing animal found in houses and fields throughout the world. **2** a small device moved by the hand, as on a flat surface, so as to make the cursor move on a computer terminal. —*pl.* **mice** (mīs)

mov·er (m̅o̅o̅v′ər) *n.* a person or thing that moves; especially, ☆one whose work is moving people's furniture from one home to another.

mug·ger (mug′ər) *n.* a person who assaults others, usually in order to rob them.

mul·ti·ply (mul′tə plī) *v.* **1** to become more, greater, etc.; increase [Our troubles *multiplied.*] **2** to repeat a certain figure a certain number of times [If you *multiply* 10 by 4, or repeat 10 four times, you get the product 40.] —**mul′ti·plied, mul′ti·ply·ing**

mus·cle (mus′l) *n.* **1** the tissue in an animal's body that makes up the fleshy parts. Muscle can be stretched or tightened to move the parts of the body. **2** any single part or band of this tissue [The biceps is a *muscle* in the upper arm.] **3** strength that comes from muscles that are developed; brawn.

mu·si·cal (my̅o̅o̅′zi kəl) *adj.* **1** of music or for making music [a *musical* score; a *musical* instrument]. **2** like music; full of melody, harmony, etc. [Wind has a *musical* sound.] **3** fond of music or skilled in music. —**mu′si·cal·ly** *adv.*

☆**musk·rat** (musk′rat) *n.* **1** a North American animal that is like a large rat. It lives in water and has glossy brown fur.

mys·ter·y (mis′tər ē *or* mis′trə) *n.* **1** any event or thing that remains unexplained or is so secret that it makes people curious [That murder is still a *mystery.*] **2** a story or play about such an event [She read a murder *mystery.*] —*pl.* **mys′ter·ies**

Nn

need (nēd) *v.* to require; want [She *needs* a car.]

neigh·bor (nā′bər) *n.* **1** a person who lives near another. **2** a person or thing that is near another [France and Spain are *neighbors.*] **3** another human being; fellow person ["Love thy *neighbor.*"]

neph·ew (nef′y̅o̅o̅) *n.]* **1** the son of one's brother or sister. **2** the son of one's brother-in-law or sister-in-law.

nerv·ous (nur′vəs) *adj.* feeling fear or expecting trouble [He is *nervous* about seeing the dentist.]

night·in·gale (nīt′n gāl) *n.* a small European thrush. The male is known for its sweet singing.

noise (noiz) *n.* sound, especially a loud, harsh, or confused sound [the *noise* of fireworks; *noises* of a city street]. —*pl.* **nois′es** ◆*v.* to make public by telling; spread [to *noise* a rumor about]. —**noised, nois′ing**

nom·i·nate (näm′ə nāt) *v.* **1** to name as a candidate for an election [Each political party *nominates* a person to run for president.] **2** to appoint to a position [The President *nominates* the members of the Cabinet.] —**nom′i·nat·ed, nom′i·nat·ing**

non·fic·tion (nän′fik′shən) *n.* a piece of writing about the real world, real people, or true events, as a biography or history.

non·prof·it (nän präf′it) *adj.* not intending to make a profit [a *nonprofit* hospital].

non·sense (nän′sens) *n.* **1** speech or writing that is foolish or has no meaning [I read the letter but it just sounded like *nonsense* to me.] **2** silly or annoying behavior [She is a teacher who will put up with no *nonsense* in the classroom.] ◆*interj.* how silly! how foolish! indeed not!

non·stop (nän′stäp′) *adj., adv.* without making a stop [to fly *nonstop* from New York to Seattle].

North America the northern continent in the Western Hemisphere. Canada, the United States, Mexico, and the countries of Central America are in North America.

north·west (nôrth west′ *or* nôr west′) *n.* **1** the direction halfway between north and west. **2** a place or region in or toward this direction. ◆*adj.* **1** in, of, or toward the northwest [the *northwest* part of the county]. **2** from the northwest [a *northwest* wind]. ◆*adv.* in or toward the northwest [to sail *northwest*].

numb (num) *adj.* not able to feel, or feeling very little; deadened [My toes were *numb* with cold. He sat *numb* with grief.] ◆*v.* to make numb. —**numb′ly** *adv.* **numb′ness** *n.*

nurse (nurs) *n.* a person who has been trained to take care of sick people and help doctors.

nu·tri·ent (n̅o̅o̅′trē ənt *or* ny̅o̅o̅′trē ənt) *adj.* nourishing. ◆*n.* any of the substances in food that are needed for health, such as proteins, minerals, vitamins, etc.

Oo

o·cean·og·ra·phy (ō′shən äg′rə fē) *n.* the science that studies the oceans and the animals and plants that live in them. —**o′cean·og′ra·pher** *n.*

muskrat

a	ask, fat
ā	ape, date
ä	car, lot
e	elf, ten
ē	even, meet
i	is, hit
ī	ice, fire
ō	open, go
ô	law, horn
oi	oil, point
o͝o	look, pull
o͞o	ooze, tool
ou	out, crowd
u	up, cut
u	fur, fern
ə	a in ago
	e in agent
	e in father
	i in unity
	o in collect
	u in focus
ch	chin, arch
ŋ	ring, singer
sh	she, dash
th	thin, truth
th	then, father
zh	s in pleasure

organ

penguin

of·ten (ôf′ən *or* ôf′tən) *adv.* many times; frequently.

o·pen (ō′pən) *adj.* not closed, shut, covered, or stopped up [*open* eyes; *open* doors; an *open* jar; an *open* drain]. ◆*v.* **1** to make or become open, or no longer closed [Please *open* that trunk. The door suddenly *opened.*] **2** to begin or start [We *opened* the program with a song.] **3** to start operating [She *opened* a new store. School will *open* in September.] —**o′pen·ly** *adv.* —**o′pen·ness** *n.*

op·er·a·tor (äp′ər ātər) *n.* ☆**1** a person who operates a machine or device [a telephone *operator*]. **2** an owner or manager of a factory, mine, etc.

or·gan (ôr′gən) *n.* **1** a musical instrument having sets of pipes that make sounds when keys or pedals are pressed to send air through the pipes. *Also called* **pipe organ.** **2** a part of an animal or plant that has some special purpose [The heart, lungs, and eyes are *organs* of the body.]

or·gan·i·za·tion (ôr′gə ni zā′shən) *n.* **1** the act of organizing or arranging. **2** a group of persons organized for some purpose.

or·gan·ize (ôr′gə nīz) *v.* to arrange or place according to a system [The library books are *organized* according to their subjects.] —**or′gan·ized, or′gan·iz·ing** —**or′gan·iz′er** *n.*

or·phan (ôr′fən) *n.* a child whose parents are dead or, sometimes, one of whose parents is dead. ◆*adj.* **1** being an orphan [an *orphan* child]. **2** of or for orphans [an *orphan* home]. ◆*v.* to cause to become an orphan [children *orphaned* by war].

os·trich (äs′trich) *n.* a very large bird of Africa and southwestern Asia, with a long neck and long legs. It cannot fly, but runs swiftly.

ot·ter (ät′ər) *n.* **1** a furry animal related to the weasel. It has webbed feet used in swimming and a long tail, and it eats small animals and fish.

☆**out·doors** (out′dôrz′) *adv.* in or into the open; outside [We went *outdoors* to play.] ◆*n.* (out dôrz′) the world outside of buildings; the open air.

out·fit (out′fit) *n.* the clothing or equipment used in some work, activity, etc. [a hiking *outfit*]. ◆*v.* to supply with what is needed [Their store *outfits* campers.] —**out′fit·ted, out′fit·ting**

out·stand·ing (out′ stan′diŋ) *adj.* that stands out as very good or important [an *outstanding* lawyer].

☆**o·ver·coat** (ō′vər kōt) *n.* a heavy coat worn outdoors in cold weather.

ox (äks) *n.* **1** a castrated male of the cattle family, used for pulling heavy loads. **2** any animal of a group that chew their cud and have cloven hoofs, including the buffalo, bison, etc. —*pl.* **ox·en** (äk′s'n)

pace (pās) *n.* **1** a step in walking or running. **2** the length of a step or stride, thought of as about 30 to 40 inches. **3** the rate of speed at which something moves or develops [The scoutmaster set the *pace* in the hike. Science goes forward at a rapid *pace.*] ◆*v.* **1** to walk back and forth across [While waiting for the verdict, I *paced* the floor nervously.] **2** to measure by paces [*Pace* off 30 yards.] —**paced, pac′ing** —**pac′er** *n.*

pad (pad) *n.* **1** anything made of or stuffed with soft material, and used to protect against blows, to give comfort, etc.; cushion [a shoulder *pad*; seat *pad*]. **2** the under part of the foot of some animals, as the wolf, lion, etc. ◆*v.* to stuff or cover with soft material [a *padded* chair]. —**pad′ded, pad′ding**

par·don (pärd′n) *n.* the act of forgiving or excusing. —*pl.* **par′dons**

par·ty (pär′tē) *n.* **1** a gathering of people to have a good time [a birthday *party*]. **2** a group of people who share the same political opinions and work together to elect certain people, to promote certain policies, etc. [the Republican *Party*]. **3** a group of people working or acting together [a hunting *party*]. —*pl.* **par′ties**

pas·sen·ger (pas′ən jər) *n.* a person traveling in a car, bus, plane, ship, etc., but not driving or helping to operate it.

pa·ti·o (pat′ē ō *or* pät′ē ō) *n.* ☆**1** in Spain and Spanish America, a courtyard around which a house is built. ☆**2** a paved area near a house, with chairs, tables, etc. for outdoor lounging, dining, etc. —*pl.* **pa′ti·os**

pa·trol (pə trōl′) *v.* to make regular trips around a place in order to guard it [The watchman *patrolled* the area all night.] —**pa·trolled′, pa·trol′ling**

peace (pēs) *n.* **1** freedom from war or fighting [a nation that lives in *peace* with all other nations]. **2** law and order [The rioters were disturbing the *peace.*] **3** calm or quiet [to find *peace* of mind].

pen·cil (pen′səl) *n.* a long, thin piece of wood, metal, etc. with a center stick of graphite or crayon that is sharpened to a point for writing or drawing. ◆*v.* to mark, write, or draw with a pencil. —**pen′ciled** or **pen′cilled, pen′cil·ing** or **pen′cil·ling**

pen·guin (peŋ′gwin) *n.* a sea bird mainly of the antarctic region, with webbed feet and flippers for swimming and diving. Penguins cannot fly.

pen·in·su·la (pə nin′sə lə) *n.* a long piece of land almost completely surrounded by water [Italy is a *peninsula*.] —**pen·in′su·lar** *adj.*

per·ceive (pər sēv′) *v.* **1** to become aware of through one of the senses, especially through seeing [to *perceive* the difference between two shades of red]. **2** to take in through the mind [I quickly *perceived* the joke.] —**per·ceived′, per·ceiv′ing**

perch (purch) *n.* **1** a small fish living in lakes and streams. It is used for food. **2** a similar saltwater fish. —*pl.* **perch** or **perch′es**

per·fect (pur′fəkt) *adj.* complete in every way and having no faults or errors [a *perfect* test paper].

per·form·er (pər fôrm′ər) *n.* one who does something to entertain an audience [The *performer* sang and danced.]

per·fume (pur′fyoom *or* pər fyoom′) *n.* **1** a sweet smell; pleasing odor; fragrance [the *perfume* of roses]. **2** a liquid with a pleasing smell, for use on the body, clothing, etc. ◆*v.* (pər fyoom′) to give a pleasing smell to, as with perfume. —**per·fumed′, per·fum′ing**

per·son (pur′sən) *n.* a human being; man, woman, or child [every *person* in this room].

pet·ri·fy (pe′tri fī) *v.* **1** to change into a substance like stone by replacing the normal cells with minerals [Trees buried under lava for a great many years can become *petrified*.] **2** to make unable to move or act, as because of fear or surprise. —**pet′ri·fied, pet′ri·fy·ing**

phase (fāz) *n.* **1** any of the sides or views of a subject by which it may be looked at, thought about, or shown [We discussed the many *phases* of the problem.] **2** any stage in a series of changes [Adolescence is a *phase* we all go through.] ◆*v.* —**phased, phas′ing**

☆**pho·ny** *or* **pho·ney** (fō′nē) *adj.* not real or genuine; fake; false. —**pho′ni·er, pho′ni·est** ◆*n.* a person or thing that is not really what it is supposed to be. —*pl.* **pho′nies** *This is a slang word.*

pho·to (fōt′ō) *n. a shorter name for* **photograph**: *used only in everyday talk.* —*pl.* **pho′tos**

pho·to·graph (fōt′ə graf) *n.* a picture made with a camera. ◆*v.* **1** to take a photograph of. **2** to look a certain way in photographs [She *photographs* taller than she is.]

pho·tog·ra·pher (fə täg′rə fər) *n.* a person who takes photographs, especially for a living.

phrase (frāz) *n.* a group of words that is not a complete sentence, but that gives a single idea, usually as a separate part of a sentence.

pi·an·o (pē ä′nō) *n.* a large musical instrument with many wire strings in a case and a keyboard. When a key is struck, it makes a small hammer hit a string so that it gives out a tone. **grand piano** *and* **upright.** —*pl.* **pi·an′os**

pic·ture (pik′chər) *n.* a likeness of a person, thing, scene, etc. made by drawing, painting, or photography; also, a printed copy of this. ◆*v.* **1** to make a picture of. **2** to show; make clear [Joy was *pictured* in her face.] **3** to describe or explain [Dickens *pictured* life in England.] **4** to form an idea or picture in the mind; imagine [You can *picture* how pleased I was!] —**pic′tured, pic′tur·ing**

pie (pī) *n.* a dish with a filling made of fruit, meat, etc., baked in a pastry crust.

piece (pēs) *n.* **1** a part broken or separated from a whole thing [The glass shattered and I swept up the *pieces*.] **2** a part or section of a whole, thought of as complete by itself [a *piece* of meat; a *piece* of land]. **3** any one of a set or group of things [a dinner set of 52 *pieces*; a chess *piece*]. ◆*v.* to join the pieces of, as in mending [to *piece* together a broken jug.]

pine·ap·ple (pīn′ap əl) *n.* **1** a juicy tropical fruit that looks a little like a large pine cone. **2** the plant it grows on, having a short stem and curved leaves with prickly edges.

pi·o·neer (pī ə nir′) *n.* ☆ a person who goes before, opening up the way for others to follow, as an early settler or a scientist doing original work [Daniel Boone was a *pioneer* in Kentucky. Marie Curie was a *pioneer* in the study of radium.] ◆*v.* to act as a pioneer; open up the way for others [The Wright brothers *pioneered* in air travel.]

Pitts·burgh (pits′burg) a city in southwestern Pennsylvania.

pit·y (pit′ē) *v.* to feel sorrow for another's suffering or trouble [to *pity* someone's misfortune]. —**pit′ied, pit′y·ing**

plain (plān) *adj.* **1** open; clear; not blocked [in *plain* view]. **2** easy to understand; clear to the mind [The meaning is *plain*.] **3** simple; easy [I can do a little *plain* cooking.] —**plain′ly** *adv.* —**plain′ness** *n.*

plane[1] (plān) *adj.* **1** flat; level; even. ◆*n.* **2** *a shorter form of* **airplane**.

plane[2] (plān) *n.* a tool used by carpenters for shaving wood in order to make it smooth or level. ◆*v.* to make smooth or level with a plane. —**planed, plan′ing**

plat·form (plat′fôrm) *n.* a flat surface or stage higher than the ground or floor around it [*platform* at a railroad station; a speaker's *platform*].

po·et·ry (pō′ə trē) *n.* **1** the art of writing poems. **2** poems [the *poetry* of Keats].

po·lit·i·cal (pə lit′i kəl) *adj.* **1** having to do with government, politics, etc. [*political* parties]. **2** of or like political parties or politicians [a *political* speech]. —**po·lit′i·cal·ly** *adv.*

perch

poll (pōl) *n.* **1** a voting or listing of opinions by persons; also, the counting of these votes or opinions [A *poll* of our class shows that most of us want a party.] **2** the number of votes cast. **3** a list of voters. ☆**4 polls,** *pl.* a place where people go to vote.

porch (pôrch) *n.* **1** a covered entrance to a building, usually with a roof that is held up by posts. **2** a room on the outside of a building, either open or enclosed by screens, etc.

por·poise (pôr′pəs) *n.* **1** a water animal that is like a small whale. It is dark above and white below and has a blunt snout. **2** *another name for* **dolphin.**

porpoise

port·hole (pôrt′hōl) *n.* a small opening in a ship's side, as for letting in light and air.

pow·er·ful (pou′ər fəl) *adj.* having much power; strong or influential [a *powerful* hand; a *powerful* leader]. —**pow′er·ful·ly** *adv.*

prac·tice (prak′tis) *v.* **1** to do or carry out regularly; make a habit of [to *practice* what one preaches; to *practice* charity]. **2** to do something over and over again in order to become skilled at it [She *practices* two hours a day on the piano.] **3** to work at as a profession or occupation [to *practice* medicine]. —**prac′ticed, prac′tic·ing**

☆**prai·rie** (prer′ē) *n.* a large area of level or rolling grassy land without many trees.

praise (prāz) *v.* **1** to say good things about; give a good opinion of [to *praise* someone's work]. **2** to worship, as in song [to *praise* God]. —**praised, prais′ing**

pre·cau·tion (prē kô′shən *or* prē kä′shən) *n.* care taken ahead of time, as against danger, failure, etc. [She took the *precaution* of locking the door before she left.] —**pre·cau′tion·ar′y** *adj.*

pre·cip·i·ta·tion (prē sip′ə tā′shən) *n.* **1** a sudden bringing about of something [the *precipitation* of a cold by getting chilled]. **2** sudden or reckless haste. **3** rain, snow, etc. or the amount of this.

pre·dict (prē dikt′) *v.* to tell what one thinks will happen in the future [I *predict* that you will win.] —**pre·dict′a·ble** *adj.*

pre·fix (prē′fiks) *n.* a syllable or group of syllables joined to the beginning of a word to change its meaning. Some common prefixes are *un-, non-, re-, anti-,* and *in-.*

pre·paid (prē pād′) *past tense and past participle of* **prepay.**

pre·pay (prē pā′) *v.* to pay for ahead of time [Postage is normally *prepaid.*] —**pre·paid′, pre·pay′ing**

pre·set (prē set′) *v.* to set or adjust ahead of time [He *presets* the oven so it will be ready for the cake.] —**pre·set′, pre·set′ting**

pret·ty (prit′ē) *adj.* **1** pleasant to look at or hear, especially in a delicate, dainty, or graceful way [a *pretty* girl; a *pretty* voice; a *pretty* garden]. **2** fine; good; nice: —**pret′ti·er, pret′ti·est**

pre·view (prē′vyoo) *n.* ☆a view or showing ahead of time; especially, a private showing of a movie before showing it to the public. ◆*v.* to give a preview of.

price (prīs) *n.* **1** the amount of money asked or paid for something; cost [What is the *price* of that coat?] **2** value or worth [a painting of great *price*]. ◆*v.* to set the price of [The rug was *priced* at $40.] —**priced, pric′ing**

pride (prīd) *n.* **1** an opinion of oneself that is too high; vanity [Her *pride* blinded her to her own faults.] **2** proper respect for oneself; dignity; self-respect [He has too much *pride* to go begging.] **3** pleasure or satisfaction in something done, owned, etc. [We take *pride* in our garden.] **4** a person or thing that makes one proud [She is her father's *pride* and joy.] —**prid′ed, prid′ing**

prince (prins) *n.* a son or grandson of a king or queen.

prin·ci·pal (prin′sə pəl) *n.* the head of a school.

print·ing (print′iŋ) *n.* **1** the act of one that prints. **2** the making of printed material, as books, newspapers, etc. **3** printed words. —**print′er** *n.*

pro·ceed (prō sēd′) *v.* **1** to go on, especially after stopping for a while [After eating, we *proceeded* to the next town.] **2** to begin and go on doing something [I *proceeded* to build a fire.]

prod·uct (präd′əkt) *n.* **1** something produced by nature or by human beings [Wood is a natural *product*. A desk is a manufactured *product*.] **2** result [The story is a *product* of her imagination.] **3** a number that is the result of multiplying [28 is the *product* of 7 multiplied by 4.]

pro·gram (prō′gram) *n.* **1** the acts, speeches, or musical pieces that make up a ceremony or entertainment [a commencement *program*]. **2** a scheduled broadcast on radio or TV.

prom·ise (präm′is) *n.* **1** an agreement to do or not to do something; vow [to make and keep a *promise*]. **2** a sign that gives reason for expecting success; cause for hope [She shows *promise* as a singer.] ◆*v.* to make a promise to [I *promised* them I'd arrive at ten.] —**prom′ised, prom′is·ing**

prompt (prämpt) *adj.* **1** quick in doing what should be done; on time [He is *prompt* in paying his bills.] **2** done, spoken, etc. without waiting [We would like a *prompt* reply.] ◆*v.* to urge or stir into action [Tyranny *prompted* them to revolt.] —**prompt′ly** *adv.* —**prompt′ness** *n.*

prop·er (präp′ər) *adj.* **1** right, correct, or suitable [the *proper* tool for this job; the *proper* clothes for a party]. **2** not to be ashamed of; decent; respectable [*proper* manners]. —**prop′er·ly** *adv.*

pro·tect (prō tekt′) *v.* to guard or defend against harm or danger; shield [armor to *protect* the knight's body]. —**pro·tec′tor** *n.*

pro·te·in (prō′tēn) *n.* a substance containing nitrogen and other elements, found in all living things and in such foods as cheese, meat, eggs, beans, etc. It is a necessary part of an animal's diet.

pro·test (prō test′ *or* prō′test) *v.* **1** to speak out against; object [They joined the march to *protest* against injustice.] **2** to say in a positive way; insist [Bill *protested* that he would be glad to help.] ◆*n.* (prō′test) the act of protesting; objection [They ignored my *protest* and continued hammering.] —**pro·test′er** or **pro·tes′tor** *n.*

prove (prōōv) *v.* **1** to show that something is true or correct [She showed us the method of *proving* our arithmetic problems.] **2** to put to a test or trial; find out about through experiments [A *proving* ground is a place for testing new equipment, as aircraft.] **3** to turn out to be [Your guess *proved* right.] —**proved, proved** or **prov′en, prov′ing**

pub·lic (pub′lik) *adj.* of or having to do with the people as a whole [*public* opinion]. ◆*n.* the people as a whole [what the *public* wants].

punc·tu·a·tion (puŋgk′chōō ā′shən) *n.* **1** the use of commas, periods, etc. in writing [rules of *punctuation*]. **2** punctuation marks [What *punctuation* is used to end sentences?]

purse (purs) *n.* a bag of leather or cloth used for carrying money, cosmetics, keys, and so on. —*pl.* **purs′es**

quit·ter (kwit′ər) *n.* ☆a person who quits or gives up too easily.

rail·road (rāl′rōd) *n.* **1** a road on which there is a track made up of parallel steel rails along which trains run. **2** a series of such roads managed as a unit, together with the cars, engines, stations, etc. that belong to it.

rai·sin (rā′zən) *n.* a sweet grape dried for eating.

rake (rāk) *n.* a tool with a long handle having a set of teeth or prongs at one end. It is used for gathering loose grass, leaves, etc. or for smoothing broken ground. ◆*v.* to gather together or smooth as with a rake [to *rake* leaves; to *rake* a gravel path]. —**raked, rak′ing**

☆**ranch** (ranch) *n.* a large farm, especially in the Western part of the U.S., where cattle, horses, or sheep are raised. —*pl.* **ranch′es** ◆*v.* to work on or manage a ranch. —**ranch′er** *n.*

rap·id (rap′id) *adj.* very swift or quick [a *rapid* journey]. ◆☆*n.* usually **rapids**, *pl.* a part of a river where the water moves swiftly. —**rap′id·ly** *adv.*

reach (rēch) *v.* **1** to stretch out one's hand, arm, etc. [He *reached* up and shook the branch.] **2** to touch, as by stretching out [Can you *reach* the top shelf?] **3** to stretch out in time, space, amount, etc. [Her fame *reaches* into all parts of the world.]

re·ac·tion (rē ak′shən) *n.* an action, happening, etc. in return or in response to some other action, happening, force, etc. [What was their *reaction* to your suggestion? A rubber ball bounces as a *reaction* to hitting the ground.]

rea·son (rē′zən) *n.* **1** something said to explain or try to explain an act, idea, etc. [Write the *reasons* for your answer.] **2** a cause for some action, feeling, etc.; motive [Noisy neighbors were our *reason* for moving.] **3** the power to think, get ideas, decide things, etc. [Human beings are the only creatures that truly have *reason*.]

re·ceipt (rē sēt′) *n.* **1** a receiving or being received [Upon *receipt* of the gift, she thanked him.] **2** a written statement that something has been received [My landlord gave me a *receipt* when I paid my rent.] **3 receipts**, *pl.* the amount of money taken in, as in a business

re·ceive (rē sēv′) *v.* **1** to take or get what has been given or sent to one [to *receive* a letter]. **2** to meet with,; be given; undergo [to *receive* punishment; to *receive* applause]. **3** to find out about; learn [He *received* the news calmly.] **4** to greet guests and let them come in [Our hostess *received* us at the door.] —**re·ceived′, re·ceiv′ing**

re·count (rē kount′) *v.* to count again [You had better *recount* your change just to make sure.]

re·duce (rē dōōs′ *or* rē dyōōs′) *v* **1** to make smaller, less, fewer, etc.; decrease [to *reduce* speed; to *reduce* taxes]. **2** to loose weight, as by dieting. **3** to make lower, as in rank or condition; bring down [to *reduce* a major to rank of captain; a family *reduced* to poverty.] —**re·duced′, re·duc′ing** —**re·duc′er** *n.* —**re·duc′i·ble** *adj.*

reel (rēl) *n.* **1** a frame or spool on which film, fishing line, wire, etc. is wound. **2** the amount of movie film, wire, etc. usually wound on one reel. ◆*v.* to wind on a reel

reel

a	ask, fat
ā	ape, date
ä	car, lot
e	elf, ten
ē	even, meet
i	is, hit
ī	ice, fire
ō	open, go
ô	law, horn
oi	oil, point
͞oo	look, pull
͞oo	ooze, tool
ou	out, crowd
u	up, cut
ʉ	fur, fern
ə	a in ago
	e in agent
	e in father
	i in unity
	o in collect
	u in focus
ch	chin, arch
ŋ	ring, singer
sh	she, dash
th	thin, truth
th	then, father
zh	s in pleasure

177

reindeer

re·fill (rē fil′) *v.* to fill again. ◆*n.* (rē′fil)**1** something to refill a special container [a *refill* for a ball point pen]. **2** any extra filling of a prescription for medicine. —**re·fill′a·ble** *adj.*

re·frig·er·a·tor (ri frij′ər āt′ər) *n.* a box or room in which the air is kept cool to keep food, etc. from spoiling.

re·fund (rē fund′) *v.* to give back money, etc.; repay [We will *refund* the full price if you are not satisfied.] ◆*n.* (rē′fund) the act of refunding or the amount refunded. —**re·fund′a·ble** *adj.*

reg·is·ter (rej′is tər) *n.* **1** a record or list of names, events, or things; also, a book in which such a record is kept [a hotel *register*; *register* of accounts]. **2** a device for counting and keeping a record of [a cash *register*]. ◆*v.* ☆**1** to keep a record of in a register [to *register* a birth]. **2** to put one's name in a register, as of voters.

reg·u·lar (reg′yə lər) *adj.* formed or arranged in an orderly way; balanced [a face with *regular* features].

rein·deer (rān′dir) *n.* a large deer found in northern regions, where it is tamed and used for work or as food. Both the male and female have antlers. —*pl.* **rein′deer**

re·lief (rē lēf′) *n.* **1** a lessening of pain, discomfort, worry, etc. [This salve will give *relief* from itching.] **2** anything that lessens pain, worry, etc. or gives a pleasing change [It's a *relief* to get out of that stuffy hall.] **3** help given to poor people, to victims of a flood, etc.

re·ly (rē lī′) *v.* to trust or depend [You can *rely* on me to be on time.] —**re·lied′, re·ly′ing**

re·mem·ber (rē mem′bər) *v.* **1** to think of again [I suddenly *remembered* I was supposed to mow the lawn.] **2** to bring back to mind by trying; recall [I just can't *remember* your name.] **3** to be careful not to forget [*Remember* to look both ways before crossing.]

re·move (rē mo͞ov′) *v.* to move to another place; take away or take off [They *removed* their coats.]

re·pair (rē per′) *v.* **1** to put into good condition again; fix; mend [to *repair* a broken toy]. **2** to set right; correct [to *repair* a mistake; to *repair* an injustice]. ◆*n.* **1** the act of repairing. **2** *usually* **repairs**, *pl.* work done in repairing [to make *repairs* on a house]. —**re·pair′a·ble** *adj.*

re·ply (rē plī′) *v.* to answer by saying or doing something [to *reply* to a question; to *reply* to the enemy's fire with a counterattack]. —**re·plied′, re·ply′ing** ◆*n.* an answer. —*pl.* **re·plies′**

re·port (rē pôrt′) *v.* **1** to tell about; give an account of [I *reported* on my trip to the Falls.] **2** to tell as news [The papers *reported* little damage as a result of the storm.] ◆*n.* an account of something, often one in written or printed form [a financial *report*].

☆**res·tau·rant** (res′tər änt *or* res′tränt) *n.* a place where meals can be bought and eaten.

re·turn (rē turn′) *v.* **1** to go or come back [When did you *return* from your trip?] **2** to bring, send, carry, or put back [Our neighbor *returned* the ladder.] **3** to pay back by doing the same [to *return* a visit; to *return* a favor]. **4** to report back [The jury *returned* a verdict of "not guilty."]

rid·er (rīd′ər) *n.* a person who rides.

rise (rīz) *v.* **1** to stand up or get up from a lying or sitting position [*rise* to greet the guests]. **2** to get up after sleeping [She *rises* early.] —**rose** (rōz), **ris′en** (riz′en), **ris′ing**

risk (risk) *n.* the chance of getting hurt, or of losing, failing, etc.; danger [He ran into the burning house at the *risk* of his life.] ◆*v.* to take the chance of [Are you willing to *risk* a fight for your beliefs?]

roast (rōst) *v.* **1** to cook with little or no liquid, as in an oven or over an open fire [to *roast* a chicken or a whole ox]. **2** to dry or brown with great heat [to *roast* coffee]. ◆*n.* a piece of roasted meat.

ro·dent (rōd′nt) *n.* an animal having sharp front teeth for gnawing. Rats, mice, rabbits, squirrels, woodchucks, and beavers are rodents.

rough·ly (ruf′lē) *adv.* **1** in a rough manner. **2** more or less; about [*Roughly* 50 people came to the party.]

roy·al·ty (roi′əl tē) *n.* **1** a royal person, or royal persons as a group [a member of British *royalty*]. **2** the rank or power of a king or queen. **3** royal quality or nature; nobility, splendor, etc. —*pl.* **roy′al·ties**

rude (ro͞od) *adj.* without respect for others; impolite [It was *rude* of them not to thank you.] —**rud′er, rud′est**

rule (ro͞ol) *n.* **1** a statement or law that is meant to guide or control the way one acts or does something [the *rules* of grammar; baseball *rules*]. **2** a usual way of doing something, behaving, etc. [to make it a *rule* never to rush]. **3** government or reign [the *rule* of Elizabeth I].

☆**run·way** (run′wā) *n.* a track or path on which something moves, as a paved strip on an airfield used by airplanes in taking off and landing.

Ss

safe (sāf) *adj.* **1** free from harm or danger; secure [a *safe* hiding place; *safe* in bed]. **2** not hurt or harmed [We emerged *safe* from the wreck.] **3** that can be trusted [a *safe* investment]. —**saf′er, saf′est** —**safe′ly** *adv.*

sal·ad (sal′əd) *n.* any mixture of vegetables, fruits, fish, eggs, etc., with a dressing of oil, vinegar, spices, etc.   It is usually served cold, often on lettuce leaves.

sand·wich (san′dwich *or* san′wich) *n.* slices of bread with a filling of meat, cheese, etc. between them. —*pl.* **sand′wich·es** ◆*v.* to squeeze in [a shed *sandwiched* between two houses].

San Fran·cis·co (san′ fran sis′kō) a city on the coast of central California.

sar·dine (sär dēn′) *n.* a small fish, as a young herring, preserved in oil and packed in cans.

sash (sash) *n.* a band, ribbon, or scarf worn over the shoulder or around the waist. —*pl.* **sash′es**

sat·el·lite (sat′l īt) *n.* **1** a heavenly body that revolves around another, larger one [The moon is a *satellite* of the earth.] **2** an artificial object put into orbit around the earth, the moon, or some other heavenly body.

sat·is·fy (sat′is fī) *v.* **1** to meet the needs or wishes of; content; please [Only first prize will *satisfy* him.] **2** to make feel sure; convince [The jury was *satisfied* that he was innocent.] —**sat′is·fied, sat′is·fy·ing**

sauce (sôs *or* säs) *n.* **1** a liquid or soft dressing served with food to make it tastier [spaghetti with tomato *sauce*].   ☆**2** fruit that has been stewed [apple*sauce*].

sauce·pan (sôs′pan *or* s'äs′pan) *n.* a small metal pot with a long handle, used for cooking.

sau·cer (sô′sər *or* sä′sər) *n.* a small, shallow dish, especially one for a cup to rest on.

save (sāv) *v.* **1** to rescue or keep from harm or danger [He was *saved* from drowning.] **2** to keep or store up for future use [She *saved* her money for a vacation.] **3** to keep from being lost or wasted [Traveling by plane *saved* many hours.] —**saved, sav′ing** —**sav′er** *n.*

scale¹ (skāl) *n.* **1** a series of marks along a line, with regular spaces in between, used for measuring [A Celsius thermometer has a basic *scale* of 100 degrees.] **2** the way that the size of a map, model, or drawing compares with the size of the thing that it stands for [One inch on a map of this *scale* equals 100 miles of real distance.] **3** a series of steps or degrees based on size, amount, rank, etc. [A passing grade on this *scale* is 70.]

scale² (skāl) *n.* **1** any of the thin, flat, hard plates that cover and protect certain fish and reptiles. **2** a thin piece or layer; flake [*scales* of rust in a water pipe]. ◆*v.* to scrape scales from [to *scale* a fish]. —**scaled, scal′ing**

scale³ (skāl) *n.* **1** either of the shallow pans of a balance. **2** *often* **scales,** *pl.* the balance itself; also, any device or machine for weighing. ◆*v.* to weigh. —**scaled, scal′ing**

scare (sker) *v.* to make or become afraid; frighten. —**scared, scar′ing** ◆*n.* a sudden fear; fright [The loud noise gave me quite a *scare.*]

scarf (skärf) *n.* **1** a long or broad piece of cloth worn about the head, neck, or shoulders for warmth or decoration. **2** a long, narrow piece of cloth used as a covering on top of a table, bureau, etc. —*pl.* **scarfs** or **scarves** (skärvz)

scent (sent) *n.* **1** a smell; odor [the *scent* of apple blossoms]. **2** the sense of smell [Lions hunt partly by *scent.*] **3** a smell left by an animal [The dogs lost the fox's *scent* at the river.]

school·house (skool′hous) *n.* a building used as a school.

scout (skout) *n.* a soldier, ship, or plane sent to spy out the strength or movements of the enemy.

scram·ble (skram′bəl) *v.* to climb or crawl in a quick, rough way [The children *scrambled* up the steep hill.] —**scram′bled, scram′bling**

scratch (skrach) *n.* **1** a mark or cut made in a surface by something sharp. **2** a slight wound. —*pl.* **scratch′es**

scrawl (skrôl) *v.* to write or draw in a hasty, careless way. ◆*n.* careless or poor handwriting that is hard to read.

screech (skrēch) *v.* to give a harsh, high shriek. ◆*n.* a harsh, high shriek.

screen (skrēn) *n.* **1** a mesh woven loosely of wires so as to leave small openings between them.   Screens are used in windows, doors, etc. to keep insects out. **2** a covered frame or curtain used to hide, separate, or protect. **3** anything that hides, separates, or protects [a smoke *screen;* a *screen* of trees].

scrub (skrub) *v.* to clean or wash by rubbing hard [to *scrub* floors]. —**scrubbed, scrub′bing** ◆*n.* the act of scrubbing.

scur·ry (skur′ē) *v.* to run quickly; scamper. —**scur′ried, scur′ry·ing** ◆*n.* the act or sound of scurrying.

sea·son (sē′zən) *n.* **1** any of the four parts into which the year is divided: spring, summer, fall, or winter. **2** a special time of the year [the Easter *season;* the hunting *season*]. **3** a period of time [the busy *season* at a factory]. ◆*v.* to add to or change the flavor of [to *season* meat with herbs].

Se·at·tle (sē at′l) a city in Washington.

satellite

a	ask, fat
ā	ape, date
ä	car, lot
e	elf, ten
ē	even, meet
i	is, hit
ī	ice, fire
ō	open, go
ô	law, horn
oi	oil, point
oo	look, pull
o͞o	ooze, tool
ou	out, crowd
u	up, cut
u	fur, fern
ə	a in ago
	e in agent
	e in father
	i in unity
	o in collect
	u in focus
ch	chin, arch
ŋ	ring, singer
sh	she, dash
th	thin, truth
th	then, father
zh	s in pleasure

seaweed

sea·weed (sē′wēd) *n.* any plant or plants growing in the sea, especially algae. There are some plants like these that grow in fresh water and are also called seaweed.

seek (sēk) *v.* **1** to try to find; search for [to *seek* gold]. **2** to try to get; aim at [to *seek* a prize]. —**sought, seek′ing**

seize (sēz) *v.* **1** to take hold of in a sudden, strong, or eager way; grasp [to *seize* a weapon and fight; to *seize* an opportunity] . **2** to capture or arrest, as a criminal. **3** to take over as by force [The troops *seized* the fort. The city *seized* the property for nonpayment of taxes.] —**seized, seiz′ing**

sense (sens) *n.* **1** any of the special powers of the body and mind that let one see, hear, feel, taste, smell, etc. **2** a feeling or sensation [a *sense* of warmth; a *sense* of guilt]. **3** an understanding or appreciation; special awareness [a *sense* of honor; a *sense* of beauty; a *sense* of rhythm; a *sense* of humor]. **4** judgment or intelligence; reasoning [He showed good *sense* in his decision. There's no *sense* in going there late.]

serve (surv) *v.* **1** to work for someone as a servant [I *served* in their household for ten years.] **2** to do services for; aid; help [She *served* her country well.] **3** to hold a certain office [She *served* as mayor for two terms.] **4** to offer or pass food, drink, etc. to [May I *serve* you some chicken?] —**served, serv′ing**

sev·en (sev′ən) *n., adj.* one more than six; the number 7.

shake (shāk) *v.* to move quickly up and down, back and forth, or from side to side [She *shook* her head in disapproval.] —**shook, shak′en, shak′ing**

share (sher) *n.* a part that each one of a group gets or has [your *share* of the cake; my *share* of the blame]. ◆*v.* **1** to divide and give out in shares [The owners *shared* the profits with their employees.] **2** to have a share of with others; have or use together [The three of you will *share* the back seat.] —**shared, shar′ing**

sharp (shärp) *adj.* **1** having a thin edge for cutting, or a fine point for piercing [a *sharp* knife; a *sharp* needle]. **2** not gradual; abrupt [a *sharp* turn]. **3** severe or harsh [a *sharp* reply]. ◆*adv.* in a sharp manner; keenly, alertly, briskly, etc. [Look *sharp* when crossing streets.] —**sharp′ly** *adv.* —**sharp′ness** *n.*

shawl (shôl) *n.* a large piece of cloth worn, especially by women, over the shoulders or head.

shawl

sheep (shēp) *n.* an animal that chews its cud and is related to the goat. Its body is covered with heavy wool and its flesh is used as food, called mutton. —*pl.* **sheep**

shelf (shelf) *n.* a thin, flat length of wood, metal, etc. fastened against a wall or built into a frame so as to hold things [the top *shelf* of a bookcase. —*pl.* **shelves**

she'll (shēl) **1** she will. **2** she shall.

shel·ter (shel′tər) *n.* a place or thing that covers or protects from the weather or danger [The *shelter* protected us from the rain.]

sher·bet (shur′bət) *n.* a frozen dessert of fruit juice, sugar, and water, milk, etc.

ship·ment (ship′mənt) *n.* **1** the shipping of goods by any means. **2** the goods shipped.

shoe (sho͞o) *n.* an outer covering for the foot, usually of leather. ◆*v.* to furnish with shoes; put shoes on [to *shoe* a horse].

shore (shôr) *n.* **1** land at the edge of a sea or lake. **2** land, not water [The retired sailor lives on *shore*.]

short·en (shôrt′n) *v.* to make or become short or shorter [to *shorten* a skirt].

should·n't (shood′nt) should not.

shov·el (shuv′əl) *n.* **1** a tool with a broad scoop and a handle, for lifting and moving loose material. **2** a machine with a part like a shovel, used for digging or moving large amounts of loose material [a steam *shovel*]. ◆*v.* to lift and move with a shovel [to *shovel* coal]. —**shov′eled** or **shov′elled, shov′el·ing** or **shov′el·ling**

show·er (shou′ər) *n.* **1** a short fall of rain or hail. **2** a sudden, very full fall or flow, as of sparks, praise, etc. ☆**3** a bath in which the body is sprayed with fine streams of water. *The full name is* **shower bath.**

shriek (shrēk) *n.* a loud, sharp, shrill cry; screech; scream. ◆*v.* to cry out with a shriek [to *shriek* in terror].

shrimp (shrimp) *n.* a small shellfish with a long tail, used as food.

shut·tle (shut′əl) *n.* **1** a device in weaving that carries a thread back and forth between the threads that go up and down. ☆**2** a bus, train, or airplane that makes frequent trips back and forth over a short route. ◆*v.* to move rapidly to and fro. —**shut′tled, shut′tling**

☆**side·walk** (sīd′wôk) *n.* a path for walking, usually paved, along the side of a street.

si·lent (sī′lənt) *adj.* **1** not speaking or not talking much. **2** with no sound or noise; noiseless [Find a *silent* place to study. We went to a *silent* movie.] **3** not spoken or told [*silent* grief; the *silent* "b" in "debt"]. —**si′lent·ly** *adv.*

sing·er (siŋ′ər) *n.* **1** a person that sings. **2** a bird that sings.

sink (siŋk) *v.* to go or put down below the surface [The boat is *sinking*.] —**sank** or **sunk, sink′ing**

sink·er (siŋk′ər) *n.* something that sinks, as a lead weight put on the end of a fishing line.

sis·ter (sis′tər) *n.* **1** a girl or woman as she is related to the other children of her parents. **2** a girl or woman who is close to one in some way; especially, a fellow member of the same race, religion, club, etc. **3** a nun.

sit (sit) *v.* **1** to rest the weight of the body upon the buttocks or haunches [She is *sitting* on a bench.   The dog *sat* still.] **2** to perch, rest, lie, etc. [A bird *sat* on the fence.   Cares *sit* lightly on him.] —**sat, sit′ting**

sit·ting (sit′iŋ) *n.* **1** the act or position of one that sits, as for a picture. **2** a meeting, as of a court or a council. **3** a period of being seated [I read the book in one *sitting*.]

skat·er (skāt′ər) *n.* one who moves along on skates [The *skater* twirled on the ice.]

skill (skil) *n.* **1** ability that comes from training, practice, etc. [He plays the violin with *skill*.] **2** an art, craft, or science, especially one that calls for use of the hands or body [Weaving is a *skill* often taught to the blind.]

skim (skim) *v.* **1** to take off floating matter from the top of a liquid [to *skim* cream from milk; to *skim* molten lead]. **2** to look through a book, magazine, etc. quickly without reading carefully. **3** to glide lightly, as over a surface [bugs *skimming* over the water]. —**skimmed, skim′ming**

☆**skunk** (skuŋk) *n.* **1** an animal having a bushy tail and black fur with white stripes down its back.   It sprays out a very bad-smelling liquid when frightened or attacked.

☆**sleigh** (slā) *n.* a carriage with runners instead of wheels, for travel over snow or ice. ◆*v.* to ride in or drive a sleigh.

slen·der (slen′dər) *adj.* small in width as compared with the length or height; long and thin [a *slender* woman].

slice (slīs) *n.* a thin, broad piece cut from something [a *slice* of cheese; a *slice* of bread] . ◆*v.* **1** to cut into slices [to *slice* a cake]. **2** to cut as with a knife [The plow *sliced* through the soft earth.] —**sliced, slic′ing** —**slic′er** *n.*

slip (slip) *v.* **1** to go or pass quietly or without being noticed; escape [We *slipped* out the door.   It *slipped* my mind.   Time *slipped* by.] **2** to pass slowly into a certain condition [to *slip* into bad habits]. **3** to move, shift, or drop, as by accident [The plate *slipped* from my hand.] **4** to slide by accident [He *slipped* on the ice.] —**slipped, slip′ping**

slip·per (slip′ər) *n.* a light, low shoe that is usually worn while a person is relaxing at home.

smooth (smōōth) *adj.* having an even or level surface, with no bumps or rough spots [*smooth* water on the lake].

snap (snap) *v.* to bite, grasp, or snatch suddenly [The frog *snapped* at the fly.] — **snapped, snap′ping**

sneeze (snēz) *v.* to blow out breath from the mouth and nose in a sudden way that cannot be controlled [My cold made me *sneeze*.] —**sneezed, sneez′ing**

soar (sôr) *v.* to rise or fly high into the air [The plane *soared* out of sight.]

sof·ten (sôf′ən *or* säf′ən) *v.* to make or become soft or softer. —**sof′ten·er** *n.*

soft·ware (sôft′wer′ *or* sft′wer) *v.* the special instructions, information, etc. that make a computer operate.

sol·id (säl′id) *adj.* **1** keeping its shape instead of flowing or spreading out like a liquid or gas; quite firm or hard [Ice is water in a *solid* form.] **2** filled with matter throughout; not hollow [a *solid* block of wood]. **3** that has length, width, and thickness [A prism is a *solid* figure.] **4** strong, firm, sound, dependable, etc. [*solid* thinking; a *solid* building]. —**sol′id·ly** *adv.*

sor·row (sär′ō) *n.* **1** a sad or troubled feeling; sadness; grief. **2** a loss, death, or trouble causing such a feeling [Our grandmother's illness is a great *sorrow* to us.] ◆*v.* to feel or show sorrow [We are *sorrowing* over his loss.]

sort (sôrt) *n.* **1** a group of things that are alike in some way; kind; class [various *sorts* of toys]. **2** quality or type [phrases of a noble *sort*]. ◆*v.* to separate or arrange according to class or kind [*Sort* out the clothes that need mending.]

sought (sôt *or* sät) *v.* past tense and past participle of **seek**.

sound (sound) *n.* **1** the form of energy that acts on the ears so that one can hear.   Sound consists of waves of vibrations carried in the air, water, etc. [In air, *sound* travels at a speed of about 332 meters per second, or 1,088 feet per second.] **2** anything that can be heard; noise, tone, etc. [the *sound* of bells]. **3** any of the noises made in speaking [a vowel *sound*]. ◆*v.* to make a sound [Your voice *sounds* hoarse.]

soup (soop) *n.* a liquid food made by cooking meat, vegetables, etc. as in water or milk.

South America the southern continent in the Western Hemisphere. —**South American**

south·east (south ēst′ *or* sou ēst′) *n.* **1** the direction halfway between south and east. **2** a place or region in or toward this direction. ◆*adj.* **1** in, of, or toward the southeast [the *southeast* part of the county]. **2** from the southeast [a *southeast* wind]. ◆*adv.* in or toward the southeast [to sail *southeast*].

south·ern (suth′ərn) *adj.* **1** in, of, or toward the south [the *southern* sky]. **2** from the south [a *southern* wind]. **3** **Southern,** of the South.

soy·bean (soi′bēn) *n.* **1** the seed, or bean, of a plant of Asia, now grown throughout the world.   The beans are ground into flour, pressed for oil, etc. **2** the plant itself.

sleigh

a	ask, fat
ā	ape, date
ä	car, lot
e	elf, ten
ē	even, meet
i	is, hit
ī	ice, fire
ō	open, go
ô	law, horn
oi	oil, point
oo	look, pull
ōō	ooze, tool
ou	out, crowd
u	up, cut
ʉ	fur, fern
ə	a in ago
	e in agent
	e in father
	i in unity
	o in collect
	u in focus
ch	chin, arch
ŋ	ring, singer
sh	she, dash
th	thin, truth
th	then, father
zh	s in pleasure

spacecraft

space (spās) *n.* **1** the area that stretches in all directions, has no limits, and contains all things in the universe [The earth, the sun, and all the stars exist in *space*.] **2** the distance or area between things or inside of something, especially as used for some purpose [a closet with much *space*; parking *space*]. **3** *a shorter name for* **outer space**. ◆*v.* to arrange with spaces in between [The trees are evenly *spaced*.] —**spaced, spac′ing**

space·craft (spās′kraft) *n.* any spaceship or satellite designed for use in outer space. —*pl.* **space′craft**

spare (sper) *v.* **1** to save or free from something [*Spare* us the trouble of listening to that story again.] **2** to get along without; give up [We can't *spare* the money or the time for a vacation trip.] —**spared, spar′ing** ◆*adj.* **1** kept for use when needed [a *spare* room; a *spare* tire]. **2** not taken up by regular work or duties; free [*spare* time]. —**spar′er, spar′est** ◆*n.* **1** an extra part or thing. ☆**2** in bowling, the act of knocking down all ten pins with two rolls of the ball. —**spare′ly** *adv.*

spark (spärk) *n.* **1** a small bit of burning matter, as one thrown off by a fire. **2** any flash of light like this [the *spark* of a firefly] . **3** the small flash of light that takes place when an electric current jumps across an open space, as in a spark plug.

spar·row (sper′ō) *n.* a small gray and brown songbird with a short beak. The common sparrow seen on city streets is the **English sparrow**.

spe·cies (spē′shēz *or* spē′sēz) *n.* a group of plants or animals that are alike in certain ways [The lion and tiger are two different *species* of cat.] —*pl.* **spe′cies**

speed (spēd) *n.* **1** fast motion; swiftness. **2** rate of motion; velocity [a *speed* of 10 miles per hour]. **3** swiftness of any action [reading *speed*]. ◆*v.* **1** to go or move fast or too fast [The arrow *sped* to its mark.] **2** to make go or move fast [He *sped* the letter on its way.] —**sped** or **speed′ed, speed′ing**

spend (spend) *v.* **1** to pay out or give up, as money, time, or effort [He *spent* $50 for food. Try to *spend* some time with me.] **2** to pass [She *spent* the summer at camp.] —**spent, spend′ing** —**spend′er** *n.*

spent (spent) *past tense and past participle of* **spend**. ◆*adj.* tired out; used up.

spice (spīs) *n.* any one of several vegetable substances used to give a special flavor or smell to food [Cinnamon, nutmeg, and pepper are kinds of *spices*.]

splash (splash) *v.* **1** to make a liquid scatter and fall in drops [to *splash* water or mud about.] **2** to dash a liquid on, so as to wet or soil [The car *splashed* my coat.] ◆*n.* the act or sound of splashing. —*pl.* **splash′es** —**splash′y** *adj.*

splen·did (splen′did) *adj.* very bright, brilliant, showy, or magnificent [a *splendid* gown].

splin·ter (splin′tər) *v.* to break or split into thin, sharp pieces [Soft pine *splinters* easily.] ◆*n.* a thin, sharp piece of wood, bone, etc. broken off.

spoil (spoil) *v.* **1** to make or become useless, worthless, rotten, etc.; damage; ruin [Ink stains *spoiled* the paper. Illness *spoiled* my attendance record. Meat *spoils* fast in warm weather.] **2** to cause a person to ask for or expect too much by giving in to all of that person's wishes [to *spoil* a child]. —**spoiled** or **spoilt, spoil′ing**

sponge (spunj) *n.* **1** a sea animal that is like a plant and grows fixed to surfaces under water. **2** the light, elastic skeleton of such an animal, that is full of holes and can soak up much water. Sponges are used for washing, bathing, etc. **3** any artificial substance like this, as of plastic or rubber, used in the same way. ◆*v.* to wipe, clean, make wet, or soak up as with a sponge [to *sponge* up gravy with a crust of bread]. —**sponged, spong′ing**

sport (spôrt) *n.* **1** active play, a game, etc. taken up for exercise or pleasure and, sometimes, as a profession [Football, golf, bowling, swimming, etc. are *sports*.] **2** fun or play [They thought it was great *sport* to fool others on the telephone.]

sprain (sprān) *v.* to twist a muscle or ligament in a joint without putting the bones out of place [to *sprain* one's wrist]. ◆*n.* an injury caused by this.

sprin·kle (spriŋ′kəl) *v.* **1** to scatter in drops or bits [to *sprinkle* salt on an egg]. **2** to scatter drops or bits on [to *sprinkle* a lawn with water]. **3** to rain lightly. —**sprin′kled, sprin′kling** ◆*n.* **1** the act of sprinkling. **2** a light rain. —**sprin′kler** *n.*

spy (spī) *n.* a person who watches others secretly and carefully. —*pl.* **spies**

squall (skwôl) *n.* a short, violent windstorm, usually with rain or snow. ◆*v.* to storm for a short time. —**squall′y** *adj.*

stage (stāj) *n.* **1** a raised platform or other area on which plays, speeches, etc. are given. **2** the profession of acting; the theater [He left the *stage* to write.] **3** *a shorter name for* **stagecoach**. **4** a period or step in growth or development [She has reached a new *stage* in her career.] ◆*v.* to present on a stage, as a play. —**staged, stag′ing**

stamp (stamp) *v.* **1** to bring one's foot down with force ["No!" she cried, *stamping* on the floor.] **2** to beat, press, or crush as with the foot [to *stamp* out a fire; to *stamp* out a revolt]. **3** to press or print marks, letters, a design, etc. on something [He *stamped* his initials on all his books.] ◆*n.* **1** a machine, tool, or die used for stamping. **2** a small piece of paper printed and sold by a government for sticking on letters, packages, etc. as proof that postage or taxes were paid.

stand (stand) **v. 1** to be or get in an upright position on one's feet [*Stand* by your desk.] **2** to be or place in an upright position on its base, bottom, etc. [Our trophy *stands* on the shelf. *Stand* the broom in the corner.] **3** to put up with; endure; bear [The boss can't *stand* noise.] —**stood, stand′ing** ◆*n.* **1** an opinion, belief, or attitude [What is the Senator's *stand* on higher taxes?] **2** *often* **stands,** *pl.* seats in rising rows, as in a stadium, from which to watch games, races, etc. **3** a booth or counter where goods are sold [a popcorn *stand*]. **4** a rack, framework, etc. for holding something [a music *stand*].

stare (ster) **v.** to look steadily with the eyes wide open [to *stare* in curiosity]. —**stared, star′ing**

starve (stärv) **v.** to die or suffer from lack of food [Many pioneers *starved* during the long winter.] —**starved, starv′ing**

sta·tion (stā′shən) **n. 1** the place where a person or thing stands or is located, as one's post when on duty, a building for a special purpose, etc. [a sentry's *station*; a police *station*]. **2** a regular stopping place, as for a bus or train; also, a building at such a place.

☆**steam·boat** (stēm′bōt) **n.** a steamship, especially a small one.

step (step) **v.** to move by taking a step or steps [We *stepped* into the car.] —**stepped, step′ping**

stern[1] (sturn) **adj.** strict or harsh; not gentle, tender, easy, etc. [*stern* parents; *stern* treatment]. —**stern′ly adv.** —**stern′ness n.**

stern[2] (sturn) **n.** the rear end of a ship or boat.

stick (stik) **n. 1** a twig or branch broken or cut off. **2** any long, thin piece of wood, with a special shape for use as a cane, club, etc. [a walking *stick*; a hockey *stick*]. **3** a long, thin piece [a *stick* of celery; a *stick* of chewing gum]. ◆*v.* **1** to press a sharp point into; pierce; stab [He *stuck* his finger with a needle.] **2** to fasten or be fastened as by pinning or gluing [I *stuck* my name tag on my coat. The stamp *sticks* to the paper.] —**stuck, stick′ing**

stiff (stif) **adj. 1** that does not bend easily; firm [*stiff* cardboard]. **2** not able to move easily [*stiff* muscles]. **3** not relaxed; tense or formal [a *stiff* smile]. —**stiff′ly adv.** —**stiff′ness n.**

stitch (stich) **n. 1** one complete movement of a needle and thread into and out of the material in sewing. **2** one complete movement done in various ways in knitting, crocheting, etc. **3** a loop made by stitching [Tight *stitches* pucker the cloth.] —**stitches**

sto·ry[1] (stôr′ē) **n. 1** a telling of some happening, whether true or made-up [the *story* of the first Thanksgiving]. **2** a made-up tale, written down, that is shorter than a novel [the *stories* of Poe]. —*pl.* **sto′ries**

sto·ry[2] (stôr′ē) **n.** the space or rooms making up one level of a building, from a floor to the ceiling above it [a building with ten *stories*]. —*pl.* **sto′ries**

stove (stōv) **n.** a device for cooking or heating by the use of gas, oil, electricity, etc.

straight (strāt) **adj. 1** having the same direction all the way; not crooked, curved, wavy, etc. [a *straight* line; *straight* hair]. **2** upright or erect [*straight* posture]. **3** level or even [a *straight* hemline]. **4** direct; staying right to the point, direction, etc. [a *straight* course; a *straight* answer].

strange (strānj) **adj. 1** not known, seen, or heard before; not familiar [I saw a *strange* person at the door.] **2** different from what is usual; peculiar; odd [wearing a *strange* costume]. **3** not familiar; without experience [She is *strange* to this job.] —**strang′er, strang′est** —**strange′ly adv.**

straw (strô *or* strä) **n. 1** hollow stalks, as of wheat or rye, after the grain has been threshed out. Straw is used as stuffing or is woven into hats, etc. **2** a tube, as of plastic, used for sucking a drink.

strength (streŋkth *or* strenth) **n.** the quality of being strong; force; power [the *strength* of a blow].

stretch (strech) **v. 1** to reach out or hold out, as a hand, object, etc. **2** to draw out to full length, to a greater size, to a certain distance, etc.; extend [She *stretched* out on the sofa. Will this material *stretch*? *Stretch* the rope between two trees. The road *stretches* for miles through the hills.] **3** to pull or draw tight; strain [to *stretch* a muscle].

strict (strikt) **adj. 1** keeping to rules in a careful, exact way [a *strict* supervisor]. **2** never changing; rigid [a *strict* rule]. —**strict′ly adv.** —**strict′ness n.**

stuff (stuf) **n. 1** what anything is made of; material; substance. **2** a collection of objects, belongings, etc. [I emptied the *stuff* from my bag.] ◆*v.* **1** to fill or pack [pockets *stuffed* with candy]. **2** to fill with seasoning, bread crumbs, etc. before roasting [to *stuff* a turkey]. **3** to force or push [I *stuffed* the money in my wallet.]

stum·ble (stum′bəl) **v.** to trip or almost fall while walking or running [to *stumble* over a curb]. —**stum′bled, stum′bling**

stur·dy (stur′dē) **adj.** strong and hardy [a *sturdy* oak]. —**stur′di·er, stur′di·est** —**stur′di·ly adv.** —**stur′di·ness n.**

sub·trac·tion (səb trak′shən) **n.** the act of subtracting one part, number, etc. from another.

☆**su·per·mar·ket** (sōō′pər mär′kət) **n.** a large food store in which shoppers serve themselves from open shelves and pay at the exit.

steamboat

a	ask, fat
ā	ape, date
ä	car, lot
e	elf, ten
ē	even, meet
i	is, hit
ī	ice, fire
ō	open, go
ô	law, horn
oi	oil, point
ᴐᴐ	look, pull
ōō	ooze, tool
ou	out, crowd
u	up, cut
u	fur, fern
ə	a in ago
	e in agent
	e in father
	i in unity
	o in collect
	u in focus
ch	chin, arch
ŋ	ring, singer
sh	she, dash
th	thin, truth
th	then, father
zh	s in pleasure

sword

telescope

sup·ply (sə plī′) **v. 1** to give what is needed; furnish [The camp *supplies* sheets and towels. The book *supplied* us with the facts.] **2** to take care of the needs of [to *supply* workers with tools]. —**sup·plied′, sup·ply′ing** ◆*n.* **1** the amount at hand; store; stock [I have a small *supply* of money but a large *supply* of books.] **2 supplies,** *pl.* things needed; materials; provisions [school *supplies*]. —*pl.* **sup·plies′**

sur·prise (sər prīz′) **v.** to cause to feel wonder by being unexpected [Her sudden anger *surprised* us.] —**sur·prised′, sur·pris′ing**

sur·pris·ing (sər prīz′iŋ) **adj.** causing surprise; strange. —**sur·pris′ing·ly adv.**

sur·vey (sər vā′) **v. 1** to look over in a careful way; examine; inspect [The lookout *surveyed* the horizon.] **2** to measure the size, shape, boundaries, etc. of a piece of land by the use of special instruments [to *survey* a farm]. ◆*n.* (sur′vā) a general study covering the main facts or points [The *survey* shows that we need more schools. This book is a *survey* of American poetry.] —*pl.* **sur′veys**

sur·viv·al (sər vī′vəl) **n.** the act or fact of surviving, or continuing to exist [Nuclear war threatens the *survival* of all nations.]

swal·low (swä′lō) **v. 1** to let food, drink, etc. go through the throat into the stomach. **2** to move the muscles of the throat as in swallowing something [I *swallowed* hard to keep from crying.] **3** to take in; engulf [The waters of the lake *swallowed* him up.]

swamp (swämp) **n.** a piece of wet, spongy land; marsh; bog: *also called* ☆**swamp′land.** —**swamp′y adj.**

sway (swā) **v. 1** to swing or bend back and forth or from side to side [The flowers *swayed* in the breeze.] **2** to lean or go to one side; veer [The car *swayed* to the right on the curve.] **3** to change the thinking or actions of; influence [We will not be *swayed* by their promises.]

sweat (swet) **v. 1** to give out a salty liquid through the pores of the skin; perspire [Running fast made me *sweat*.] —**sweat** or **sweat′ed, sweat′ing** ◆*n.* **1** the salty liquid given out through the pores of the skin.

sweat shirt (swet shʉrt) **n.** a heavy, loose cotton shirt with long or short sleeves.

swift (swift) **adj. 1** moving or able to move very fast [a *swift* runner]. **2** coming, happening, or done quickly [a *swift* reply]. **3** acting quickly; prompt [They were *swift* to help us.] —**swift′ly adv.** —**swift′ness n.**

sword (sôrd) **n.** a weapon having a long, sharp blade, with a handle, or hilt, at one end.

syl·la·ble (sil′ə bəl) **n. 1** a word or part of a word spoken with a single sounding of the voice ["Moon" is a word of one *syllable*. "Moonlight" is a word of two *syllables*.] **2** any of the parts into which a written word is divided to show where it may be broken at the end of a line [The *syllables* of the entry words in this dictionary are divided by tiny dots.]

syn·o·nym (sin′ə nim) **n.** a word having the same or almost the same meaning as another ["Big" and "large" are *synonyms*.]

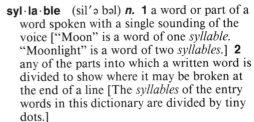

tail (tāl) **n. 1** the part at the rear of an animal's body that sticks out beyond the backbone. **2** any thing or part like this [the *tail* of a shirt; a pig*tail*]. **3** the hind or last part [the *tail* of a parade]. **tails,** *pl.* —**tail′less adj.**

tai·lor (tā′lər) **n.** a person who makes or repairs suits, coats, etc. ◆*v.* **1** to work as a tailor or make as a tailor does [suits *tailored* for stout people]. **2** to make or change so as to fit a certain need [That movie was *tailored* to please children.]

tale (tāl) **n.** a story, especially about things that are imagined or made up [The sitter read the child both folk *tales* and fairy *tales*.]

tar·dy (tär′dē) **adj.** not on time; late; delayed [to be *tardy* for class]. —**tar′di·er, tar′di·est** —**tar′di·ly adv.** —**tar′di·ness n.**

tast·y (tās′tē) **adj.** tasting good; full of flavor [a *tasty* meal] —**tast′i·er, tast′i·est**

tax (taks) **n.** money that citizens and businesses must pay to help support a government. —*pl.* **tax′es**

tax·pay·er (taks′pā ər) **n.** a person who pays a tax or taxes.

teach·er (tēch′ər) **n.** a person who teaches, especially in a school or college.

tea·spoon (tē′spoon) **n. 1** a spoon for stirring tea, coffee, etc. and eating some soft foods. **2** *a shorter form of* **teaspoonful.**

teeth (tēth) **n.** *plural of* **tooth.**

tel·e·scope (tel′ə skōp) **n.** a device for making far-off things seem closer and larger, used especially in astronomy. It consists of one or more tubes containing lenses and, often, mirrors.

tel·e·vi·sion (tel′ə vizhən) **n. 1** a way of sending pictures through space by changing the light rays into electric waves which are picked up by a receiver that changes them back to light rays shown on a screen. The sound that goes with the picture is sent by radio at the same time. **2** such a receiver, usually in a cabinet.

tem·per·ate (tem′pər ət *or* tem′prət) *adj.* **1** using or showing temperance in one's actions, appetites, etc.; moderate [Although she was angry, she made a *temperate* reply.] **2** neither very hot nor very cold [a *temperate* climate]. —**tem′per·ate·ly** *adv.*

ten·der (ten′dər) *adj.* **1** soft or delicate and easily chewed, cut, etc. [*tender* meat; *tender* blades of grass]. **2** that is hurt or feels pain easily; sensitive [My sprained ankle still feels *tender*.] —**ten′der·ly** *adv.* —**ten′der·ness** *n.*

tense[1] (tens) *adj.* **1** stretched tight; taut [a *tense* rope; *tense* muscles]. **2** feeling or showing nervous strain; anxious [a *tense* silence]. **3** causing a nervous feeling [a *tense* situation]. —**tens′er, tens′est** ◆*v.* to make or become tense; tighten, as muscles. —**tensed, tens′ing** —**tense′ly** *adv.*

tense[2] (tens) *n.* any of the forms of a verb that show the time of the action or condition [Present, past, and future *tenses* of "sail" are "sail" or "sails," "sailed," and "will sail."]

☆**te·pee** (tē′pē) *n.* a tent made of animal skins and shaped like a cone, used by some Native Americans.

ter·ri·to·ry (ter′ə tôr′ē) *n.* **1** the land ruled by a nation or state. **2 Territory,** a large division of a country or empire, that does not have the full rights of a province or state, as in Canada or Australia [the Northwest *Territories*]. **3** any large stretch of land; region. **4** the particular area chosen as its own by an animal or group of animals. —*pl.* **ter′ri·to·ries**

thank·ful (thaŋk′fəl) *adj.* feeling or showing thanks; grateful.

their (*th*er) *adj.* of them or done by them. *This possessive form of* **they** *is used before a noun and thought of as an adjective* [*their* house; *their* work].

there (*th*er) *adv.* **1** at or in that place [Who lives *there*?] **2** to, toward, or into that place [Go *there*.]

there·fore (*th*er′fôr) *adv.* for this or that reason; as a result of this or that; hence. *This word is often used as a conjunction* [We missed the bus; *therefore*, we were late.]

there's (*th*erz) there is.

these (*th*ēz) *pron., adj. plural of* **this.**

they'll (*th*āl) **1** they will. **2** they shall.

thief (thēf) *n.* a person who steals, especially secretly. —*pl.* **thieves** (thēvz)

think (thiŋk) *v.* to use the mind; reason [*Think* before you act.] —**thought, think′ing**

this (*th*is) *pron.* **1** the person or thing mentioned or understood [*This* is Juan. *This* tastes good.] **2** the thing that is present or nearer [*This* is prettier than that.] **3** the fact, idea, etc. about to be told [Now hear *this*!] —*pl.* **these** (*th*ēz) ◆*adj.* **1** being the one that is mentioned or understood [Copy down *this* rule.] **2** being the one that is present or nearer [*This* house is newer than that one.] ◆*adv.* to such a degree; so [It was *this* big.]

thought[1] (thôt *or* thät) *n.* **1** the act or process of thinking [When deep in *thought*, he doesn't hear.] **2** what one thinks; idea, opinion, plan, etc. [a penny for your *thoughts*].

thought[2] (thôt *or* thät) *past tense and past participle of* **think.**

thou·sand (thou′zənd) *n., adj.* ten times one hundred; the number 1,000.

thumb (thum) *n.* the short, thick finger nearest the wrist.

thun·der (thun′dər) *n.* **1** the loud noise that comes after a flash of lightning. It is caused when the discharge of electricity disturbs the air. **2** any loud, rumbling noise like this [We heard the *thunder* of stampeding cattle.]

Thurs·day (thurz′dē) *n.* the fifth day of the week.

tight (tīt) *adj.* **1** put together firmly or closely [a *tight* knot]. **2** fitting too closely [a *tight* shirt]. **3** stretched and strained; taut [a *tight* wire; *tight* nerves]. —**tight′ly** *adv.* —**tight′ness** *n.*

tim·id (tim′id) *adj.* feeling or showing fear or shyness.

tip·toe (tip′tō) *n.* the tip of a toe. ◆*v.* to walk on one's tiptoes in a quiet or careful way. —**tip′toed, tip′toe·ing**

to·ma·to (tə māt′ō *or* tə mät′ō) *n.* a red or yellow, round fruit with a juicy pulp. —*pl.* **to·ma′toes**

tooth (to͞oth) *n.* **1** any of the white, bony parts growing from the jaws and used for biting and chewing. **2** any part more or less like a tooth, as on a saw, comb, gearwheel, etc. —*pl.* **teeth** (tēth) —**tooth′less** *adj.*

tooth·ache (to͞oth′āk) *n.* pain in or near a tooth.

tooth·brush (to͞oth′brush) *n.* a small brush for cleaning the teeth. —*pl.* **tooth′brush·es**

tor·na·do (tôr nā′dō) *n.* a high, narrow column of air that is whirling very fast. It is often seen as a slender cloud shaped like a funnel, that usually destroys everything in its narrow path. —*pl.* **tor·na′does** *or* **tor·na′dos**

toss (tôs *or* täs) *v.* **1** to throw from the hand in a light, easy way [to *toss* a ball]. **2** to throw about; fling here and there [The waves *tossed* the boat.]

tough (tuf) *adj.* **1** able to bend or twist without tearing or breaking [*tough* rubber]. **2** not able to be cut or chewed easily [*tough* meat]. **3** very difficult or hard [a *tough* job].

town (toun) *n.* **1** a place where there are a large number of houses and other buildings, larger than a village but smaller than a city. **2** *another name for* **city. 3** the business center of a city or town.

tepee

a	ask, fat
ā	ape, date
ä	car, lot
e	elf, ten
ē	even, meet
i	is, hit
ī	ice, fire
ō	open, go
ô	law, horn
oi	oil, point
o͝o	look, pull
o͞o	ooze, tool
ou	out, crowd
u	up, cut
u	fur, fern
ə	a in ago
	e in agent
	e in father
	i in unity
	o in collect
	u in focus
ch	chin, arch
ŋ	ring, singer
sh	she, dash
th	thin, truth
th	then, father
zh	s in pleasure

185

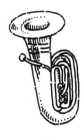

tuba

trace (trās) *n.* **1** a mark, track, sign, etc. left by someone or something [no human *trace* on the island]. **2** a very small amount [a *trace* of garlic in the dressing]. ◆*v.* **1** to follow the trail of; track [The hunter *traced* the lions to their den.] **2** to follow or study the course of [We *traced* the history of Rome back to Caesar.] **3** to copy a picture, drawing, etc. by following its lines on a thin piece of paper placed over it. —**traced, trac′ing**

trade (trād) *n.* **1** any work done with the hands that needs special skill got by training [the plumber's *trade*]. **2** all those in a certain business or kind of work [the book *trade*]. **3** the act of giving one thing for another; exchange [an even *trade* of my comic books for your football]. ◆*v.* **1** to carry on a business; buy and sell [This company *trades* in tea. Our country *trades* with other countries.] **2** to exchange [I *traded* my stamp collection for a camera.] —**trad′ed, trad′ing**

traf·fic (traf′ik) *n.* the movement or number of automobiles, persons, ships, etc. along a road or route of travel [to direct *traffic* on city streets; the heavy *traffic* on weekends]. —**traf′ficked, traf′fick·ing**

trail·er (trā′lər) *n.* a wagon, van, cart, etc. made to be pulled by an automobile, truck, or tractor. Some trailers are outfitted as homes.

treat (trēt) *v.* **1** to deal with or act toward in a certain way [We were *treated* with respect. Don't *treat* this matter lightly.] **2** to try to cure or heal, as with medicine [The doctor *treated* my cuts.] **3** to act upon, as by adding something [The water is *treated* with chlorine.]

tribe (trīb) *n.* a group of people or families living together under a leader or chief [a North American Indian *tribe*; the *tribes* of ancient Israel]. —**trib′al adj.**

trim (trim) *v.* **1** to make neat or tidy, especially by clipping, smoothing, etc. [She had her hair *trimmed*.] **2** to cut, clip, etc. [He *trimmed* dead branches off the tree.] —**trimmed, trim′ming** ◆*n.* good condition or order [An athlete must keep in *trim*.] —**trim′mer, trim′mest** —**trim′ly adv.** —**trim′ness n.**

trip (trip) *v.* to stumble or make stumble [She *tripped* over the rug. Bill put out his foot and *tripped* me.] —**tripped, trip′ping**

tro·phy (trō′fē) *n.* anything kept as a token of victory or success, as a deer's head from a hunting trip, a silver cup from a sports contest, or a sword from a battle. —*pl.* **tro′phies**

trop·i·cal (träp′i·kəl) *adj.* of, in, or like the tropics [heavy *tropical* rains; *tropical* heat].

trou·ble (trub′əl) *n.* **1** worry, care, annoyance, suffering, etc. [My mind is free of *trouble*.] **2** a difficult or unhappy situation; disturbance [We've had no *trouble* with our neighbors.] —**trou′bled, trou′bling**

trust (trust) *n.* a strong belief that some person or thing is honest or can be depended on; faith [You can put your *trust* in that bank.] ◆*v.* **1** to have or put trust in; rely; depend [I *trust* him to be on time. Don't *trust* that rickety ladder.] **2** to put something in the care of [Her mother *trusted* her with the car.] **3** to believe [I *trust* her story.]

try (trī) *v.* **1** to make an effort; attempt [We must *try* to help them.] **2** to seek to find out about, as by experimenting; test [Please *try* my recipe. *Try* the other window, which may not be locked.] **3** to put to a severe test or strain [Such exercise *tried* my strength.] —**tried, try′ing** ◆*n.* an effort; attempt; trial [He made a successful jump on his third *try*.] —*pl.* **tries**

tu·ba (too′bə *or* tyoo′bə) *n.* a large brass-wind instrument with a full, deep tone.

tun·dra (tun′drə *or* toon′drə) *n.* a large, flat plain without trees in the arctic regions.

turn (turn) *v.* **1** to move around a center point or axis; revolve; rotate [The wheels *turn*. *Turn* the key.] **2** to do by moving in a circle [*Turn* a somersault.] **3** to change in position or direction [*Turn* your chair around. *Turn* to the left. The tide has *turned*.]

twelve (twelv) *n., adj.* two more than ten; the number 12.

twist·er (twis′tər) *n.* **1** a person or thing that twists. ☆**2** a tornado or cyclone.

type·writ·er (tīp′rīt ər) *n.* a machine with a keyboard for making printed letters or figures on paper.

um·pire (um′pīr) *n.* **1** a person who rules on the plays of a game, as in baseball. **2** a person chosen to settle an argument. ◆*v.* to be an umpire in a game or dispute. —**um′pired, um′pir·ing**

un·cle (uŋ′kəl) *n.* **1** the brother of one's father or mother. **2** the husband of one's aunt.

un·clear (un klir′) *adj.* not clear; hard to see or understand.

un·fold (un fōld′) *v.* **1** to open and spread out something that has been folded [to *unfold* a map]. **2** to make or become known [to *unfold* one's plans].

u·ni·verse (yōōn′ə vʉrs) *n.* all space and everything in it; earth, the sun, stars, and all things that exist.

u·ni·ver·si·ty (yōōn′ə vʉr′sə tē) *n.* a school of higher education, made up of a college or colleges. —*pl.* **u′ni—′ver′si·ties**

un·known (un nōn′) *adj.* **1** not known, seen, or heard before [a song *unknown* to me]. **2** not discovered, identified, etc. [an *unknown* writer]. ◆*n.* an unknown person or thing.

un·pleas·ant (un plez′ənt) *adj.* not pleasant or agreeable; offensive; disagreeable [an *unpleasant* taste]. —**un·pleas′ant·ly** *adv.* —**un·pleas′ant·ness** *n.*

un·pre·pared (un′prē perd′) *adj.* not prepared or ready [We are still *unprepared* for the visitors.]

un·re·al (un rēl′) *adj.* not real; imaginary or made up. —**un·re·al·i·ty** (un′rē al′ə tē) *n.*

un·re·lat·ed (un rē lāt′əd) *adj.* not of the same family or kind.

un·til (un til′) *prep.* **1** up to the time of; till [Wait *until* noon.] **2** before [Don't leave *until* tomorrow.] ◆*conj.* **1** up to the time when [He was lonely *until* he met her.] **2** to the point, degree, or place that [She ate *until* she was full.] **3** before [Don't stop *until* he does.]

un·wise (un wīz′) *adj.* not wise; not showing good sense; foolish. —**un·wise′ly** *adv.*

ur·gent (ʉr′jənt) *adj.* **1** needing quick action [an *urgent* situation]. **2** demanding in a strong and serious way; insistent [an *urgent* call for help]. —**ur′gent·ly** *adv.*

Vv

vague (vāg) *adj.* not clear, definite, or distinct, as in form, meaning, or purpose [*vague* figures in the fog; a *vague* answer]. —**va′guer, va′guest** —**vague′ly** *adv.* —**vague′ness** *n.*

val·ley (val′ē) *n.* **1** low land lying between hills or mountains. **2** the land that is drained or watered by a large river and its branches [the Mississippi *valley*]. —*pl.* **val′leys**

veil (vāl) *n.* a piece of thin cloth, such as net or gauze, worn especially by women over the face or head [a bride's *veil*].

ves·sel (ves′əl) *n.* a ship or large boat.

Vi·et·nam (vē′ət näm′) a country in southeastern Asia. —**Vi·et·nam·ese** (vē′et nə mēz′ *or* vē′et nə mēs′) *adj., n.*

vi·ta·min (vīt′ə min) *n.* any of certain substances needed by the body to keep healthy. Vitamin A is found in fish-liver oil, yellow vegetables, egg yolk, etc. One kind of vitamin B, called vitamin B₁, is found in cereals, green peas, beans, liver, etc. Vitamin C is found in citrus fruits, tomatoes, etc. Vitamin D is found in fish-liver oil, milk, eggs, etc. Lack of these vitamins or others can cause certain diseases.

voice (vois) *n.* **1** sound made through the mouth, especially by human beings in talking, singing, etc. **2** anything thought of as like speech or the human voice [the *voice* of the sea; the *voice* of one's conscience]. **3** the right to say what one wants, thinks, or feels [Each voter has a *voice* in the government.] ◆*v.* to put into words, as an idea, feeling, etc.; utter. —**voiced, voic′ing** —**voice′less** *adj.*

vote (vōt) *n.* one's decision on some plan or idea, or one's choice between persons running for office, shown on a ballot, by raising one's hand, etc. ◆*v.* **1** to give or cast a vote [For whom did you *vote*?] **2** to decide, elect, or bring about by vote [Congress *voted* new taxes.] —**vot′ed, vot′ing**

walrus

Ww

waist (wāst) *n.* **1** the part of the body between the ribs and the hips. **2** the part of a garment that covers the body from the shoulders to the waistline.

wait·er (wāt′ər) *n.* **1** a man who waits on table, as in a restaurant. **2** one who waits.

wait·ress (wā′trəs) *n.* a woman who waits on table, as in a restaurant.

walk·er (wôk′ər) *n.* **1** a person or animal that walks. ☆**2** a frame with or without wheels for use by babies in learning to walk or by people who have trouble walking because of injuries or disease.

wal·rus (wôl′rəs) *n.* a large sea animal like the seal, found in northern oceans. It has two tusks and a thick layer of blubber.

Wash·ing·ton (wôsh′iŋ tən *or* wäsh′iŋ tən) the capital of the U.S., in the District of Columbia.

watch (wäch *or* wôch) *v.* **1** to keep one's sight on; look at [We *watched* the parade.] **2** to pay attention to; observe [I've *watched* her career with interest.] **3** to take care of; look after; guard [The shepherd *watched* his flock.]

a	ask, fat
ā	ape, date
ä	car, lot
e	elf, ten
ē	even, meet
i	is, hit
ī	ice, fire
ō	open, go
ô	law, horn
oi	oil, point
oo	look, pull
ōō	ooze, tool
ou	out, crowd
u	up, cut
ʉ	fur, fern
ə	a in ago
	e in agent
	e in father
	i in unity
	o in collect
	u in focus
ch	chin, arch
ŋ	ring, singer
sh	she, dash
th	thin, truth
th	then, father
zh	s in pleasure

wheat

wa·ter·fall (wôt'ər fôl *or* wät'ər fôl) **n.** a steep fall of water, as from a high cliff.

wax (waks) **n. 1** a yellow substance that bees make and use for building honeycombs; beeswax. **2** any substance like this, as paraffin. Wax is used to make candles, polishes, etc. ◆**v.** to put wax or polish on.

wea·ry (wir'ē) **adj. 1** tired; worn out [*weary* after a day's work]. **2** having little or no patience or interest left; bored [I grew *weary* of listening to them.] —**wea'ri·er, wea'ri·est** —**wea'ried, wea'ry·ing** —**wea'ri·ly** **adv.** —**wea'ri·ness n.**

Wednes·day (wenz'dē) **n.** the fourth day of the week.

weigh (wā) **v. 1** to use a scales, balance, etc. to find out how heavy a thing is [to *weigh* oneself]. **2** to have a certain weight [The suitcase *weights* six pounds.]

we're (wir) we are.

west·ward (west'wərd) **adv., adj.** in the direction of the west.

wheat (hwēt *or* wēt) **n. 1** the cereal grass whose grain is used in making the most common type of flour. **2** this grain.

where (hwer *or* wer) **adv. 1** in or at what place? [*Where* is the car?] **2** in what way? how? [*Where* is she at fault?]

where's (hwerz *or* werz) **1** where is. **2** where has.

wheth·er (hweth'ər *or* weth'ər) **conj. 1** if it is true or likely that [I don't know *whether* I can go.] **2** in either case that [It makes no difference *whether* he comes or not.]

which (hwich *or* wich) **pron. 1** what one or what ones of those being talked about or suggested [*which* will you choose?] **2** the one or the ones that [I know *which* I like best.] **3** that [the story *which* we all know]. ◆**adj.** what one or ones [*Which* apples are the best for baking?]

whisk·er (hwis'kər *or* wis'kər) **n. 1** **whiskers,** *pl.* the hair growing on a man's face, especially the beard on the cheeks. **2** a single hair of a man's beard **3** any of the long, stiff hairs on the upper lip of a cat, rat, etc. —**whisk'ered adj.**

whis·tle (hwis'əl *or* wis'əl) **n.** a device for making high, shrill sounds.

who's (hōōz) **1** who is. **2** who has.

whose (hōōz) **pron.** the one or the ones belonging to whom [*Whose* are these books?]

wife (wīf) **n.** the woman to whom a man is married. —*pl.* **wives**

wild (wīld) **adj. 1** living or growing in nature; not tamed or cultivated by human beings [*wild* animals; *wild*flowers]. **2** not civilized; savage [*wild* tribes]. **3** not controlled; unruly, rough, noisy, etc. [*wild* children]. —**wild'ly adv.** —**wild'ness n.**

win·ner (win'ər) **n. 1** one that wins. **2** a person who seems very likely to win or be successful: *used only in everyday talk.*

wish (wish) **v. 1** to have a longing for; want; desire [You may have whatever you *wish*.] **2** to have or express a desire about [I *wish* you were here. We *wished* her good luck.] ◆**n.** something wanted or hoped for [He got his *wish*.] —*pl.* **wish'·es**

witch (wich) **n. 1** a person, now especially a woman, who is imagined to have magic power with the help of the devil. **2** an ugly and mean old woman.

with·out (with out' *or* with out') **prep.** free from; not having [a person *without* a worry; a cup *without* a saucer].

wit·ness (wit'nəs) **n.** a person who saw or heard something that happened [A *witness* saw the fire start.] —*pl.* **wit'nes·ses**

wives (wīvz) **n.** *plural of* **wife.**

wom·an (woom'ən) **n.** an adult, female human being. —*pl.* **wom'en**

wom·en (wim'ən) **n.** *plural of* **woman.**

wor·ry (wur'ē) **v. 1** to be or make troubled in mind; feel or make uneasy or anxious [Don't *worry*. Her absence *worried* us.] **2** to annoy, bother, etc. [Stop *worrying* me with such unimportant matters.] —**wor'ried, wor'ry·ing** ◆**n. 1** a troubled feeling; anxiety; care [sick with *worry*]. **2** a cause of this [He has many *worries*.] —*pl.* **wor'ries**

would·n't (wood'nt) would not.

wrap (rap) **v. 1** to wind or fold around something [She *wrapped* a scarf around her head.] **2** to cover in this way [They *wrapped* the baby in a blanket.] **3** to cover with paper, etc. [to *wrap* a present]. —**wrapped** *or* **wrapt** (rapt), **wrap'ping**

wreck (rek) **n. 1** the loss of a ship, or of a building, car, etc. through storm, accident, etc. **2** the remains of something that has been destroyed or badly damaged [an old *wreck* stranded on the reef]. ◆**v. 1** to destroy or damage badly; ruin [to *wreck* a car in an accident; to *wreck* one's plans for a picnic]. **2** to tear down; raze [to *wreck* an old house].

wrench (rench) **n. 1** a sudden, sharp twist or pull [With one *wrench*, he loosened the lid.] **2** an injury, as to the back or an arm, caused by a twist. **3** a sudden feeling of sadness, as at parting with someone. **4** a tool for holding and turning nuts, bolts, pipes, etc.

wrin·kle (riŋ'kəl) **n.** a small or uneven crease or fold [*wrinkles* in a blouse].

wrist (rist) **n.** the joint or part of the arm between the hand and forearm.

writ·ing (rīt'iŋ) **n. 1** the act of one who writes. **2** something written, as a letter, article, poem, book, etc. [the *writings* of Thomas Jefferson]. **3** written form [to put a request in *writing*]. **4** handwriting [Can you read her *writing*?]

yacht (yät) *n.* a large boat or small ship for racing, taking pleasure cruises, etc. ◆*v.* to sail in a yacht. —**yacht'ing** *n.*

yak (yak) *n.* an ox with long hair, found wild or raised in Tibet and central Asia.

yawn (yôn *or* yän) *v.* to open the mouth wide and breathe in deeply in a way that is not controlled, as when one is sleepy or tired.

your·self (yoor self') *pron.* **1** your own self. *This form of* **you is used when the object is** *the same as the subject of the verb* [Did you cut *yourself*?] **2** your usual or true self [You are not *yourself* today.] *Yourself* is also used to give force to the subject [You *yourself* told me so.] —*pl.* **your·selves** (yoor selvz')

a	ask, fat
ā	ape, date
ä	car, lot
e	elf, ten
ē	even, meet
i	is, hit
ī	ice, fire
ō	open, go
ô	law, horn
oi	oil, point
oo	look, pull
ōō	ooze, tool
ou	out, crowd
u	up, cut
ʉ	fur, fern
ə	a in ago
	e in agent
	e in father
	i in unity
	o in collect
	u in focus
ch	chin, arch
ŋ	ring, singer
sh	she, dash
th	thin, truth
th	then, father
zh	s in pleasure

Level D Student Record Chart

Name _____

			Pretest	Final Test
Lesson	1	Consonant Sounds		
Lesson	2	Short-Vowel Sounds		
Lesson	3	Long-Vowel Sounds		
Lesson	4	Hard and Soft **c** and **g**		
Lesson	5	Beginning Consonant Blends		
Lesson	6	Instant Replay	■	
Lesson	7	Consonant Blends		
Lesson	8	Vowels with **r**		
Lesson	9	Consonant Digraphs		
Lesson	10	Silent Letters		
Lesson	11	/f/ Sound		
Lesson	12	Instant Replay	■	
Lesson	13	Suffixes **ed, er,** and **ing**		
Lesson	14	Suffixes **ed, er,** and **ing**: Doubling Final Consonants		
Lesson	15	Suffixes **ed, er,** and **ing**: Dropping the Final **e**		
Lesson	16	Suffixes **ed, es,** and **ing**: Words Ending with **y**		
Lesson	17	Suffixes **er** and **est**: Words Ending with **y**		
Lesson	18	Instant Replay	■	
Lesson	19	Vowel Digraphs **ee, ea, oa, oe,** and **ue**		
Lesson	20	Vowel Digraphs **ie** and **ei**		
Lesson	21	Vowel Digraphs **au** and **aw**		
Lesson	22	Vowel Digraphs **ai, ay**; Diphthongs **oi, oy**		
Lesson	23	**ou** and **ow**		
Lesson	24	Instant Replay	■	
Lesson	25	Plurals		
Lesson	26	Plurals of Words That End in **y**		
Lesson	27	Irregular Plurals: Plurals of Words That End in **f** or **fe**		
Lesson	28	Possessives and Contractions		
Lesson	29	Plurals and Plural Possessives		
Lesson	30	Instant Replay	■	
Lesson	31	Prefixes **pre, re, im, non,** and **con**		
Lesson	32	Prefixes **ex, de, dis, un,** and **ad**		
Lesson	33	Compound Words		
Lesson	34	Synonyms and Antonyms		
Lesson	35	Homonyms		
Lesson	36	Instant Replay	■	

Lesson	6	12	18	24	30	36
Standardized Instant Replay Test						

Instant Replay Test

ANSWER KEY

Lesson 6

1.	d	11.	c
2.	c	12.	b
3.	a	13.	c
4.	d	14.	a
5.	b	15.	d
6.	b	16.	b
7.	c	17.	d
8.	a	18.	a
9.	d	19.	b
10.	a	20.	c

Lesson 12

1.	b	11.	c
2.	c	12.	a
3.	b	13.	d
4.	d	14.	a
5.	b	15.	d
6.	c	16.	c
7.	c	17.	b
8.	d	18.	d
9.	b	19.	d
10.	a	20.	a

Lesson 18

1.	a	11.	c
2.	c	12.	c
3.	b	13.	b
4.	b	14.	a
5.	d	15.	d
6.	c		
7.	a		
8.	d		
9.	c		
10.	b		

Lesson 24

1.	d	11.	d
2.	c	12.	a
3.	a	13.	c
4.	c	14.	c
5.	d	15.	d
6.	b	16.	b
7.	c	17.	a
8.	a	18.	a
9.	d	19.	c
10.	a	20.	b

Lesson 30

1.	c	11.	d
2.	b	12.	d
3.	c	13.	c
4.	a	14.	b
5.	a	15.	a
6.	d	16.	d
7.	b	17.	b
8.	b	18.	c
9.	d	19.	a
10.	b	20.	b

Lesson 36

1.	d	11.	d
2.	d	12.	a
3.	a	13.	b
4.	b	14.	d
5.	c	15.	b
6.	c	16.	b
7.	b	17.	d
8.	c	18.	d
9.	a	19.	a
10.	d	20.	b

List Words

Word	Lesson
absent	7
admit	32
adopt	2
advance	32
adventure	32
adverb	32
advice	32
after	11
aircraft	33
airlines'	29
allows	23
alphabet	11
although	23
amount	23
amplifies	20
ancient	34
angrier	17
angriest	17
answer	10
applied	16
appointed	22
approach	19
Arizona's	28
armies'	29
arrive	3
artist	8
ashes	25
audience	21
aunt's	28
autograph	11
awhile	9
awkward	21
axes	25
baggage	4
banjos'	29
banner	1
barrel	1
batteries	26
beginning	14
believe	20
benches'	29
bending	13
between	19
bicycle's	28
birthdays	26
bison	27
blended	7
boards	8
boasted	19
bobbing	14
bodies'	29

Word	Lesson
boiling	22
bosses	25
bother	9
bottles	1
bouncing	15
bouquet	23
brains	5
brake	35
break	35
breakfast	33
breeze	19
brief	20
broiling	22
brother	9
brought	23
buffaloes	27
bumps	2
buries	16
businesses'	29
buying	16
cactus	4
calves	27
carried	16
carton	8
catcher	13
category	4
causing	21
cautious	34
celery	4
cement	4
center	4
chains	25
charge	9
chatting	14
checking	13
cheerfully	8
cherries	26
chicken	9
chiefly	20
chiefs	27
children's	29
child's	28
chimney	9
chowder	23
churches	25
circle	4
clapping	14
clashes	25
clasp	2
claws	21
cleaned	13

Word	Lesson
clover	3
clues	19
colder	7
comb	10
coming	15
common	4
communities	26
comparing	15
conduct	31
construct	31
contest	2
control	31
convince	31
copied	16
copies	26
corner	4
costume	3
cough	11
counties	26
courage	34
cousin's	28
crack	2
craft	5
crashes	25
crayon	22
crept	7
cries	16
crime	3
crumb	10
crunch	7
crush	9
cubes	3
curb	8
current	34
daisies'	29
dancer	15
dawn	21
deceive	20
decide	4
defend	32
denies	16
dentist	2
deny	3
descend	34
desert's	28
design	32
destroyed	22
died	20
diet	20
different	7
difficult	34

Word	Lesson
dirty	8
disagree	32
disappoint	22
disbelief	34
disclose	32
dishonest	32
disinterested	32
disloyal	22
displays	22
ditches	25
doctor's	28
dollar	1
dolphin	11
downtown	33
dragging	14
drawings	21
dream	5
dresses'	29
dropped	14
drowsy	34
drying	16
dusk	7
duties	26
eagle	19
earlier	17
earliest	17
easier	17
easiest	17
eastern	19
edge	4
eighteen	20
elephants	11
eleven	1
employ	22
emptied	16
energy	4
enormous	34
enough	11
equal	3
error	8
everybody	33
excuse	32
expensive	34
explore	32
express	32
eyelashes	25
fair	8
fame	1
families'	29
fancier	17
fanciest	17

List Words

Word	Lesson	Word	Lesson	Word	Lesson	Word	Lesson
farther	9	halt	7	known	10	orphan	11
fault	21	halves	27	knuckle	10	outdoors	33
fawns	21	hammer	1	ladies	26	outfitted	14
fearless	8	handkerchiefs	27	landing	13	outstanding	33
feathers	9	hands	2	later	1	overcoat	33
fender	2	happier	17	laughs	11	oxen	27
fields	20	happiest	17	launch	21	paces	25
film	1	harbor	8	leading	13	padded	14
finishing	13	hare	35	learner	13	parties	26
flashes	25	hasn't	28	leash	9	passengers'	29
fleet	19	haunt	21	leaves	27	peace	35
flies	26	heal	35	lengthy	34	pencil	2
flight	10	heart	8	let's	28	perceive	20
Florida's	28	heavier	17	letters	1	perfume	8
folks	10	heaviest	17	libraries	26	person's	28
following	13	heel	35	lifted	2	petrified	16
foolish	9	highways	26	listen	10	phase	11
force	4	hobbies	26	lives	27	phony	11
foxes	25	hoed	19	loaned	19	photo	11
fraud	21	holidays	26	loaves	27	pianos'	29
fray	22	hollow	23	locate	3	pictured	15
freedom	19	homework	33	locked	2	piece	35
freighter	20	honest	10	lonelier	17	pies	20
front	5	hoofs	27	loneliest	17	pineapple	1
frying	16	horseshoes	33	loved	15	plain	35
funnier	17	hostesses'	29	matches	25	plane	35
funniest	17	hours	23	meadow	19	powerful	23
gallon	1	how's	28	meaning	19	practice	2
garbage	8	humming	14	measure	19	praised	22
gather	9	hundred	1	melodies	26	precaution	31
gaunt	21	hurrying	16	members'	29	predict	31
geese	27	idea	3	men's	29	prepaid	31
gentle	4	immovable	31	mice	27	prettier	17
geography	11	imperfect	31	milk	7	prettiest	17
gerbil	4	impersonal	31	missed	13	preview	31
ghost	10	impractical	31	moose	27	prices	4
gifts	4	impure	31	mountain	23	pride	3
giraffe	11	independent	7	mover	15	printing	7
giving	15	injuries	26	multiplied	16	product	7
gloves	5	instead	19	musical	3	promised	15
glued	19	island	10	neighbors	20	proper	5
gnaw	21	jaw	21	nephew	11	protect	5
governments'	29	joggers	14	noises	22	protesting	7
grabbing	14	journal	8	nonprofit	31	proved	15
graceful	4	journey	34	nonsense	31	quitter	14
graphs	11	judge	2	nonstop	31	railroad	22
greedy	5	juicier	17	northwest	33	raking	15
groceries	26	juiciest	17	numb	10	ranches'	29
guessed	13	kisses	25	often	10	rapidly	34
hair	35	knapsack	33	opened	3	reaches	9
halfway	10	knives	27	organ	8	reaction	31

List Words

Word	Lesson	Word	Lesson	Word	Lesson	Word	Lesson
reason	19	sherbet	8	strange	4	tuba	3
receipt	20	shipment	9	straw	21	turning	13
receive	20	shoes	25	stretch	7	twelve	1
reduced	15	shore	8	strict	5	twister	7
refills	31	shovel	9	stuff	5	typewriter	33
refund	7	shower	23	sturdy	34	umpires'	29
relief	20	shriek	20	supermarket	33	uncle's	28
relying	16	shrimp	2	supplied	16	unclear	32
remembered	13	sidewalk	33	surprising	15	unfold	7
repaired	34	silent	1	surveys	26	unknown	32
replies	16	singer	13	swallowed	23	unpleasant	32
report	31	sister's	28	swaying	22	unprepared	32
restaurant	21	sitting	14	swift	1	unreal	32
returned	31	skill	5	tail	35	until	1
rider	15	skimming	14	tale	35	unwise	32
risk	7	skunk	7	teacher	13	vague	34
roasted	19	sleigh	20	teaspoon	33	valleys	26
rodent	3	sliced	15	teeth	27	voices	22
roughly	11	slipping	14	televisions'	29	waist	22
royalty	22	soften	10	tender	34	walker	13
rules	3	solid	2	tense	34	watching	13
safely	3	sorrow	34	their	35	waterfall	33
sandwiches	25	sorted	13	there	35	waxes	25
sashes	25	sought	23	therefore	33	weary	34
satisfied	16	sounds	7	these	3	Wednesday	10
sauce	21	southeast	33	they'll	28	weigh	20
saved	15	southern	23	thieves'	29	we're	28
scale	3	soybean	22	thought	23	wheat	9
scared	5	spaces	5	thousand	23	where's	28
scarves	27	spare	8	thumb	10	which	35
scents	35	sparks	8	thunder	9	whiskers	9
schoolhouse	33	sparrows	23	Thursday	9	who's	35
scrawl	21	speed	5	tight	3	whose	35
screech	5	spent	2	tiptoes	19	wild	1
screens	5	splashes	25	toothache	33	winners	14
scrubbing	14	splinter	5	toothbrushes	25	wishing	13
scurrying	16	spoiled	22	tossed	13	witch	35
season's	28	sports	8	towns	23	without	23
seize	20	sprain	22	trace	5	women	27
sense	35	sprinkle	5	traded	15	worries	16
served	15	stage	4	traffic	1	wouldn't	28
seven	1	stamp	2	treating	19	wrapped	14
sharing	15	stand	2	tries	16	wrecks	10
sharply	9	sticks	2	trimmer	14	wrench	10
shawl	21	stiff	11	tripped	14	wrist	10
sheep	27	stories	26	trophy	11	writing	15
shelf	11	stove	3	trouble	23	yawn	21
she'll	28	straight	5	trust	2	yourselves	27

All-Star Words

Word	Lesson	Word	Lesson	Word	Lesson	Word	Lesson
achieve	20	driving	15	loyal	22	sinking	13
advantage	32	drowned	23	luckiest	17	skater	15
affection	11	dues	19	magnifying	16	slender	7
allies	20	earmuffs	11	marshmallow	23	slipper	1
arithmetic	9	easygoing	33	mascot	2	smooth	34
author	21	embroider	22	mending	13	snapping	14
automatic	21	enemy	1	mugger	14	sneeze	19
bask	7	entertain	22	mysteries	16	soared	13
beliefs	27	essays	26	need	35	species'	29
bomb	10	exchange	32	nervous	8	spice	3
branch	7	extend	2	nonfiction	31	spies'	29
breakdown	33	factory's	28	nurse	8	splendid	1
brilliant	34	familiar	34	pardons	25	stared	15
broccoli	27	fish's	29	patios	27	starve	8
ceiling	20	flew	35	patrolling	14	stepped	14
champion	9	flu	35	perfect	11	strength	5
cheat	19	flue	35	performer	13	stumble	7
classes'	29	fond	2	phrase	11	sweatshirt	33
clumsier	17	forehead	19	pitying	16	tastier	17
college	4	forth	8	preset	31	taxes	25
cone	3	fought	23	prince	4	taxpayer	33
contact	31	gasp	4	principal's	28	thankful	9
convoys	26	glow	5	program	5	there's	28
couple	23	gobble	4	public	2	timid	2
crazy	5	grizzlies	26	purses	25	tomato	3
curlier	17	groan	19	raisin	22	tough	11
dairies	16	gulped	13	recount	31	universities	26
damage	4	harvest	7	regular	34	unrelated	32
daughter	10	hearth	8	remove	3	veil	20
deer	27	horrified	16	rising	15	vessel	1
define	32	hygiene	20	rude	3	westward	33
delay	22	impatient	31	saucer	21	whether	9
deliveries	26	instant	1	scouts	23	whistle	10
diaries'	29	intelligent	34	scramble	5	witnesses	25
dimmed	14	knead	35	scratches	25	wives	27
disgrace	32	knowledge	10	shaking	15	wrinkle	10
doesn't	28	lawyer	21	shelter	9		
drawn	21	loveliest	17	shouldn't	28		

Spelling Enrichment

Bulletin-Board Suggestion

Eggs-pert Spellers Display a picture of a large hen sitting near a nest. Make large eggs out of white construction paper. Encourage students to write words on the eggs that are similar in structure to the words in the week's spelling list. Post the eggs on the nest.

You may also want to display a chart showing the number of eggs each student has posted to the bulletin board during the year. It might then be fun to keep a basket in the classroom that contains plastic eggs with little surprises in them. The surprise might be a note telling them they can skip an assignment or have extra minutes of free time, or it could be a small trinket. Students could then pick an egg from the basket after they have posted a predetermined number of eggs on the bulletin board.

Group Practice

Fill-In Write spelling words on the board. Omit some of the letters and replace them with dashes. Have the first student in Row One come to the board to fill in any of the missing letters in any of the words. Then have the first student in Row Two continue the procedure. Continue having students in each row take turns coming up to the board to fill in letters until all the words are completed. Any student who is able to correctly fill in a word earns a point for his or her row. The row with the most points at the end of the game wins.

Erase Write List Words on the board. Then ask the class to put their heads down while you call on a student to come to the board and erase one of the words. This student then calls on a class member to identify the erased word. The identified word is then restored and the student who correctly identified the erasure can be the person who erases next.

Crossword Relay First draw a large grid on the board. Then, divide the class into several teams. Teams compete against each other to form separate crossword puzzles on the board. Individuals on each team take turns racing against members of the other teams to join List Words until all possibilities have been exhausted. A List Word may appear on each crossword puzzle only once. The winning team is the team whose crossword puzzle contains the greatest number of correctly spelled List Words or the team who finishes first.

Scramble Prepare letter cards sufficient to spell all the List Words. Distribute letter cards to all students. Some students may be given more than one letter card. The teacher then calls out a List Word. Students holding the letters contained in the word race to the front of the class to form the word by standing in the appropriate sequence with their letter cards.

Proofreading Relay Write two columns of misspelled List Words on the board. Although the errors can differ, be sure that each list has the same number of errors. Divide the class into two teams and assign each team to a different column. Teams then compete against each other to correct their assigned lists by team members taking turns erasing and replacing an appropriate letter. Each member may correct only one letter per turn. The team that corrects its entire word list first wins.

Detective Call on a student to be a detective. The detective must choose a spelling word from the list and think of a structural clue, definition, or synonym that will help classmates identify it. The detective then states the clue using the format, "I spy a word that . . . ." Students are called on to guess and spell the mystery word. Whoever answers correctly gets to take a turn being the detective.

Spelling Tic-Tac-Toe Draw a tic-tac-toe square on the board. Divide the class into *X* and *O* teams. Take turns dictating spelling words to members of each team. If the word is spelled correctly, allow the team member to place an *X* or *O* on the square. The first team to place three *X*'s or *O*'s in a row wins.

Words of Fortune Have students put their heads down while you write a spelling word on the board in large letters. Then cover each letter with a sheet of sturdy paper. The paper can be fastened to the board with magnets. Call on a student to guess any letter of the alphabet they think may be hidden. If that particular letter is hidden, then reveal the letter in every place where it appears in the word by removing the paper.

The student continues to guess letters until an incorrect guess is made or the word is revealed. In the event that an incorrect guess is made, a different student continues the game. Continue the game until every List Word has been hidden and then revealed.

Spelling Enrichment

Dictionary Activities

Around the World   Designate the first person in the first row to be the traveler. The traveler must stand next to the student seated behind him or her. Then dictate any letter of the alphabet at random. Instruct the two students to quickly name the letter of the alphabet that precedes the given letter. The student who is first to respond with the correct answer becomes the traveler while the other student sits at that desk. The traveler then moves to compete with the next person in the row. The game continues with the traveler moving up and down the rows as the teacher dictates various alphabet letters. See who can be the traveler who has moved the farthest around the classroom. For variety, you may want to require students to state the letter that follows the given letter. You may also want to dictate pairs of List Words and have students name which word comes first.

Stand-Up   While the teacher pronounces a word from the spelling dictionary, students look up the entry word and point to it. Tell students to stand up when they have located the entry. See who is the first student to stand up.

This game can be played using the following variations:

1. Have students stand when they have located the guide words for a given word.

2. Have students stand when they are able to tell on what page a given List Word appears in the dictionary.

Guide Word Scramble   Prepare tagboard cards with spelling words written on them in large letters. Distribute the cards to students. Call on two students to come to the front of the room to serve as guide words. Then call one student at a time to hold their word card either in front of, in between, or behind the guide words so that the three words are in alphabetical order. You may want to vary the guide words occasionally.

Cut-Off   Distribute a strip of paper to each student. Instruct students to write any four spelling words on the strip. All but one of the words should be in alphabetical order. Then have students exchange their strip with a partner. Students use scissors to cut off the word that is not in alphabetical sequence and tape the remaining words strips together. If students find this activity too difficult, you might have them cut all four words off the strip and arrange them alphabetically on their desks.

Applied Spelling

Journal   Allow time each day for students to write in a journal. A spiral bound notebook can be used for this purpose. Encourage students to express their feelings about events that are happening in their lives at home or at school. Or they could write about what their plans are for the day. To get them started, you may have to provide starter phrases. Allow them to use "invented" spelling for words they can't spell.

Collect the journals periodically to write comments that echo what the student has written. For example, a student's entry might read, "I'm hape I gt to plae bazball todae." The teacher's response could be, "Baseball is my favorite game, too. I'd be happy to watch you play baseball today at recess." This method allows students to learn correct spelling and sentence structure without emphasizing their errors in a negative way.

Letter to the Teacher   On a regular basis, invite students to write a note to you. At first you may have to suggest topics or provide a starter sentence. It may be possible to suggest a topic that includes words from the spelling list. Write a response at the bottom of each letter that provides the student with a model of any spelling or sentence structure that apparently needs improvement.

Daily Edit   Each day, provide a brief writing sample on the board that contains errors in spelling, capitalization, or punctuation. Have students rewrite the sample correctly. Provide time later in the day to have the class correct the errors on the board. Discuss why the spelling is as it is while students self-correct their work.

Spelling Enrichment

Acrostic Poems   Have students write a word from the spelling list vertically. Then instruct them to join a word horizontally to each letter of the List Word. The horizontal words must begin with the letters in the List Word. They also should be words that describe or relate feelings about the List Word. Encourage students to refer to a dictionary for help in finding appropriate words. Here is a sample acrostic poem:

Zebras

Otters

Ostriches

Words-in-a-Row   Distribute strips of writing paper to each student. Ask students to write three spelling words in a row. Tell them to misspell two of the words. Then have students take turns writing their row of words on the board. They can call on a classmate to identify and underline the correctly spelled word in the row. Continue until all students have had a chance to write their row of words.

Partner Spelling   Assign spelling buddies. Allow partners to alternate dictating or writing sentences that contain words from the spelling list. The sentences can be provided by the teacher or generated by students. Have students check their own work as their partner provides the correct spelling for each sentence.

Scrap Words   Provide each student with several sheets of tagboard, scraps of fabric or wallpaper, and some glue. Ask students to cut letters out of the scrap materials and glue them to the tagboard to form words from the spelling list. Display the colorful scrap words around the classroom.

Punch Words   Set up a work center in the classroom with a supply of construction paper strips, a hole puncher, sheets of thin paper, and crayons. Demonstrate to students how the hole puncher can be used to create spelling words out of the construction paper. Permit students to take turns working at the center in their free time. Students may also enjoy placing a thin sheet of paper over the punch words and rubbing them with a crayon to make colorful word designs. You can then display their punch word and crayon creations.

Word Cut-Outs   Distribute scissors, glue, a sheet of dark-colored construction paper, and a supply of old newspapers and magazines to the class. Have students look through the papers and magazines for spelling List Words. Tell them to cut out any List Words they find and glue them onto the sheet of construction paper. See who can find the most spelling List Words. This technique may also be used to have students construct sentences or cut out individual letters to form words.

Word Sorts   Invite students to write each List Word on a separate card. Then ask them how many different ways the words can be organized (e.g., animate vs. inanimate, past-tense or vowel patterns, similarity or contrast in meaning). As students sort the words into each category, have them put words that don't belong in a category into an exception pile.

Word Locker

Definitions and Rules

The alphabet has two kinds of letters. The **vowels** are a, e, i, o, and **u** (and sometimes **y** and **w**). All the rest of the letters are **consonants.**

Each **syllable** in a word must have a vowel sound. If a word or syllable has only one vowel and it comes at the beginning or between two consonants, the vowel usually stands for a **short** sound.

cat   sit   cup

A **long-vowel** sound usually has the same sound as its letter name.

When **y** comes at the end of a word with one syllable, the **y** at the end spells /ī/, as in <u>dry</u> and <u>try</u>. When **y** comes at the end of a word with more than one syllable, it usually has the sound of /ē/, as in <u>city</u> and <u>funny</u>.

When two or more **consonants** come together in a word, their sounds may blend together. In a **consonant blend,** you can hear the sound of each letter.

smile   **sl**ide   **fr**iend

A **consonant digraph** consists of two consonants that go together to make one sound.

sharp   four**th**   ea**ch**

A **consonant cluster** is three consonants together in one syllable.

thrills   pa**tch**   **spl**ash

A **suffix** is an addition made at the **end** of a **root word.**

rain**ed**   help**ed**

A **prefix** is a word part that is added to the beginning of another word called a **root word.** A prefix changes the meaning of the root.

unhappy   **dis**trust

When you write words in **alphabetical order,** use these rules:

1. If the <u>first letter</u> of two words is the same, use the second letter.

2. If the <u>first two letters</u> are the same, use the third letter.

There are two **guide words** at the top of each page in the dictionary. The word on the left tells you the first word on the page. The word on the right tells you the last word on the page. All the words in between are in **alphabetical order.**

The dictionary puts an **accent mark** (´) after the syllable with the strong sound.

per´son

There is a vowel sound that can be spelled by any of the vowels. It is often found in a syllable that is *not accented,* or stressed, in a word. This vowel sound has the sound-symbol /ə/. It is called the **schwa.**

The word <u>I</u> is always a **capital** letter.

A **contraction** is a short way of writing two words. It is formed by writing two words together and leaving out one or more letters. Use an **apostrophe** (') to show where something is left out.

it is = it's   we will = we'll

A **compound word** is a word made by joining two or more words.

cannot   anyway   maybe